SPICE & WOLF

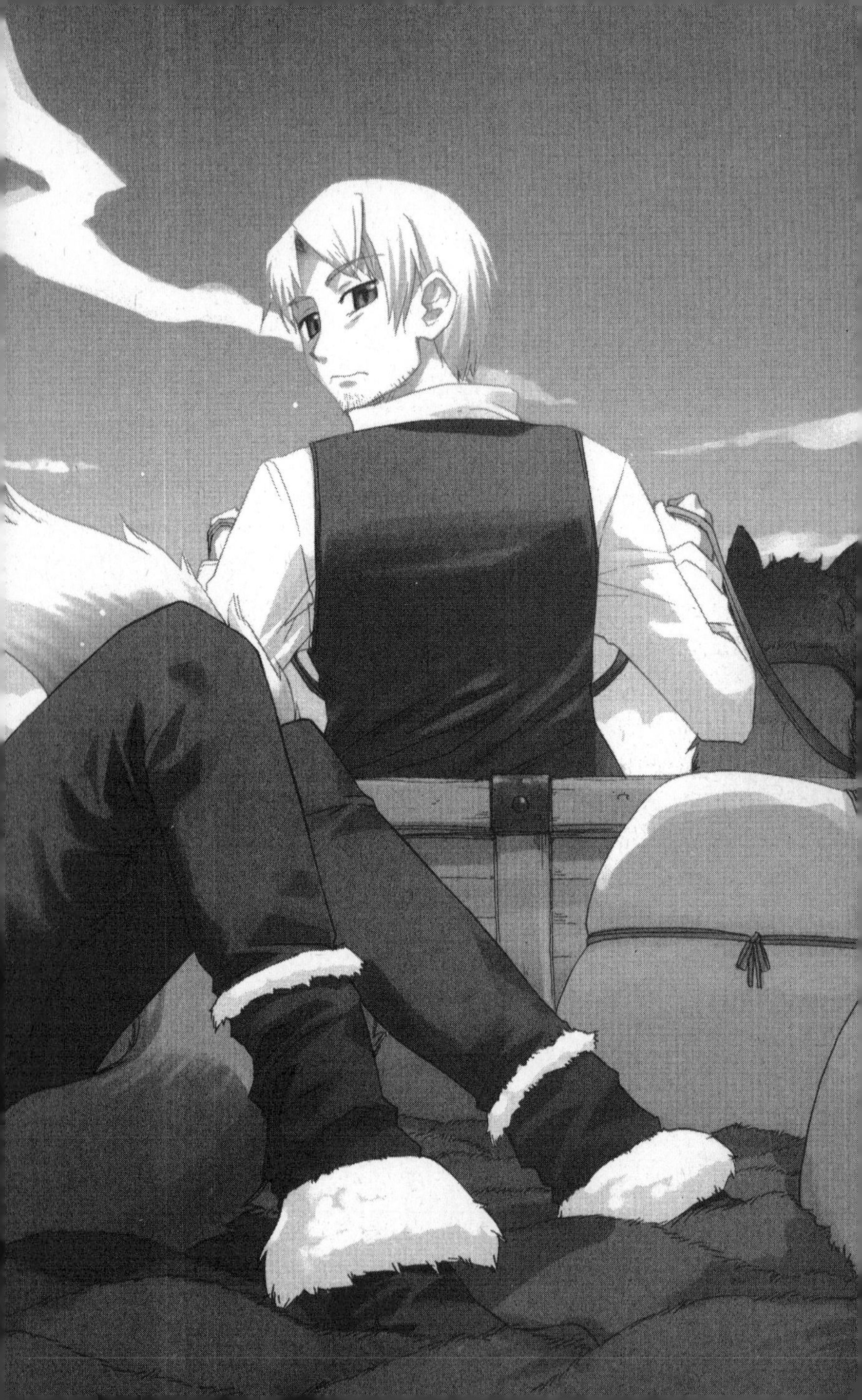

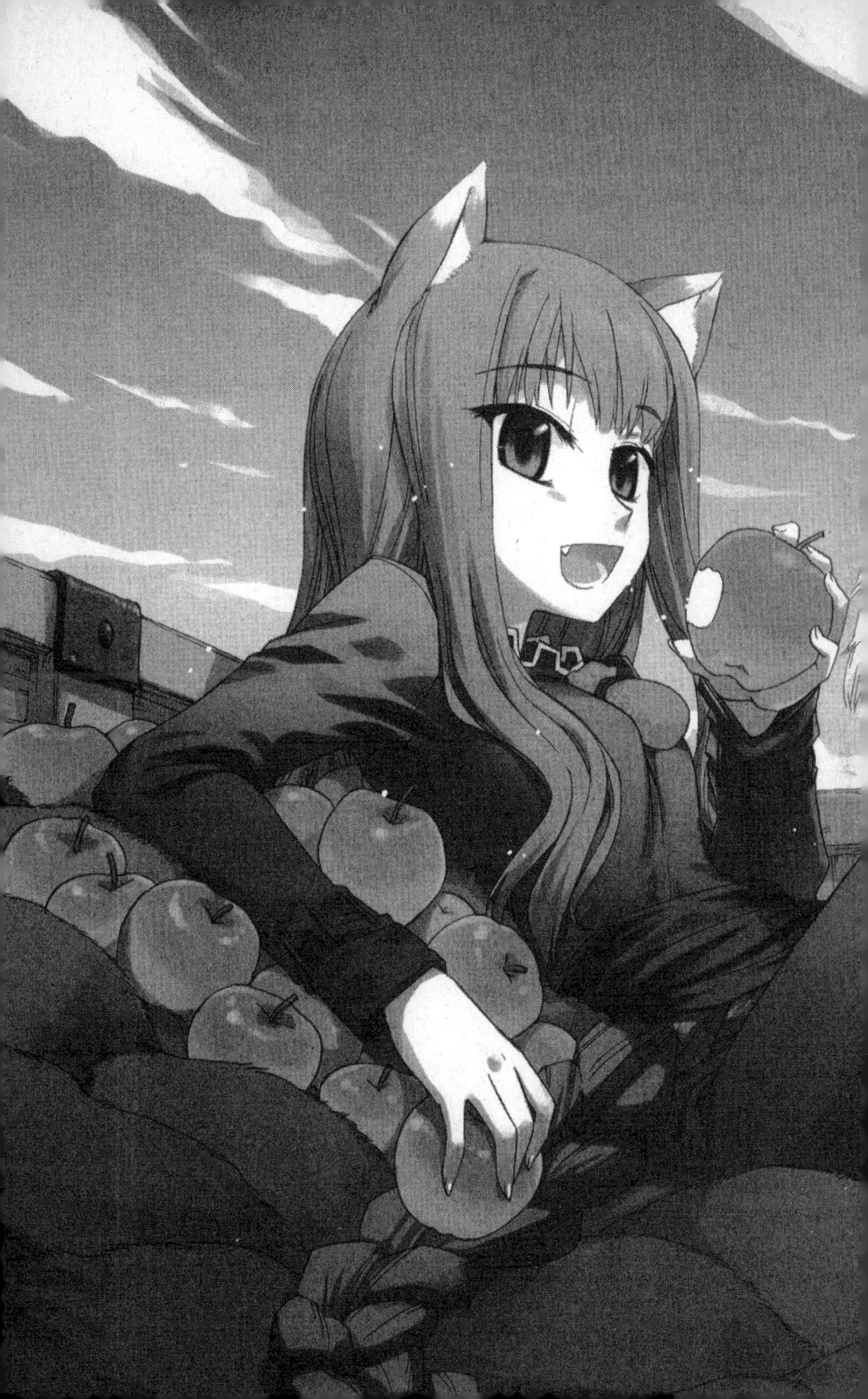

Lawrence

A traveling merchant in the seventh year of his career, age 25. He is quite clever, but as a merchant, there are still many areas he knows little about.

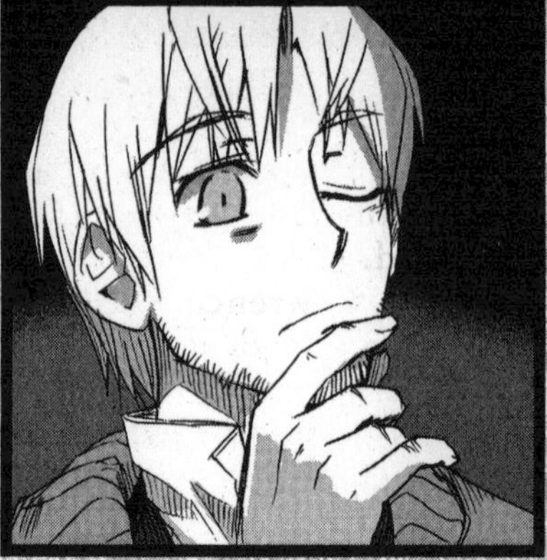

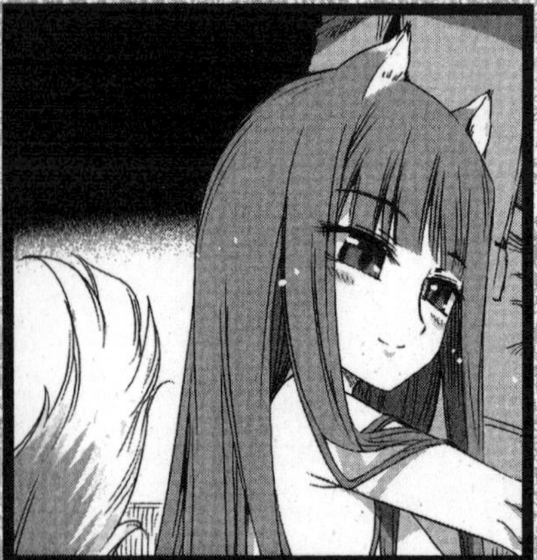

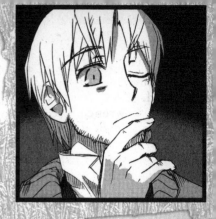

Holo

Introducing herself as the God of the Harvest for the village of Pasloe, this strange girl has wolf ears and a tail.

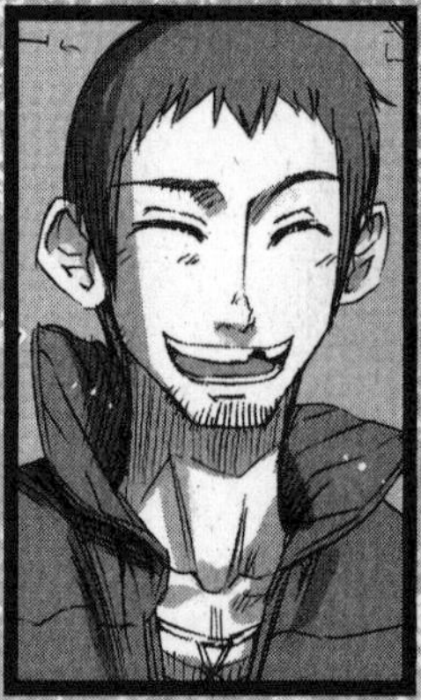

Zheren

A novice merchant who is staying at the church. He proposes a peculiar deal to Lawrence.

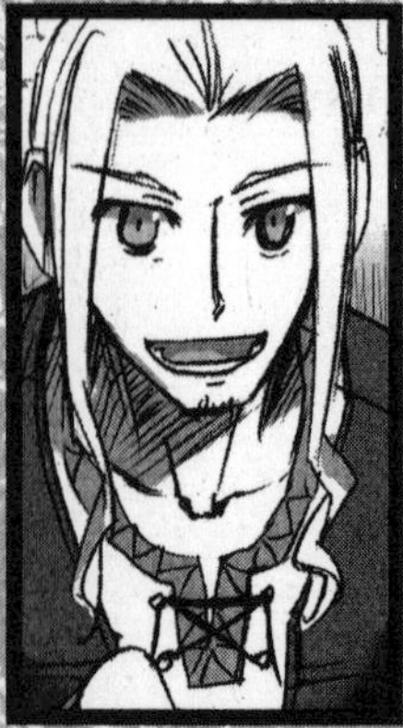

Weiz

A cambist working at the bridge in the port town of Pazzio, and a good friend of Lawrence's.

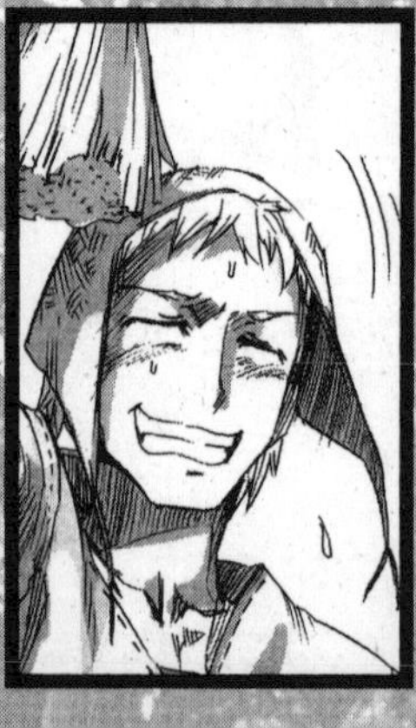

Yarei

A peasant of the village of Pasloe. He was the village's agent in the days when Lawrence traded wheat.

Introduction

The Church's influence is waning, and the time when all in the land prostrated themselves before its authority has passed.

Lawrence, who dreams of one day opening his own shop in a town somewhere, is driving his wagon—piled high with marten furs—to the village of Pasloe. He makes camp at the outskirts of the village, which is holding a festival in honor of the wolf-god of the harvest, when a strange thing happens...

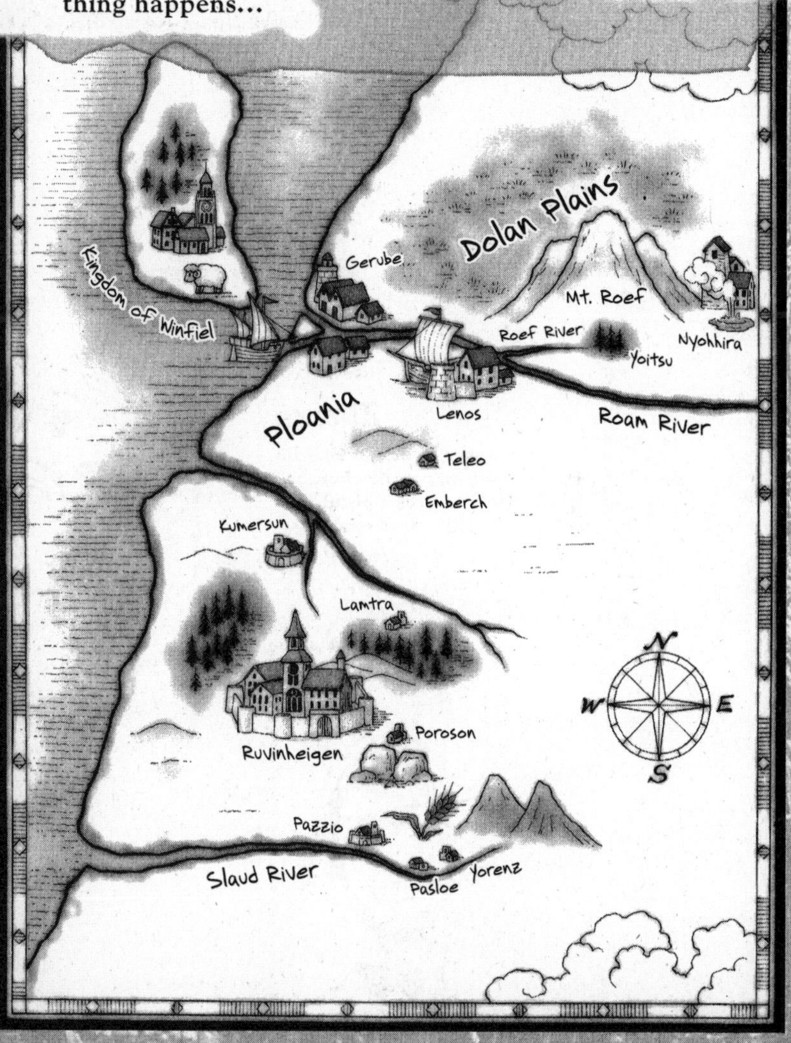
Kingdom of Winfiel
Gerube
Dolan Plains
Mt. Roef
Roef River
Nyohhira
Yoitsu
Ploania
Lenos
Roam River
Teleo
Emberch
Kumersun
Lamtra
N
W
E
S
Poroson
Ruvinheigen
Pazzio
Slaud River
Pasloe
Yorenz

Map Illustration: Hidetada Idemitsu

SPICE & WOLF
CONTENTS

Trenni Silver

The most common currency in the Pazzio area, it is regarded as being reliably pure in silver. The individual pictured on the coin above is the 11th king of the Trenni dynasty.

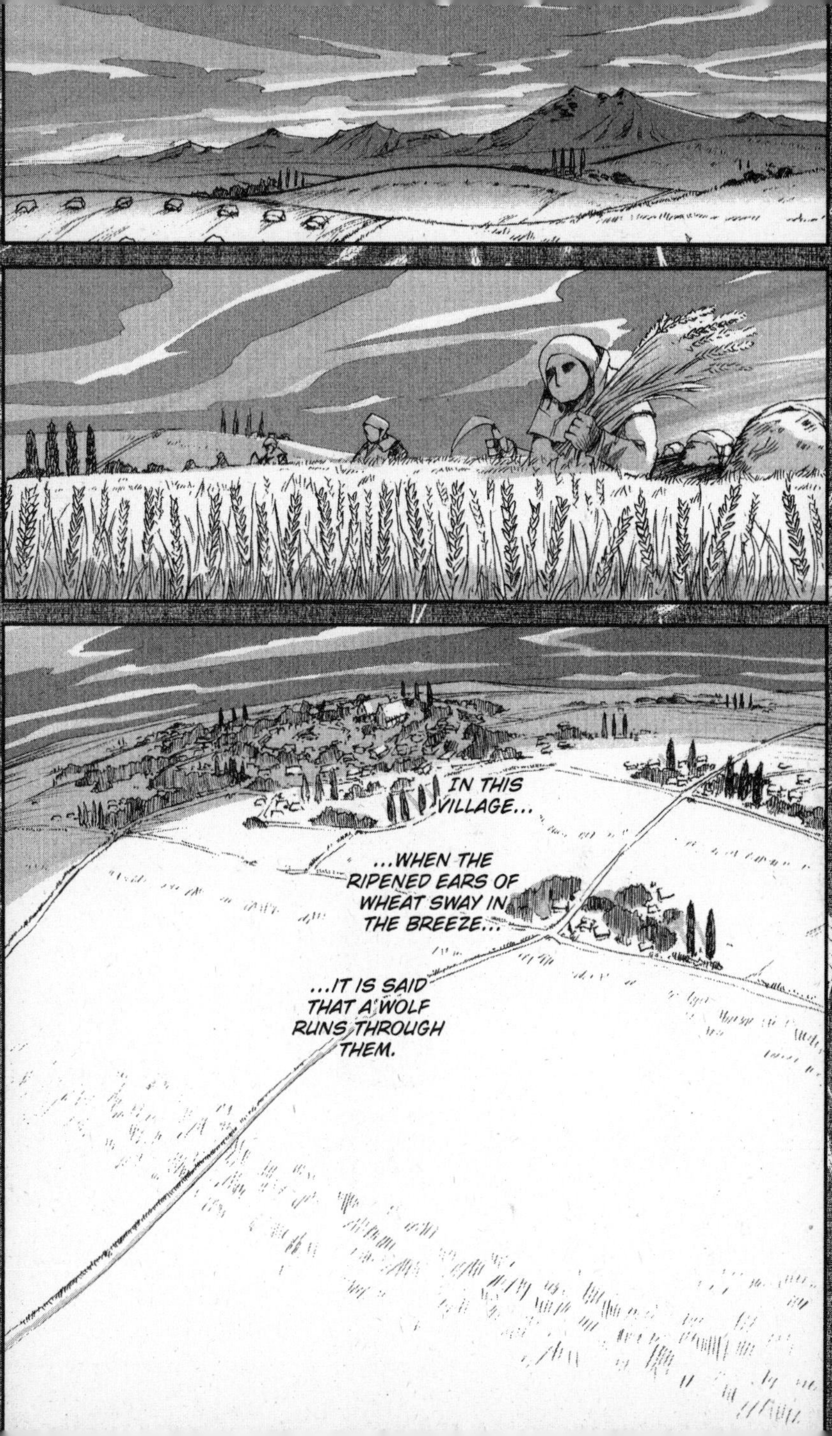
IN THIS VILLAGE...
...WHEN THE RIPENED EARS OF WHEAT SWAY IN THE BREEZE...
...IT IS SAID THAT A WOLF RUNS THROUGH THEM.

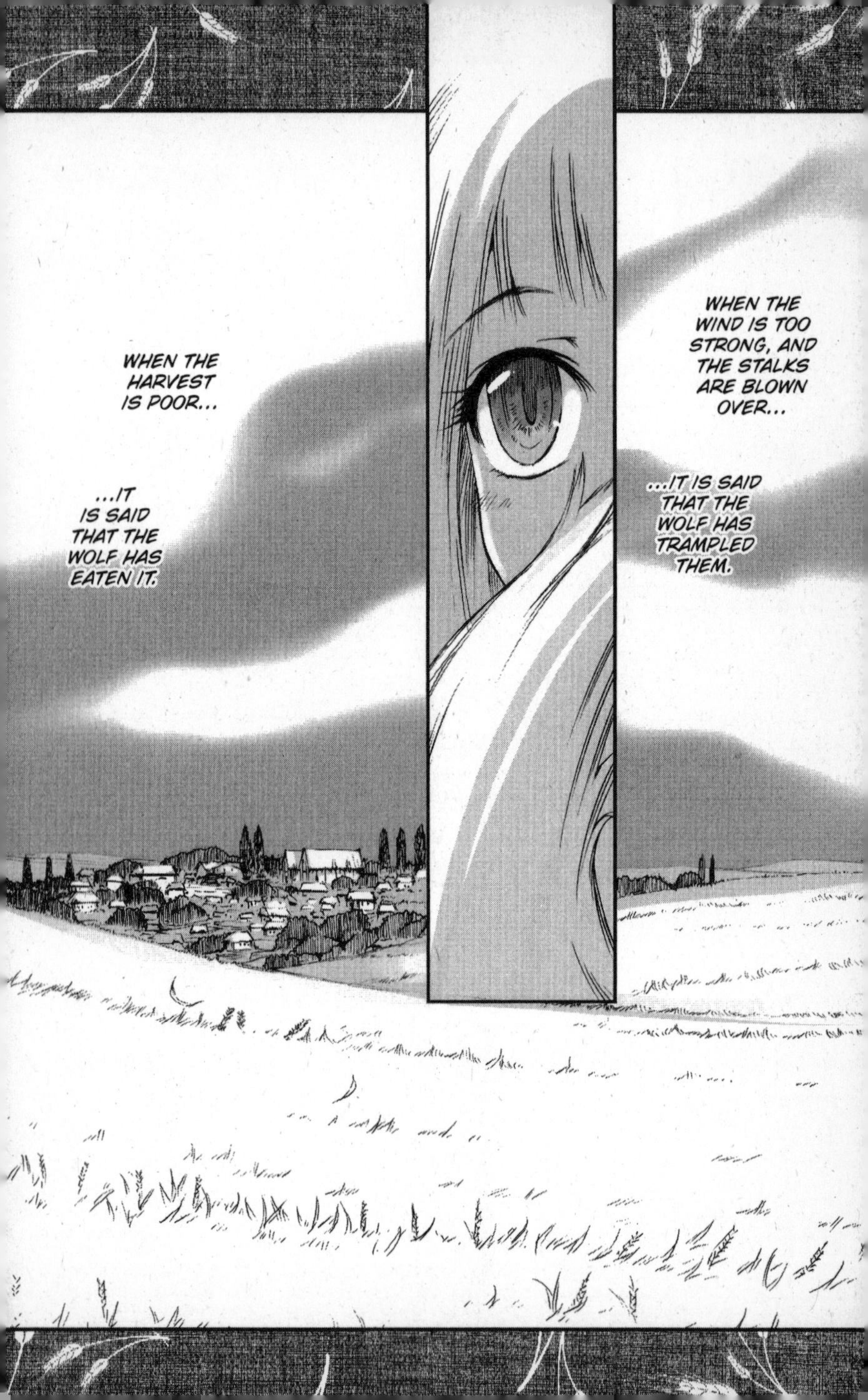
WHEN THE WIND IS TOO STRONG, AND THE STALKS ARE BLOWN OVER...
...IT IS SAID THAT THE WOLF HAS TRAMPLED THEM.
WHEN THE HARVEST IS POOR...
...IT IS SAID THAT THE WOLF HAS EATEN IT.

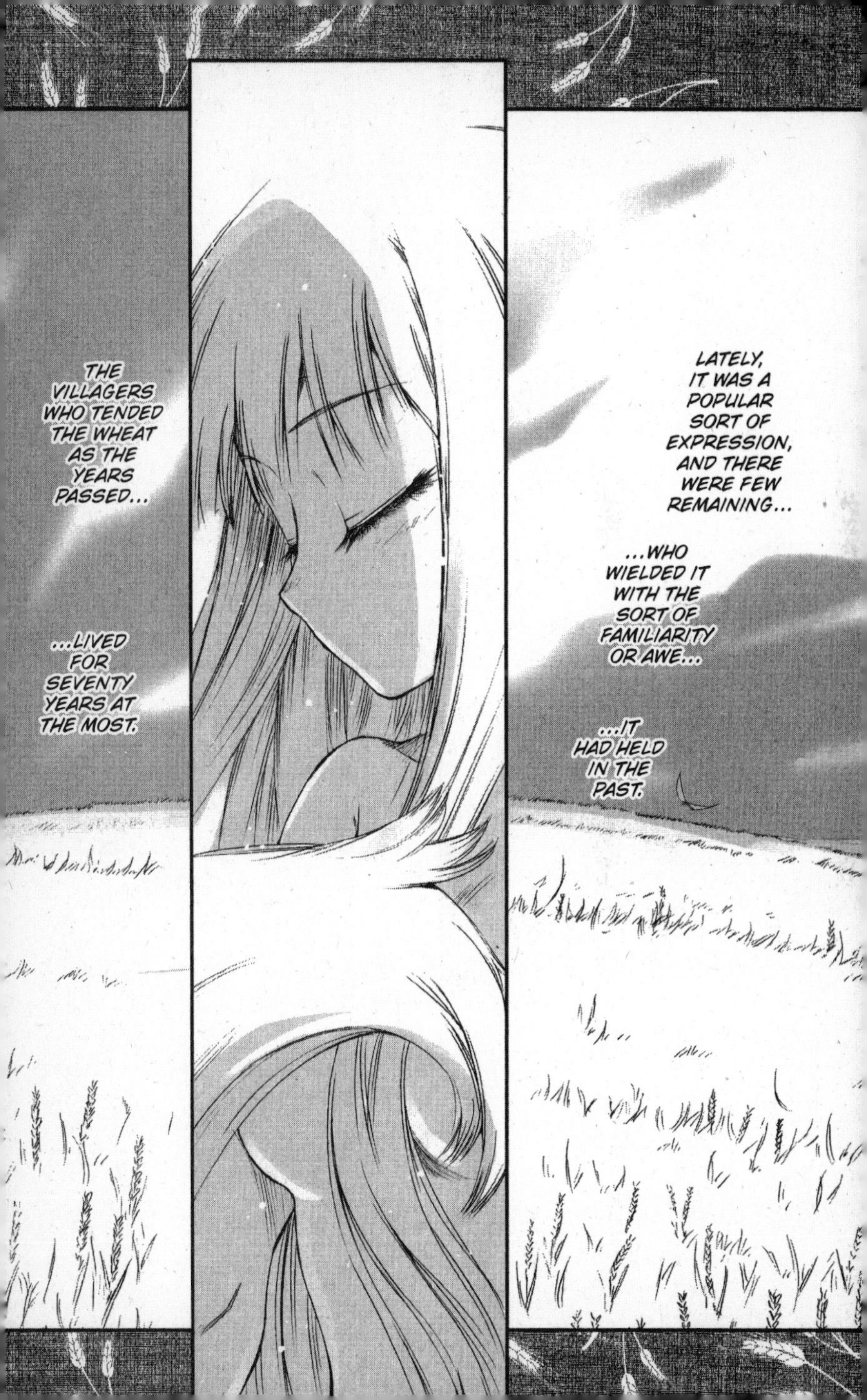
LATELY, IT WAS A POPULAR SORT OF EXPRESSION, AND THERE WERE FEW REMAINING...
...WHO WIELDED IT WITH THE SORT OF FAMILIARITY OR AWE...
...IT HAD HELD IN THE PAST.
THE VILLAGERS WHO TENDED THE WHEAT AS THE YEARS PASSED...
...LIVED FOR SEVENTY YEARS AT THE MOST.

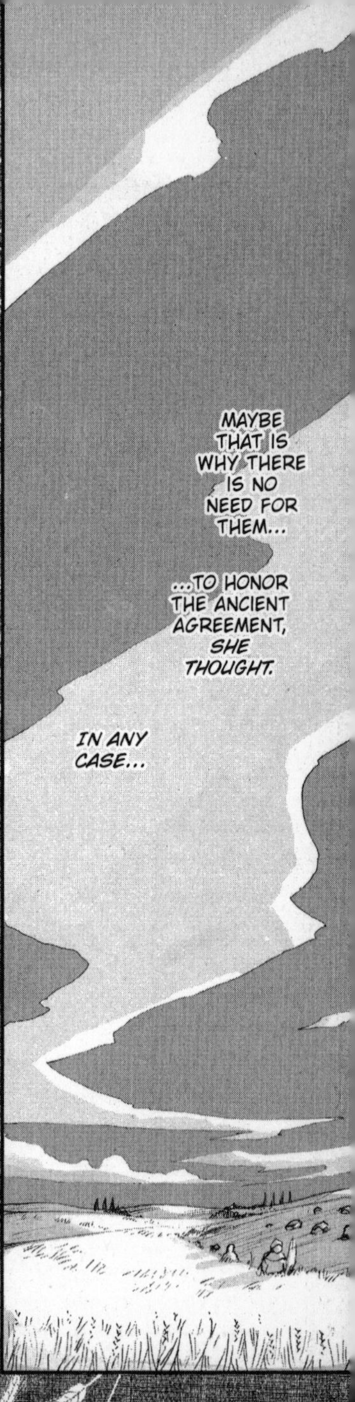
MAYBE THAT IS WHY THERE IS NO NEED FOR THEM...
...TO HONOR THE ANCIENT AGREEMENT, SHE THOUGHT.
IN ANY CASE...
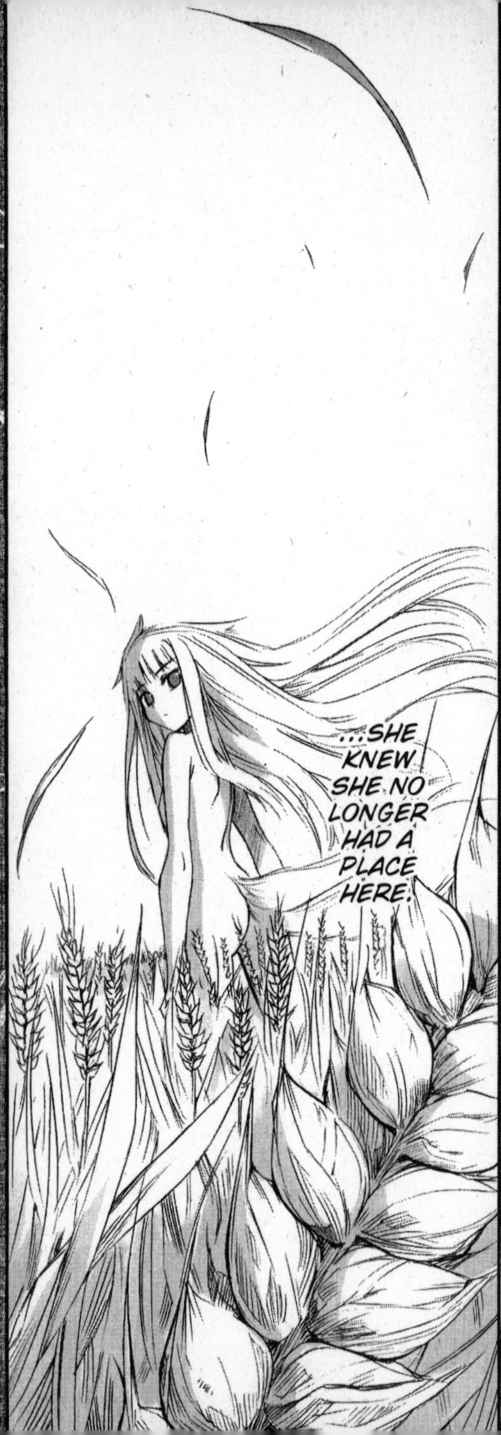
...SHE KNEW SHE NO LONGER HAD A PLACE HERE.

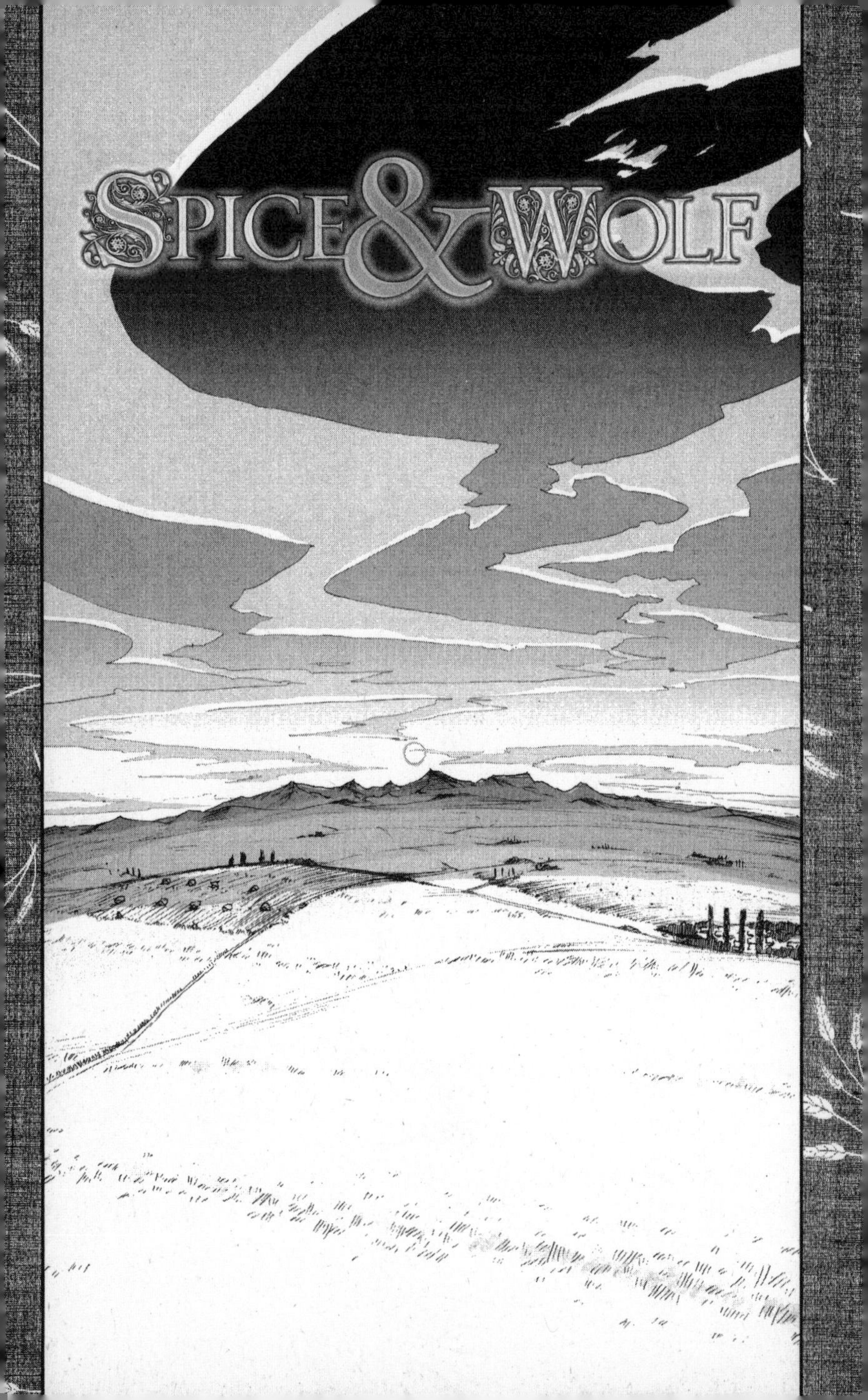
SPICE & WOLF

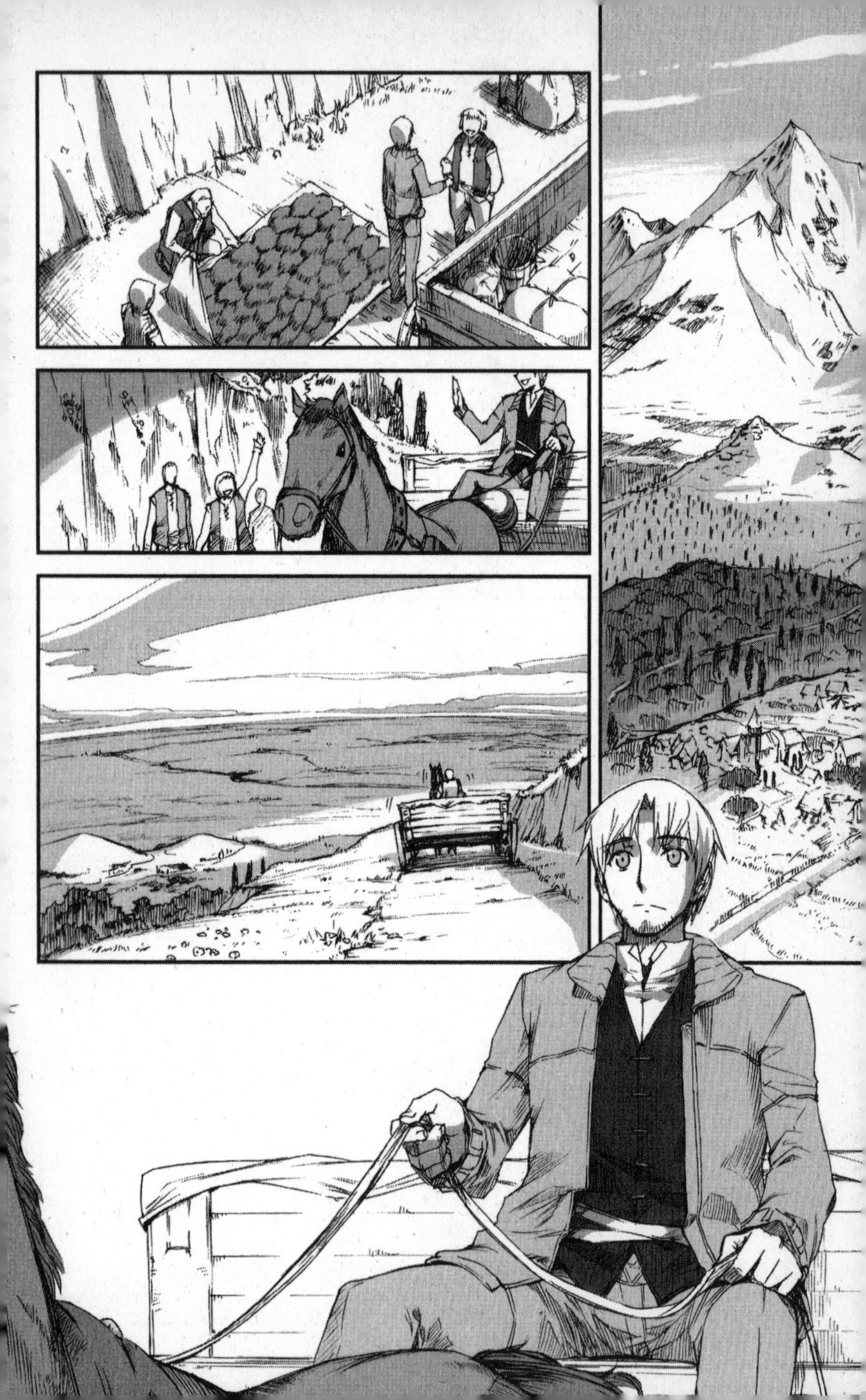

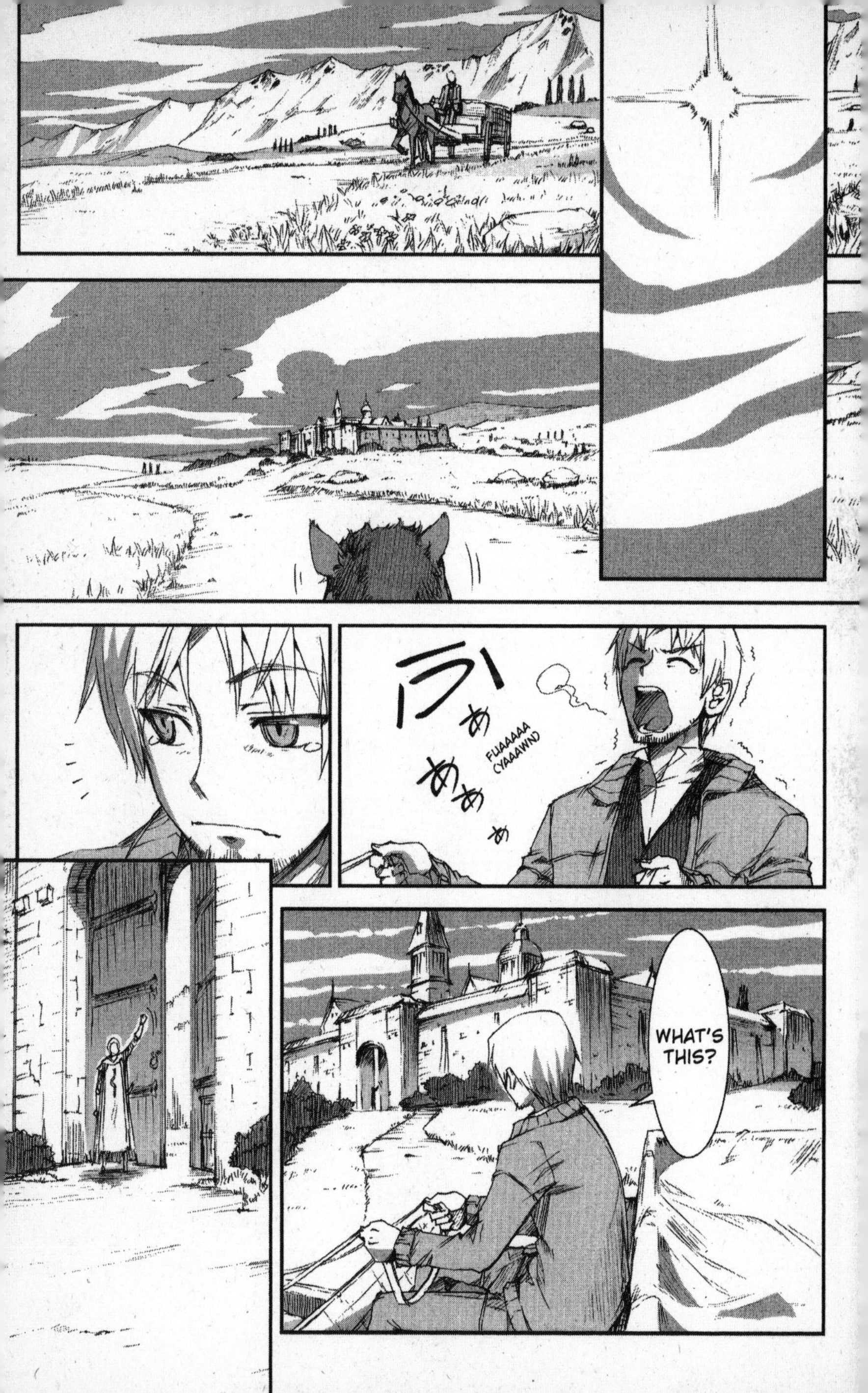
ふぁあぁぁ
FUAAAAA (YAAAWN)
WHAT'S THIS?

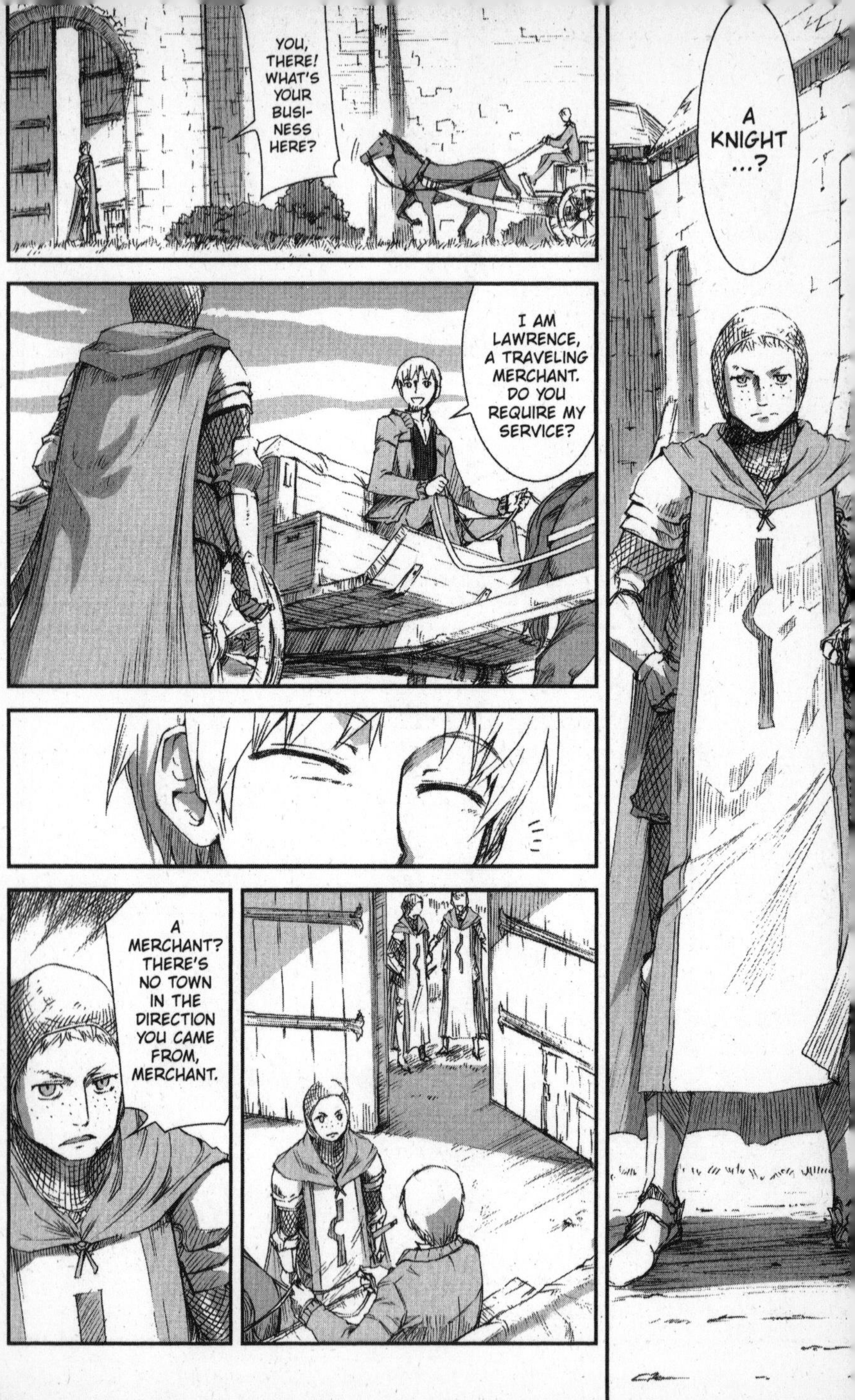
A KNIGHT ...?
YOU, THERE! WHAT'S YOUR BUSINESS HERE?
I AM LAWRENCE, A TRAVELING MERCHANT. DO YOU REQUIRE MY SERVICE?
A MERCHANT? THERE'S NO TOWN IN THE DIRECTION YOU CAME FROM, MERCHANT.

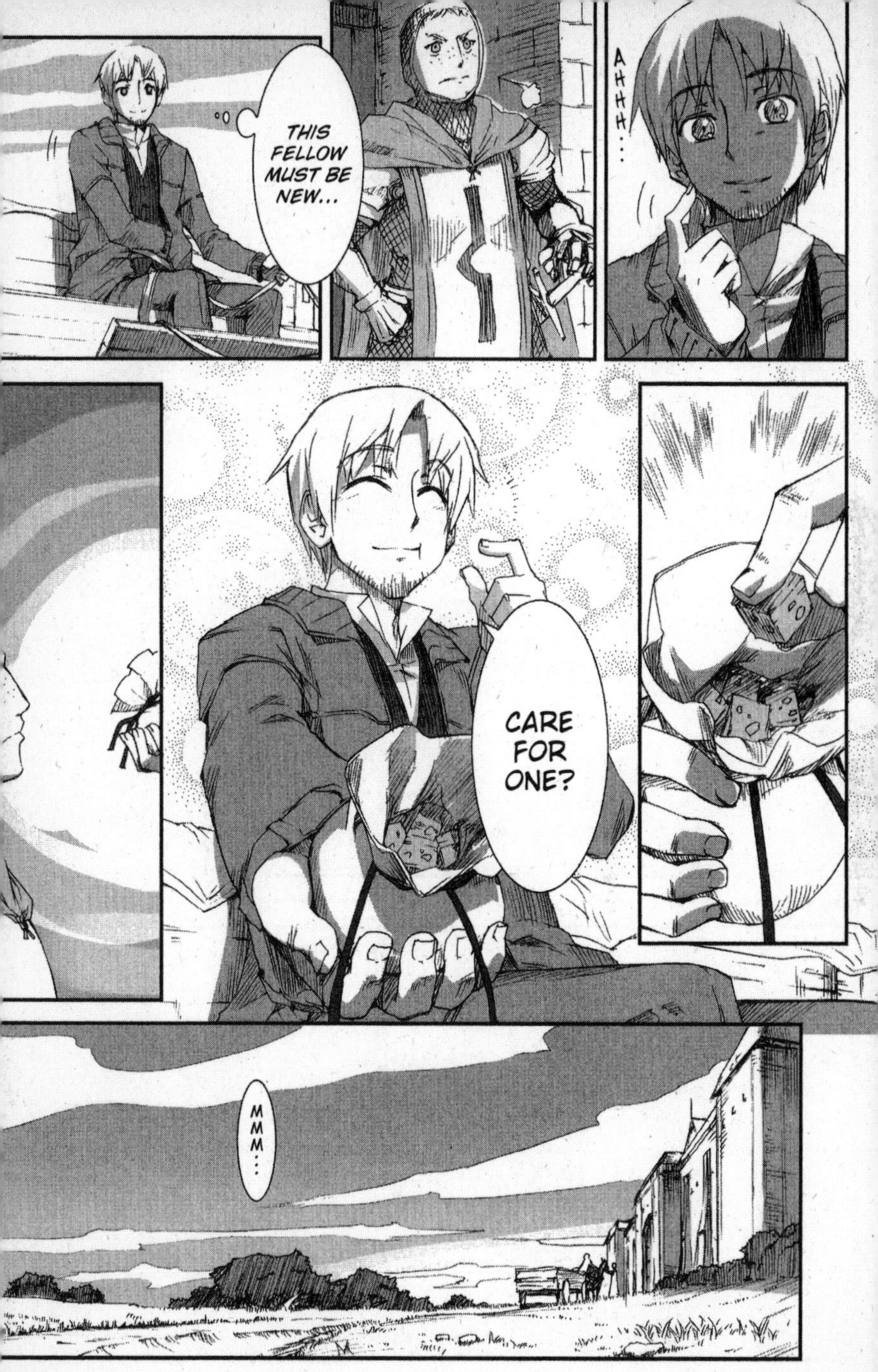
AHHH...
THIS FELLOW MUST BE NEW...
CARE FOR ONE?
MMM...

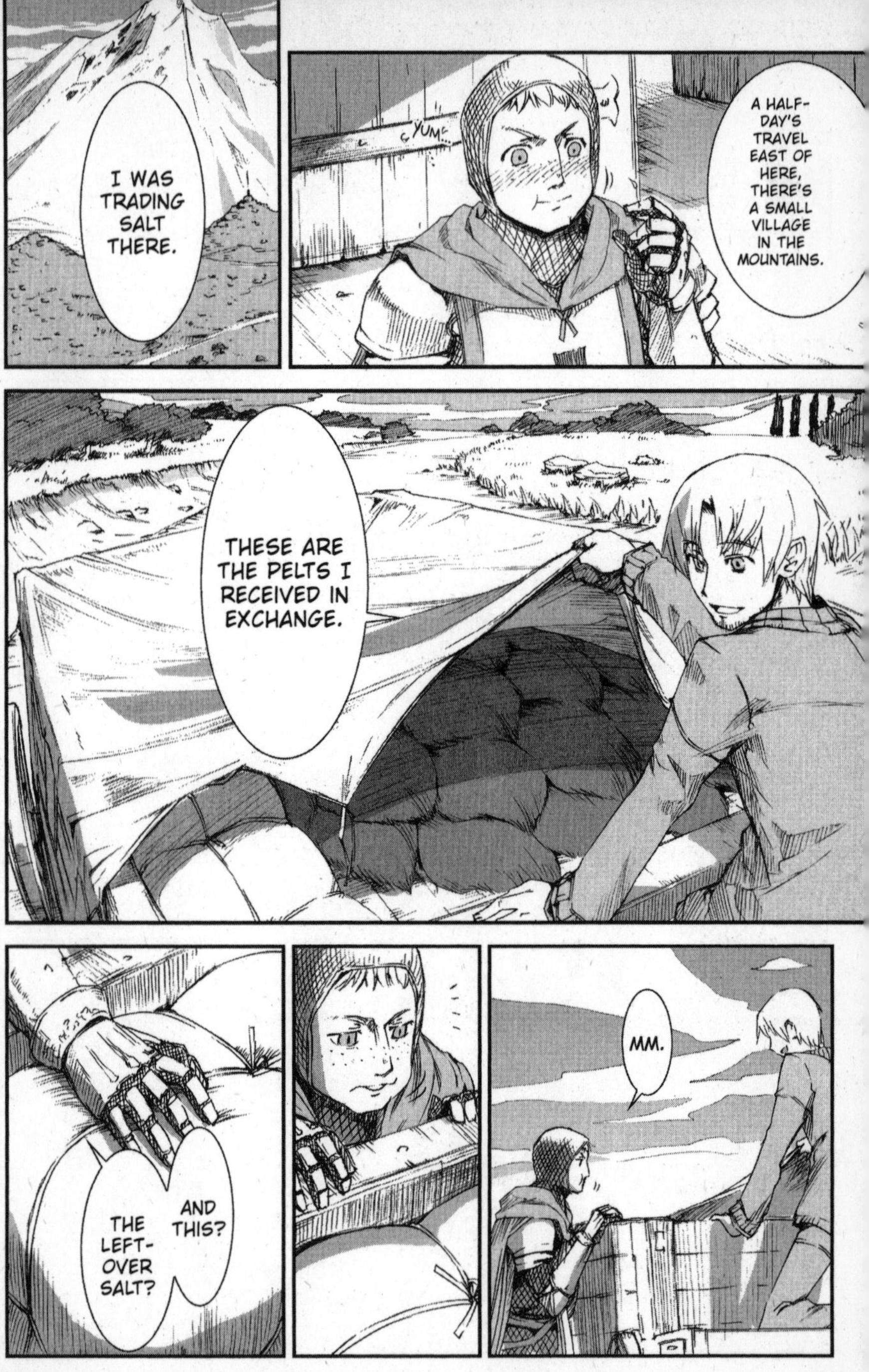
A HALF-DAY'S TRAVEL EAST OF HERE, THERE'S A SMALL VILLAGE IN THE MOUNTAINS.
YUM...
I WAS TRADING SALT THERE.
THESE ARE THE PELTS I RECEIVED IN EXCHANGE.
MM.
AND THIS?
THE LEFT-OVER SALT?

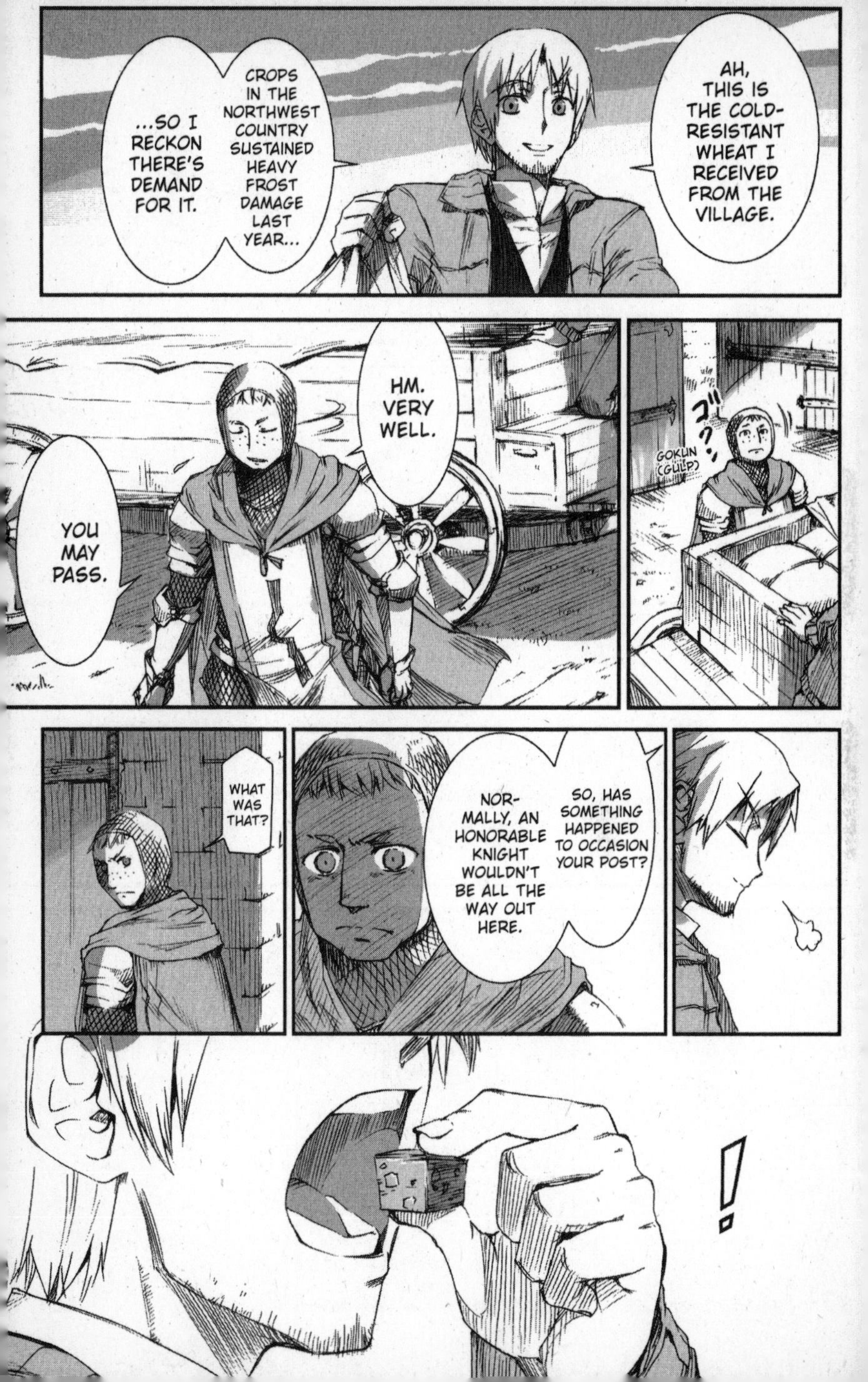
AH, THIS IS THE COLD-RESISTANT WHEAT I RECEIVED FROM THE VILLAGE.
CROPS IN THE NORTHWEST COUNTRY SUSTAINED HEAVY FROST DAMAGE LAST YEAR...
...SO I RECKON THERE'S DEMAND FOR IT.
GOKUN (GULP)
HM. VERY WELL.
YOU MAY PASS.
SO, HAS SOMETHING HAPPENED TO OCCASION YOUR POST?
NOR-MALLY, AN HONORABLE KNIGHT WOULDN'T BE ALL THE WAY OUT HERE.
WHAT WAS THAT?
!

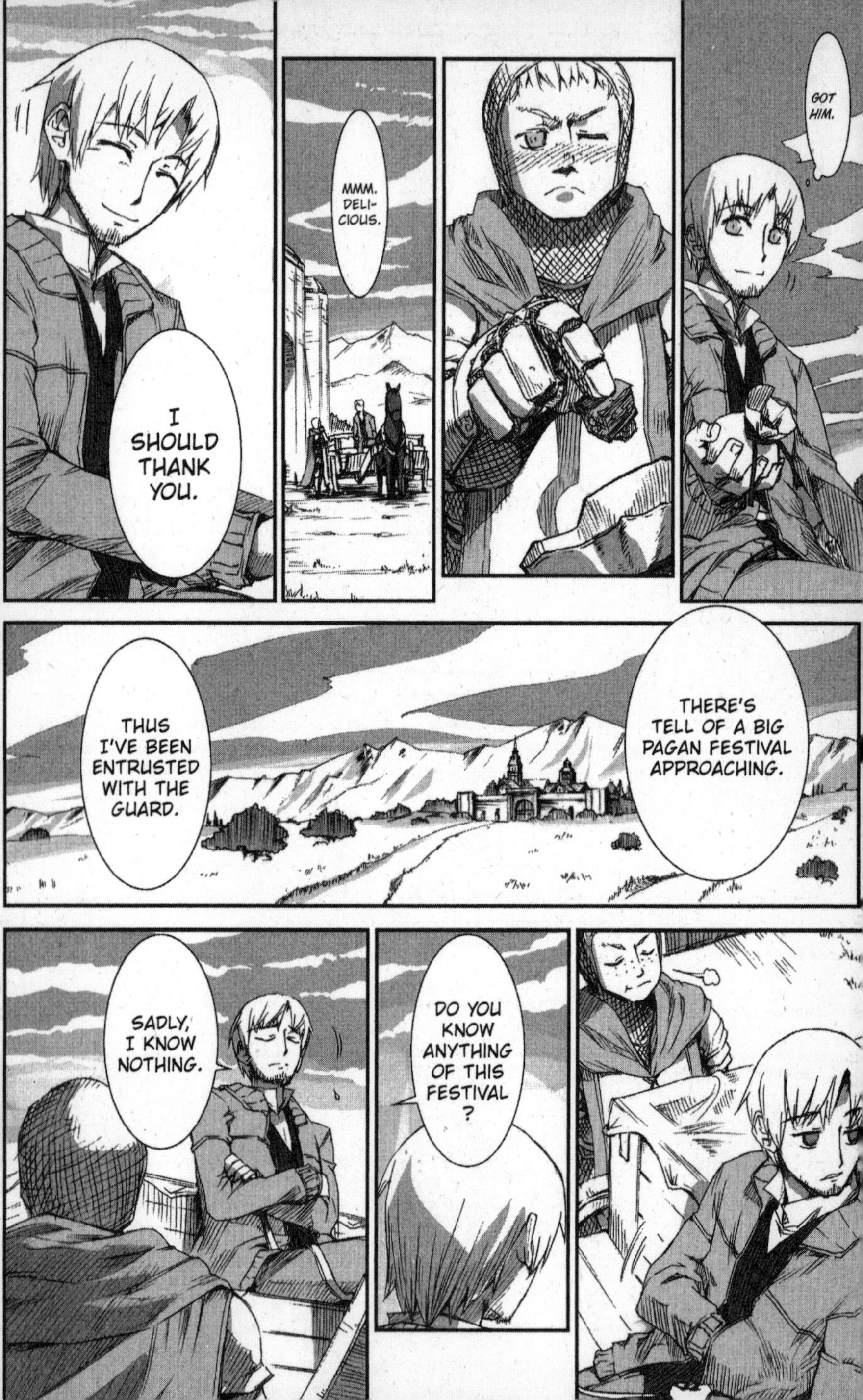
GOT HIM.
MMM. DELICIOUS.
I SHOULD THANK YOU.
THERE'S TELL OF A BIG PAGAN FESTIVAL APPROACHING.
THUS I'VE BEEN ENTRUSTED WITH THE GUARD.
DO YOU KNOW ANYTHING OF THIS FESTIVAL?
SADLY, I KNOW NOTHING.

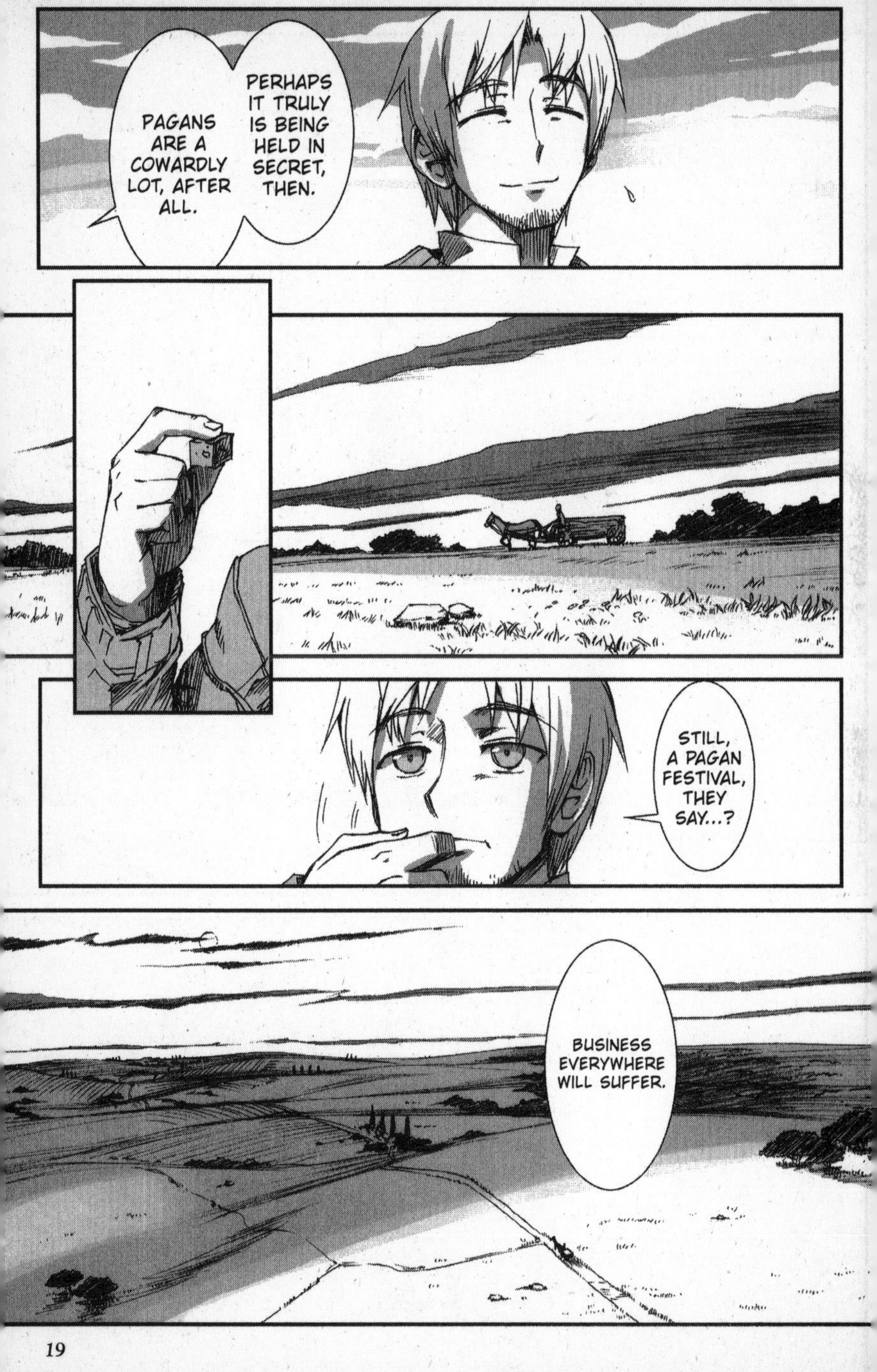
PERHAPS IT TRULY IS BEING HELD IN SECRET, THEN.
PAGANS ARE A COWARDLY LOT, AFTER ALL.
STILL, A PAGAN FESTIVAL, THEY SAY...?
BUSINESS EVERYWHERE WILL SUFFER.

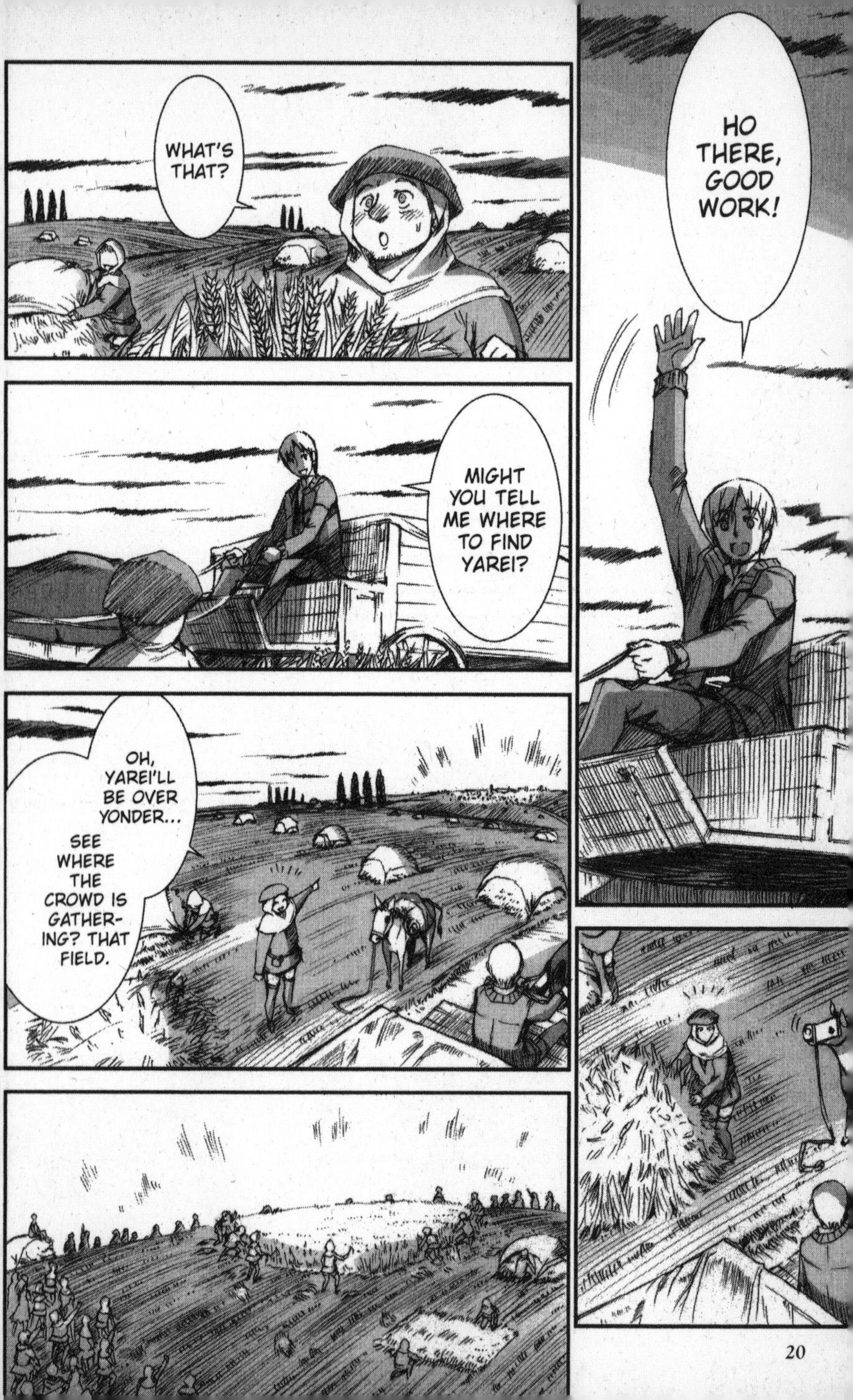
HO THERE, GOOD WORK!
WHAT'S THAT?
MIGHT YOU TELL ME WHERE TO FIND YAREI?
OH, YAREI'LL BE OVER YONDER... SEE WHERE THE CROWD IS GATHER-ING? THAT FIELD.

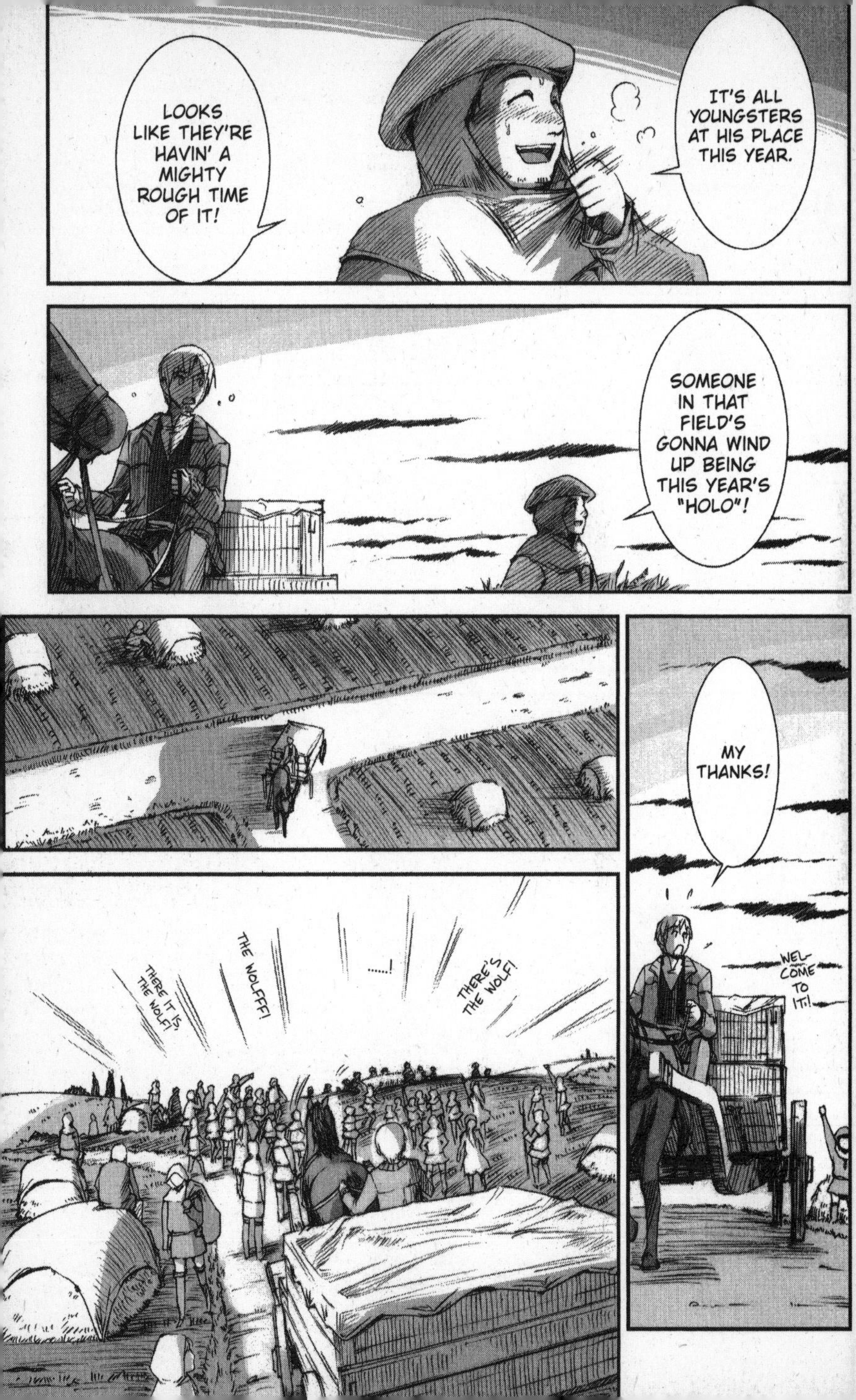
IT'S ALL YOUNGSTERS AT HIS PLACE THIS YEAR.
LOOKS LIKE THEY'RE HAVIN' A MIGHTY ROUGH TIME OF IT!
SOMEONE IN THAT FIELD'S GONNA WIND UP BEING THIS YEAR'S "HOLO"!
MY THANKS!
WEL-COME TO IT!
THERE'S THE WOLF!
......!
THE WOLFFF!
THERE IT IS, THE WOLF!

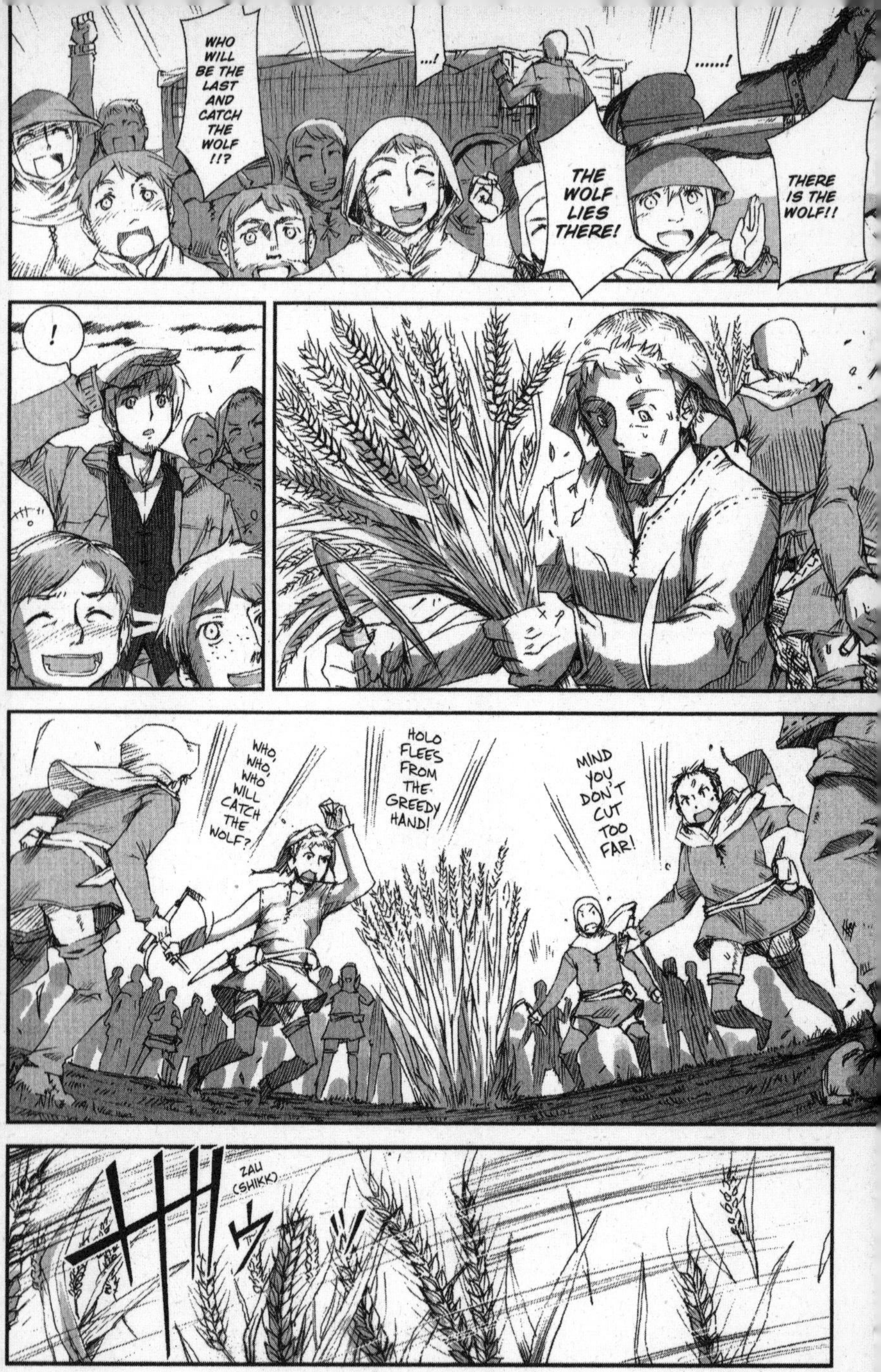
THERE IS THE WOLF!!
......!
THE WOLF LIES THERE!
...!
WHO WILL BE THE LAST AND CATCH THE WOLF!!?
!
MIND YOU DON'T CUT TOO FAR!
HOLO FLEES FROM THE GREEDY HAND!
WHO, WHO, WHO WILL CATCH THE WOLF?
ZAU (SHIKK)

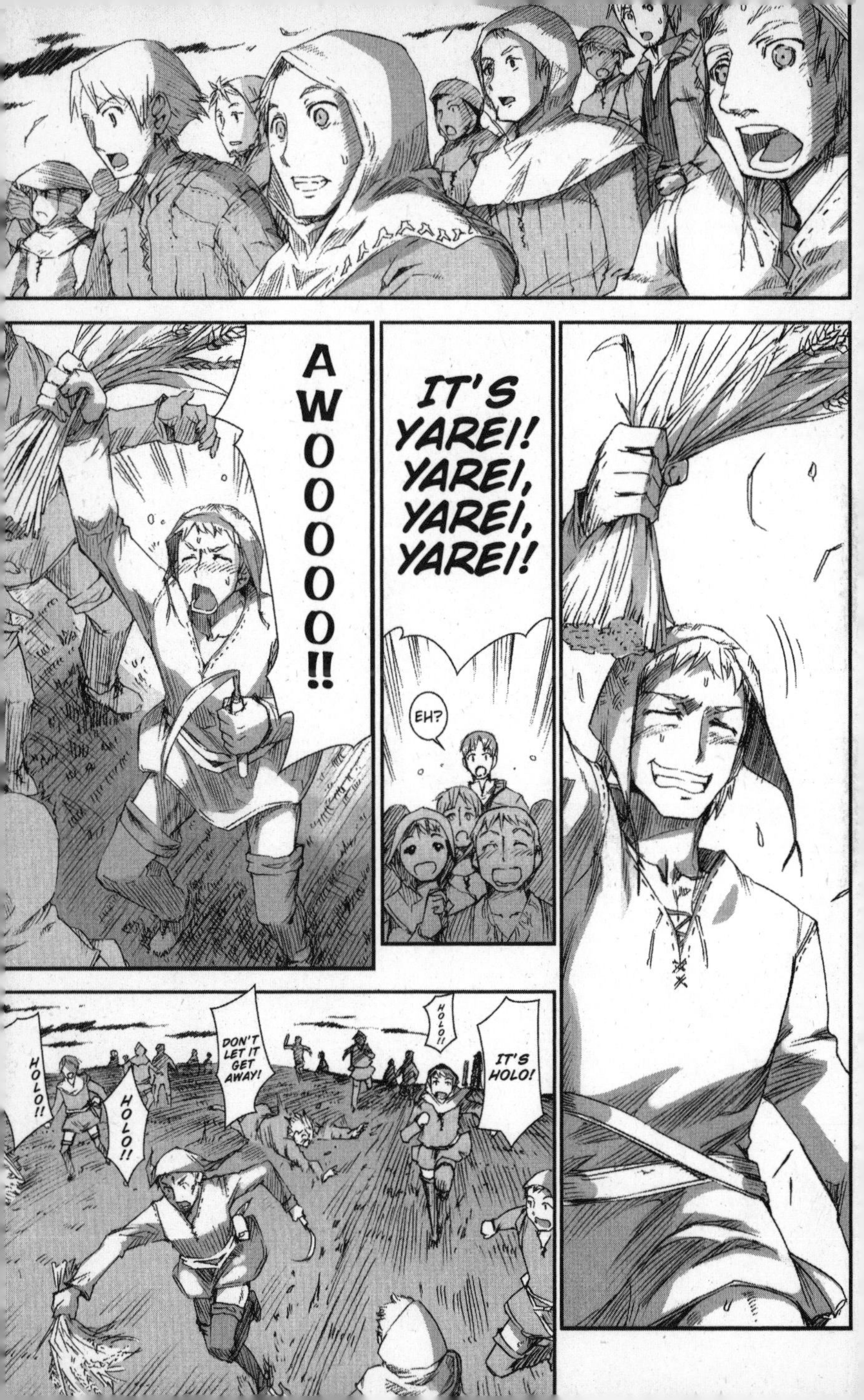
IT'S YAREI! YAREI, YAREI, YAREI!
EH?
AWOOOOOO!!
IT'S HOLO!
HOLO!!
DON'T LET IT GET AWAY!
HOLO!!
HOLO!!

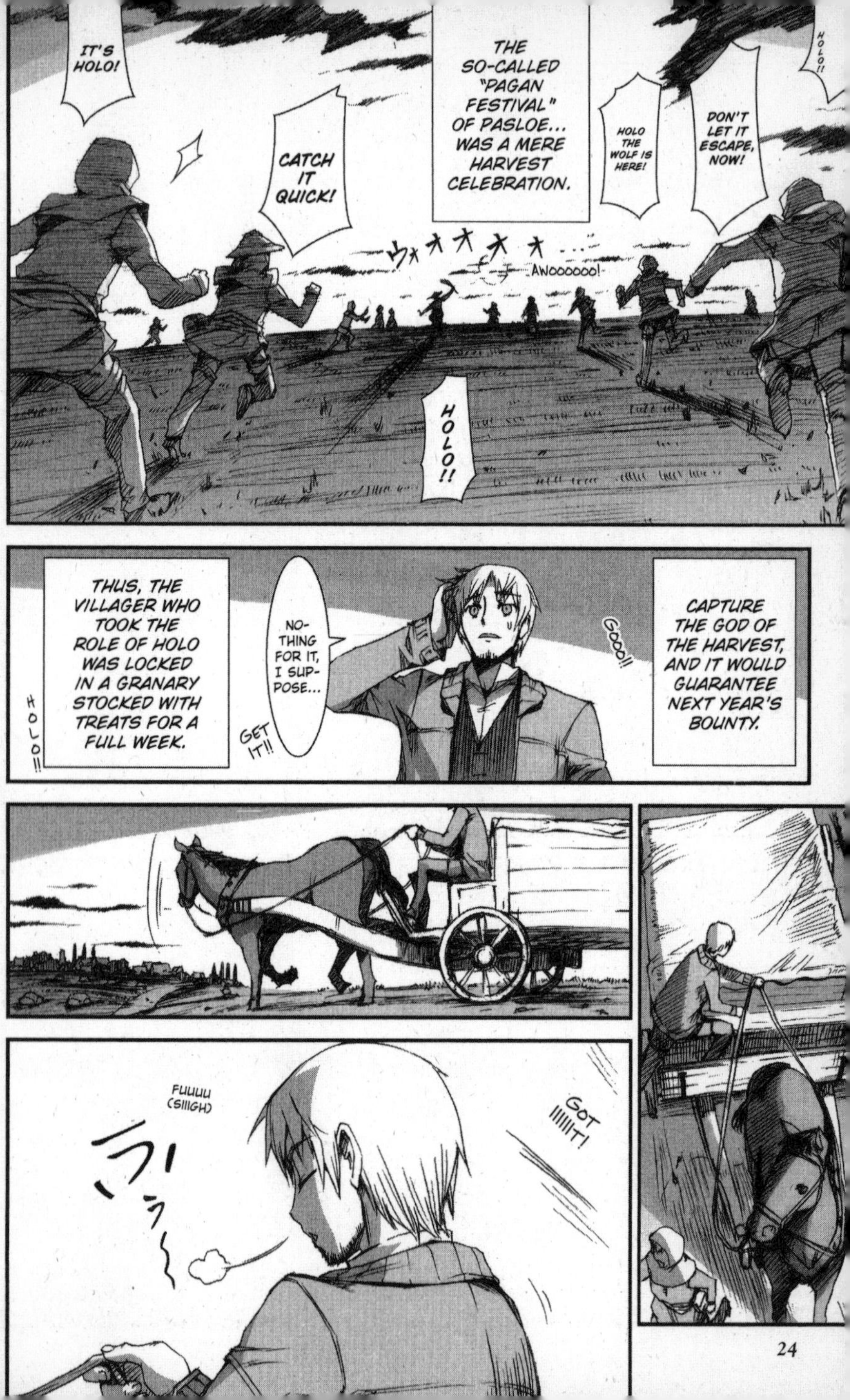
HOLO!!
DON'T LET IT ESCAPE, NOW!
HOLO THE WOLF IS HERE!
THE SO-CALLED "PAGAN FESTIVAL" OF PASLOE... WAS A MERE HARVEST CELEBRATION.
CATCH IT QUICK!
IT'S HOLO!
ウォォォォォ...
AWOOOOOO!
HOLO!!
CAPTURE THE GOD OF THE HARVEST, AND IT WOULD GUARANTEE NEXT YEAR'S BOUNTY.
GOOO!!
NOTHING FOR IT, I SUPPOSE...
GET IT!!
THUS, THE VILLAGER WHO TOOK THE ROLE OF HOLO WAS LOCKED IN A GRANARY STOCKED WITH TREATS FOR A FULL WEEK.
HOLO!!
GOT IIIIIT!
FUUUU (SIIIGH)
ふぅ~

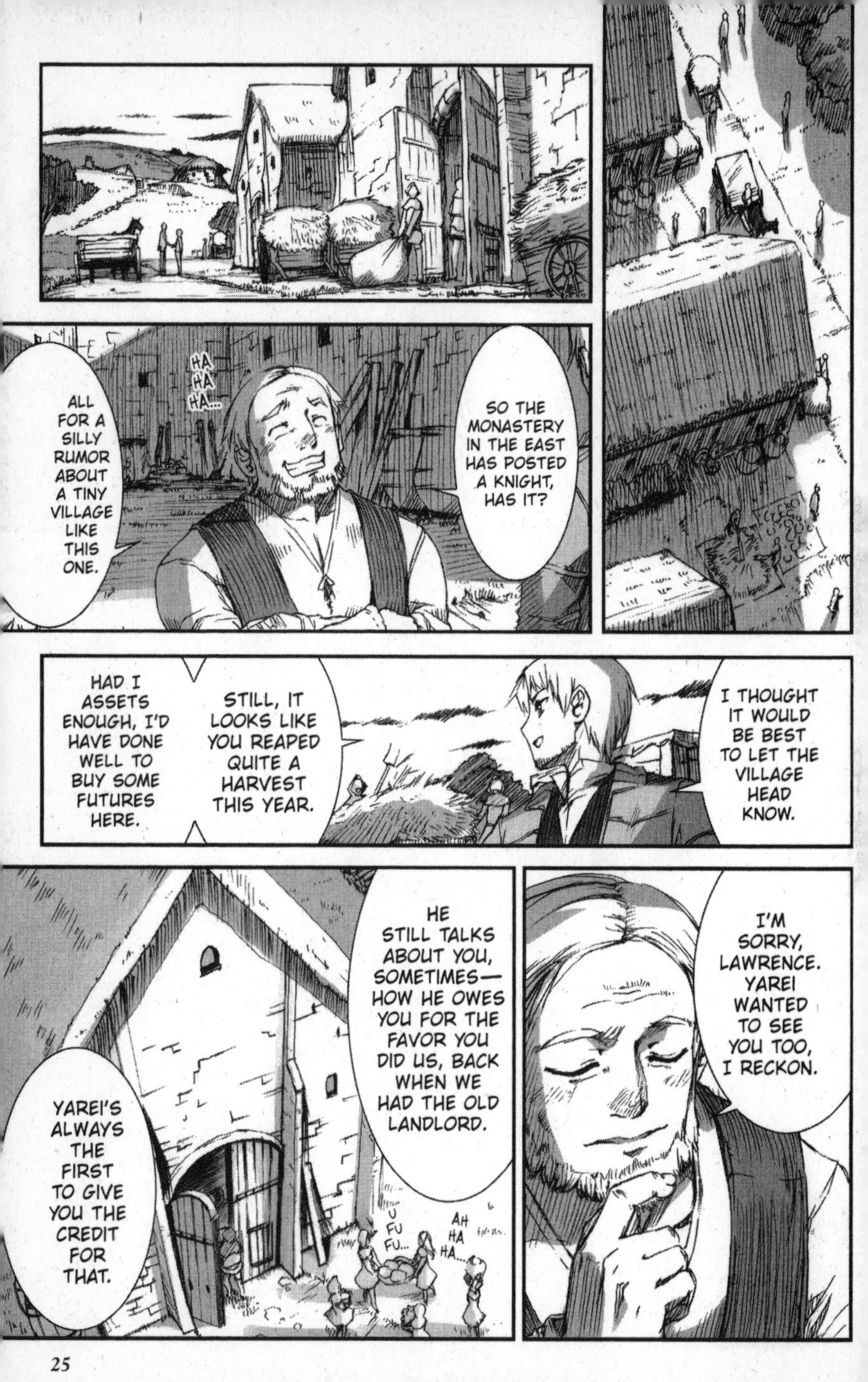
SO THE MONASTERY IN THE EAST HAS POSTED A KNIGHT, HAS IT?
HA HA HA...
ALL FOR A SILLY RUMOR ABOUT A TINY VILLAGE LIKE THIS ONE.
I THOUGHT IT WOULD BE BEST TO LET THE VILLAGE HEAD KNOW.
STILL, IT LOOKS LIKE YOU REAPED QUITE A HARVEST THIS YEAR.
HAD I ASSETS ENOUGH, I'D HAVE DONE WELL TO BUY SOME FUTURES HERE.
I'M SORRY, LAWRENCE. YAREI WANTED TO SEE YOU TOO, I RECKON.
HE STILL TALKS ABOUT YOU, SOMETIMES— HOW HE OWES YOU FOR THE FAVOR YOU DID US, BACK WHEN WE HAD THE OLD LANDLORD.
YAREI'S ALWAYS THE FIRST TO GIVE YOU THE CREDIT FOR THAT.
AH HA HA...
U FU FU...

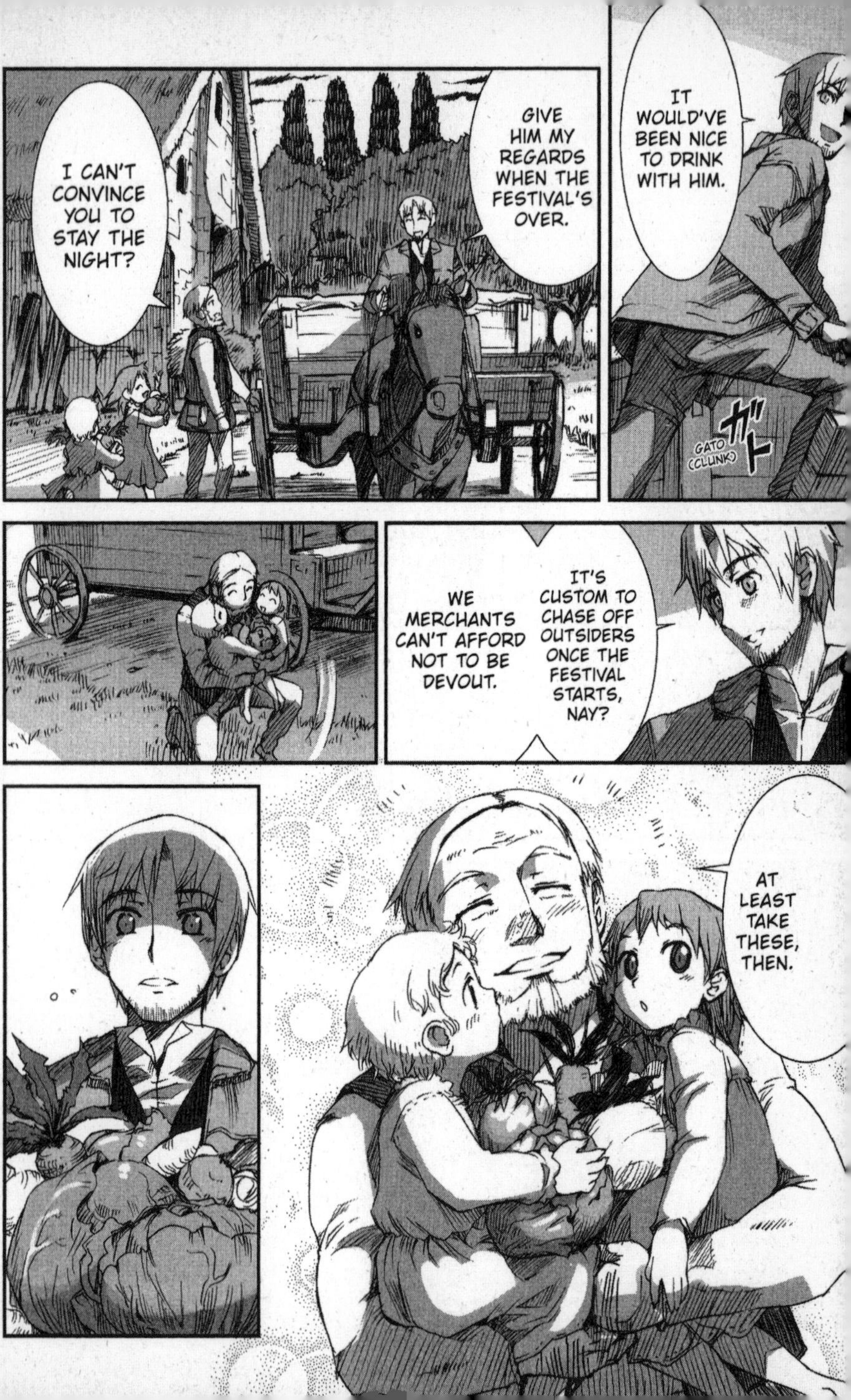
IT WOULD'VE BEEN NICE TO DRINK WITH HIM.
ガト
GATO (CLUNK)
GIVE HIM MY REGARDS WHEN THE FESTIVAL'S OVER.
I CAN'T CONVINCE YOU TO STAY THE NIGHT?
IT'S CUSTOM TO CHASE OFF OUTSIDERS ONCE THE FESTIVAL STARTS, NAY?
WE MERCHANTS CAN'T AFFORD NOT TO BE DEVOUT.
AT LEAST TAKE THESE, THEN.

DON
(BOOM)
ドン♪
TEN
(STING)
テン♪
DON
(BOOM)
ドン♪
TEN
テン
TY TEN
テン♪

SFX: GEFU (BURP)

GOTO
(CLOP)
ゴト
GOTO
ゴト

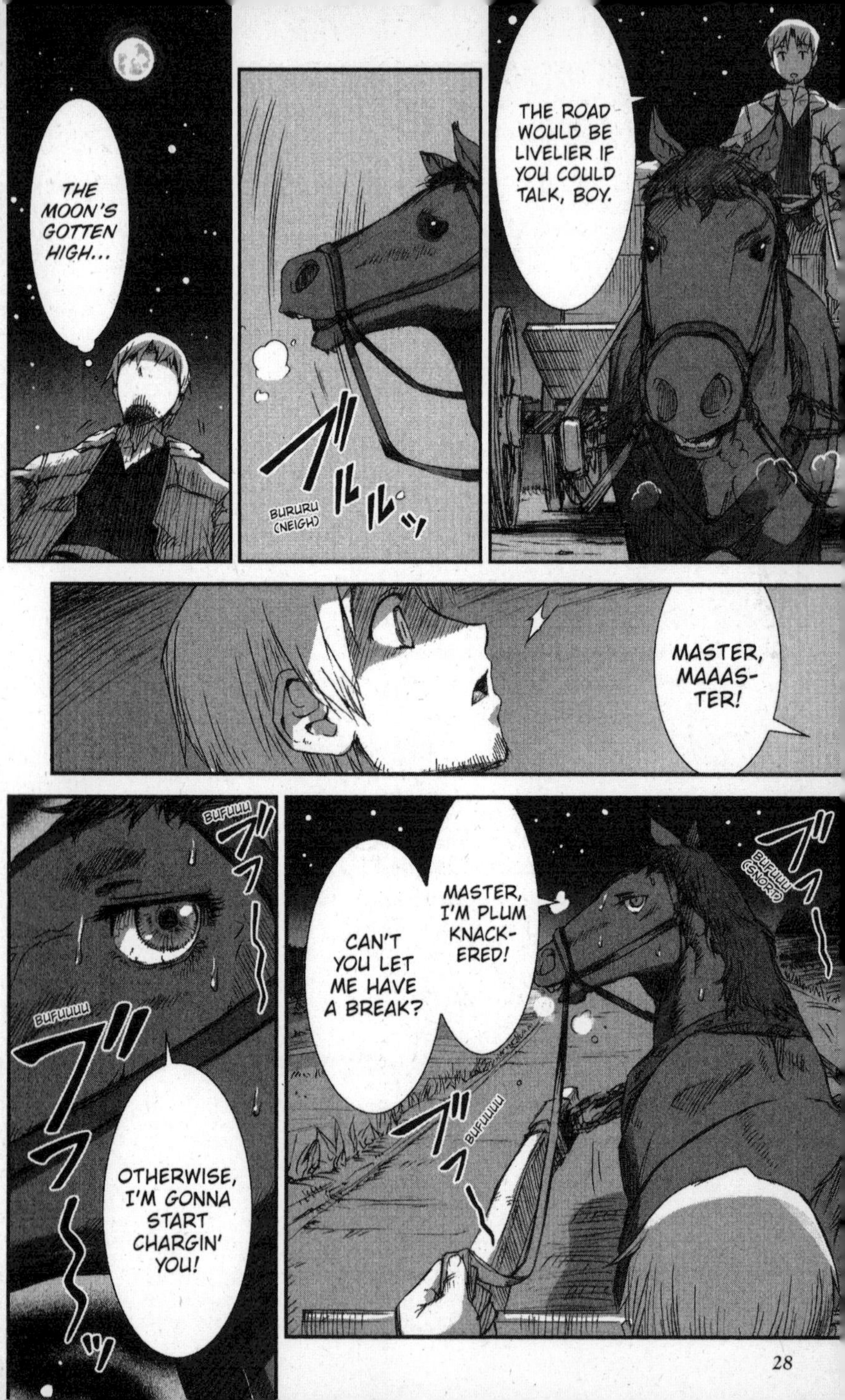
THE ROAD WOULD BE LIVELIER IF YOU COULD TALK, BOY.
BURURU (NEIGH)
THE MOON'S GOTTEN HIGH...
MASTER, MAAAS-TER!
BUFUUU (SNORT)
MASTER, I'M PLUM KNACK-ERED!
CAN'T YOU LET ME HAVE A BREAK?
BUFUUUU
BUFUUU
BUFUUUU
OTHERWISE, I'M GONNA START CHARGIN' YOU!

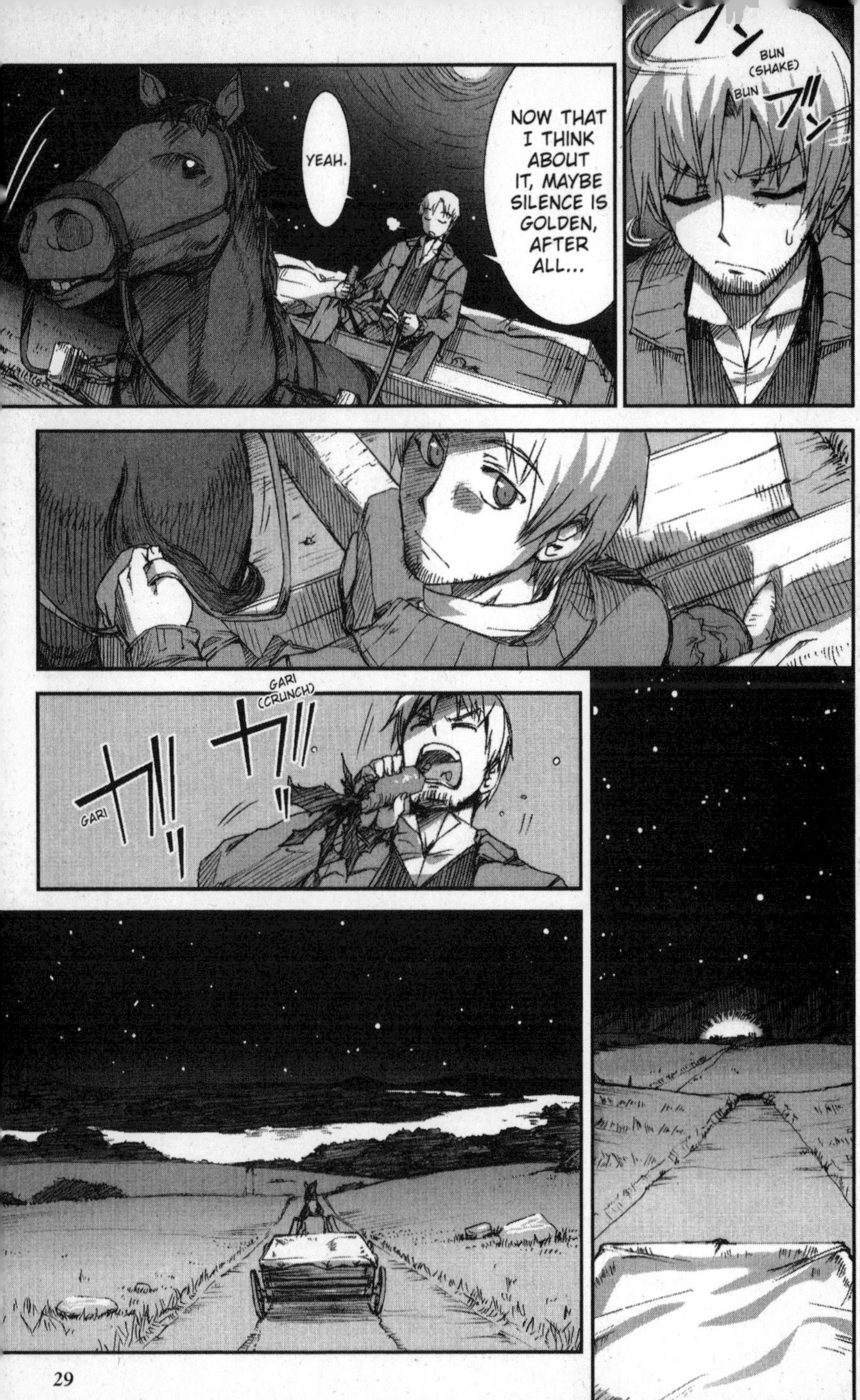
BUN (SHAKE)
BUN
NOW THAT I THINK ABOUT IT, MAYBE SILENCE IS GOLDEN, AFTER ALL...
YEAH.
GARI (CRUNCH)
GARI

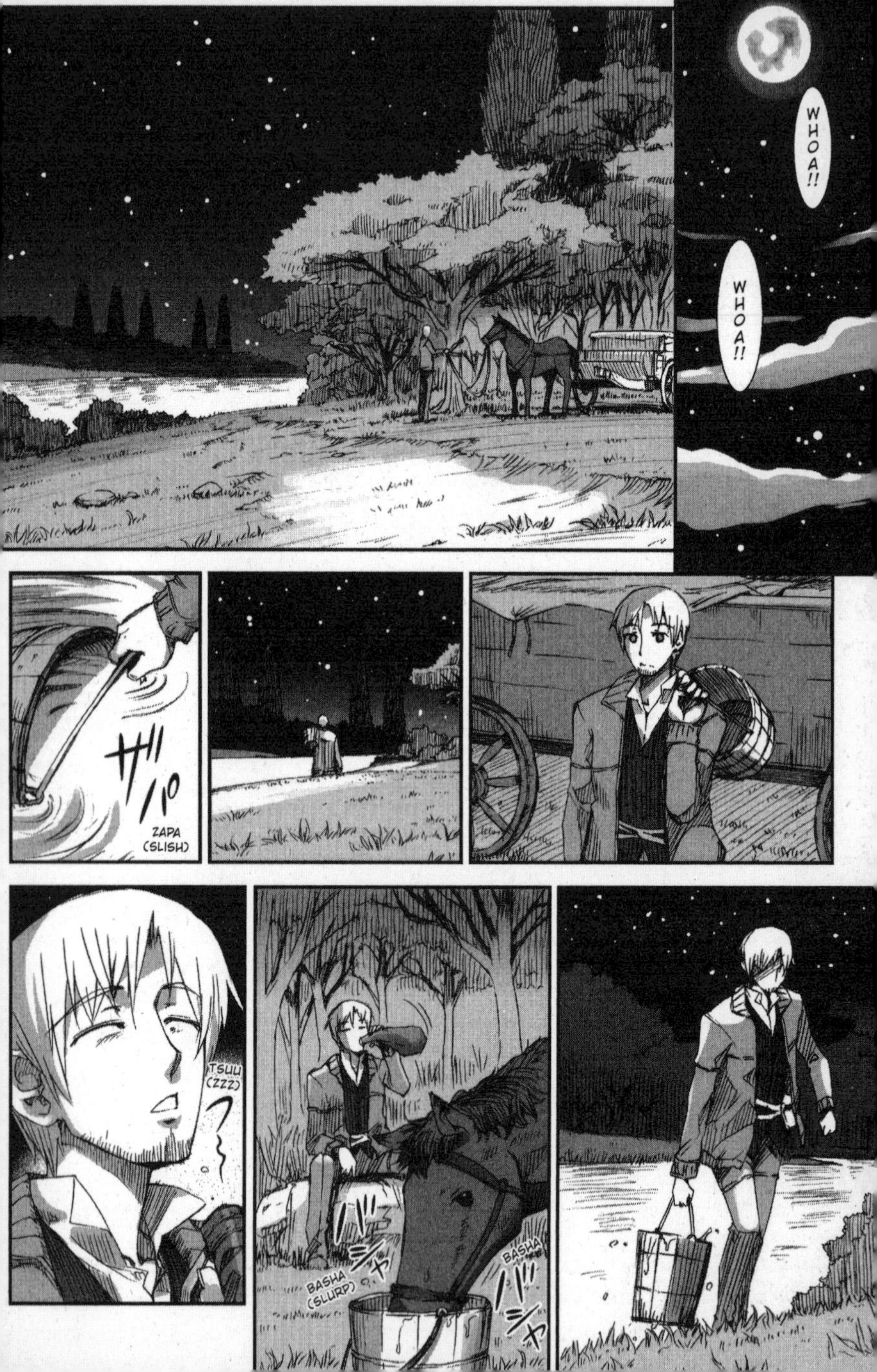
WHOA!!
WHOA!!
ZAPA (SLISH)
BASHA
BASHA (SLURP)
TSUU (ZZZ)

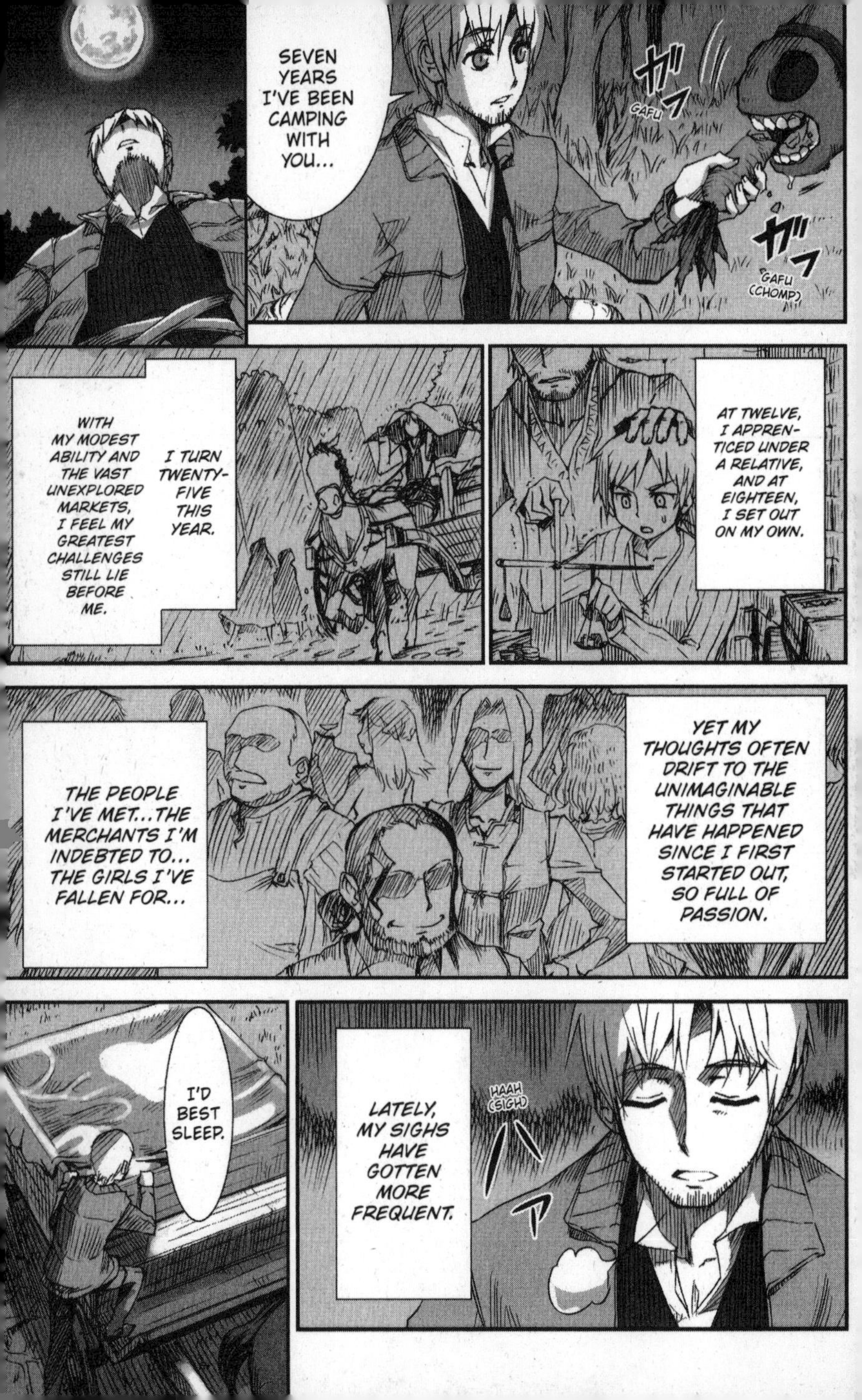
SEVEN YEARS I'VE BEEN CAMPING WITH YOU...
GAFU
GAFU (CHOMP)
AT TWELVE, I APPRENTICED UNDER A RELATIVE, AND AT EIGHTEEN, I SET OUT ON MY OWN.
I TURN TWENTY-FIVE THIS YEAR.
WITH MY MODEST ABILITY AND THE VAST UNEXPLORED MARKETS, I FEEL MY GREATEST CHALLENGES STILL LIE BEFORE ME.
YET MY THOUGHTS OFTEN DRIFT TO THE UNIMAGINABLE THINGS THAT HAVE HAPPENED SINCE I FIRST STARTED OUT, SO FULL OF PASSION.
THE PEOPLE I'VE MET...THE MERCHANTS I'M INDEBTED TO... THE GIRLS I'VE FALLEN FOR...
HAAH (SIGH)
LATELY, MY SIGHS HAVE GOTTEN MORE FREQUENT.
I'D BEST SLEEP.

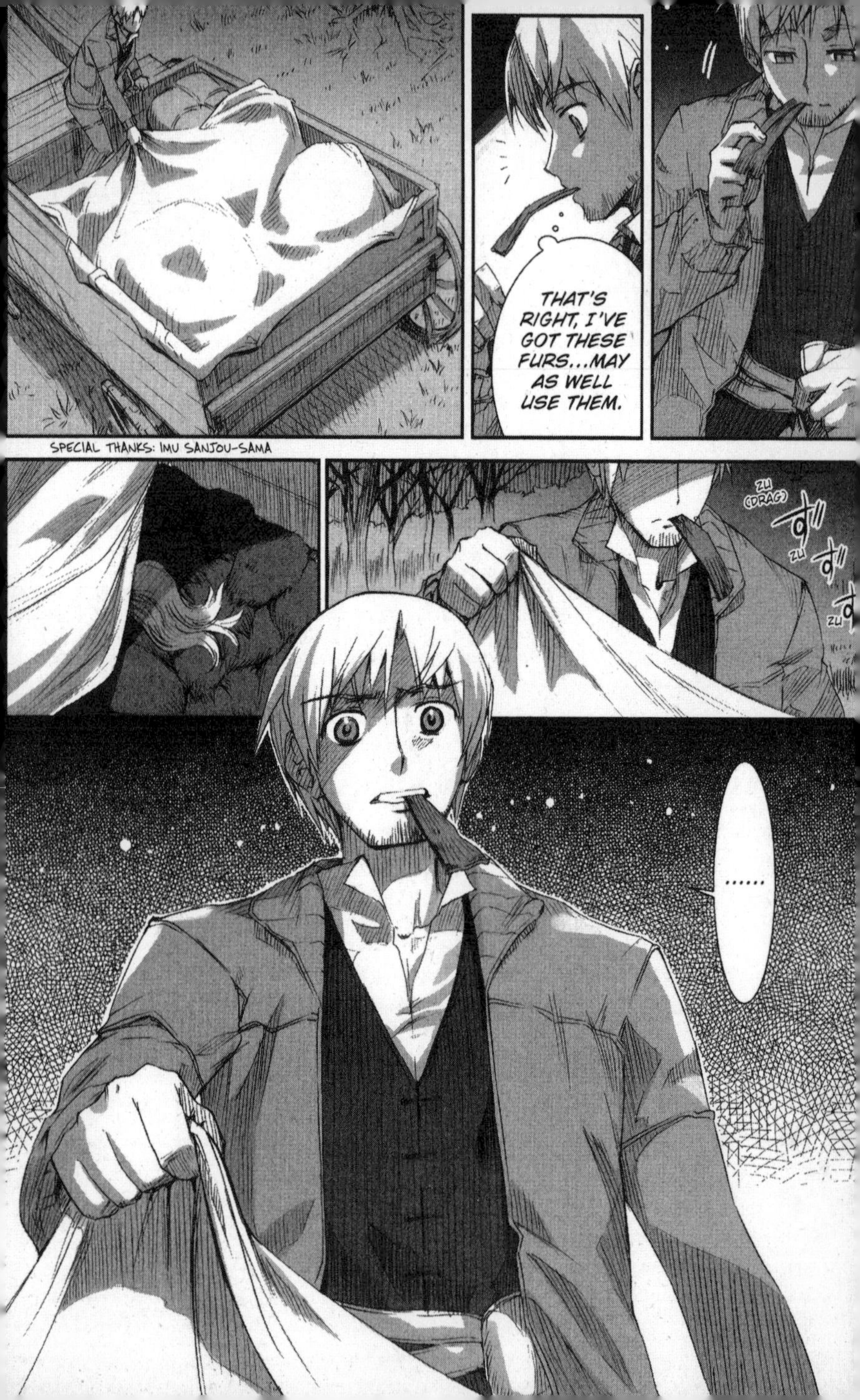
THAT'S RIGHT, I'VE GOT THESE FURS...MAY AS WELL USE THEM.
ZU (DRAG)
ZU
ZU
......

SPECIAL THANKS: IMU SANJOU-SAMA

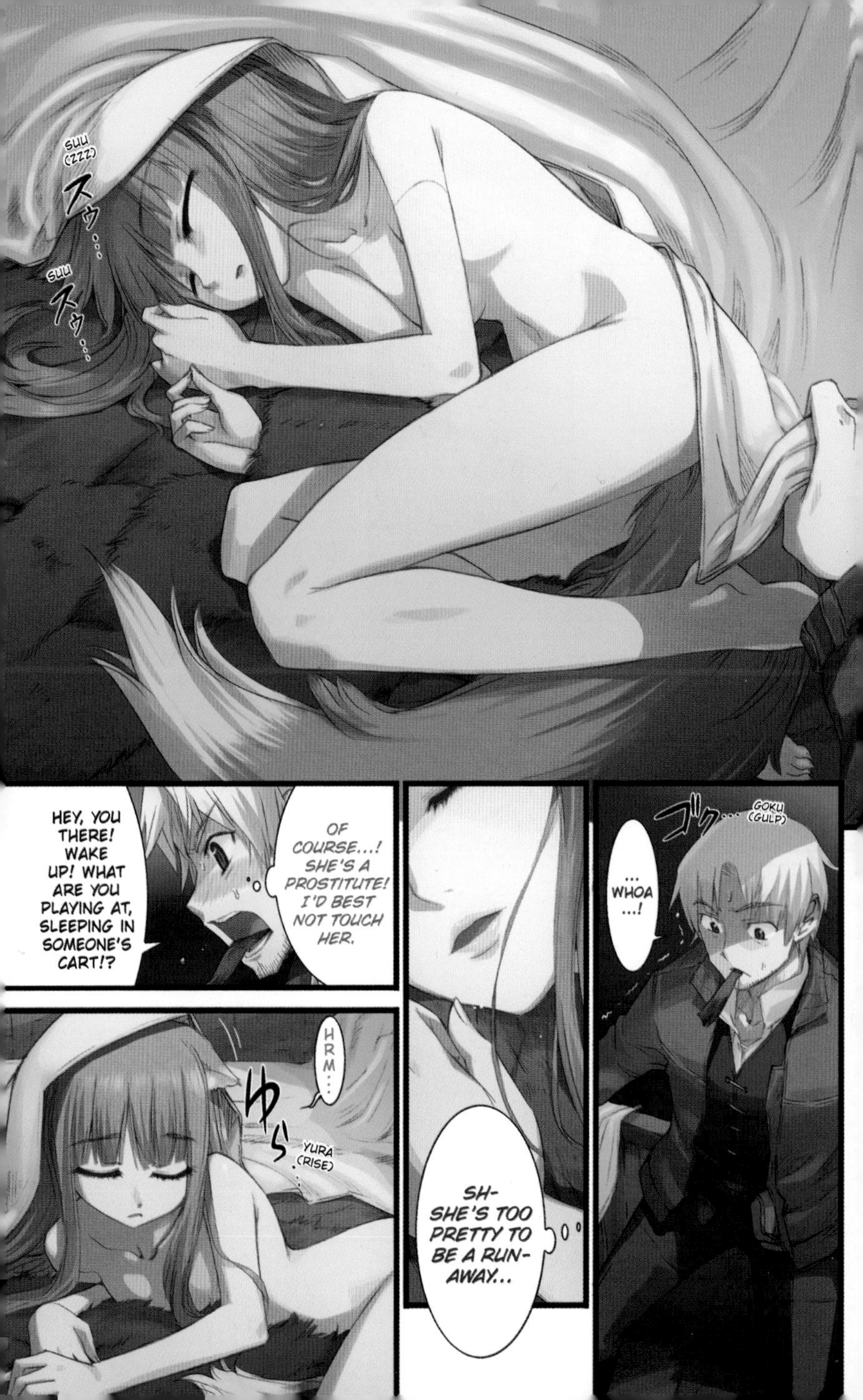
SUU (ZZZ)
スゥ…
SUU
スゥ…
ゴク…
GOKU (GULP)
…WHOA…!
SH-SHE'S TOO PRETTY TO BE A RUN-AWAY…
OF COURSE…! SHE'S A PROSTITUTE! I'D BEST NOT TOUCH HER.
HEY, YOU THERE! WAKE UP! WHAT ARE YOU PLAYING AT, SLEEPING IN SOMEONE'S CART!?
HRM…
ゆら
YURA (RISE)

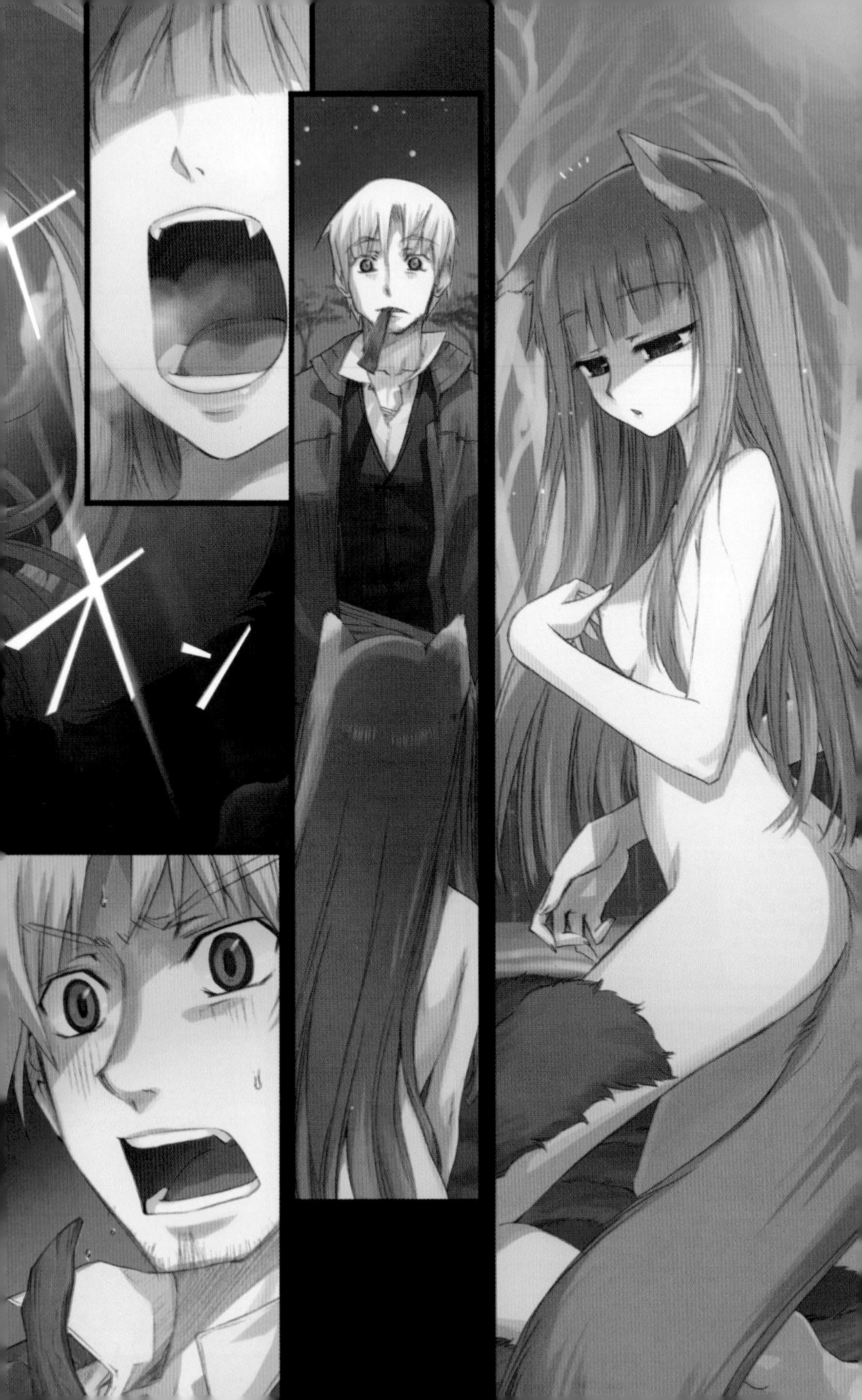

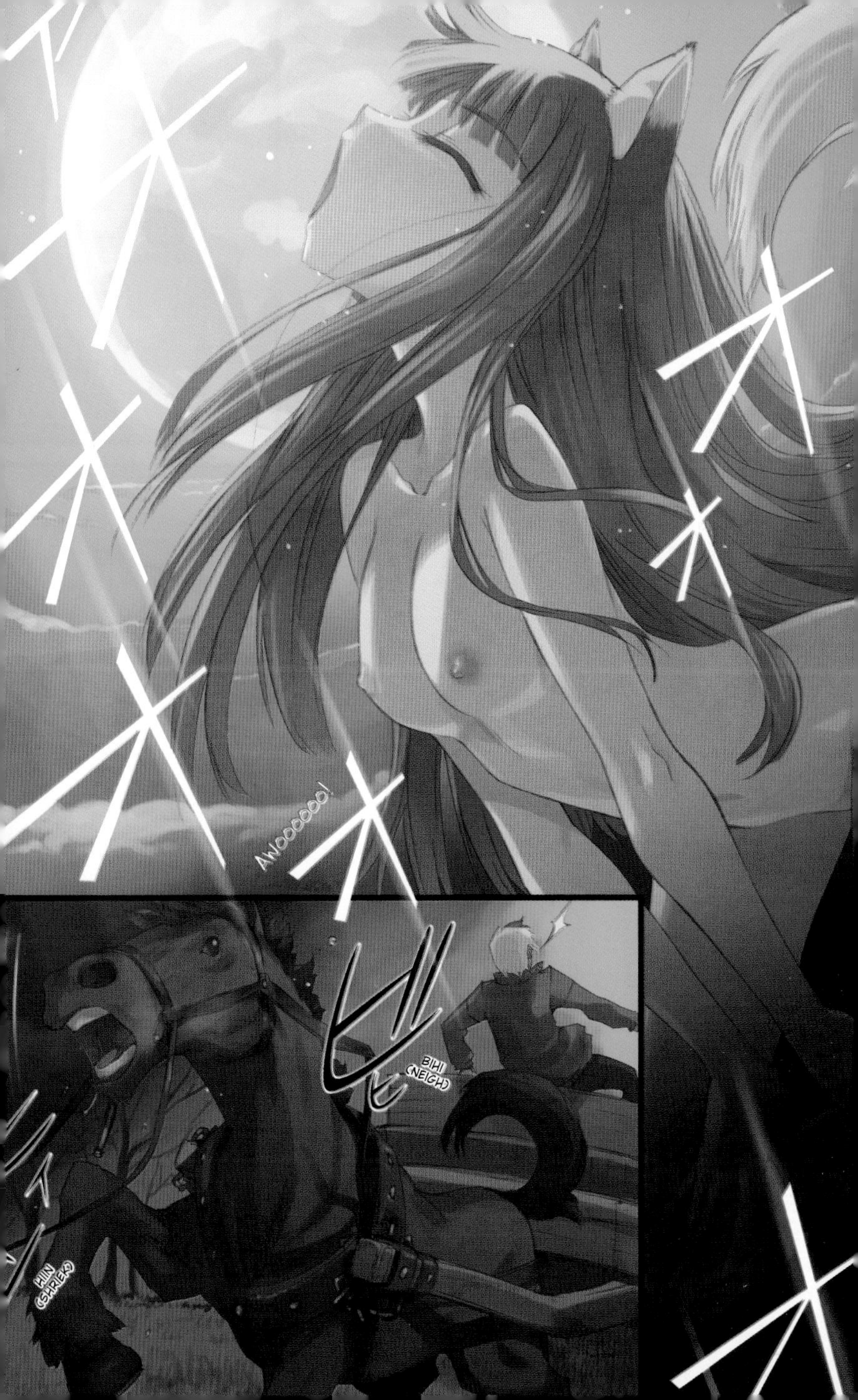
AWOOOOOOO!
BIHI (NEIGH)
HIIN (SHRIEK)

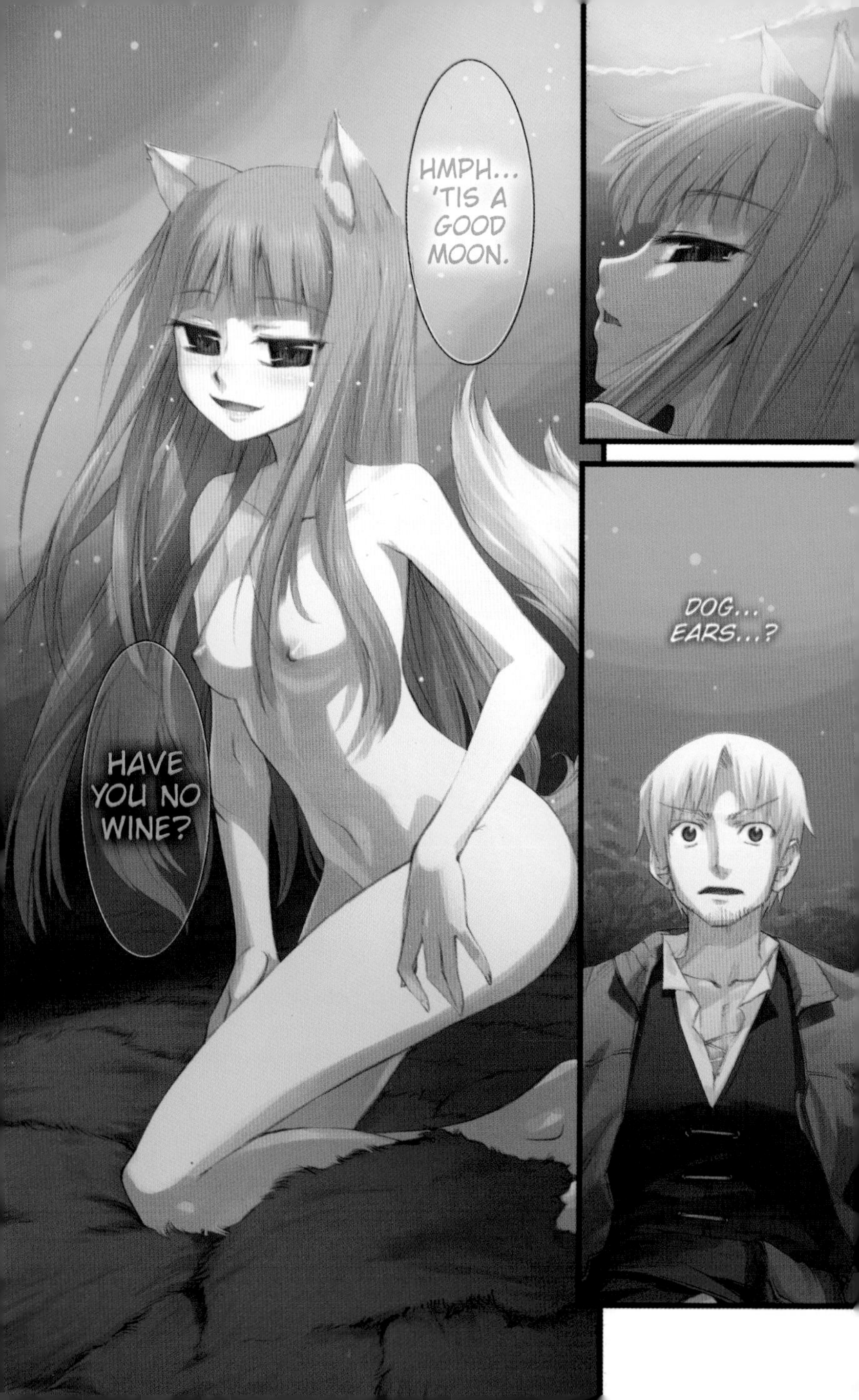
DOG... EARS...?
HMPH... 'TIS A GOOD MOON.
HAVE YOU NO WINE?

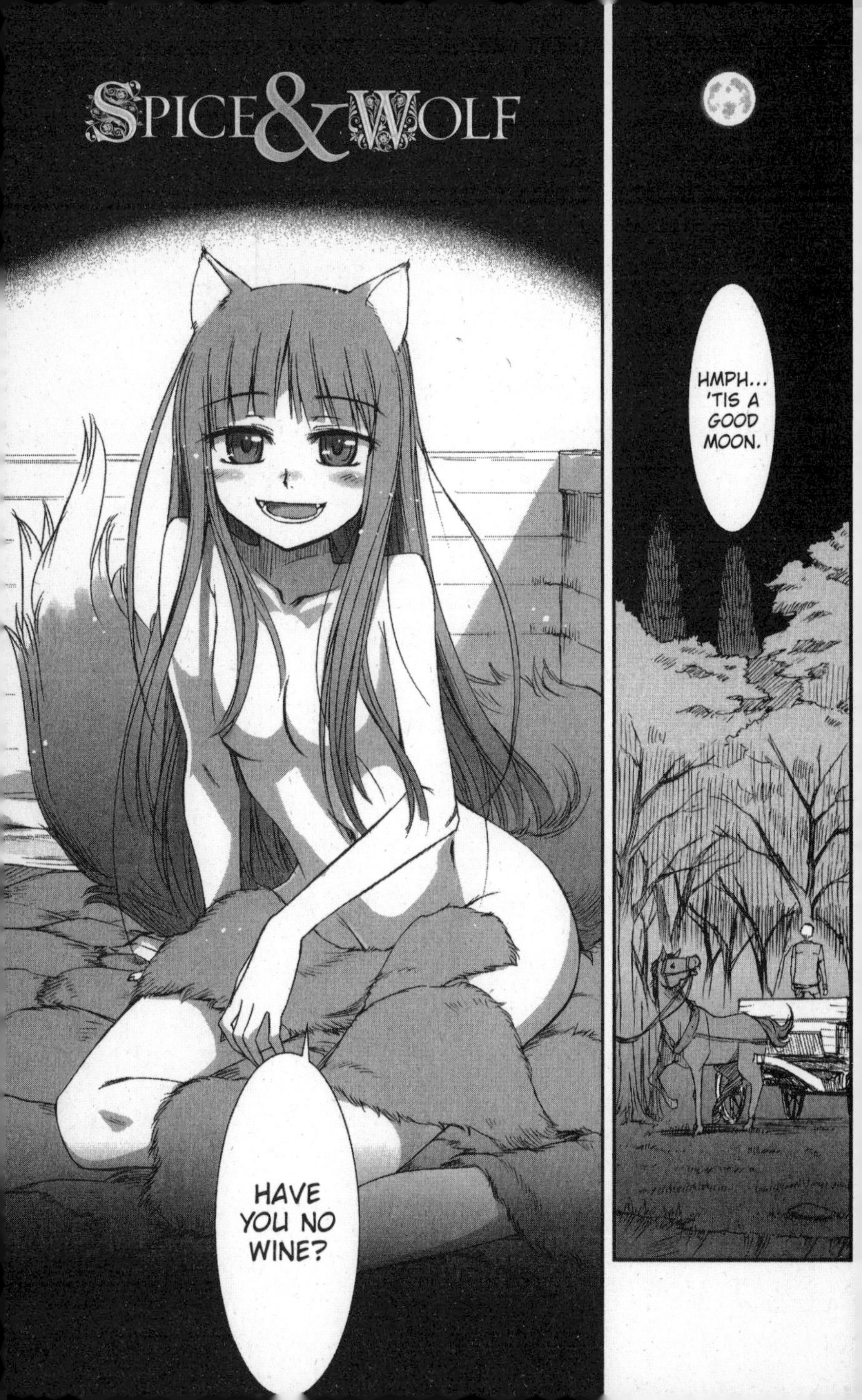
HMPH... 'TIS A GOOD MOON.
SPICE & WOLF
HAVE YOU NO WINE?

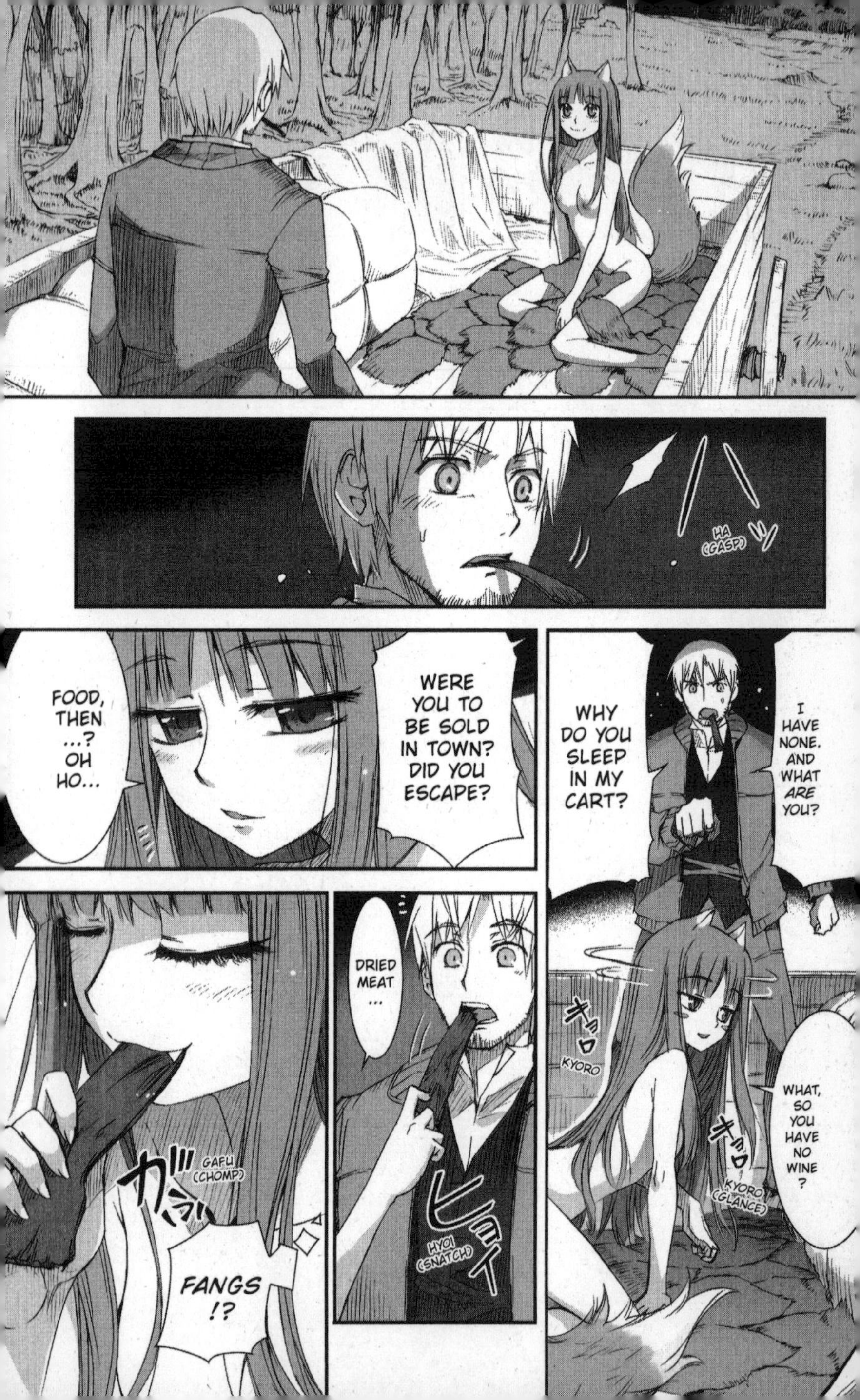
HA (GASP)
I HAVE NONE. AND WHAT *ARE* YOU?
WHY DO YOU SLEEP IN MY CART?
KYORO
WHAT, SO YOU HAVE NO WINE?
KYORO (GLANCE)
WERE YOU TO BE SOLD IN TOWN? DID YOU ESCAPE?
FOOD, THEN ...? OH HO...
DRIED MEAT ...
HYOI (SNATCH)
GAFU (CHOMP)
FANGS !?

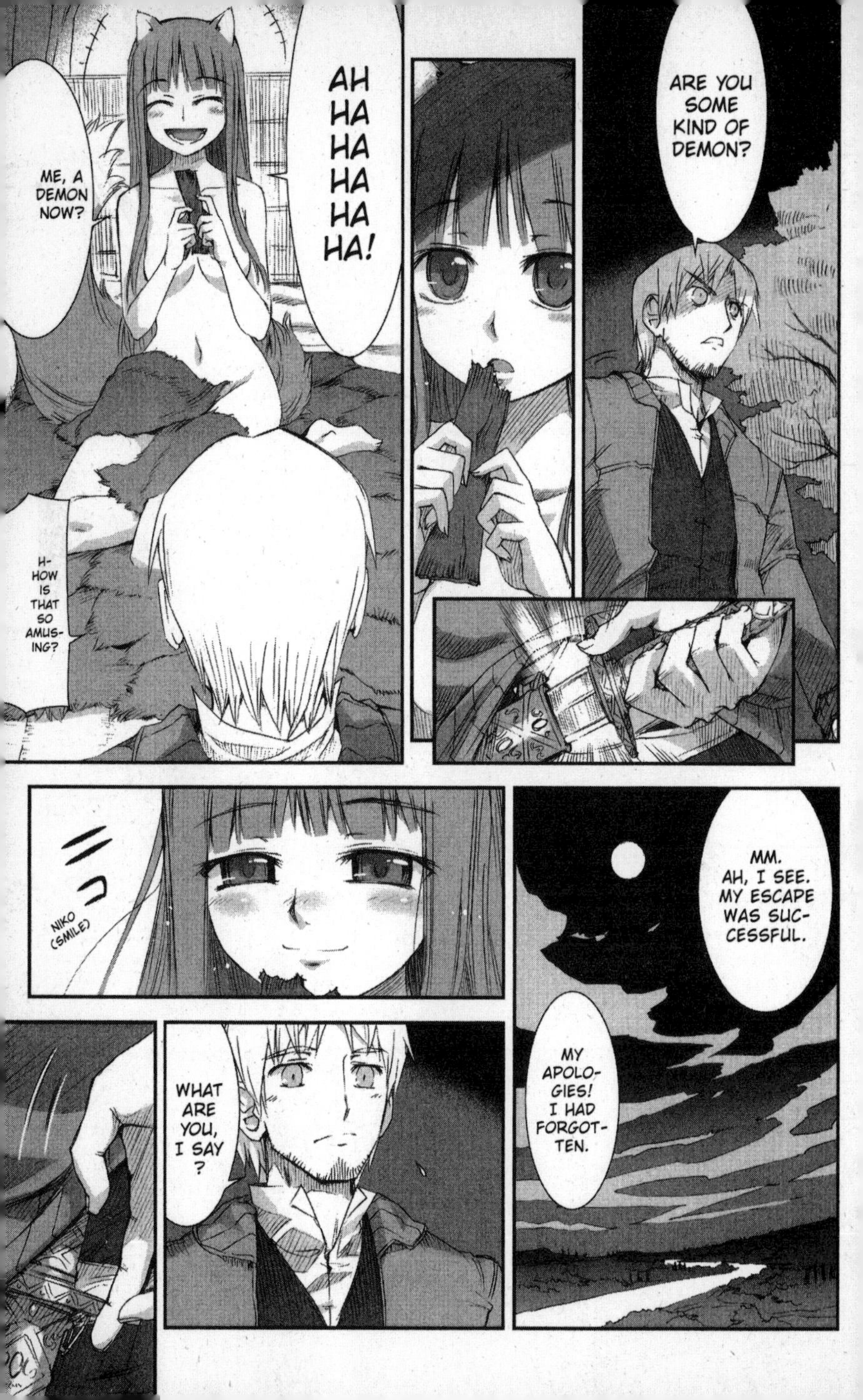

ARE YOU SOME KIND OF DEMON?
AH HA HA HA HA HA HA!
ME, A DEMON NOW?
H-HOW IS THAT SO AMUSING?
MM. AH, I SEE. MY ESCAPE WAS SUCCESSFUL.
MY APOLOGIES! I HAD FORGOTTEN.
NIKO (SMILE)
WHAT ARE YOU, I SAY?

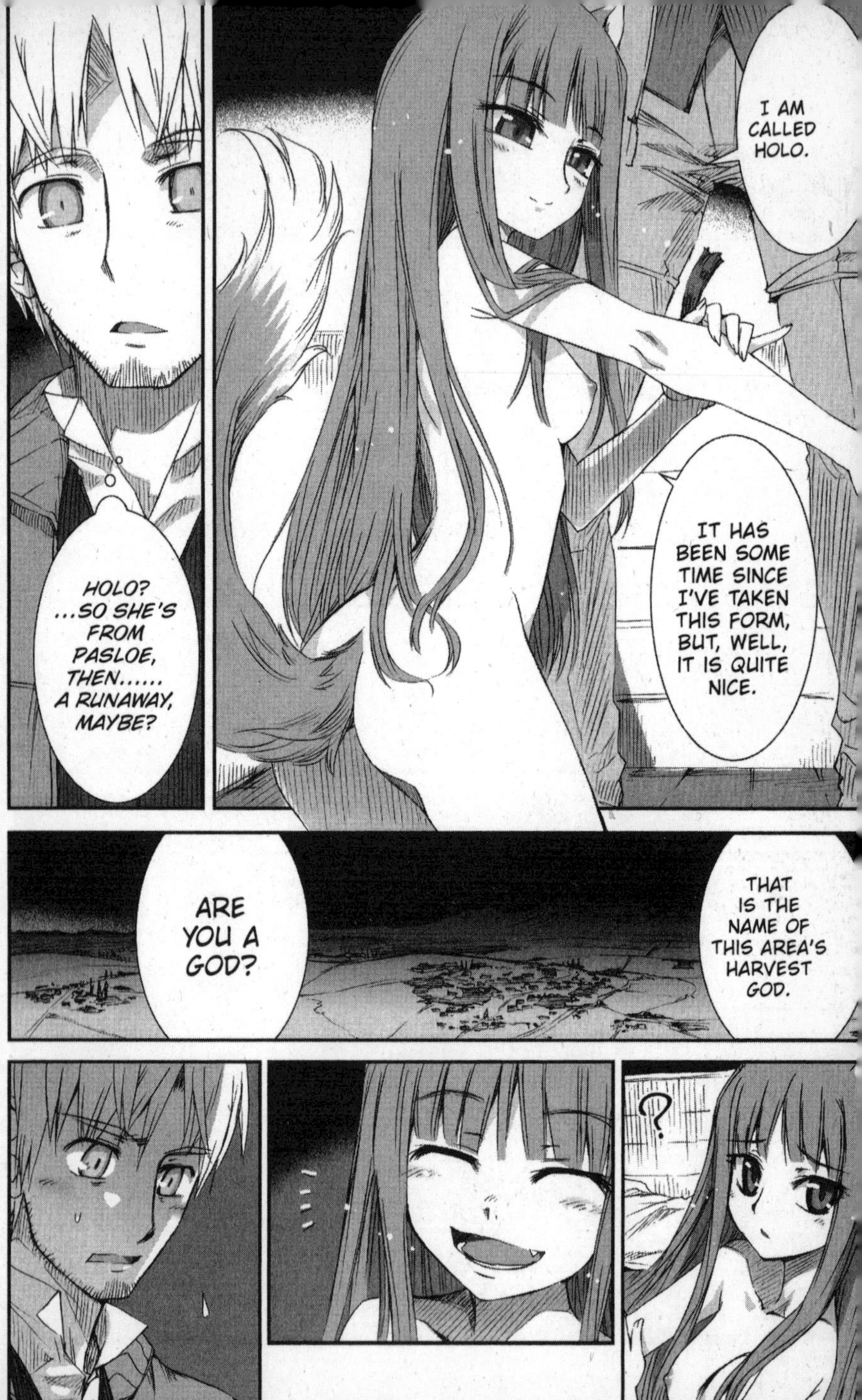
I AM CALLED HOLO.
IT HAS BEEN SOME TIME SINCE I'VE TAKEN THIS FORM, BUT, WELL, IT IS QUITE NICE.
HOLO? ...SO SHE'S FROM PASLOE, THEN...... A RUNAWAY, MAYBE?
THAT IS THE NAME OF THIS AREA'S HARVEST GOD.
ARE YOU A GOD?
?

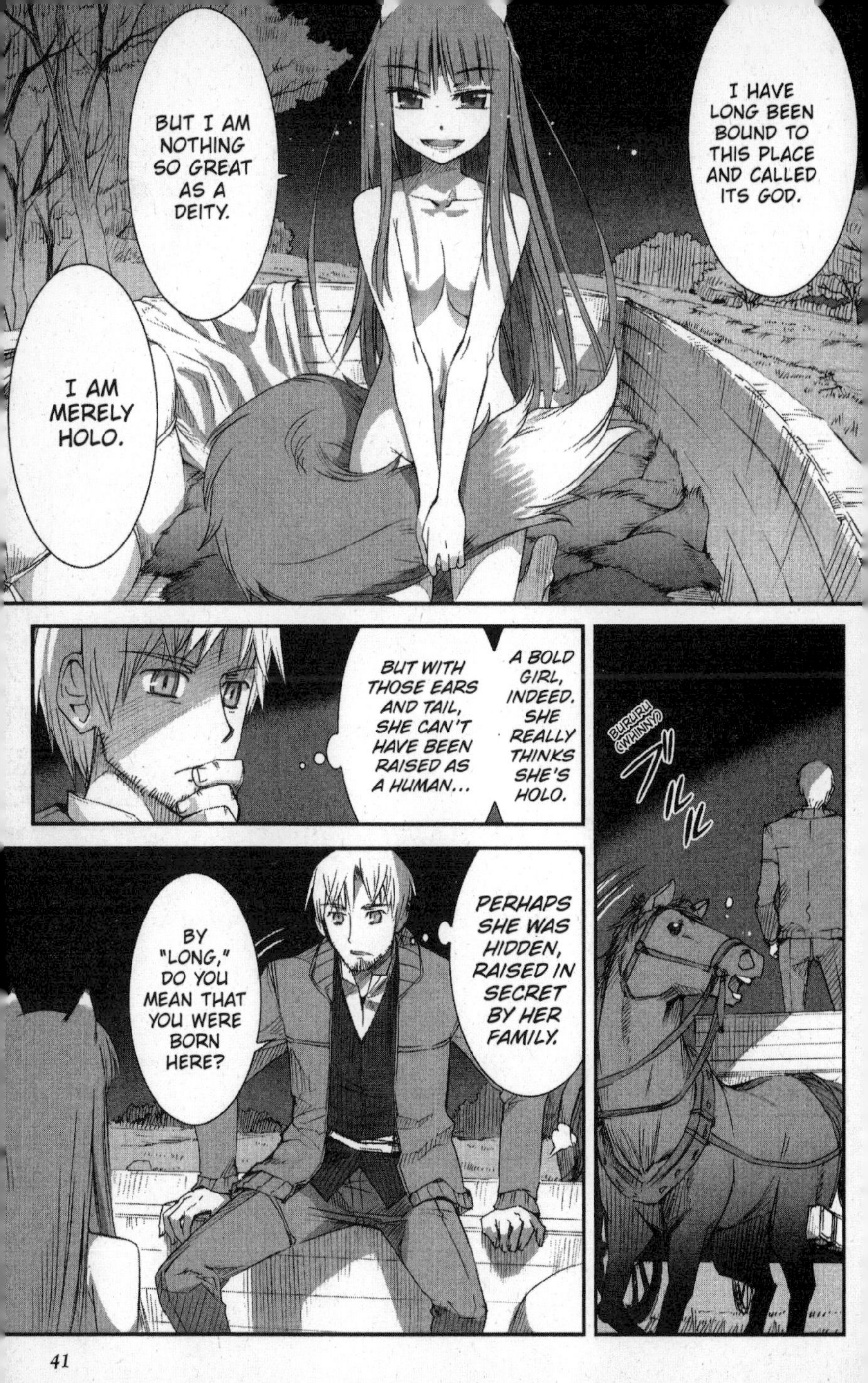
I HAVE LONG BEEN BOUND TO THIS PLACE AND CALLED ITS GOD.
BUT I AM NOTHING SO GREAT AS A DEITY.
I AM MERELY HOLO.
BURURU (WHINNY)
ブルル
A BOLD GIRL, INDEED. SHE REALLY THINKS SHE'S HOLO.
BUT WITH THOSE EARS AND TAIL, SHE CAN'T HAVE BEEN RAISED AS A HUMAN...
PERHAPS SHE WAS HIDDEN, RAISED IN SECRET BY HER FAMILY.
BY "LONG," DO YOU MEAN THAT YOU WERE BORN HERE?

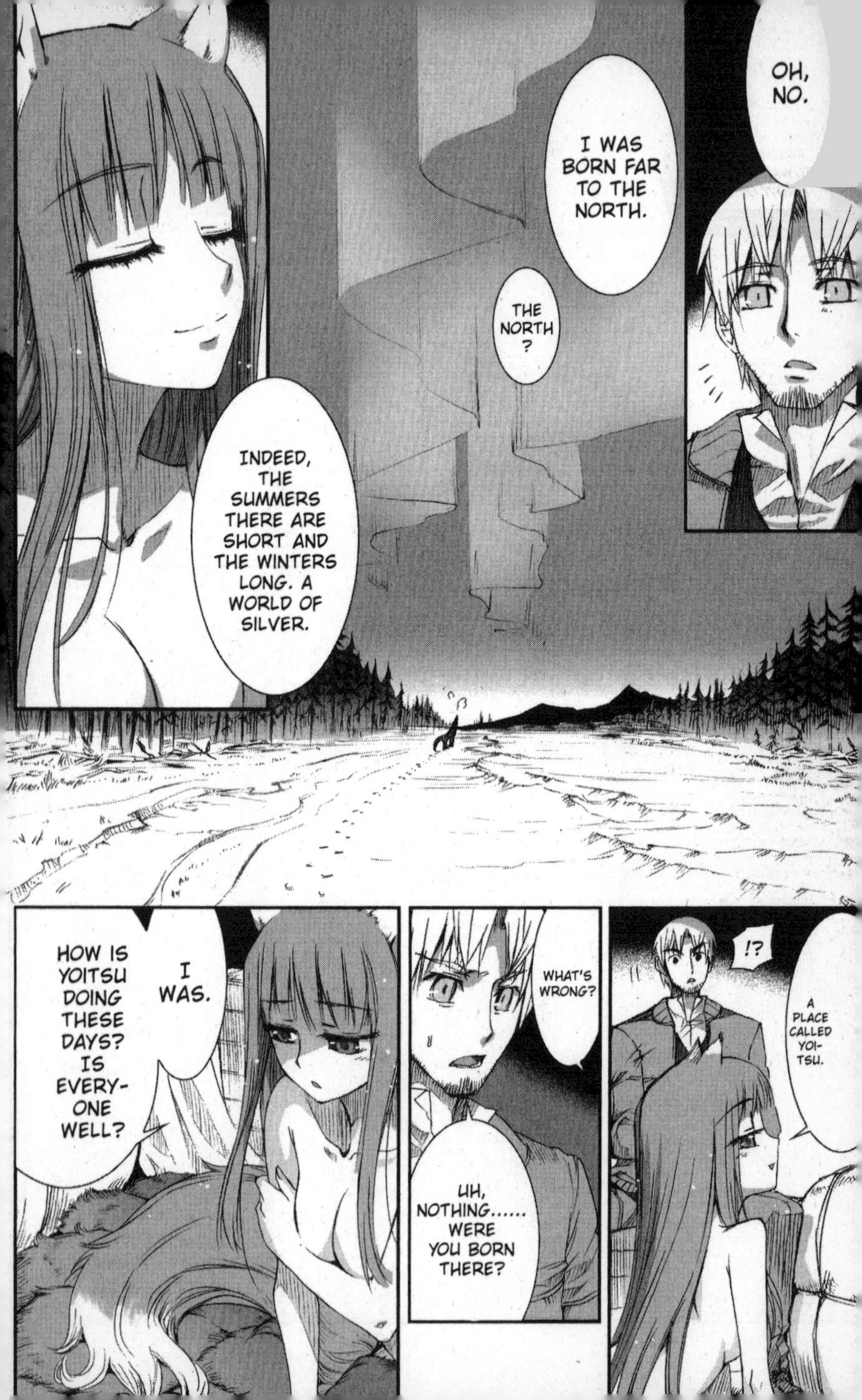
OH, NO.
I WAS BORN FAR TO THE NORTH.
THE NORTH?
INDEED, THE SUMMERS THERE ARE SHORT AND THE WINTERS LONG. A WORLD OF SILVER.
A PLACE CALLED YOI-TSU.
!?
WHAT'S WRONG?
UH, NOTHING...... WERE YOU BORN THERE?
I WAS.
HOW IS YOITSU DOING THESE DAYS? IS EVERY-ONE WELL?

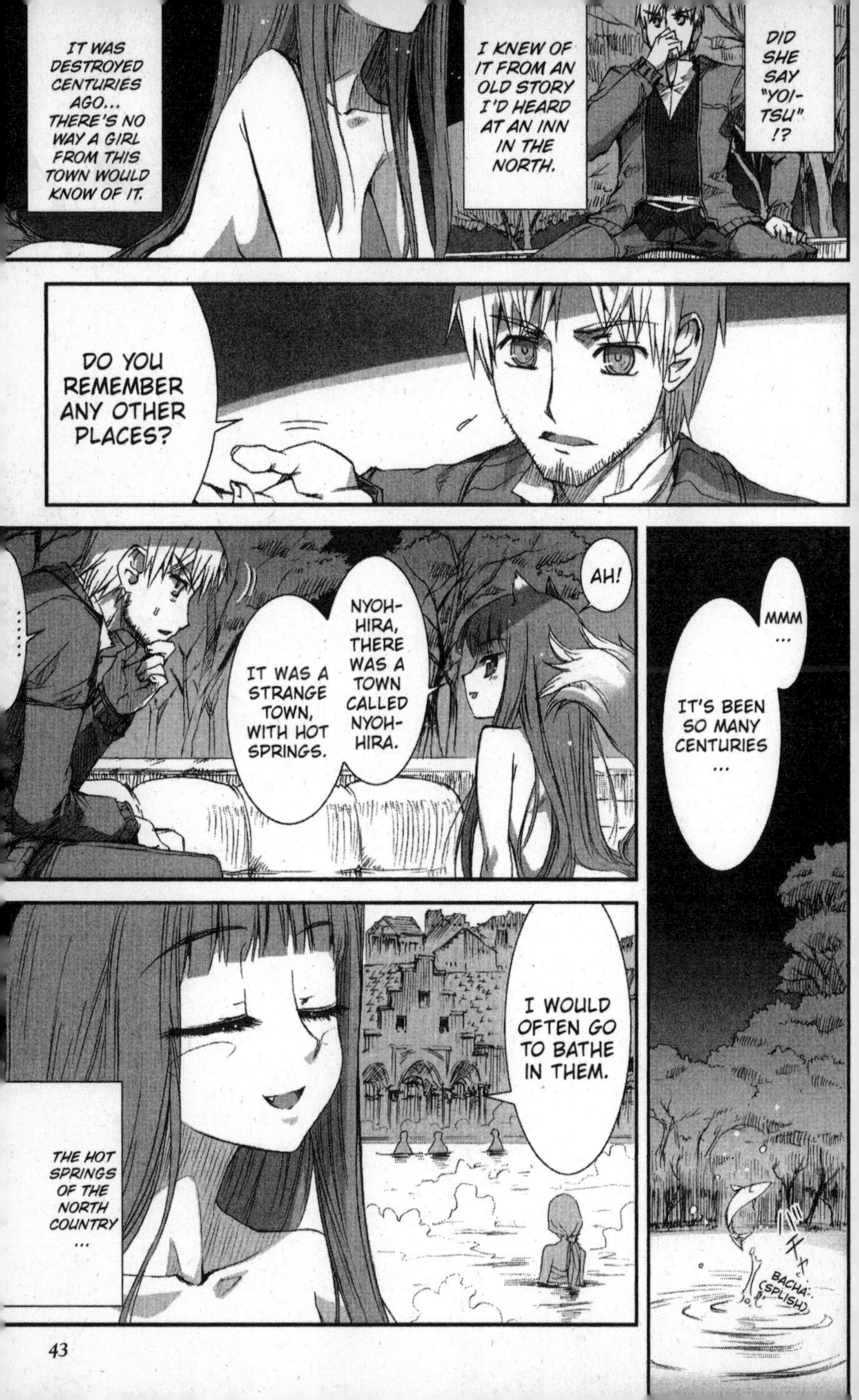
DID SHE SAY "YOI-TSU" !?
I KNEW OF IT FROM AN OLD STORY I'D HEARD AT AN INN IN THE NORTH.
IT WAS DESTROYED CENTURIES AGO... THERE'S NO WAY A GIRL FROM THIS TOWN WOULD KNOW OF IT.
DO YOU REMEMBER ANY OTHER PLACES?
MMM...
IT'S BEEN SO MANY CENTURIES...
BACHA (SPLISH)
AH!
NYOH-HIRA, THERE WAS A TOWN CALLED NYOH-HIRA.
IT WAS A STRANGE TOWN, WITH HOT SPRINGS.
...
I WOULD OFTEN GO TO BATHE IN THEM.
THE HOT SPRINGS OF THE NORTH COUNTRY...

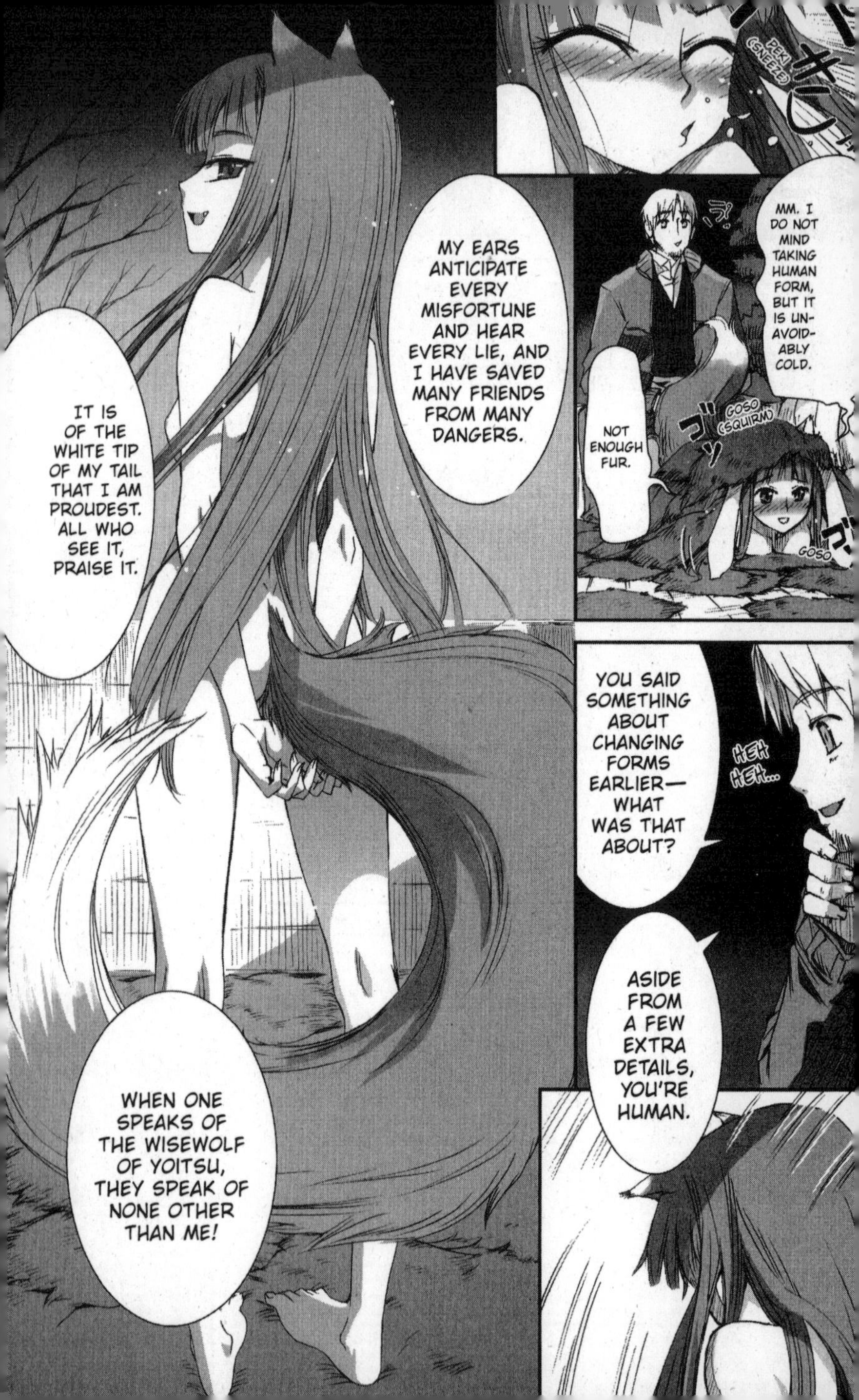
PEKI (SNEEZE)
MM. I DO NOT MIND TAKING HUMAN FORM, BUT IT IS UN-AVOID-ABLY COLD.
GOSO (SQUIRM)
NOT ENOUGH FUR.
GOSO
YOU SAID SOMETHING ABOUT CHANGING FORMS EARLIER— WHAT WAS THAT ABOUT?
HEH HEH...
ASIDE FROM A FEW EXTRA DETAILS, YOU'RE HUMAN.
MY EARS ANTICIPATE EVERY MISFORTUNE AND HEAR EVERY LIE, AND I HAVE SAVED MANY FRIENDS FROM MANY DANGERS.
IT IS OF THE WHITE TIP OF MY TAIL THAT I AM PROUDEST. ALL WHO SEE IT, PRAISE IT.
WHEN ONE SPEAKS OF THE WISEWOLF OF YOITSU, THEY SPEAK OF NONE OTHER THAN ME!

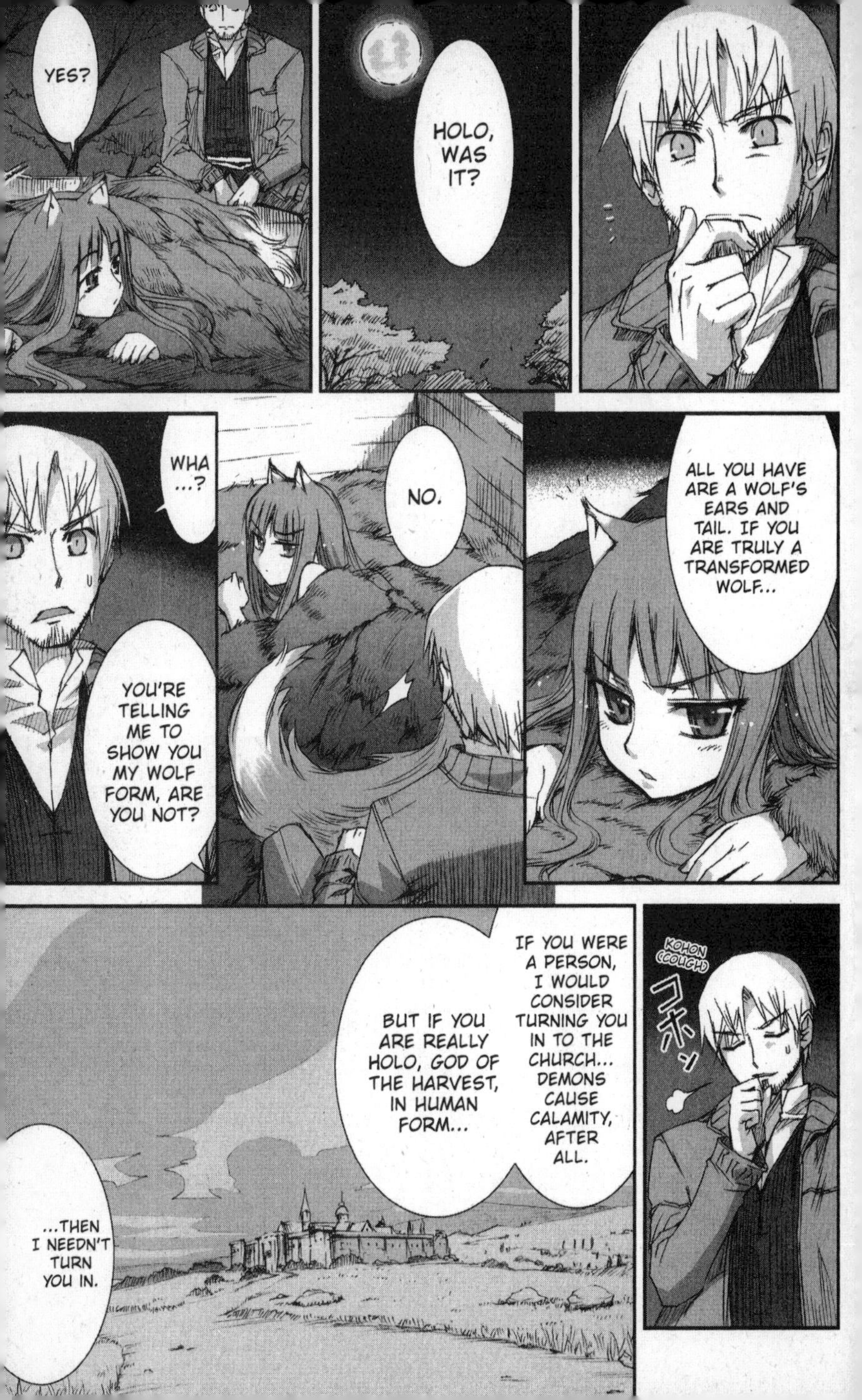
HOLO, WAS IT?
YES?
ALL YOU HAVE ARE A WOLF'S EARS AND TAIL. IF YOU ARE TRULY A TRANSFORMED WOLF...
NO.
WHA...?
YOU'RE TELLING ME TO SHOW YOU MY WOLF FORM, ARE YOU NOT?
KOHON (COUGH)
コホン
IF YOU WERE A PERSON, I WOULD CONSIDER TURNING YOU IN TO THE CHURCH... DEMONS CAUSE CALAMITY, AFTER ALL.
BUT IF YOU ARE REALLY HOLO, GOD OF THE HARVEST, IN HUMAN FORM...
...THEN I NEEDN'T TURN YOU IN.

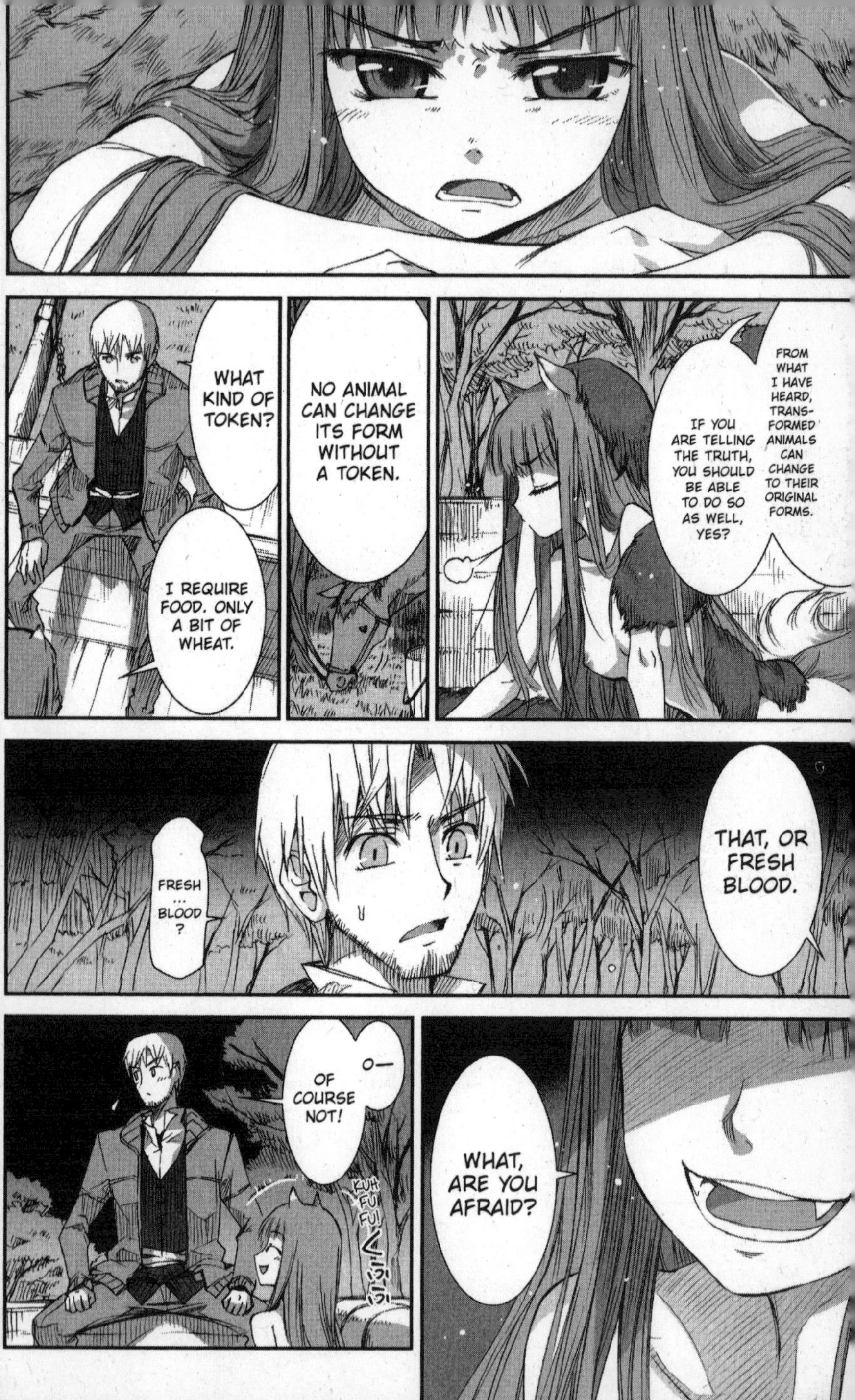
FROM WHAT I HAVE HEARD, TRANS-FORMED ANIMALS CAN CHANGE TO THEIR ORIGINAL FORMS.
IF YOU ARE TELLING THE TRUTH, YOU SHOULD BE ABLE TO DO SO AS WELL, YES?
NO ANIMAL CAN CHANGE ITS FORM WITHOUT A TOKEN.
WHAT KIND OF TOKEN?
I REQUIRE FOOD. ONLY A BIT OF WHEAT.
THAT, OR FRESH BLOOD.
FRESH ... BLOOD?
WHAT, ARE YOU AFRAID?
O— OF COURSE NOT!
KUH FU FU!
くふふ

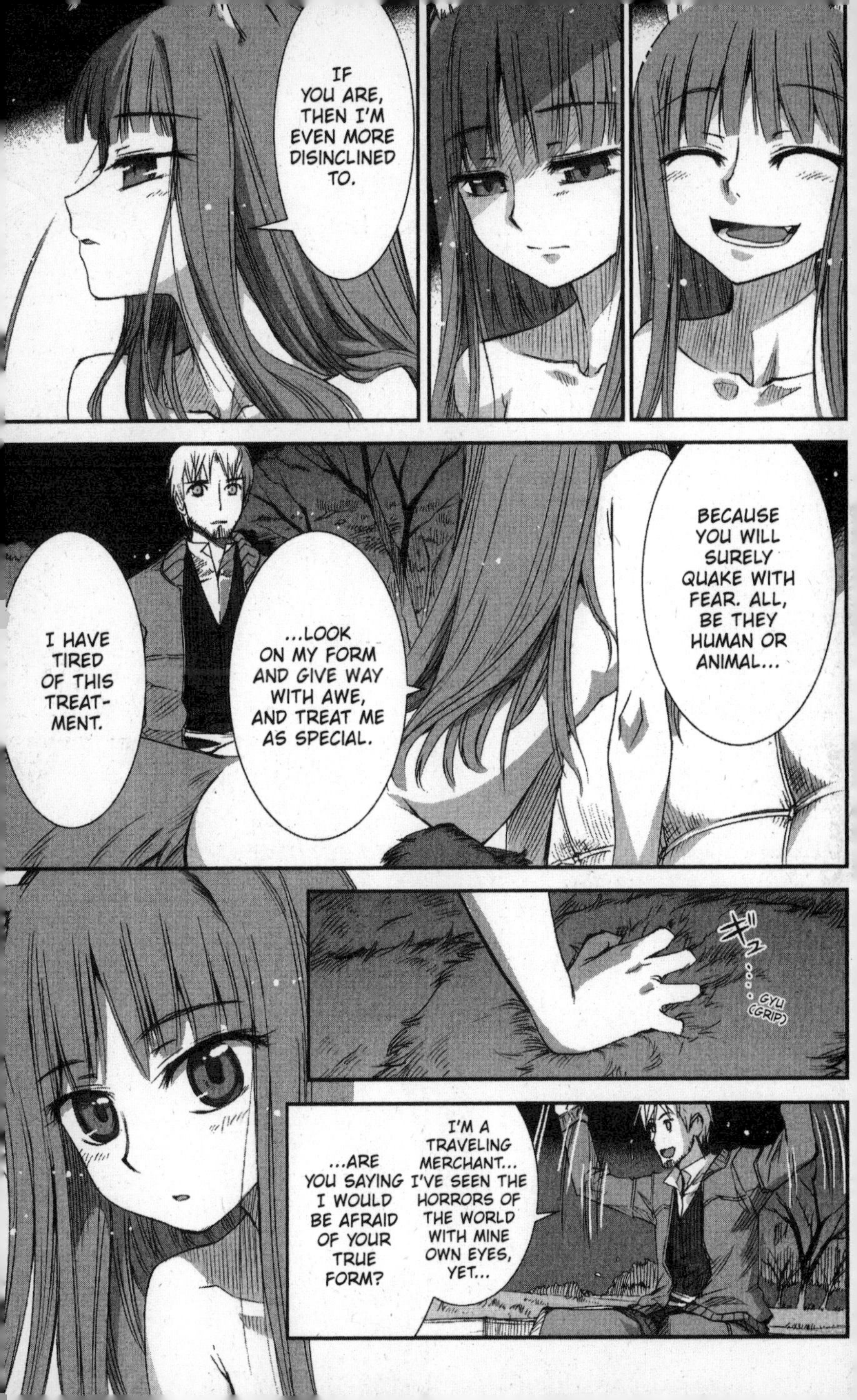
IF YOU ARE, THEN I'M EVEN MORE DISINCLINED TO.
BECAUSE YOU WILL SURELY QUAKE WITH FEAR. ALL, BE THEY HUMAN OR ANIMAL...
...LOOK ON MY FORM AND GIVE WAY WITH AWE, AND TREAT ME AS SPECIAL.
I HAVE TIRED OF THIS TREAT-MENT.
ギュ
GYU (GRIP)
I'M A TRAVELING MERCHANT... I'VE SEEN THE HORRORS OF THE WORLD WITH MINE OWN EYES, YET...
...ARE YOU SAYING I WOULD BE AFRAID OF YOUR TRUE FORM?

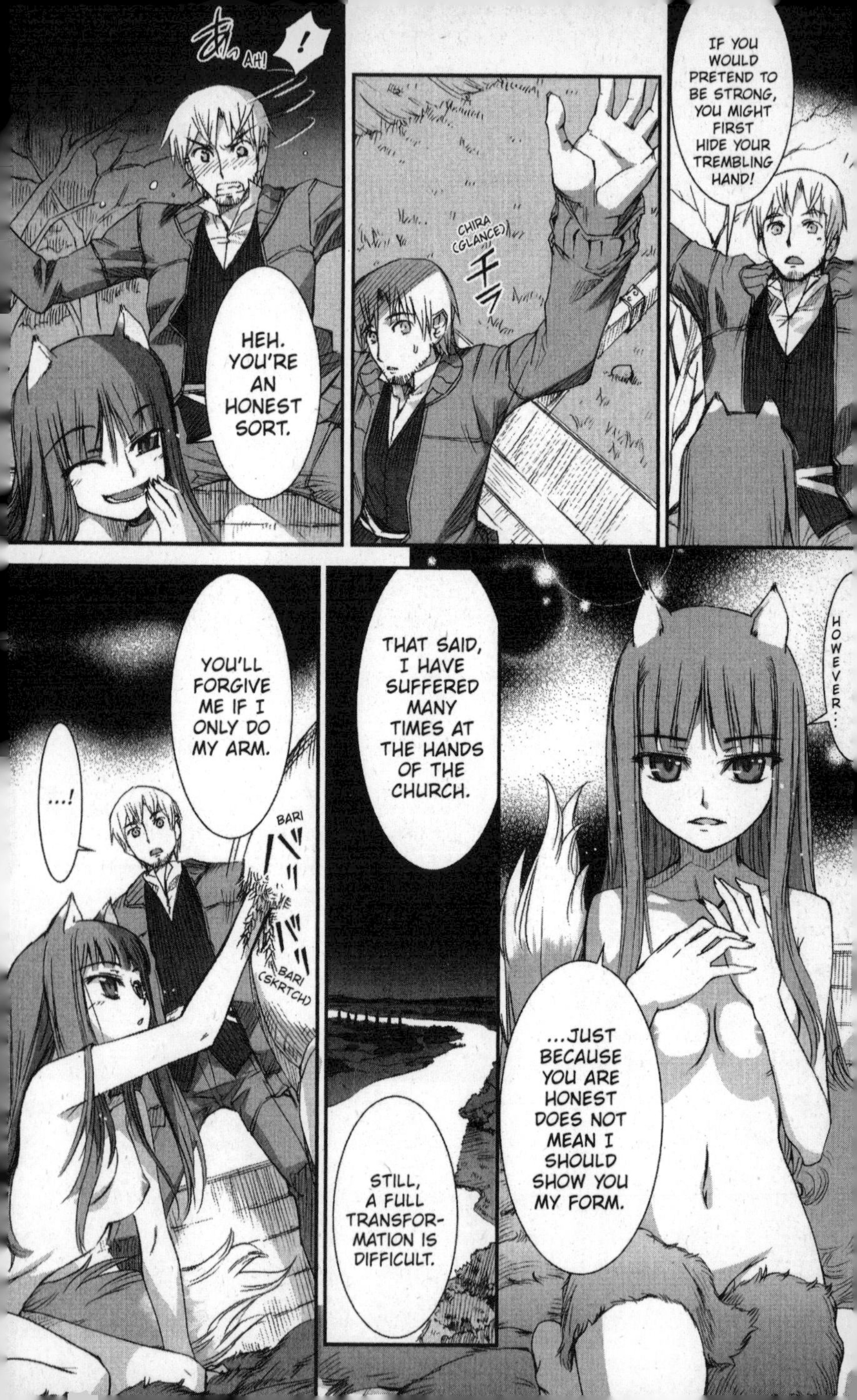
IF YOU WOULD PRETEND TO BE STRONG, YOU MIGHT FIRST HIDE YOUR TREMBLING HAND!
CHIRA (GLANCE)
チラ
あっ AH!
!
HEH. YOU'RE AN HONEST SORT.
HOWEVER...
...JUST BECAUSE YOU ARE HONEST DOES NOT MEAN I SHOULD SHOW YOU MY FORM.
THAT SAID, I HAVE SUFFERED MANY TIMES AT THE HANDS OF THE CHURCH.
STILL, A FULL TRANSFORMATION IS DIFFICULT.
YOU'LL FORGIVE ME IF I ONLY DO MY ARM.
BARI
バリバリ
BARI (SKRTCH)
...!

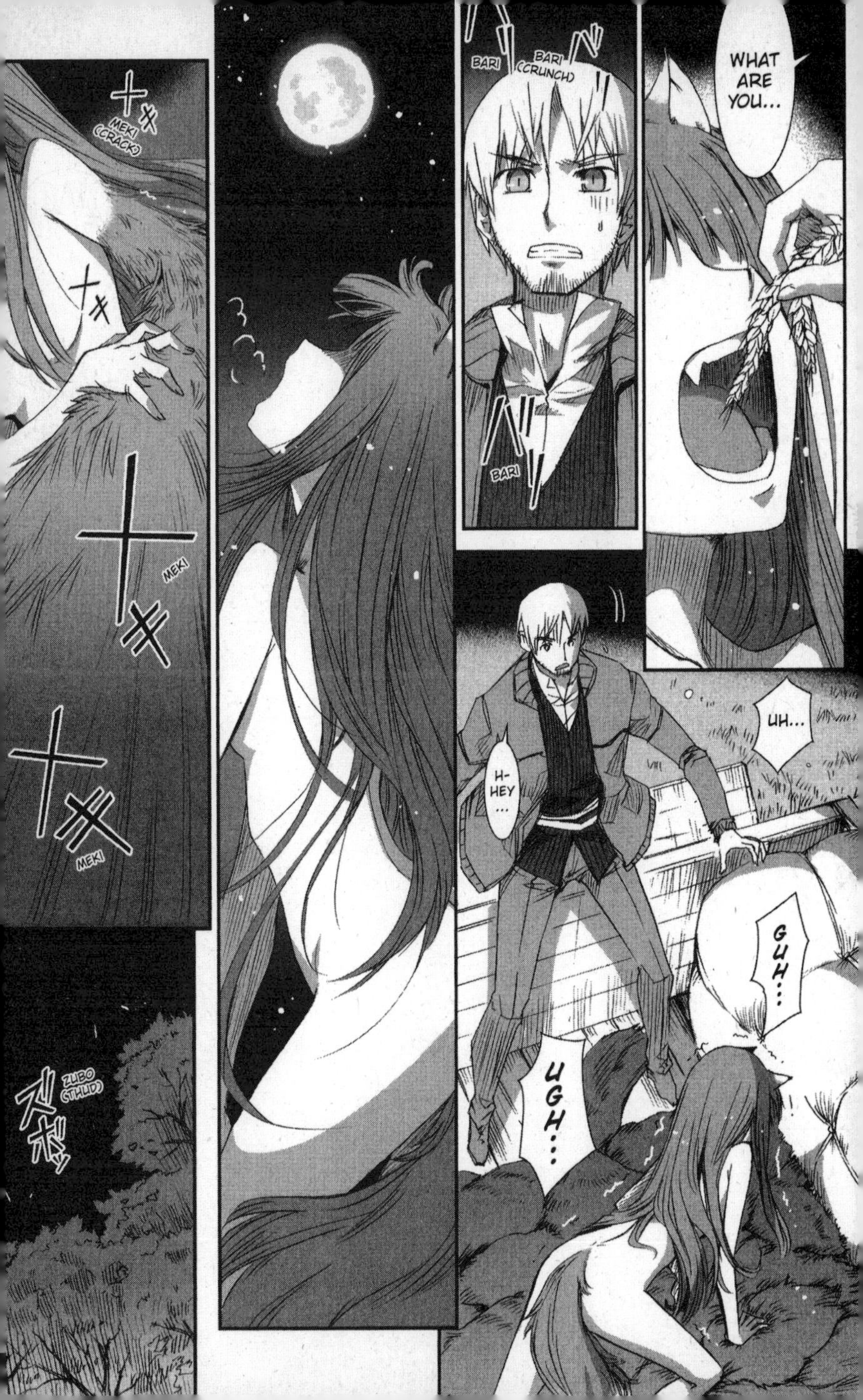
WHAT ARE YOU...
BARI
BARI (CRUNCH)
BARI
UH...
H-HEY...
GUH...
UGH...
MEKI (CRACK)
MEKI
MEKI
ZUBO (THUD)

HIHII
(NEIGH)

HIIN
(NEIGH)

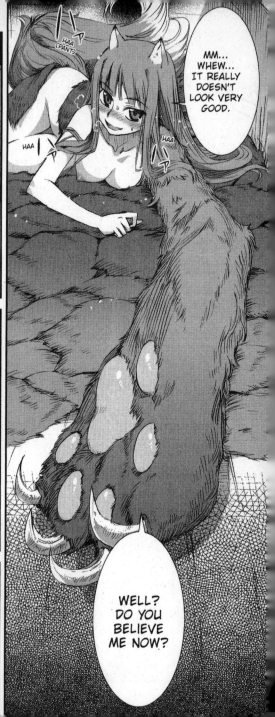

HAA
(PANT)

HAA

HAA

MM...
WHEW...
IT REALLY
DOESN'T
LOOK VERY
GOOD.

WELL?
DO YOU
BELIEVE
ME NOW?

BASHA

BASHA
(SPLASH)

AREN'T
YOU THE
DOUBTFUL
ONE. IF YOU
STILL THINK
IT'S AN
ILLUSION,
GO AHEAD
AND TOUCH
IT.

UH...
MM...

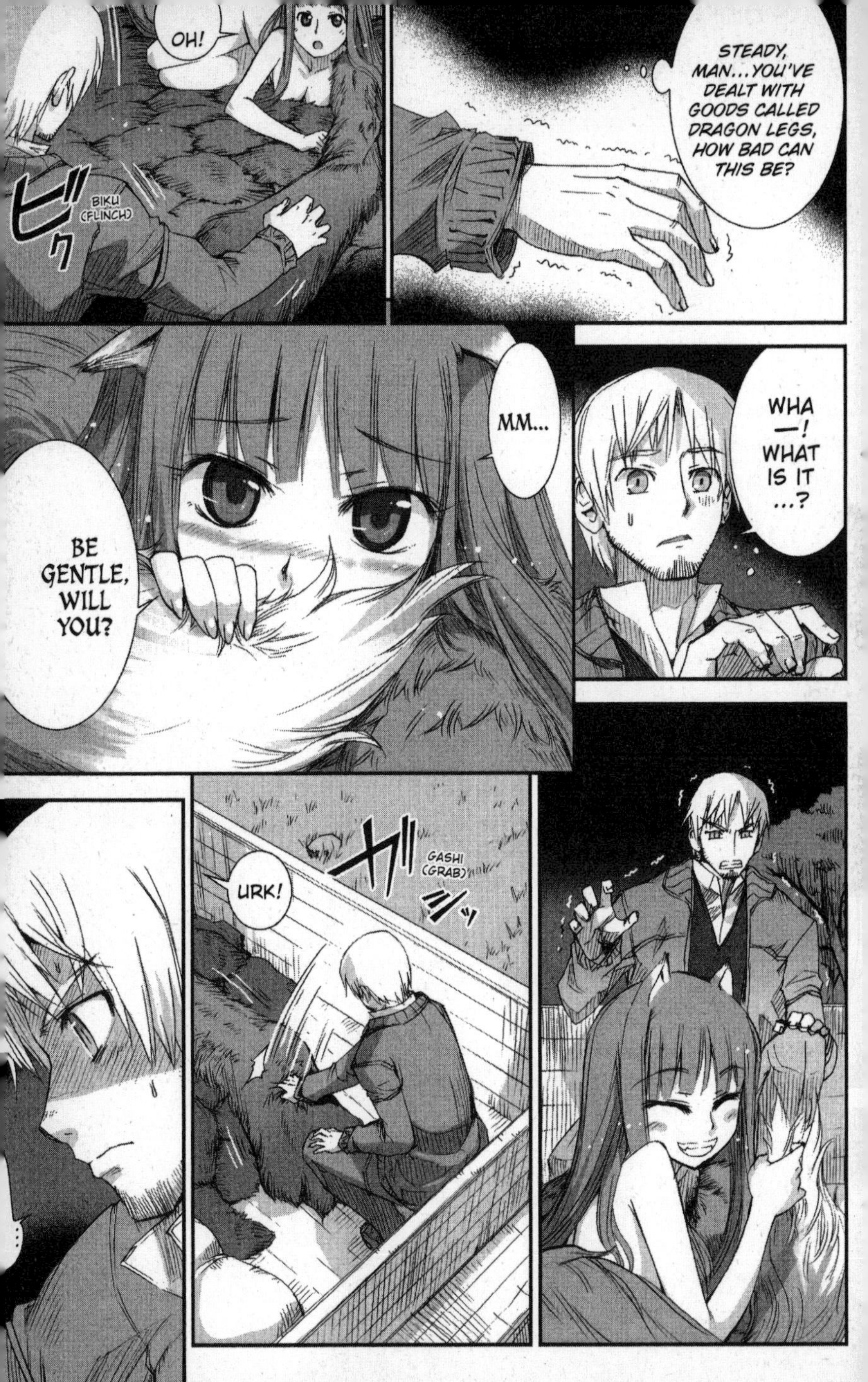
STEADY, MAN...YOU'VE DEALT WITH GOODS CALLED DRAGON LEGS, HOW BAD CAN THIS BE?
OH!
BIKU (FLINCH)
WHA—! WHAT IS IT ...?
MM...
BE GENTLE, WILL YOU?
GASHI (GRAB)
URK!

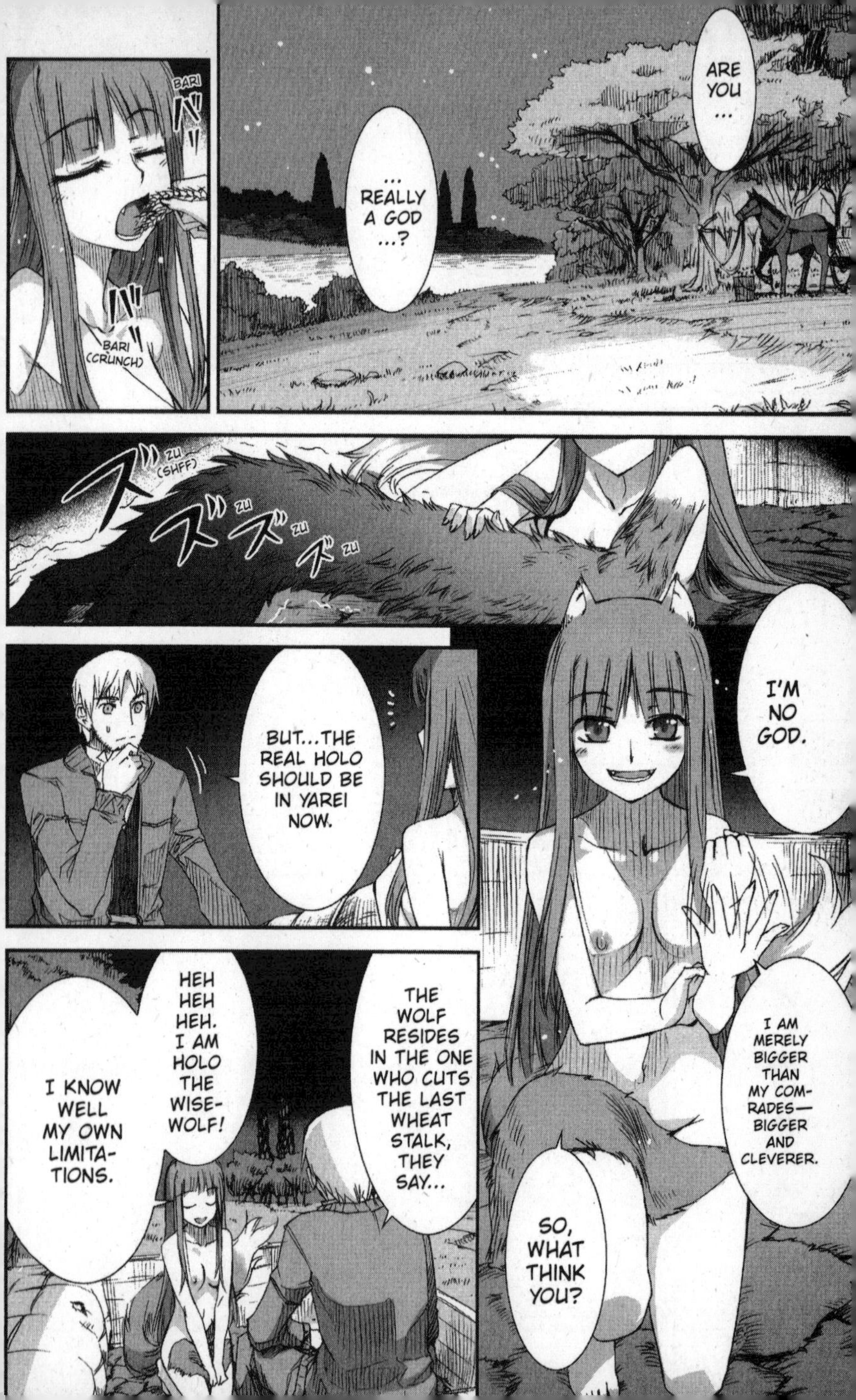
ARE YOU ...
... REALLY A GOD ...?
BARI
BARI (CRUNCH)
ZU (SHFF)
ZU
ZU
ZU
I'M NO GOD.
I AM MERELY BIGGER THAN MY COM-RADES— BIGGER AND CLEVERER.
SO, WHAT THINK YOU?
BUT...THE REAL HOLO SHOULD BE IN YAREI NOW.
THE WOLF RESIDES IN THE ONE WHO CUTS THE LAST WHEAT STALK, THEY SAY...
HEH HEH HEH. I AM HOLO THE WISE-WOLF!
I KNOW WELL MY OWN LIMITA-TIONS.

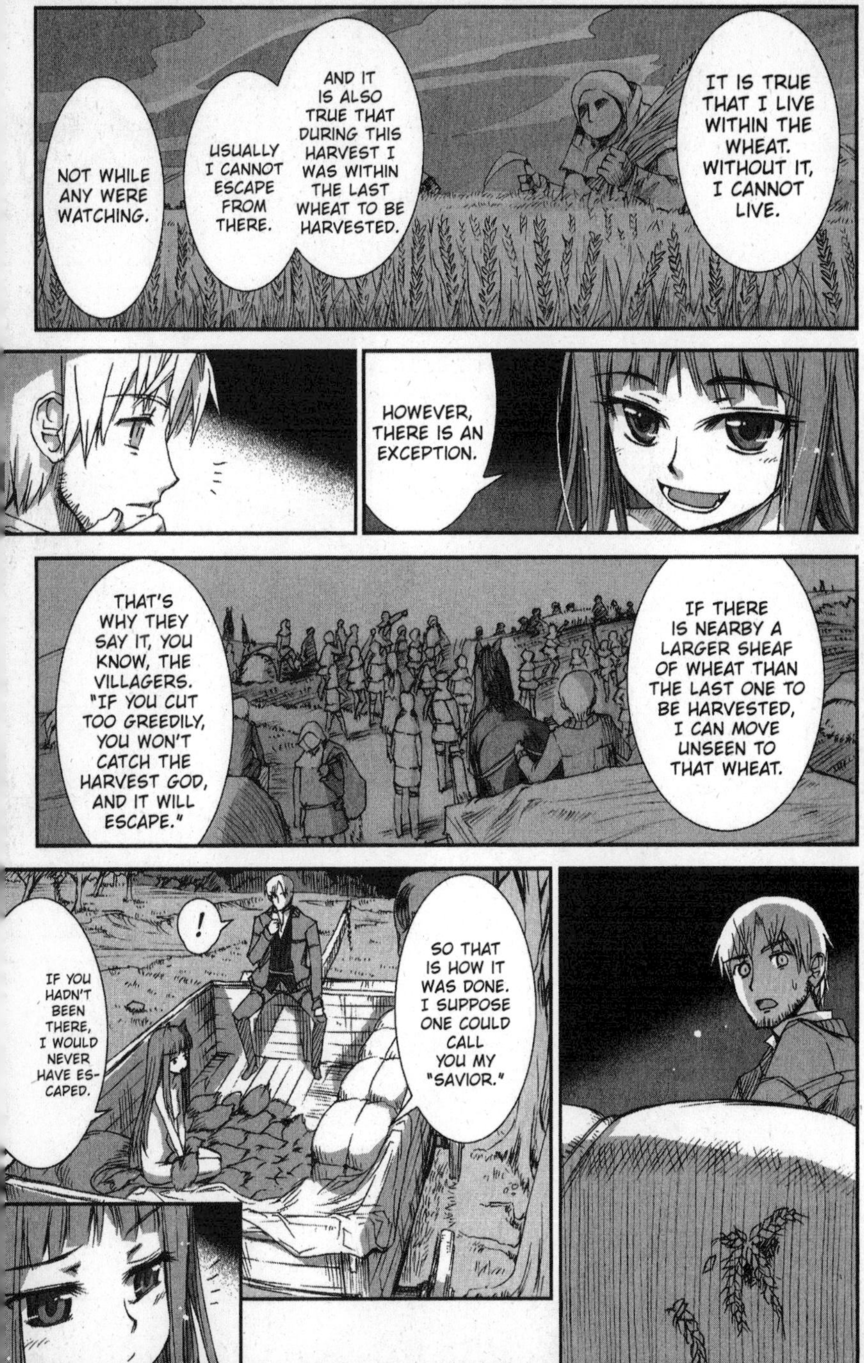
IT IS TRUE THAT I LIVE WITHIN THE WHEAT. WITHOUT IT, I CANNOT LIVE.
AND IT IS ALSO TRUE THAT DURING THIS HARVEST I WAS WITHIN THE LAST WHEAT TO BE HARVESTED.
USUALLY I CANNOT ESCAPE FROM THERE.
NOT WHILE ANY WERE WATCHING.
HOWEVER, THERE IS AN EXCEPTION.
IF THERE IS NEARBY A LARGER SHEAF OF WHEAT THAN THE LAST ONE TO BE HARVESTED, I CAN MOVE UNSEEN TO THAT WHEAT.
THAT'S WHY THEY SAY IT, YOU KNOW, THE VILLAGERS. "IF YOU CUT TOO GREEDILY, YOU WON'T CATCH THE HARVEST GOD, AND IT WILL ESCAPE."
SO THAT IS HOW IT WAS DONE. I SUPPOSE ONE COULD CALL YOU MY "SAVIOR."
!
IF YOU HADN'T BEEN THERE, I WOULD NEVER HAVE ES-CAPED.

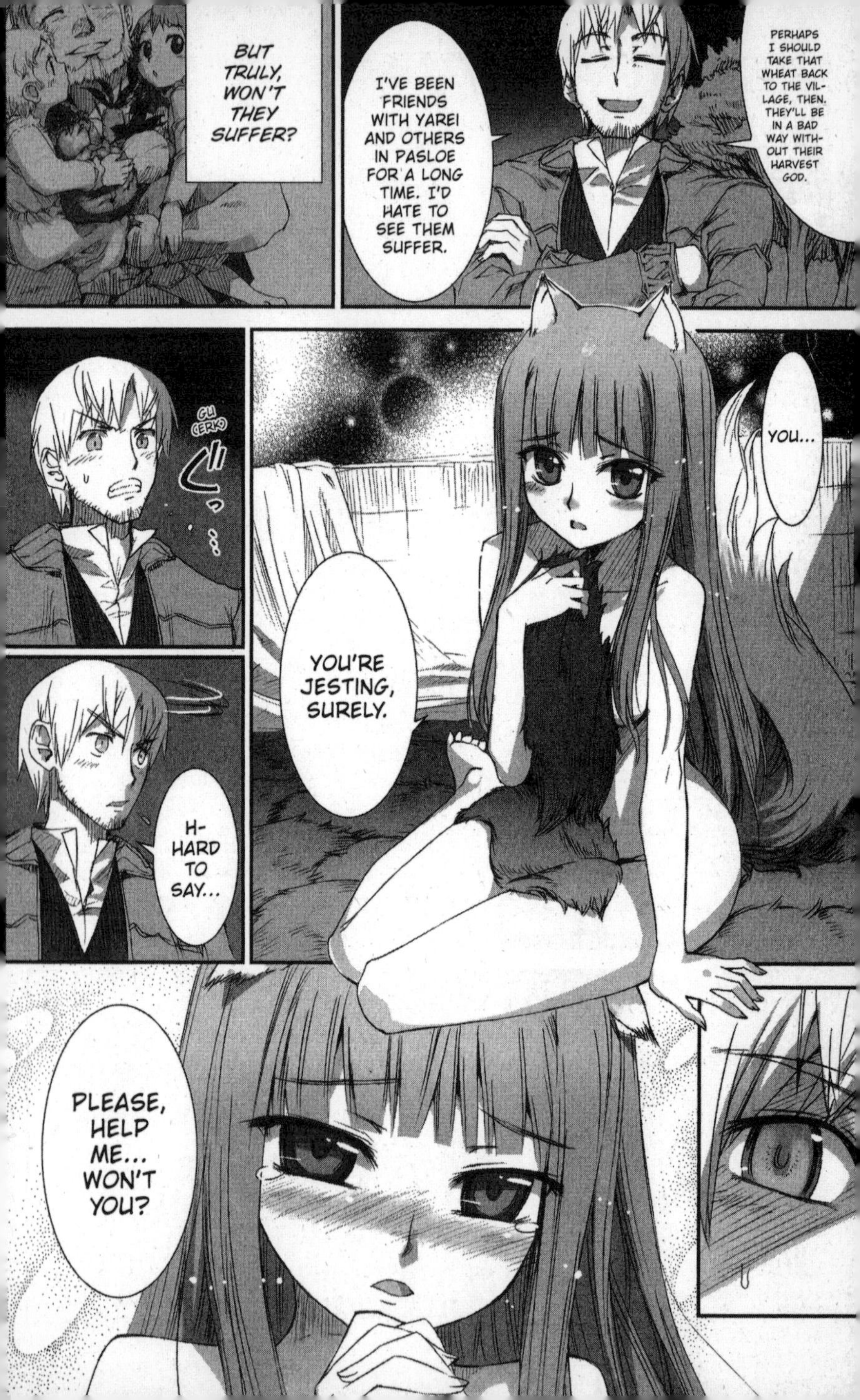
PERHAPS I SHOULD TAKE THAT WHEAT BACK TO THE VIL-LAGE, THEN. THEY'LL BE IN A BAD WAY WITH-OUT THEIR HARVEST GOD.
I'VE BEEN FRIENDS WITH YAREI AND OTHERS IN PASLOE FOR A LONG TIME. I'D HATE TO SEE THEM SUFFER.
BUT TRULY, WON'T THEY SUFFER?
YOU...
YOU'RE JESTING, SURELY.
GU (ERK)
...
H-HARD TO SAY...
PLEASE, HELP ME... WON'T YOU?

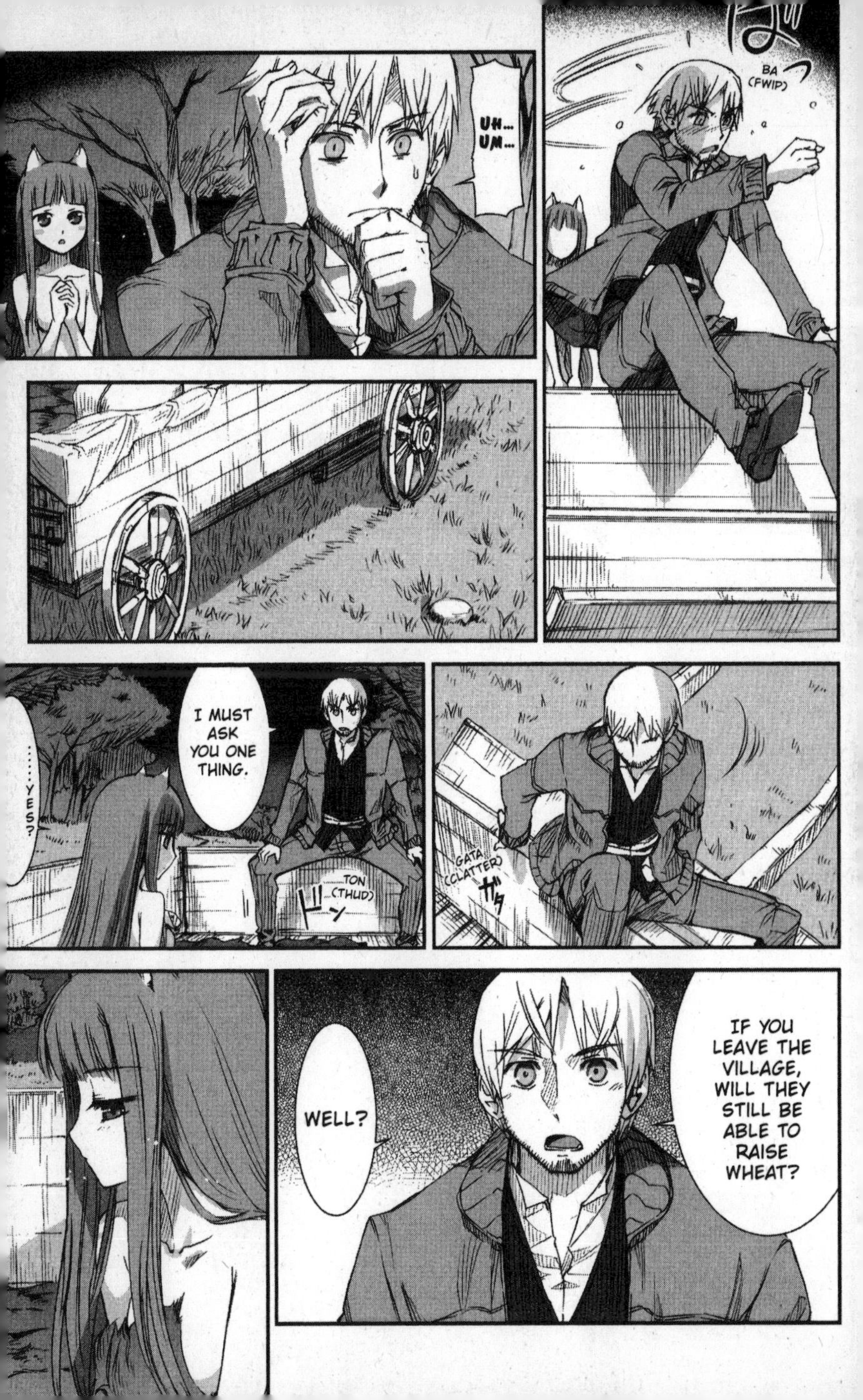
BA (FWIP)
UH... UM...
GATA (CLATTER)
I MUST ASK YOU ONE THING.
......YES?
TON (THUD)
IF YOU LEAVE THE VILLAGE, WILL THEY STILL BE ABLE TO RAISE WHEAT?
WELL?

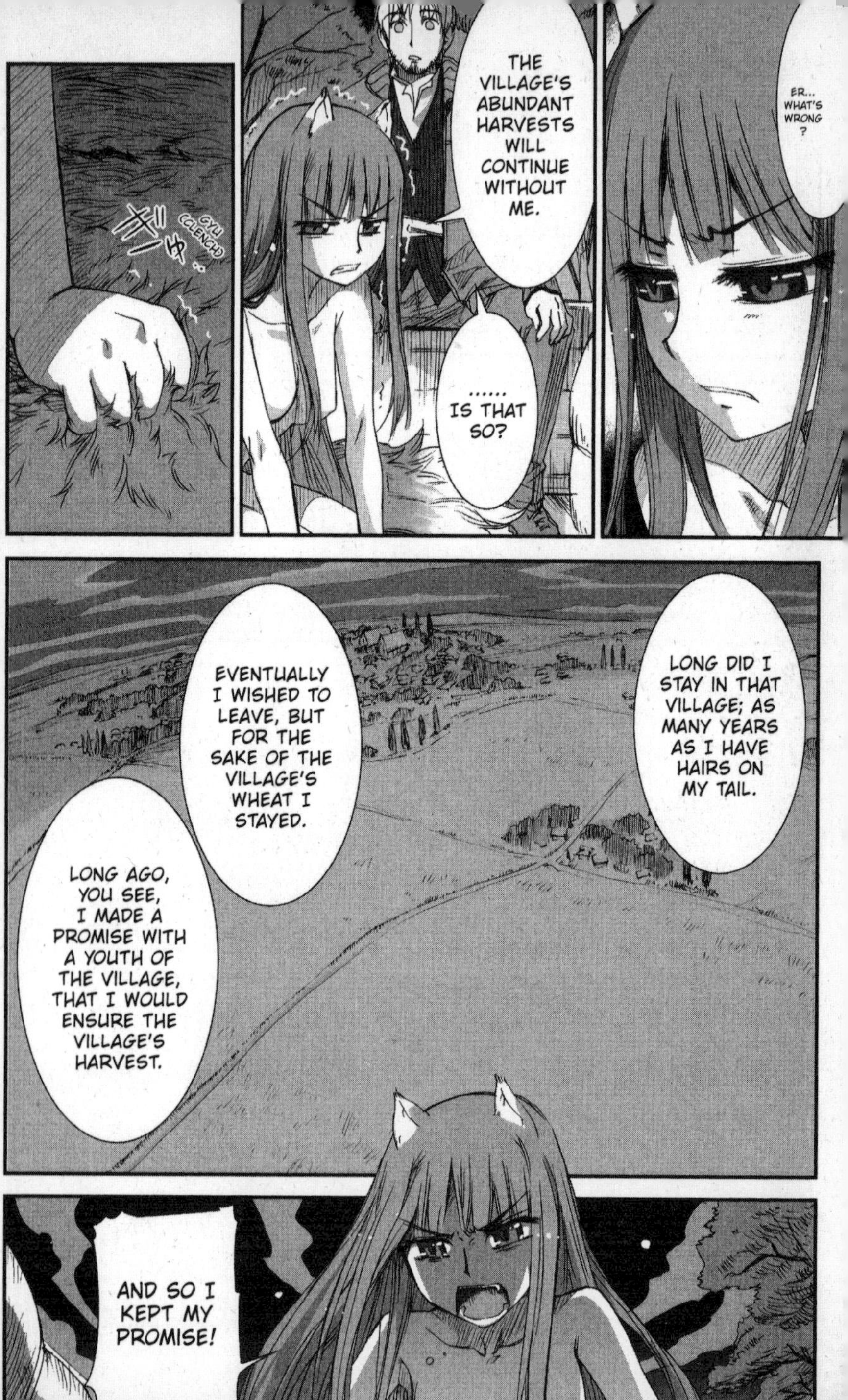
ER... WHAT'S WRONG?
THE VILLAGE'S ABUNDANT HARVESTS WILL CONTINUE WITHOUT ME.
...... IS THAT SO?
GYU (CLENCH)
LONG DID I STAY IN THAT VILLAGE; AS MANY YEARS AS I HAVE HAIRS ON MY TAIL.
EVENTUALLY I WISHED TO LEAVE, BUT FOR THE SAKE OF THE VILLAGE'S WHEAT I STAYED.
LONG AGO, YOU SEE, I MADE A PROMISE WITH A YOUTH OF THE VILLAGE, THAT I WOULD ENSURE THE VILLAGE'S HARVEST.
AND SO I KEPT MY PROMISE!

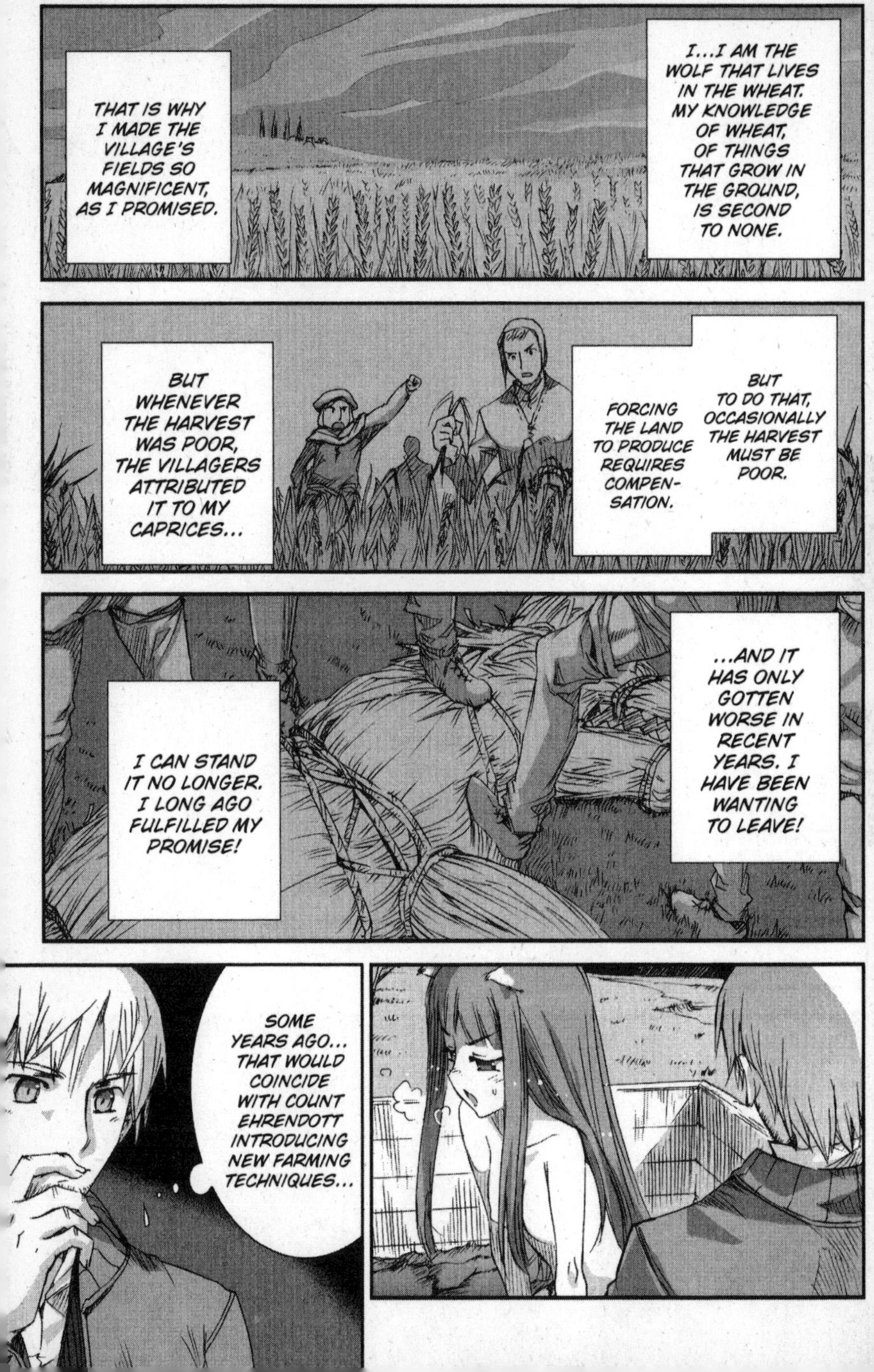
I…I AM THE WOLF THAT LIVES IN THE WHEAT. MY KNOWLEDGE OF WHEAT, OF THINGS THAT GROW IN THE GROUND, IS SECOND TO NONE.
THAT IS WHY I MADE THE VILLAGE'S FIELDS SO MAGNIFICENT, AS I PROMISED.
BUT TO DO THAT, OCCASIONALLY THE HARVEST MUST BE POOR.
FORCING THE LAND TO PRODUCE REQUIRES COMPEN-SATION.
BUT WHENEVER THE HARVEST WAS POOR, THE VILLAGERS ATTRIBUTED IT TO MY CAPRICES…
…AND IT HAS ONLY GOTTEN WORSE IN RECENT YEARS. I HAVE BEEN WANTING TO LEAVE!
I CAN STAND IT NO LONGER. I LONG AGO FULFILLED MY PROMISE!
SOME YEARS AGO… THAT WOULD COINCIDE WITH COUNT EHRENDOTT INTRODUCING NEW FARMING TECHNIQUES…

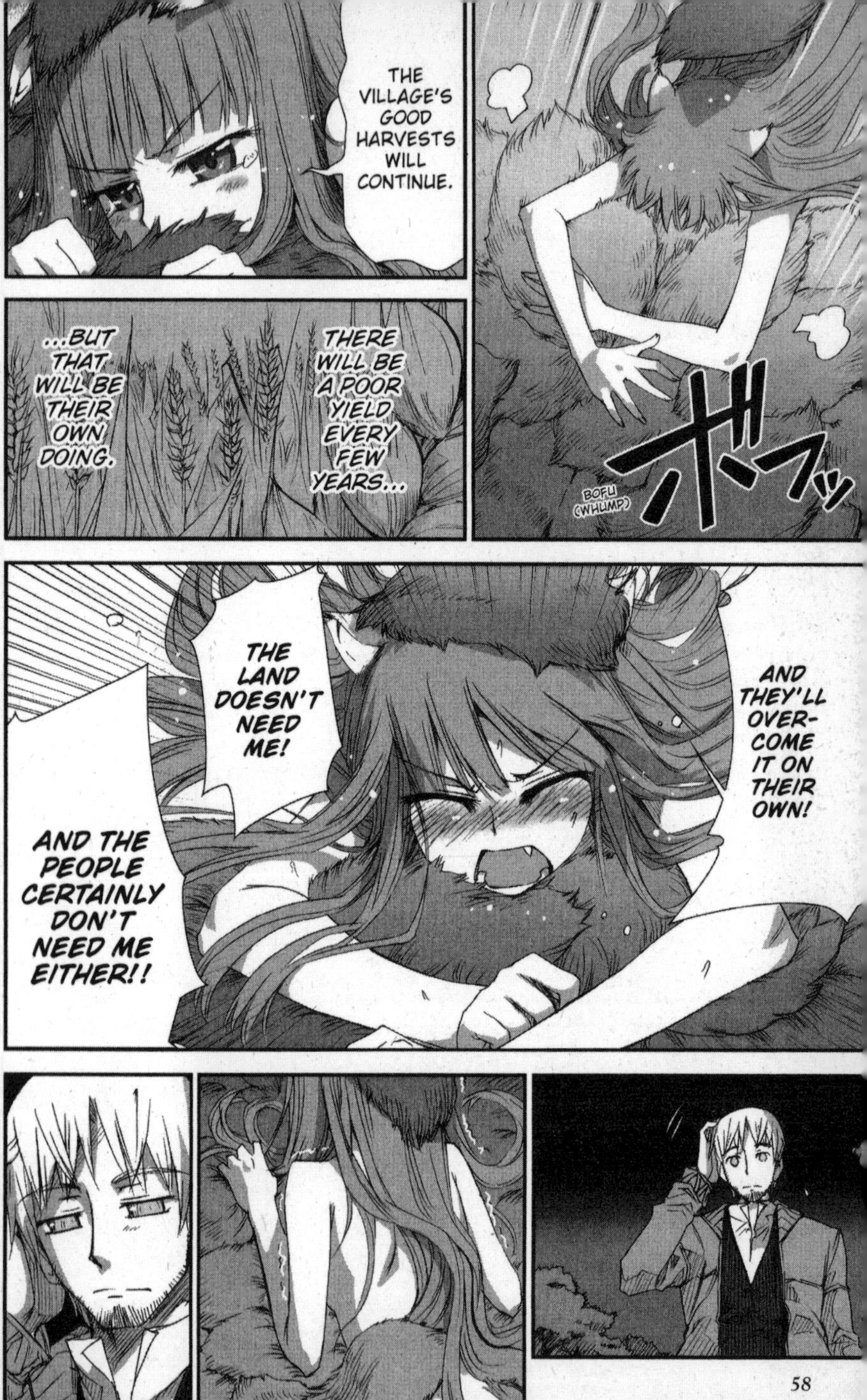
ボフッ
BOFU (WHUMP)
THE VILLAGE'S GOOD HARVESTS WILL CONTINUE.
THERE WILL BE A POOR YIELD EVERY FEW YEARS...
...BUT THAT WILL BE THEIR OWN DOING.
THE LAND DOESN'T NEED ME!
AND THEY'LL OVER-COME IT ON THEIR OWN!
AND THE PEOPLE CERTAINLY DON'T NEED ME EITHER!!

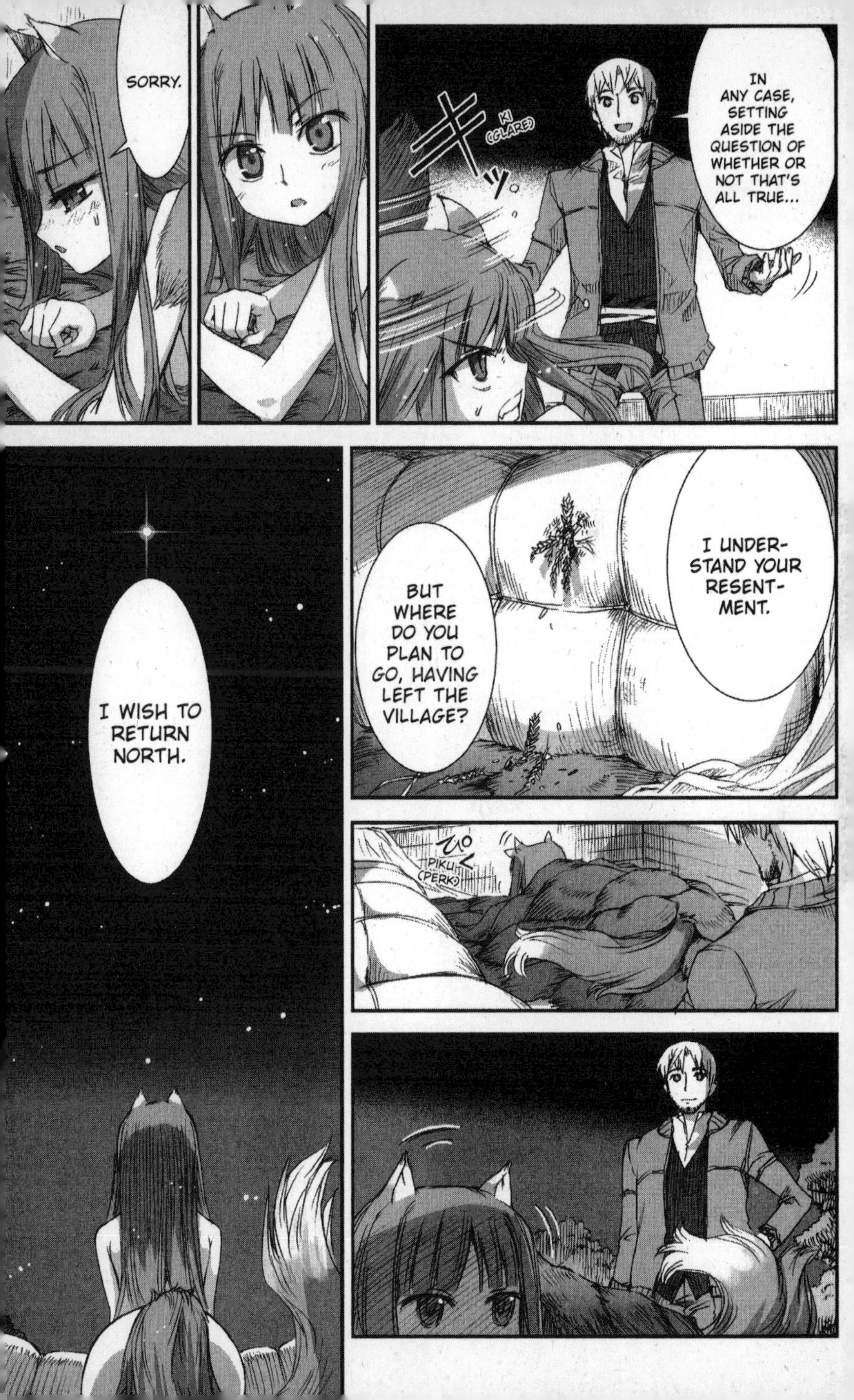
IN ANY CASE, SETTING ASIDE THE QUESTION OF WHETHER OR NOT THAT'S ALL TRUE...
KI (GLARE)
SORRY.
I UNDER-STAND YOUR RESENT-MENT.
BUT WHERE DO YOU PLAN TO GO, HAVING LEFT THE VILLAGE?
PIKU (PERK)
I WISH TO RETURN NORTH.

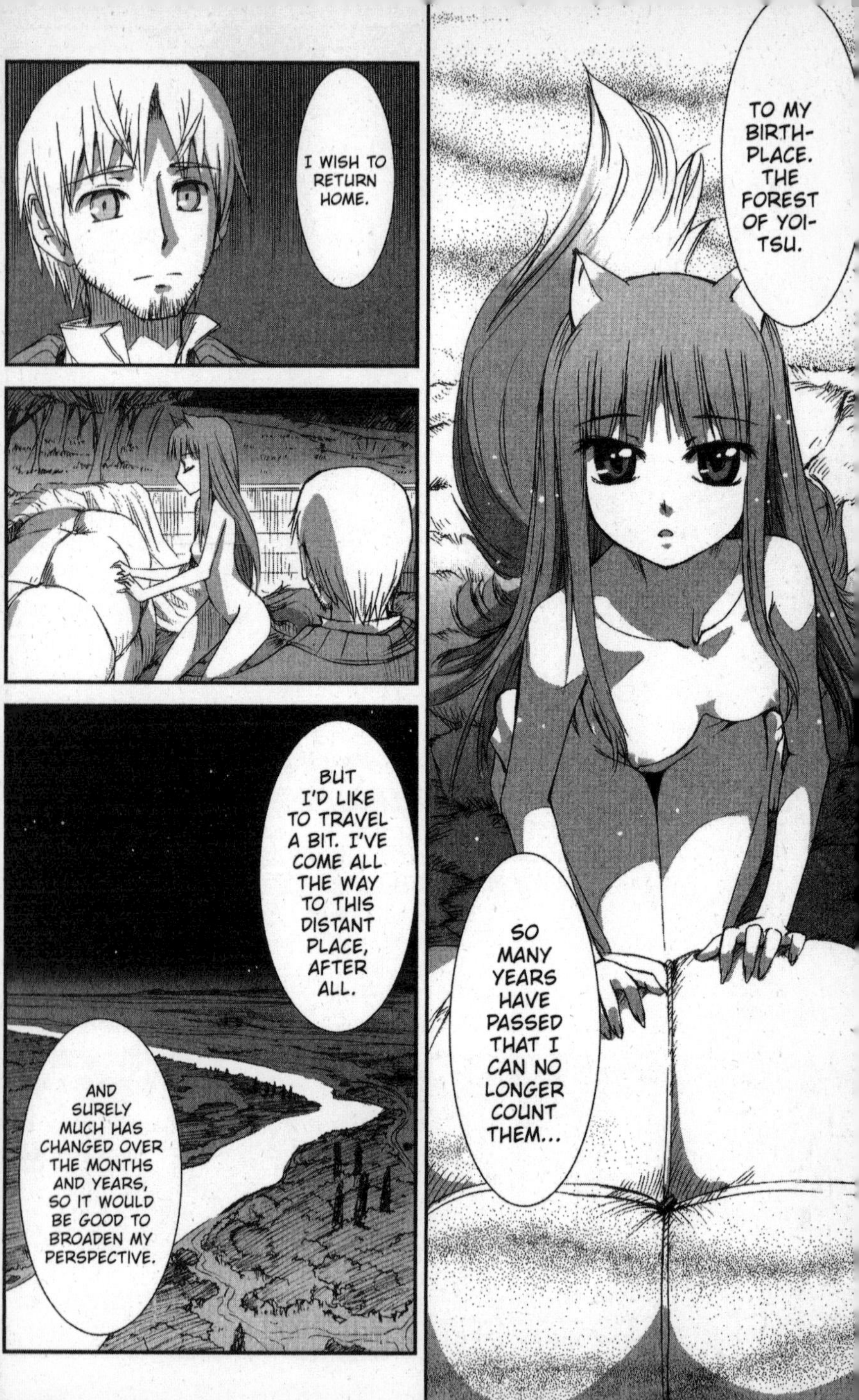
TO MY BIRTH-PLACE. THE FOREST OF YOI-TSU.
SO MANY YEARS HAVE PASSED THAT I CAN NO LONGER COUNT THEM...
I WISH TO RETURN HOME.
BUT I'D LIKE TO TRAVEL A BIT. I'VE COME ALL THE WAY TO THIS DISTANT PLACE, AFTER ALL.
AND SURELY MUCH HAS CHANGED OVER THE MONTHS AND YEARS, SO IT WOULD BE GOOD TO BROADEN MY PERSPECTIVE.

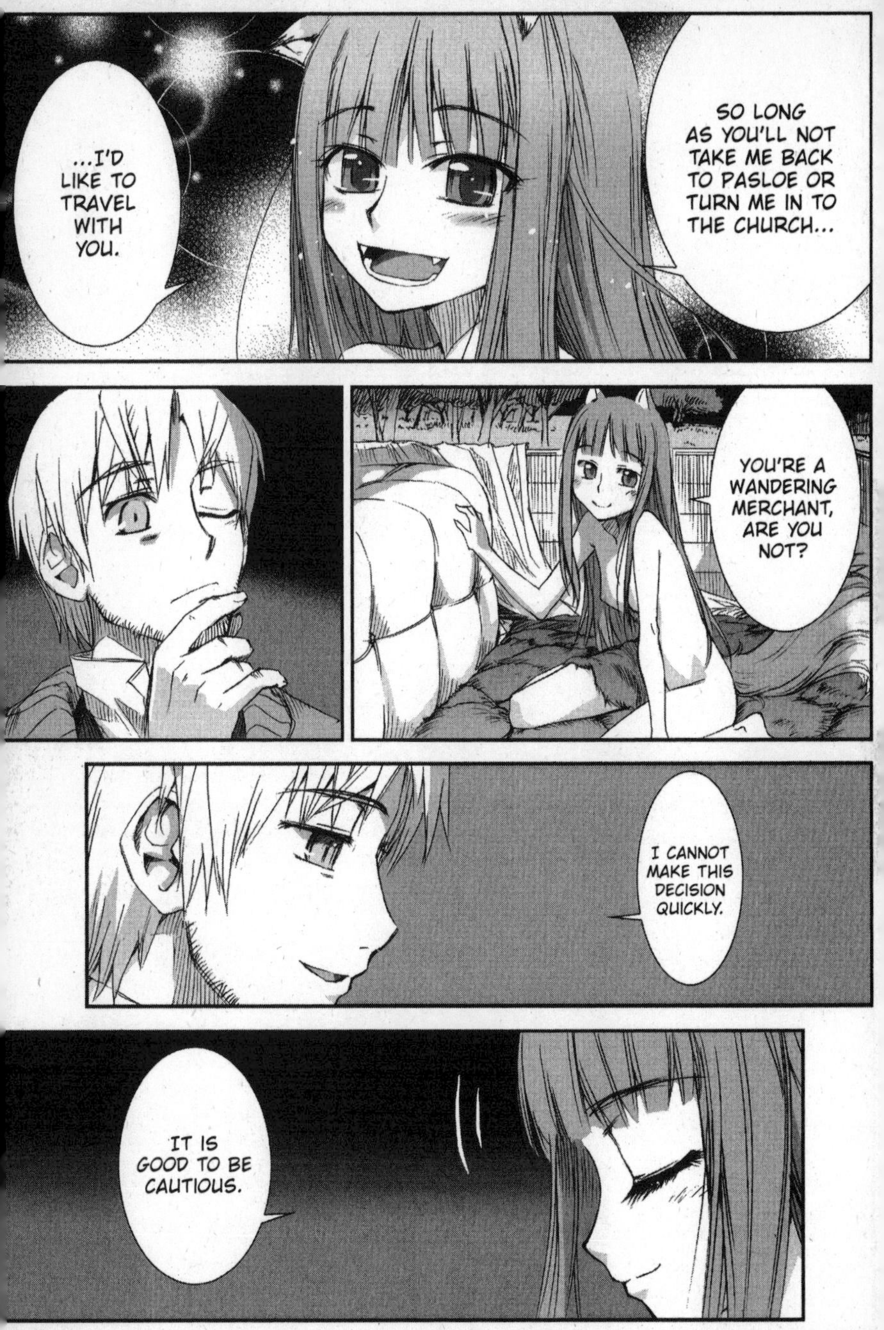
SO LONG AS YOU'LL NOT TAKE ME BACK TO PASLOE OR TURN ME IN TO THE CHURCH...
...I'D LIKE TO TRAVEL WITH YOU.
YOU'RE A WANDERING MERCHANT, ARE YOU NOT?
I CANNOT MAKE THIS DECISION QUICKLY.
IT IS GOOD TO BE CAUTIOUS.

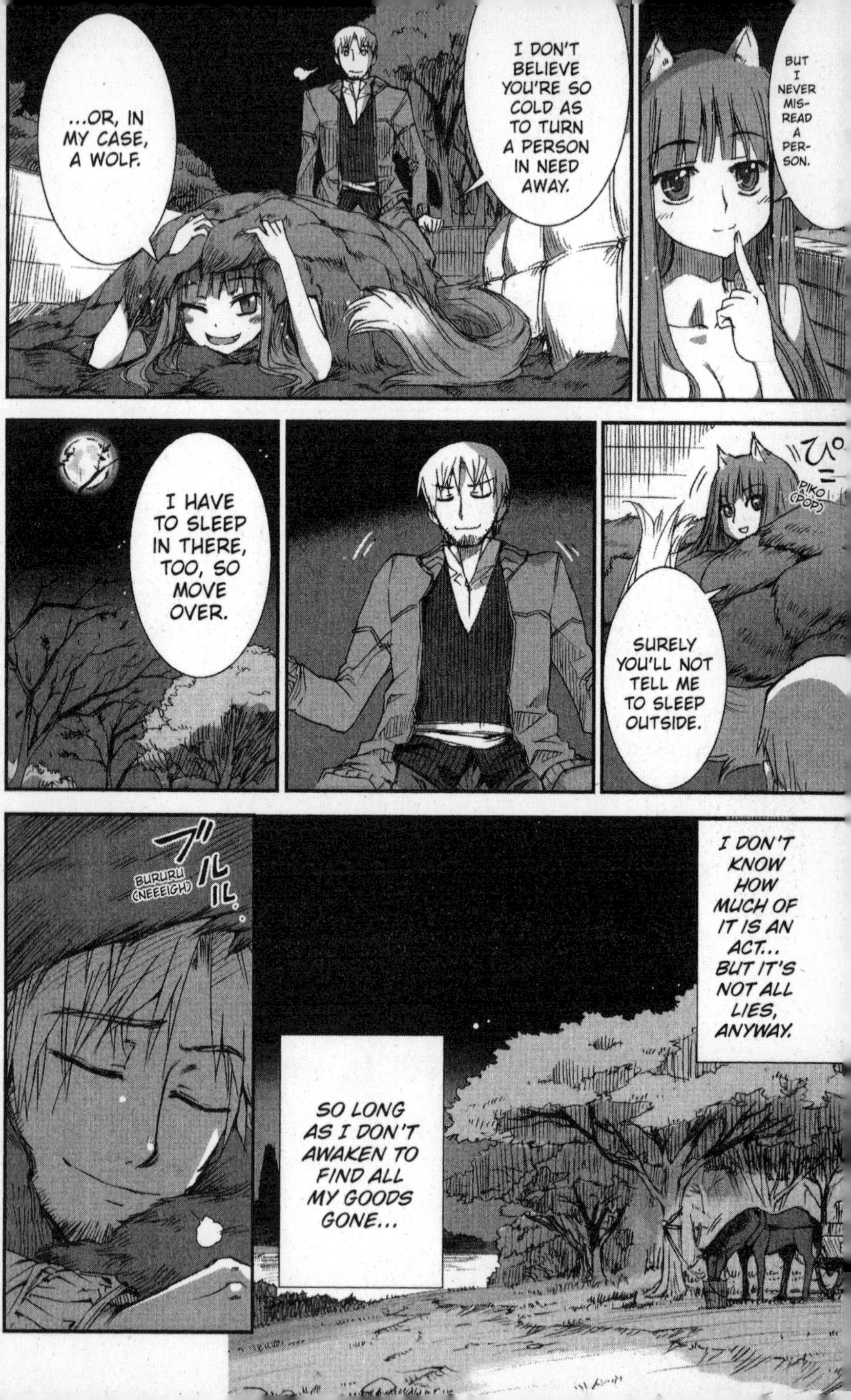
BUT I NEVER MIS-READ A PER-SON.
I DON'T BELIEVE YOU'RE SO COLD AS TO TURN A PERSON IN NEED AWAY.
...OR, IN MY CASE, A WOLF.
PIKO (POP)
SURELY YOU'LL NOT TELL ME TO SLEEP OUTSIDE.
I HAVE TO SLEEP IN THERE, TOO, SO MOVE OVER.
I DON'T KNOW HOW MUCH OF IT IS AN ACT... BUT IT'S NOT ALL LIES, ANYWAY.
SO LONG AS I DON'T AWAKEN TO FIND ALL MY GOODS GONE...
ブルル。
BURURU (NEEEIGH)

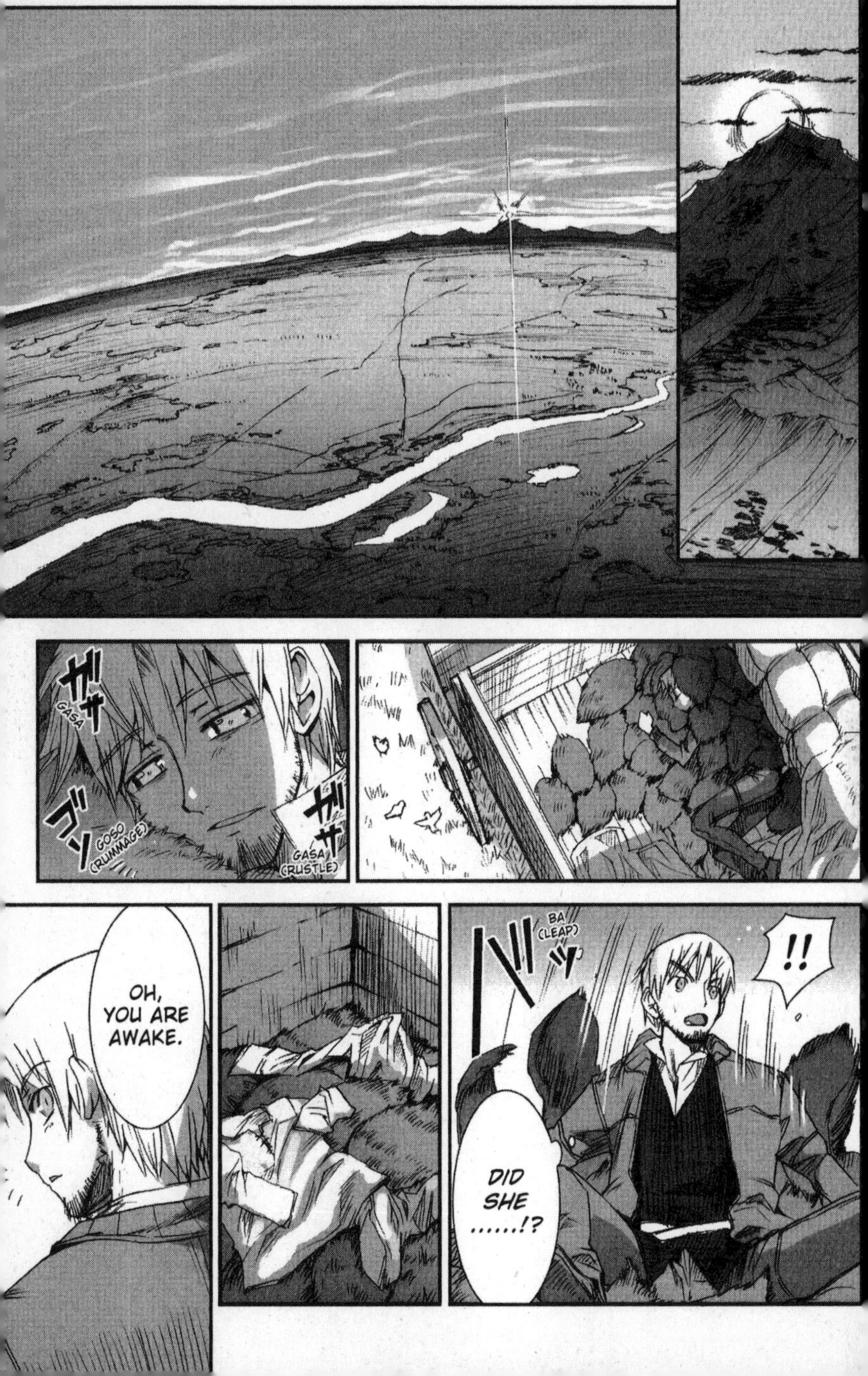
GASA
GOSO (RUMMAGE)
GASA (RUSTLE)
BA (LEAP)
!!
DID SHE ......!?
OH, YOU ARE AWAKE.

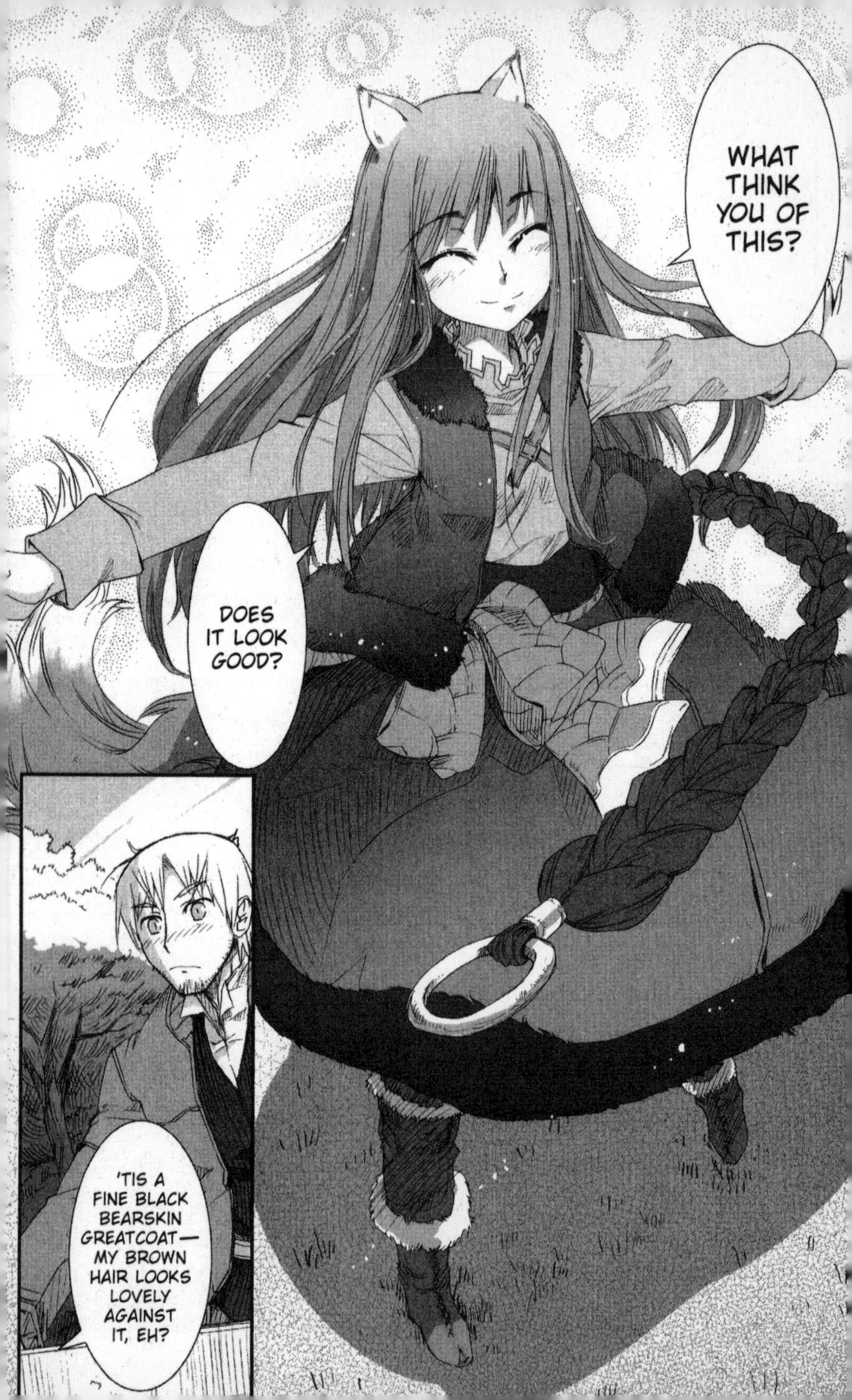
WHAT THINK YOU OF THIS?
DOES IT LOOK GOOD?
'TIS A FINE BLACK BEARSKIN GREATCOAT—MY BROWN HAIR LOOKS LOVELY AGAINST IT, EH?

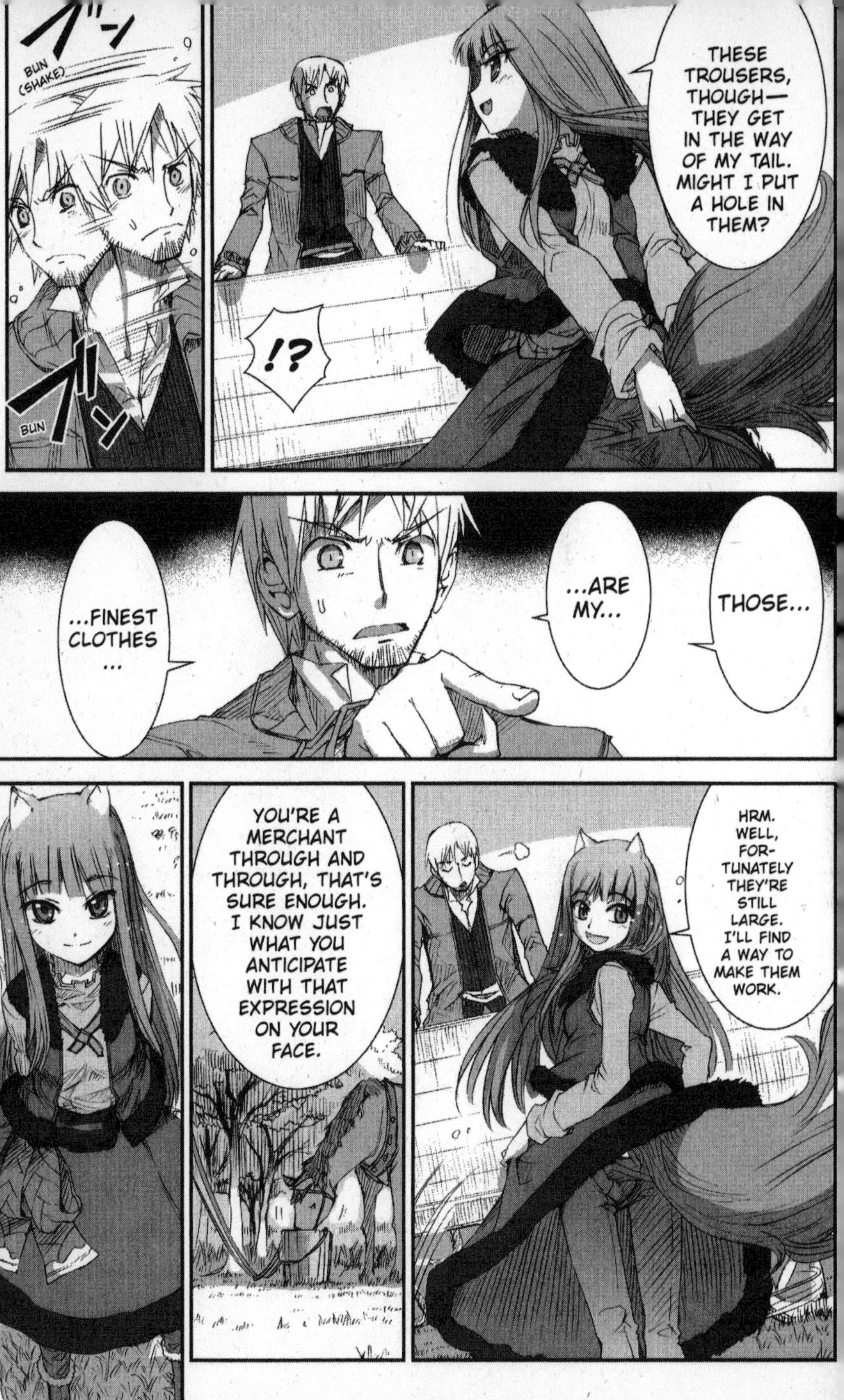
THESE TROUSERS, THOUGH— THEY GET IN THE WAY OF MY TAIL. MIGHT I PUT A HOLE IN THEM?
!?
ブン
BUN (SHAKE)
ブン
BUN
THOSE...
...ARE MY...
...FINEST CLOTHES ...
HRM. WELL, FOR-TUNATELY THEY'RE STILL LARGE. I'LL FIND A WAY TO MAKE THEM WORK.
YOU'RE A MERCHANT THROUGH AND THROUGH, THAT'S SURE ENOUGH. I KNOW JUST WHAT YOU ANTICIPATE WITH THAT EXPRESSION ON YOUR FACE.

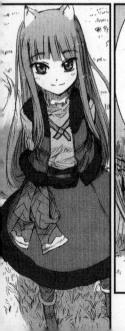

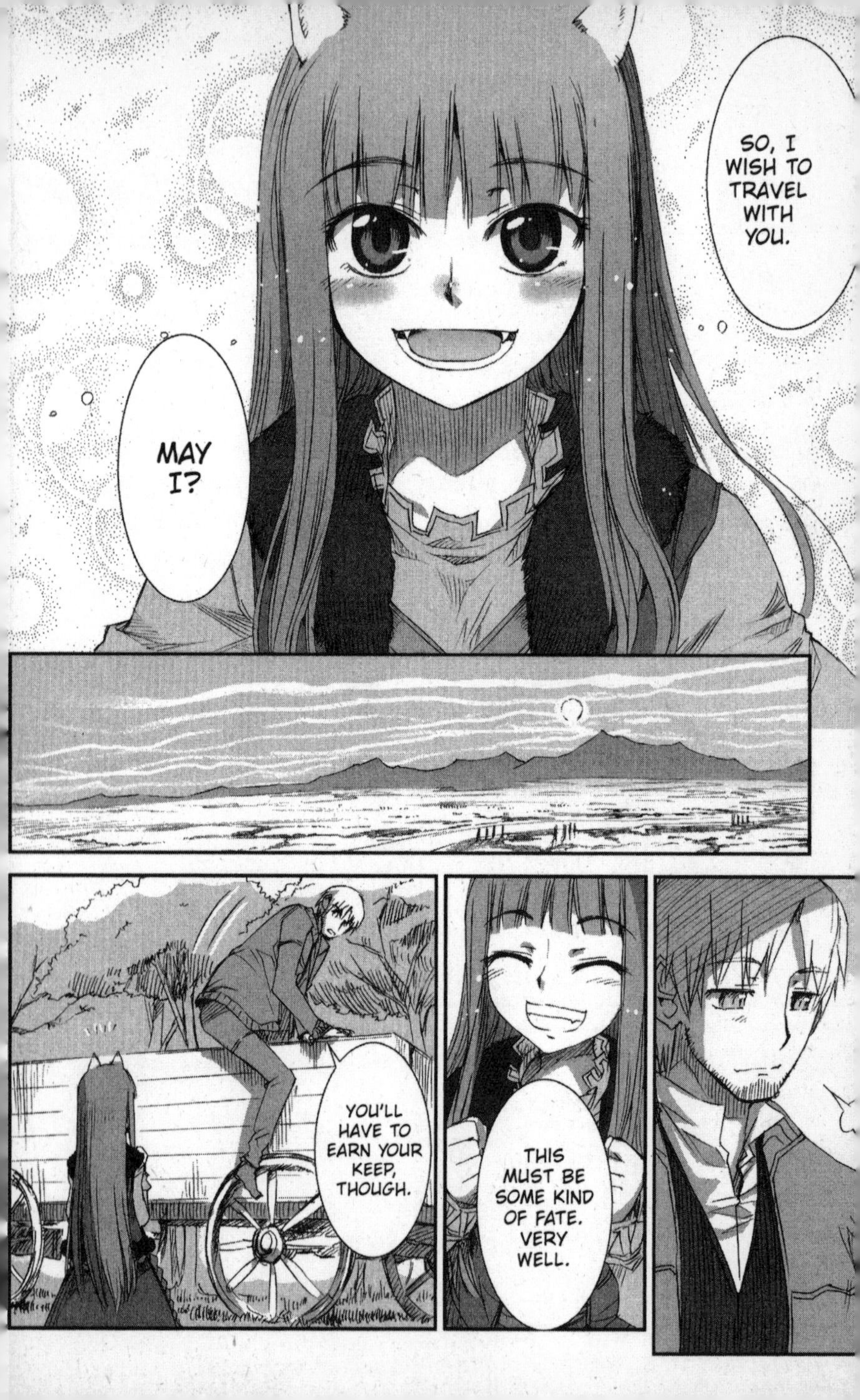
SO, I WISH TO TRAVEL WITH YOU.
MAY I?
THIS MUST BE SOME KIND OF FATE. VERY WELL.
YOU'LL HAVE TO EARN YOUR KEEP, THOUGH.

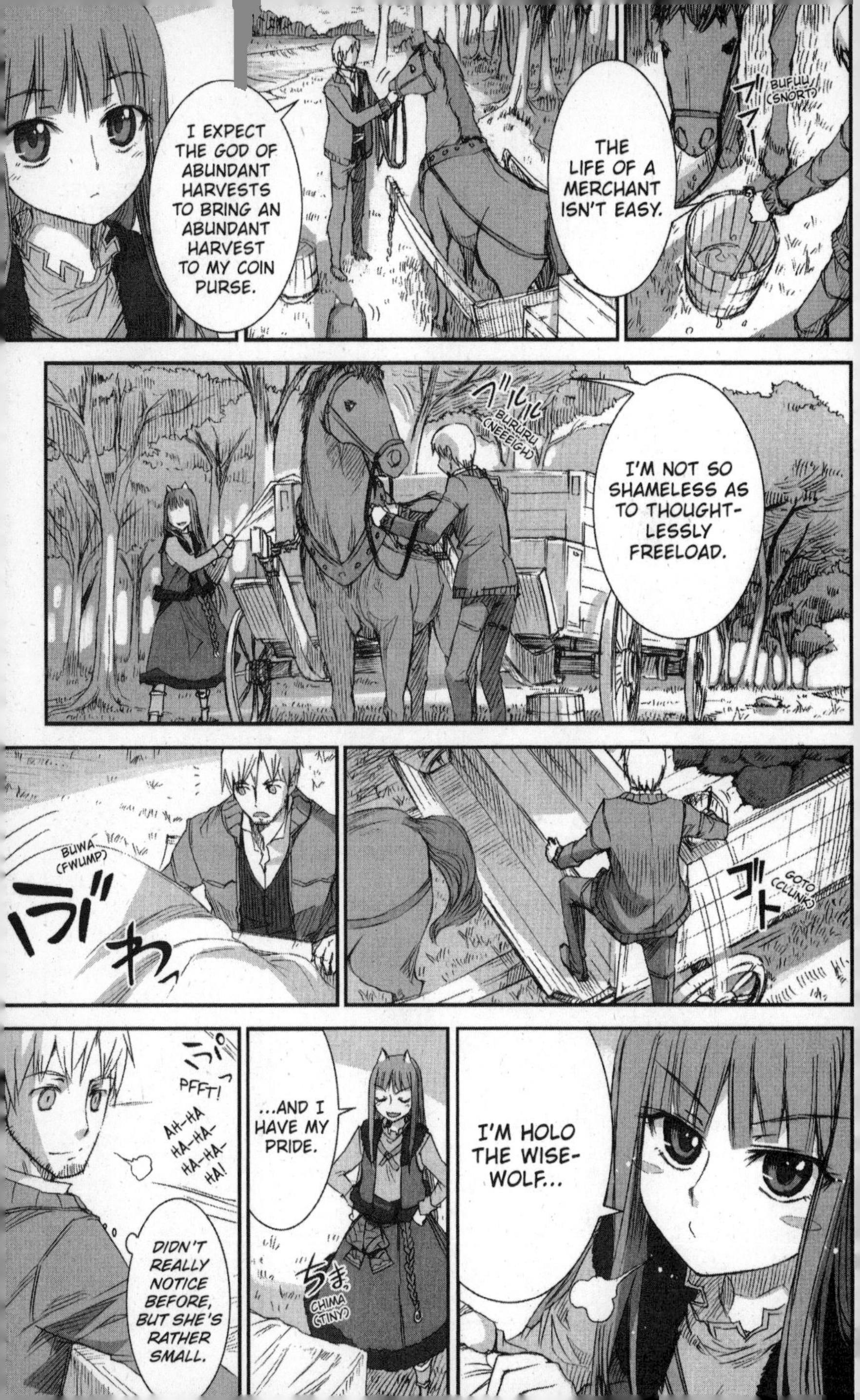
BUFUU (SNORT)
THE LIFE OF A MERCHANT ISN'T EASY.
I EXPECT THE GOD OF ABUNDANT HARVESTS TO BRING AN ABUNDANT HARVEST TO MY COIN PURSE.
BURURU (NEEEIGH)
I'M NOT SO SHAMELESS AS TO THOUGHT-LESSLY FREELOAD.
GOTO (CLUNK)
BUWA (FWUMP)
I'M HOLO THE WISE-WOLF...
...AND I HAVE MY PRIDE.
CHIMA (TINY)
PFFT!
AH-HA HA-HA-HA-HA-HA!
DIDN'T REALLY NOTICE BEFORE, BUT SHE'S RATHER SMALL.

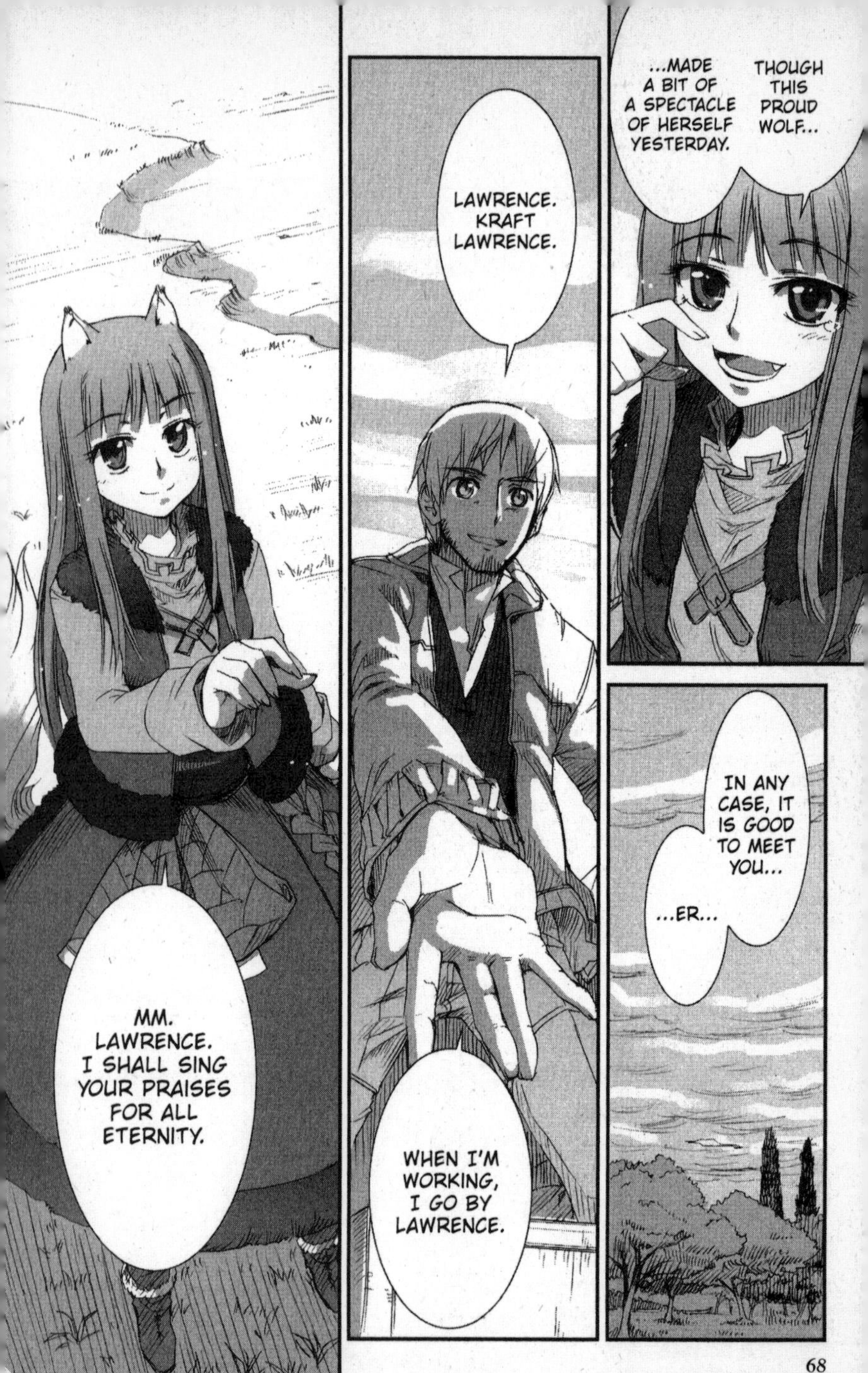
THOUGH THIS PROUD WOLF...
...MADE A BIT OF A SPECTACLE OF HERSELF YESTERDAY.
IN ANY CASE, IT IS GOOD TO MEET YOU...
...ER...
LAWRENCE. KRAFT LAWRENCE.
WHEN I'M WORKING, I GO BY LAWRENCE.
MM. LAWRENCE. I SHALL SING YOUR PRAISES FOR ALL ETERNITY.

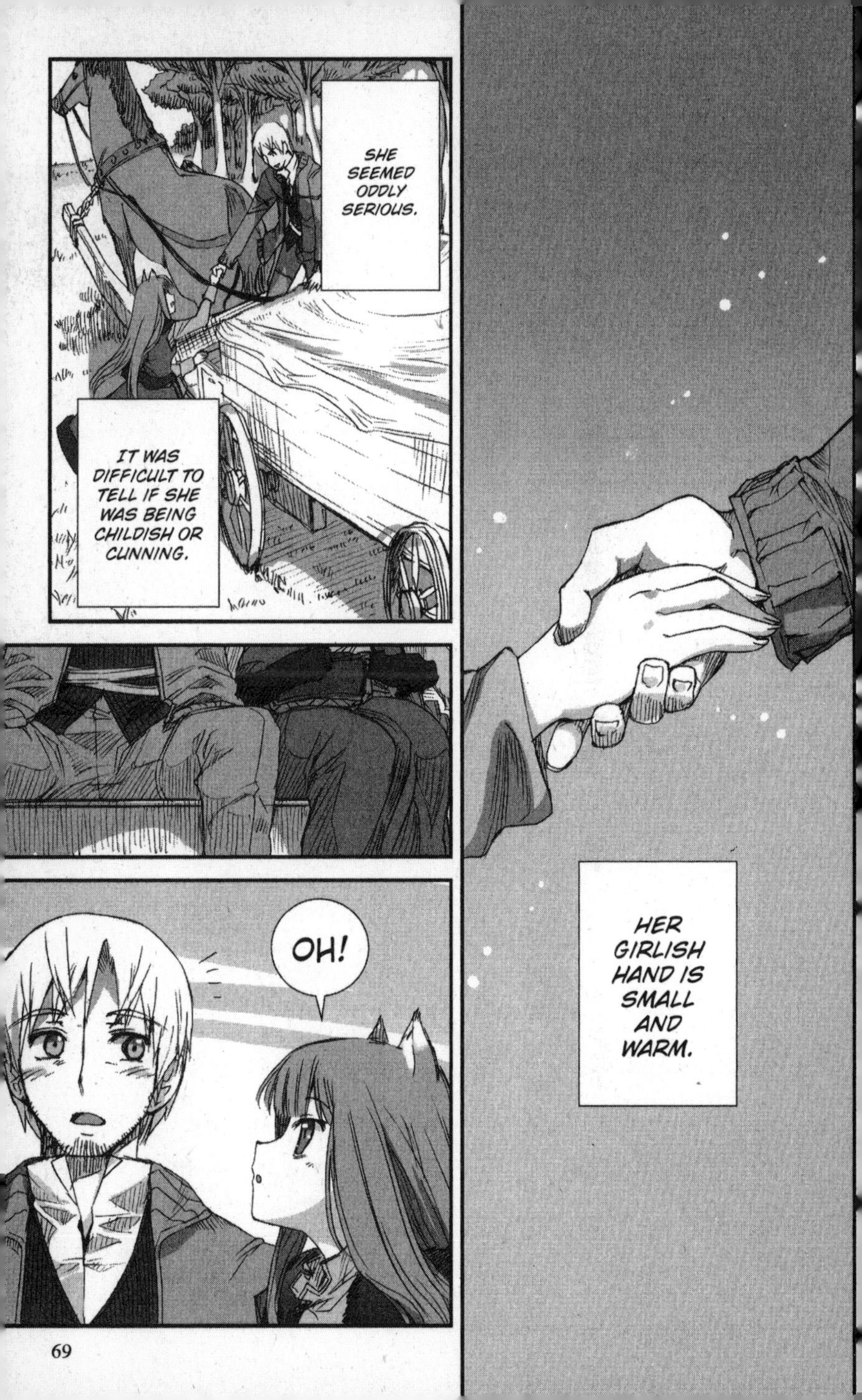
HER GIRLISH HAND IS SMALL AND WARM.
SHE SEEMED ODDLY SERIOUS.
IT WAS DIFFICULT TO TELL IF SHE WAS BEING CHILDISH OR CUNNING.
OH!

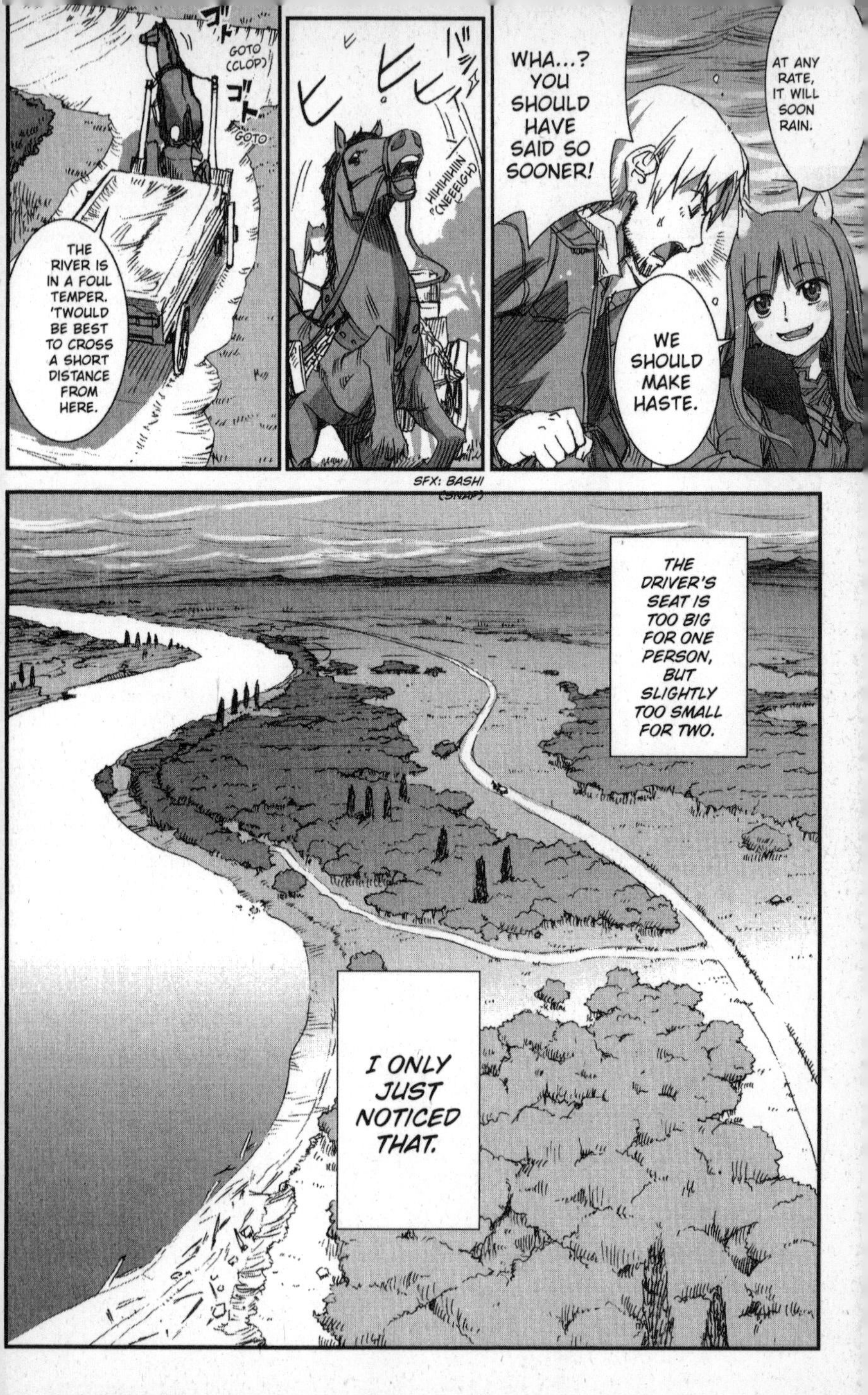
AT ANY RATE, IT WILL SOON RAIN.
WHA...? YOU SHOULD HAVE SAID SO SOONER!
WE SHOULD MAKE HASTE.
SFX: BASHI (SNAP)
HIHIHIHIN (NEEEIGH)
GOTO (CLOP)
GOTO
THE RIVER IS IN A FOUL TEMPER. 'TWOULD BE BEST TO CROSS A SHORT DISTANCE FROM HERE.
THE DRIVER'S SEAT IS TOO BIG FOR ONE PERSON, BUT SLIGHTLY TOO SMALL FOR TWO.
I ONLY JUST NOTICED THAT.

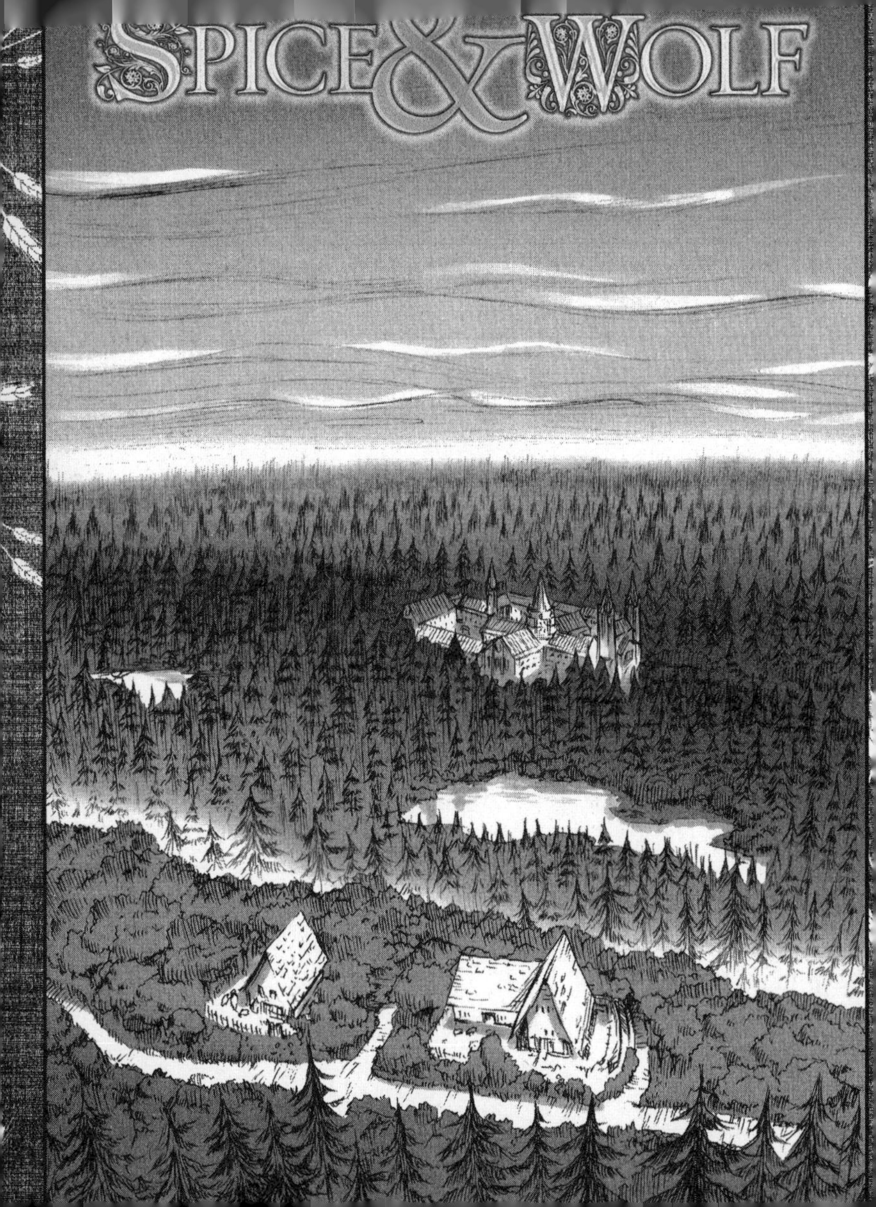
SPICE&WOLF

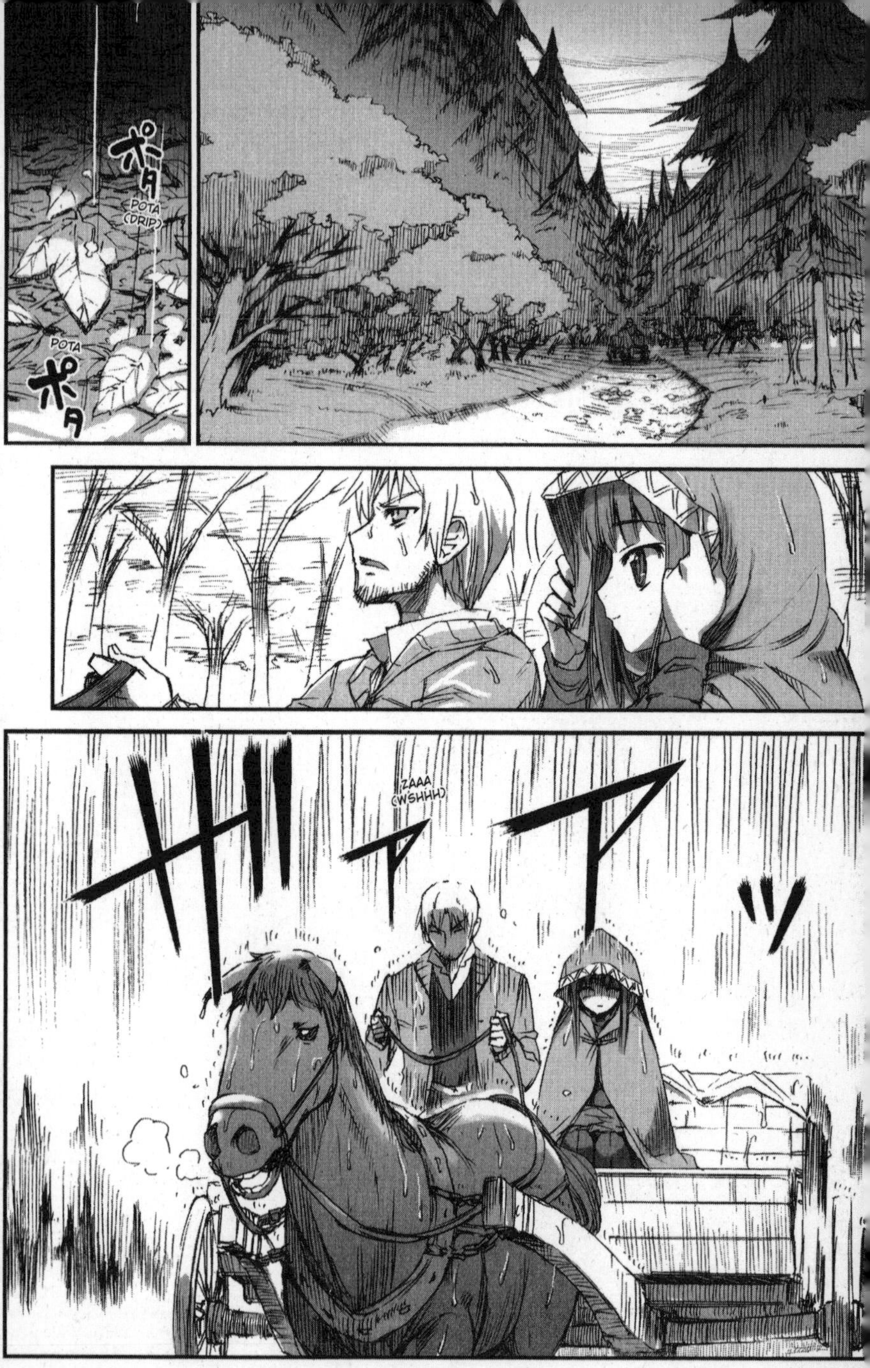
ポタ
POTA (DRIP)
POTA
ポタ
ザァアッ
ZAAA (WSHHH)

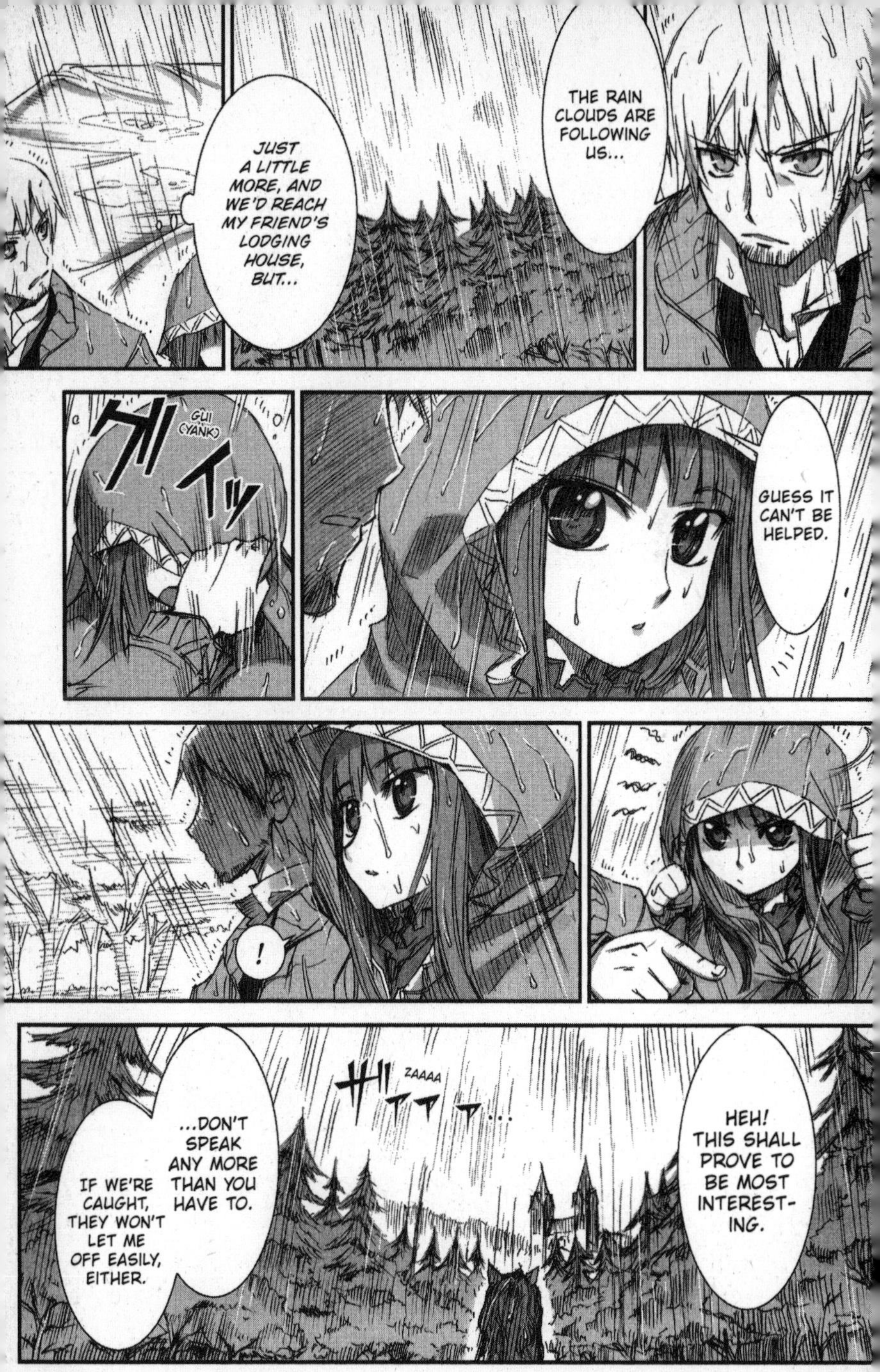
THE RAIN CLOUDS ARE FOLLOWING US...
JUST A LITTLE MORE, AND WE'D REACH MY FRIEND'S LODGING HOUSE, BUT...
GUESS IT CAN'T BE HELPED.
グイッ
GUI (YANK)
!
HEH! THIS SHALL PROVE TO BE MOST INTEREST-ING.
ザァァァ...
ZAAAA
...DON'T SPEAK ANY MORE THAN YOU HAVE TO.
IF WE'RE CAUGHT, THEY WON'T LET ME OFF EASILY, EITHER.

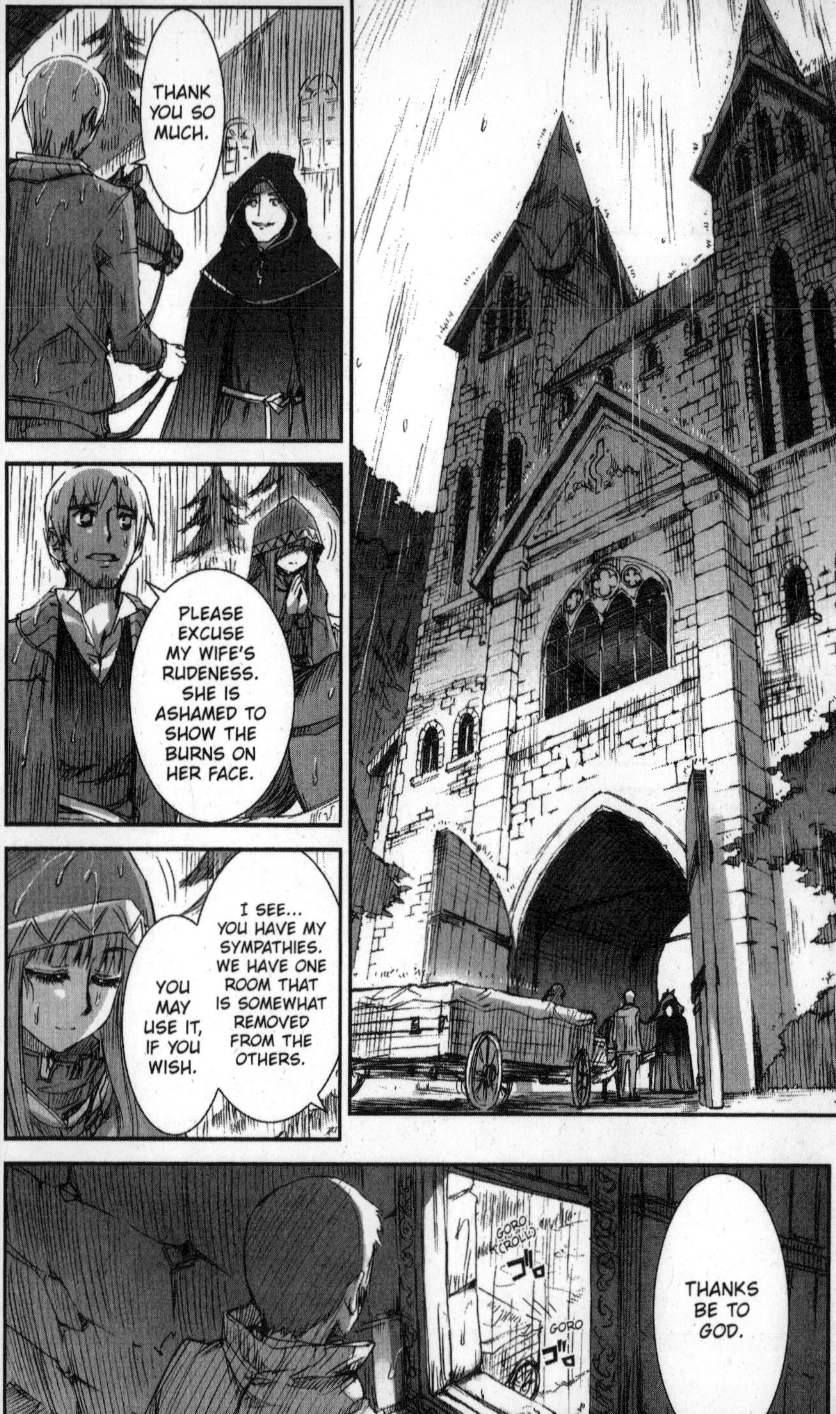
THANK YOU SO MUCH.
PLEASE EXCUSE MY WIFE'S RUDENESS. SHE IS ASHAMED TO SHOW THE BURNS ON HER FACE.
I SEE... YOU HAVE MY SYMPATHIES. WE HAVE ONE ROOM THAT IS SOMEWHAT REMOVED FROM THE OTHERS.
YOU MAY USE IT, IF YOU WISH.
THANKS BE TO GOD.
GORO (ROLL)
GORO

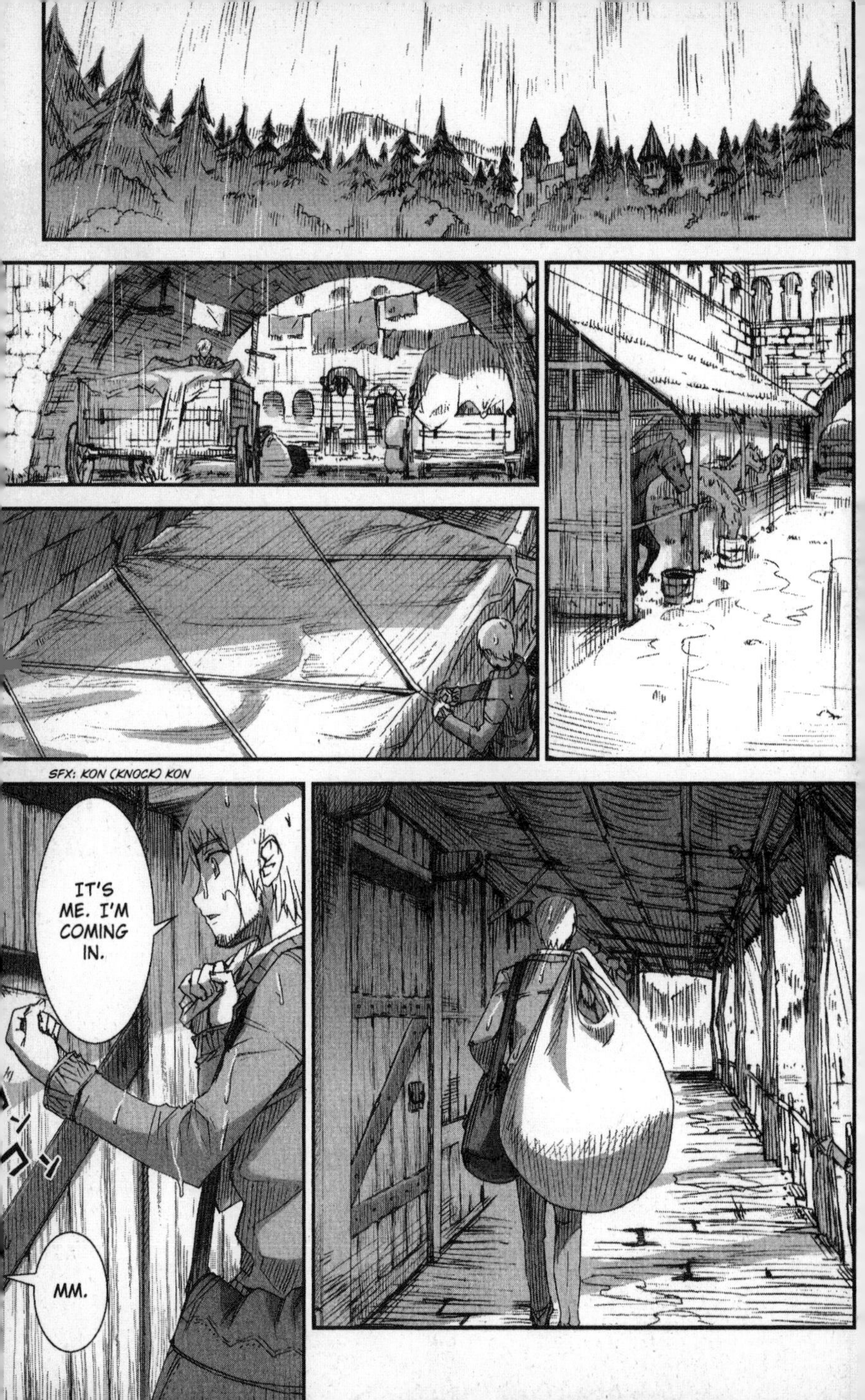
SFX: KON (KNOCK) KON
IT'S ME. I'M COMING IN.
MM.

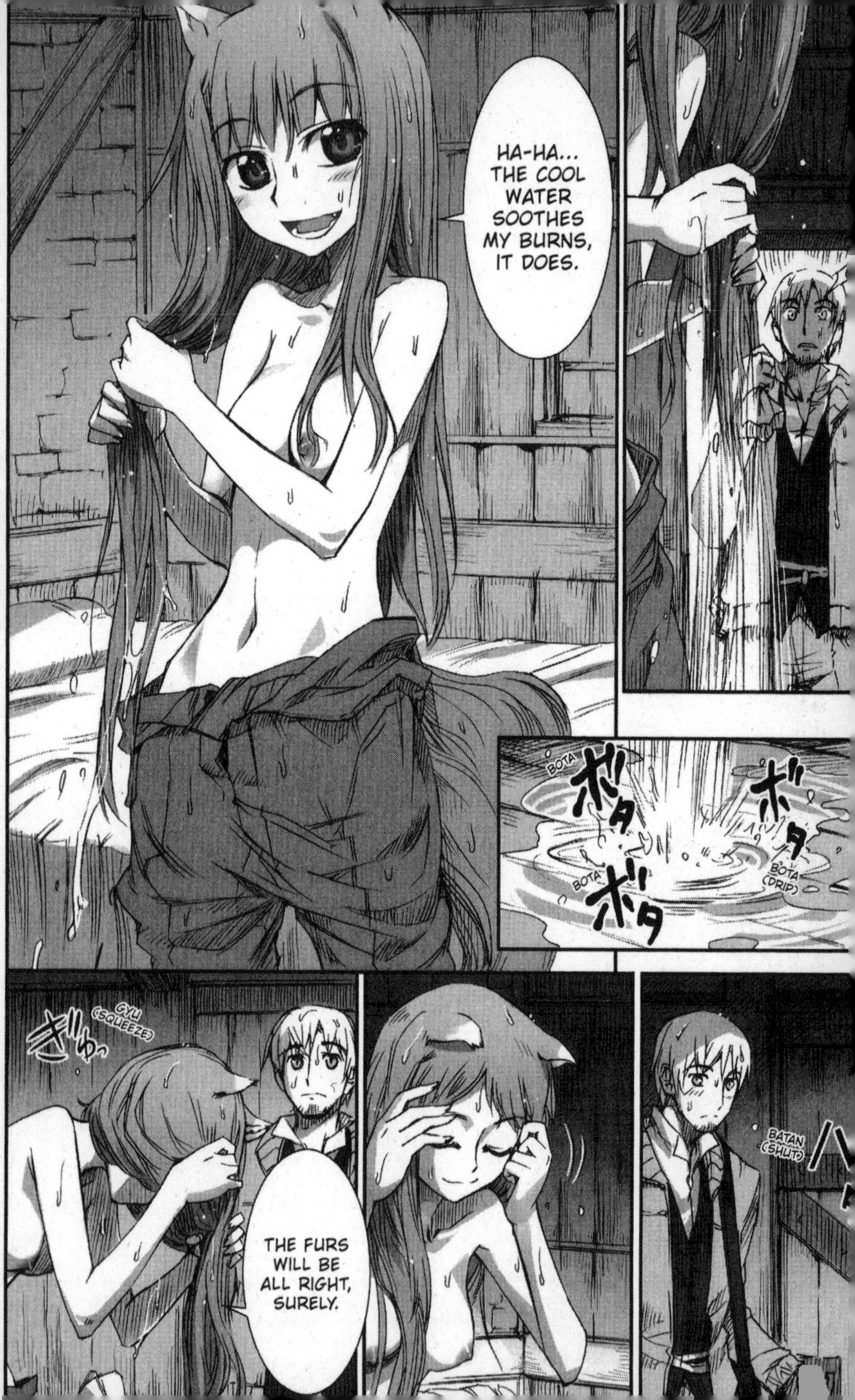
BOTA
BOTA
BOTA (DRIP)
HA-HA... THE COOL WATER SOOTHES MY BURNS, IT DOES.
BATAN (SHUT)
GYU (SQUEEZE)
THE FURS WILL BE ALL RIGHT, SURELY.

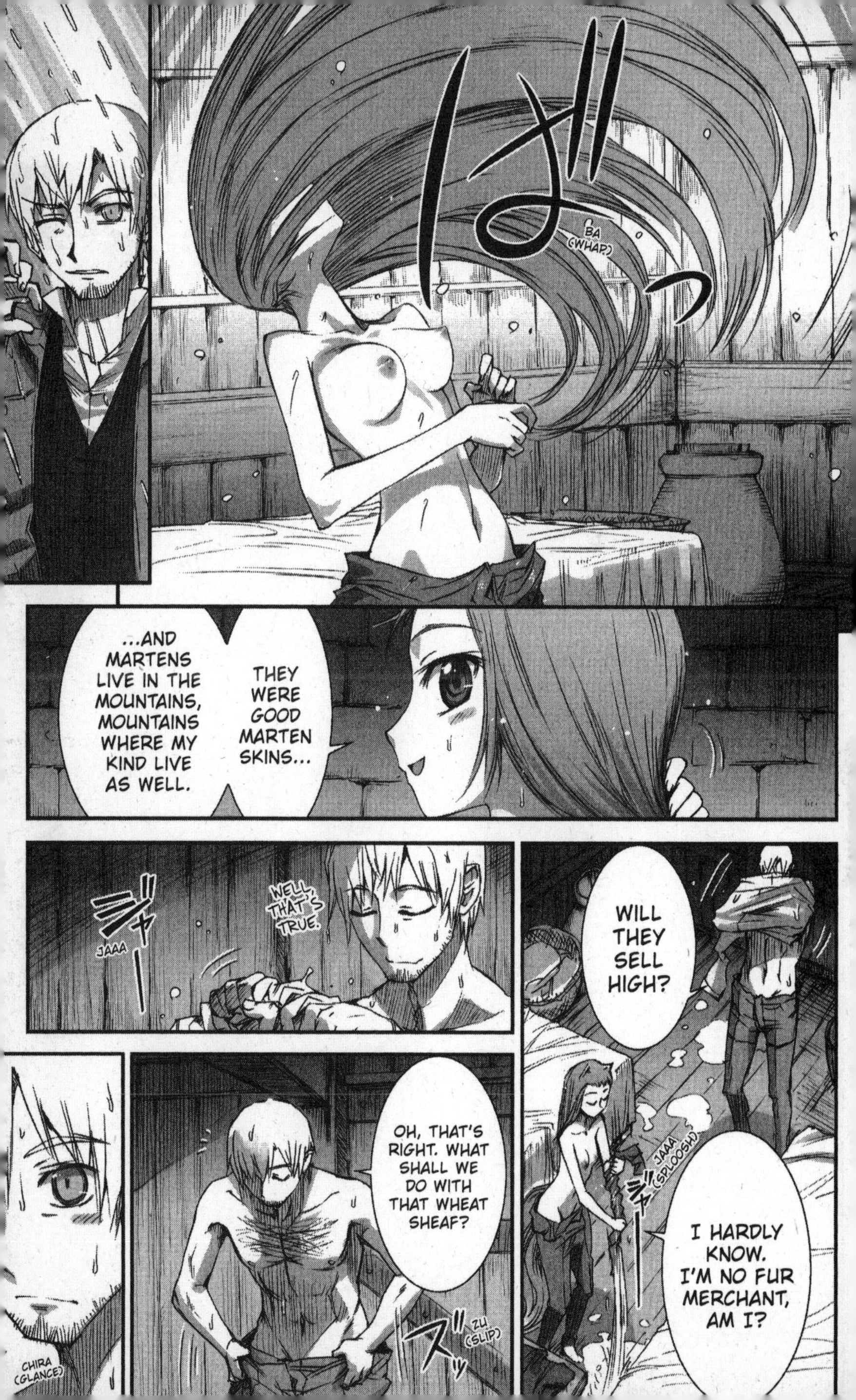
BA (WHAP)
THEY WERE GOOD MARTEN SKINS...
...AND MARTENS LIVE IN THE MOUNTAINS, MOUNTAINS WHERE MY KIND LIVE AS WELL.
WILL THEY SELL HIGH?
JAAA (SPLOOSH)
I HARDLY KNOW. I'M NO FUR MERCHANT, AM I?
WELL, THAT'S TRUE.
JAAA
OH, THAT'S RIGHT. WHAT SHALL WE DO WITH THAT WHEAT SHEAF?
ZU (SLIP)
CHIRA (GLANCE)

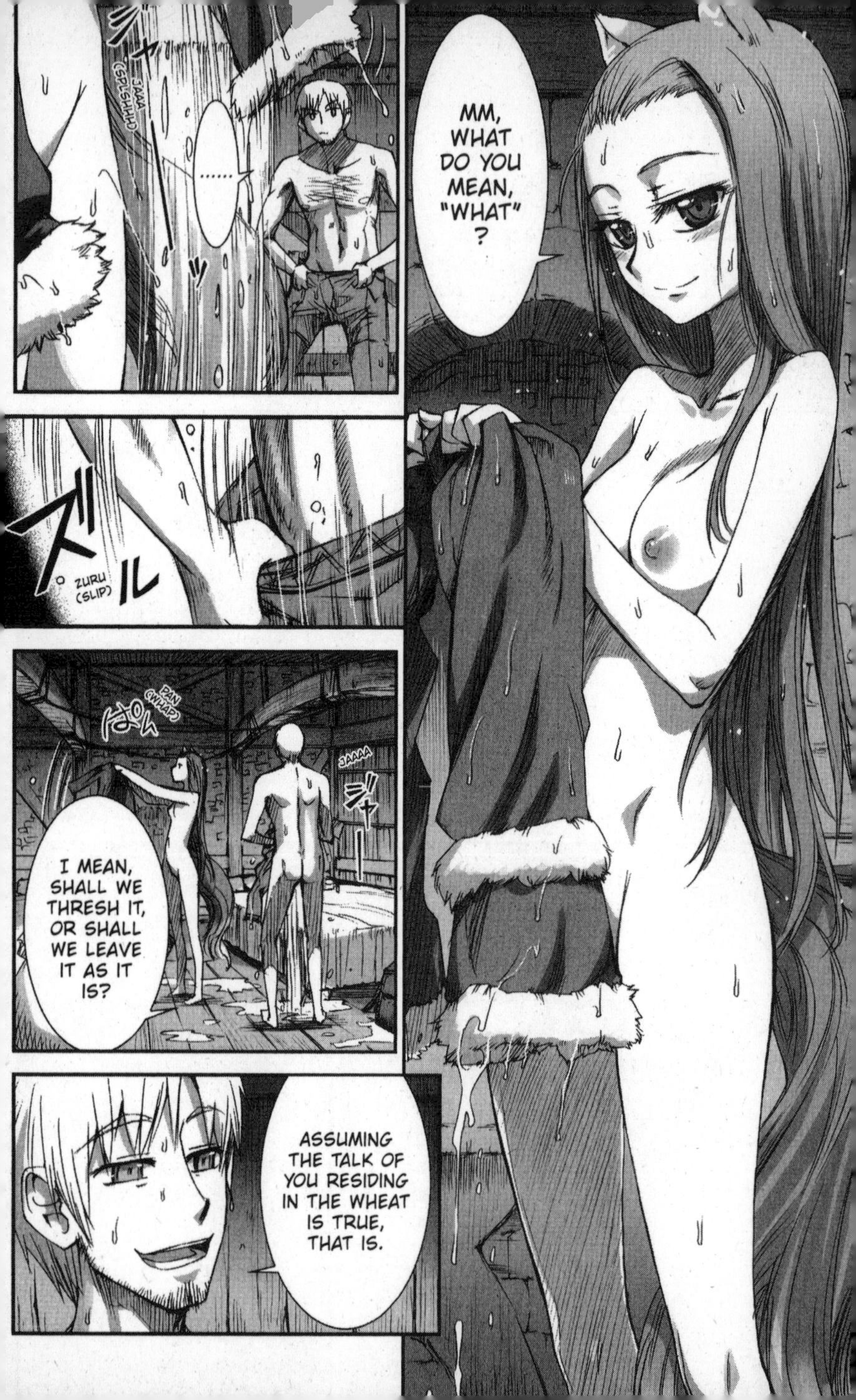
MM, WHAT DO YOU MEAN, "WHAT"?
JAAA (SPLSHHH)
......
ZURU (SLIP)
PAN (WHAP)
JAAAA
I MEAN, SHALL WE THRESH IT, OR SHALL WE LEAVE IT AS IT IS?
ASSUMING THE TALK OF YOU RESIDING IN THE WHEAT IS TRUE, THAT IS.

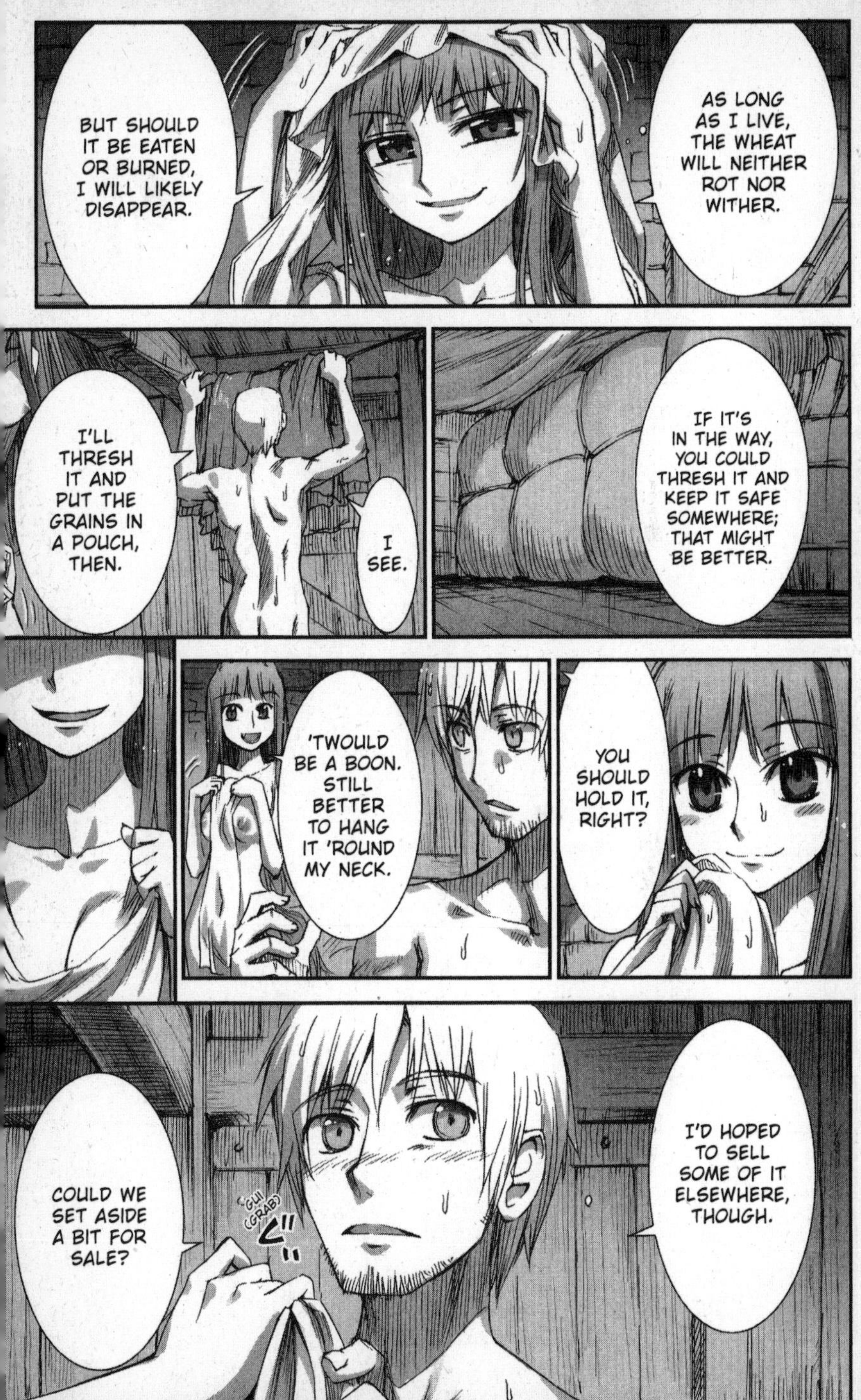
AS LONG AS I LIVE, THE WHEAT WILL NEITHER ROT NOR WITHER.
BUT SHOULD IT BE EATEN OR BURNED, I WILL LIKELY DISAPPEAR.
IF IT'S IN THE WAY, YOU COULD THRESH IT AND KEEP IT SAFE SOMEWHERE; THAT MIGHT BE BETTER.
I SEE.
I'LL THRESH IT AND PUT THE GRAINS IN A POUCH, THEN.
YOU SHOULD HOLD IT, RIGHT?
'TWOULD BE A BOON. STILL BETTER TO HANG IT 'ROUND MY NECK.
I'D HOPED TO SELL SOME OF IT ELSEWHERE, THOUGH.
GUI (GRAB)
COULD WE SET ASIDE A BIT FOR SALE?

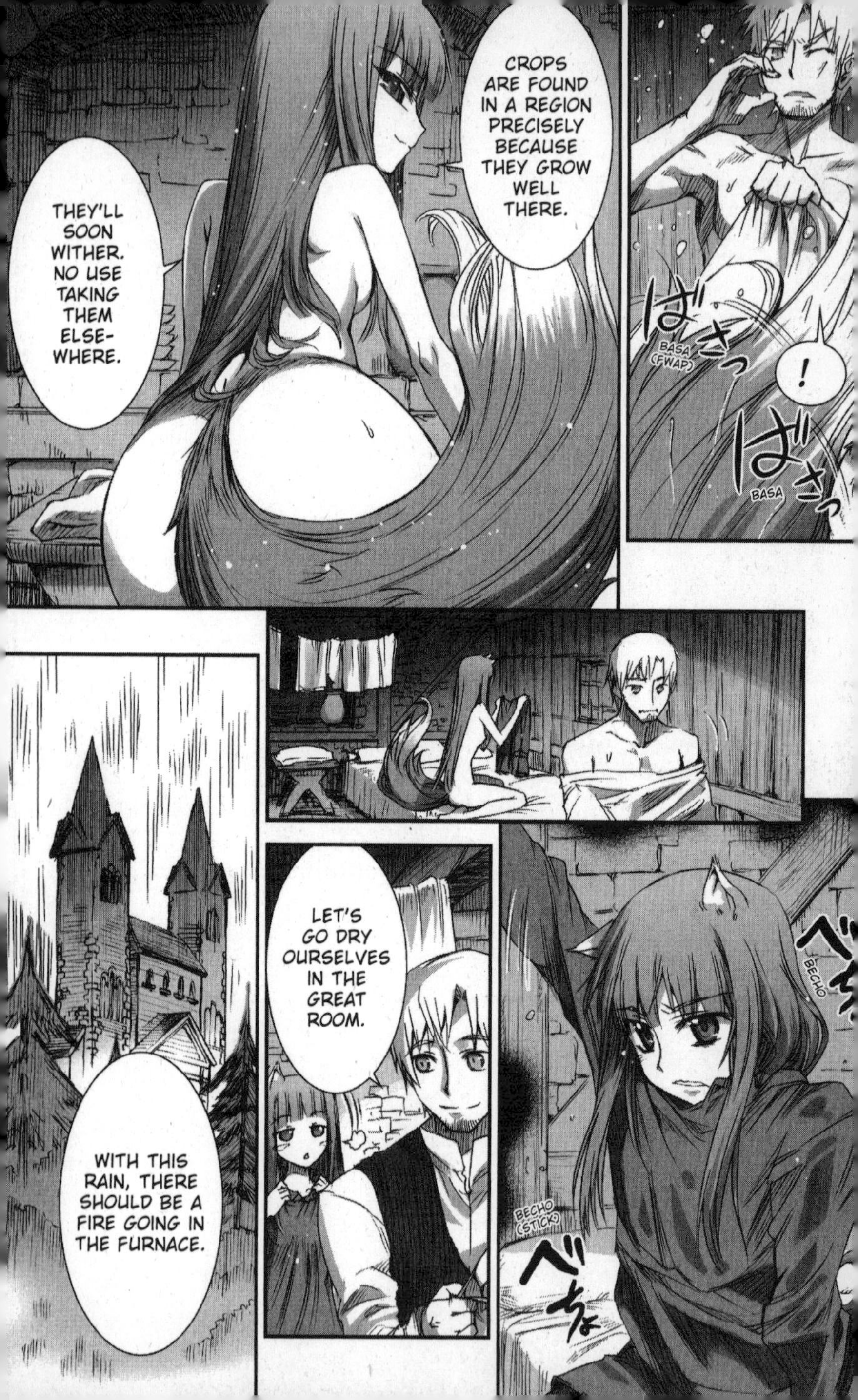
ばさっ
BASA (FWAP)
!
ばさっ
BASA
CROPS ARE FOUND IN A REGION PRECISELY BECAUSE THEY GROW WELL THERE.
THEY'LL SOON WITHER. NO USE TAKING THEM ELSE-WHERE.
べちょ
BECHO
べちょ
BECHO (STICK)
LET'S GO DRY OURSELVES IN THE GREAT ROOM.
WITH THIS RAIN, THERE SHOULD BE A FIRE GOING IN THE FURNACE.

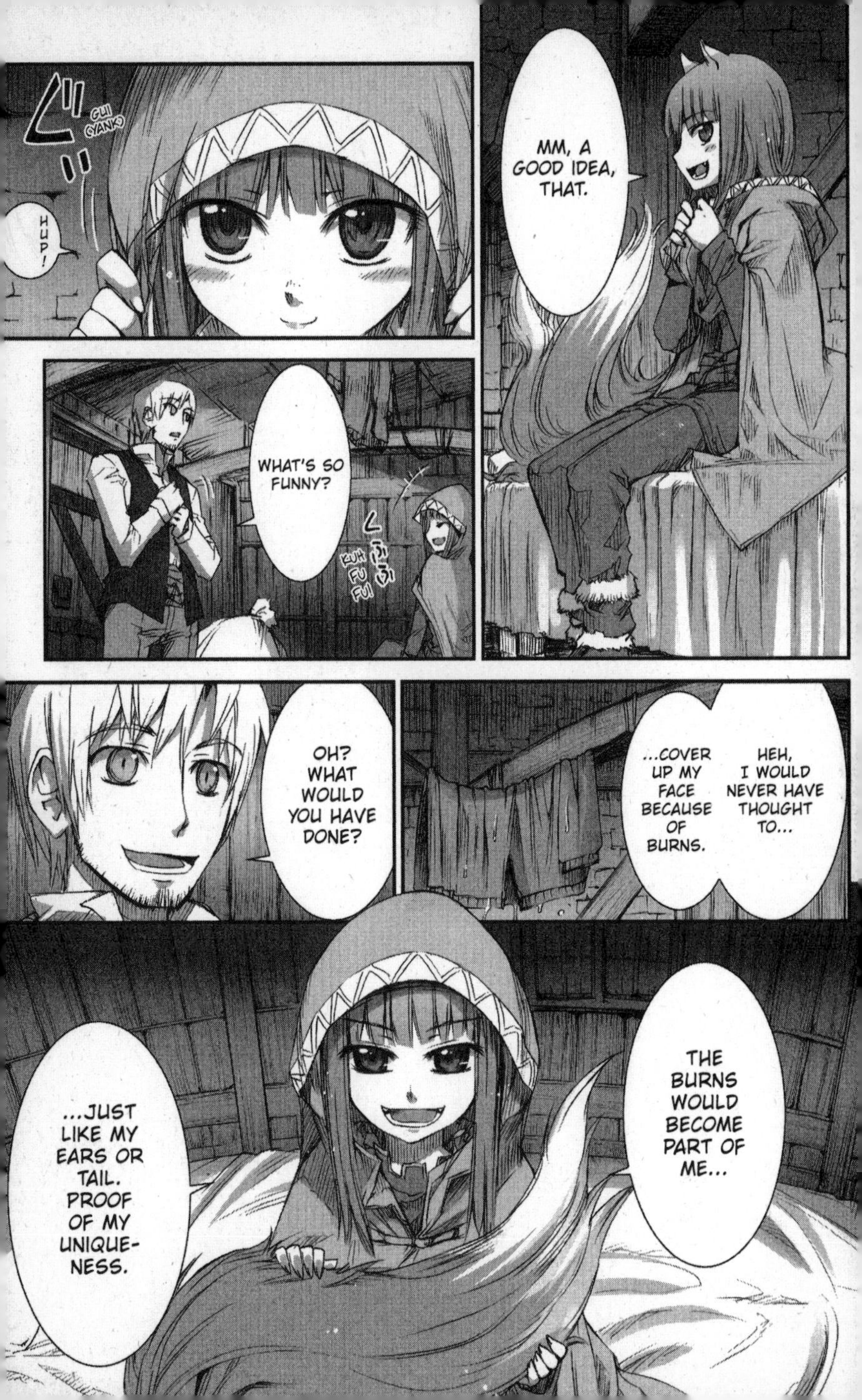
MM, A GOOD IDEA, THAT.
GUI (YANK)
HUP!
WHAT'S SO FUNNY?
KUH FU FU!
HEH, I WOULD NEVER HAVE THOUGHT TO...
...COVER UP MY FACE BECAUSE OF BURNS.
OH? WHAT WOULD YOU HAVE DONE?
THE BURNS WOULD BECOME PART OF ME...
...JUST LIKE MY EARS OR TAIL. PROOF OF MY UNIQUENESS.

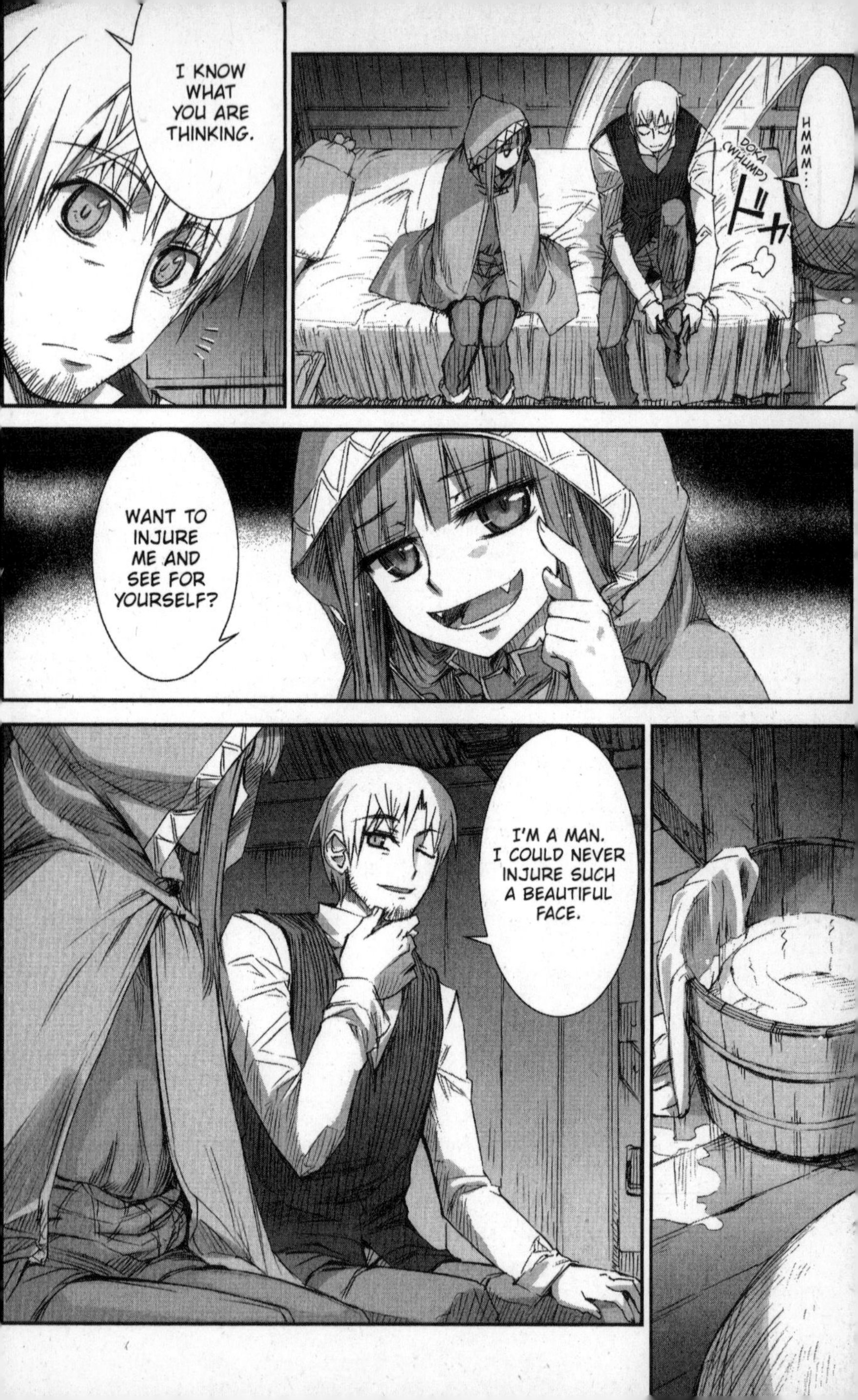
HMMM...
ドカ
DOKA (WHUMP)
I KNOW WHAT YOU ARE THINKING.
WANT TO INJURE ME AND SEE FOR YOURSELF?
I'M A MAN. I COULD NEVER INJURE SUCH A BEAUTIFUL FACE.

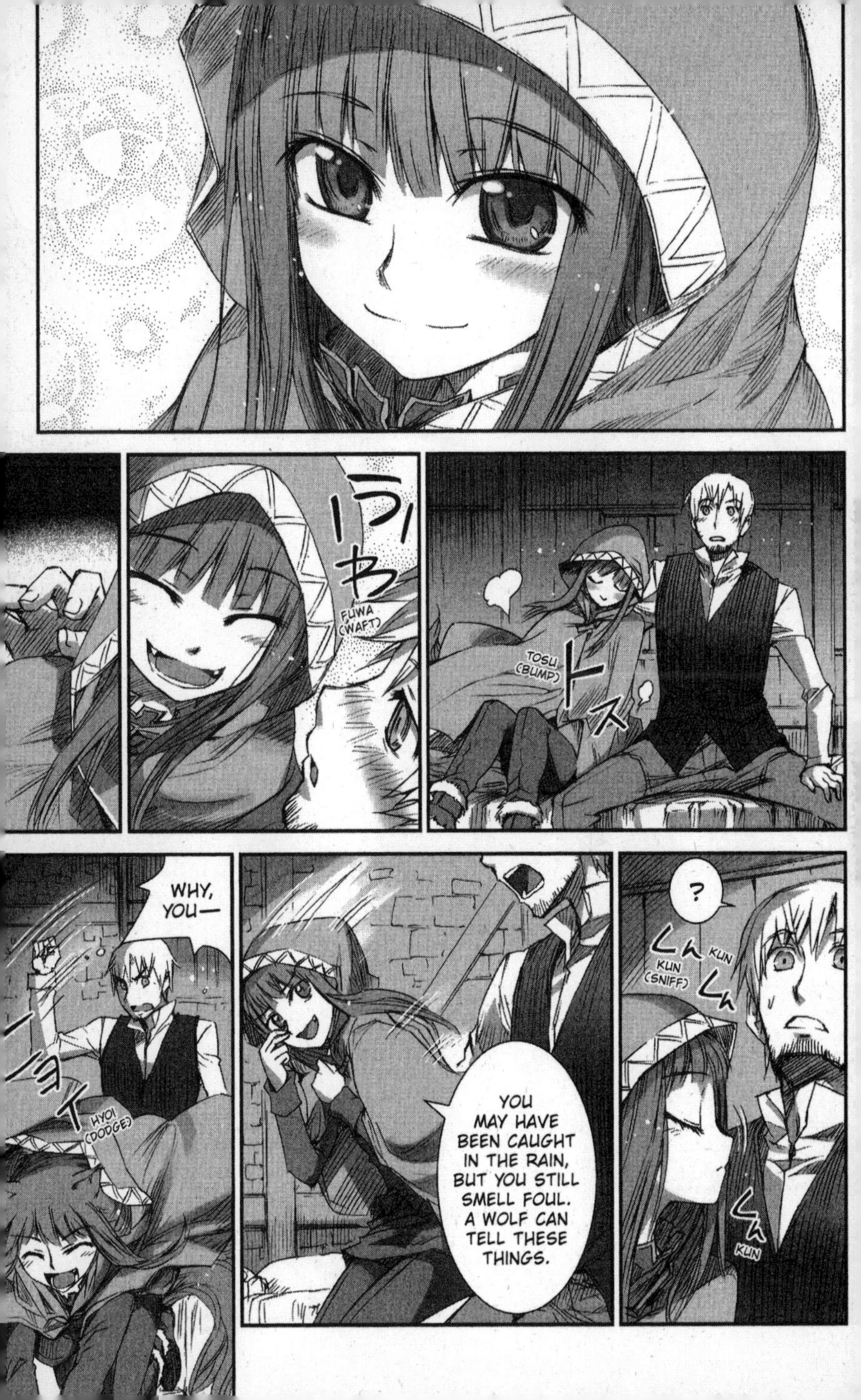

トス
TOSU (BUMP)
ふわ
FUWA (WAFT)
?
くん
KUN
くん
KUN (SNIFF)
くん
KUN
YOU MAY HAVE BEEN CAUGHT IN THE RAIN, BUT YOU STILL SMELL FOUL. A WOLF CAN TELL THESE THINGS.
WHY, YOU—
HYOI (DODGE)

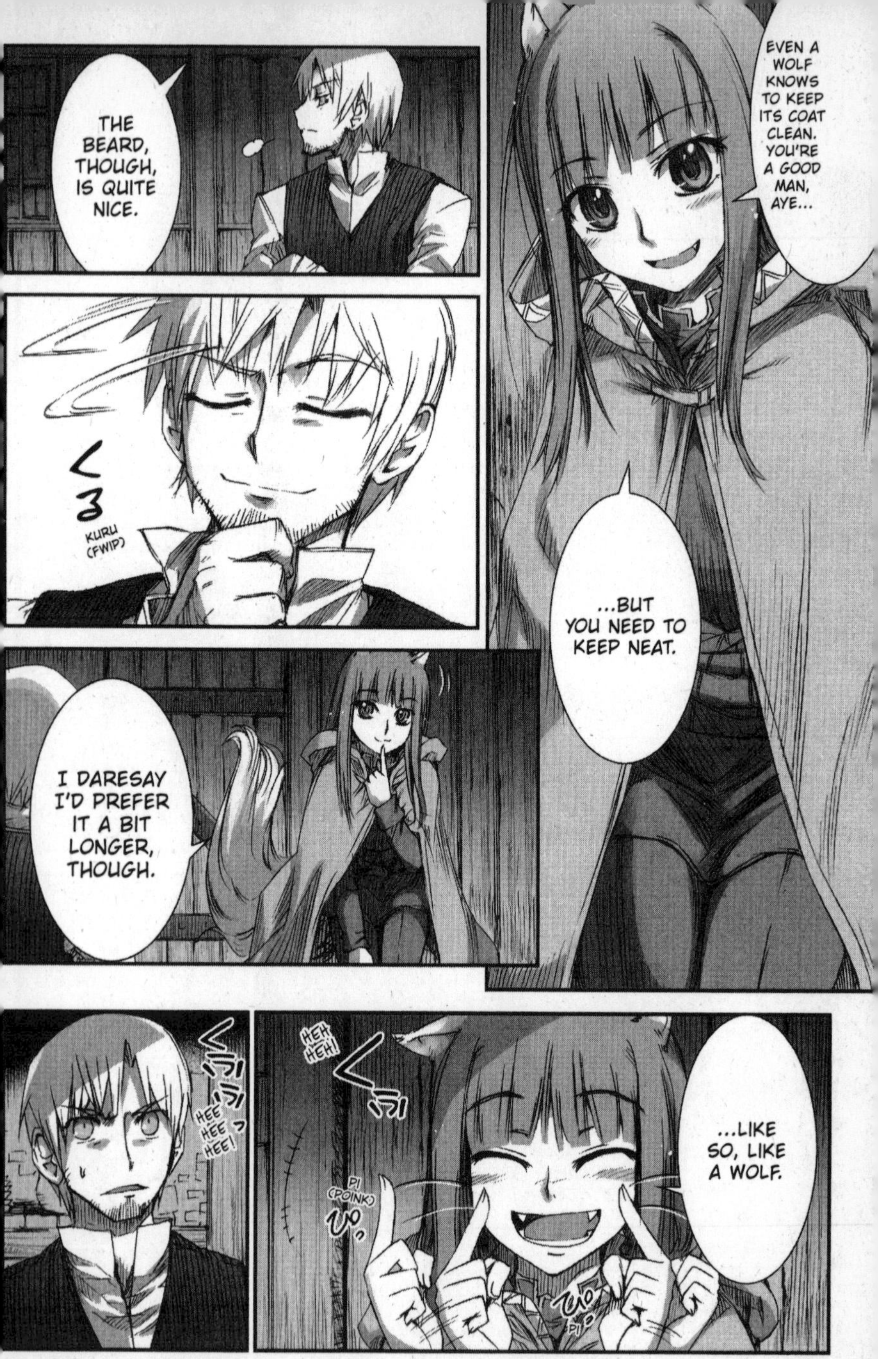
EVEN A WOLF KNOWS TO KEEP ITS COAT CLEAN. YOU'RE A GOOD MAN, AYE...
...BUT YOU NEED TO KEEP NEAT.
THE BEARD, THOUGH, IS QUITE NICE.
くる
KURU (FWIP)
I DARESAY I'D PREFER IT A BIT LONGER, THOUGH.
...LIKE SO, LIKE A WOLF.
HEH HEH!
PI (POINK)
HEE HEE HEE!

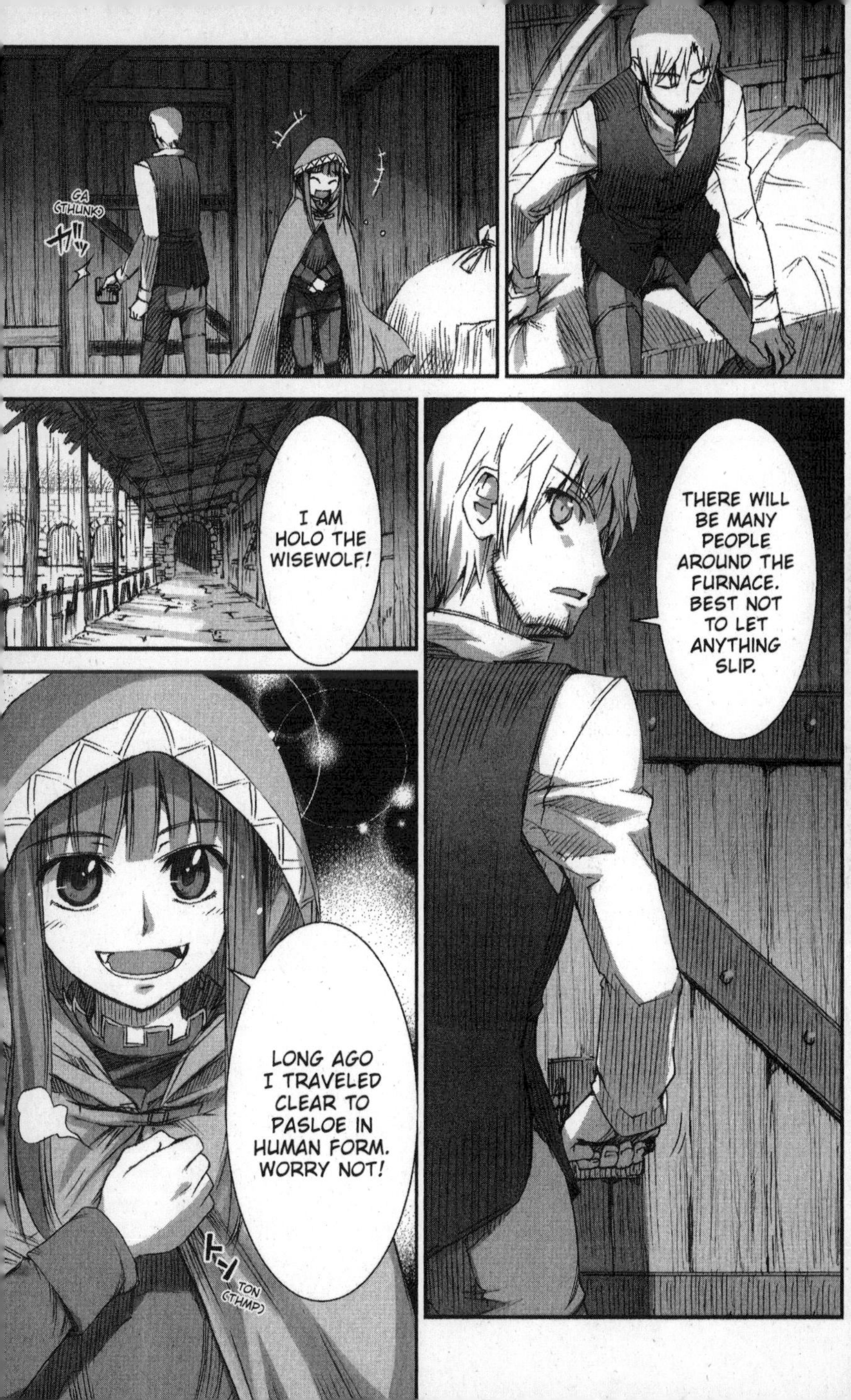

ガッ
GA (THLINK)
THERE WILL BE MANY PEOPLE AROUND THE FURNACE. BEST NOT TO LET ANYTHING SLIP.
I AM HOLO THE WISEWOLF!
LONG AGO I TRAVELED CLEAR TO PASLOE IN HUMAN FORM. WORRY NOT!
トン
TON (THMP)

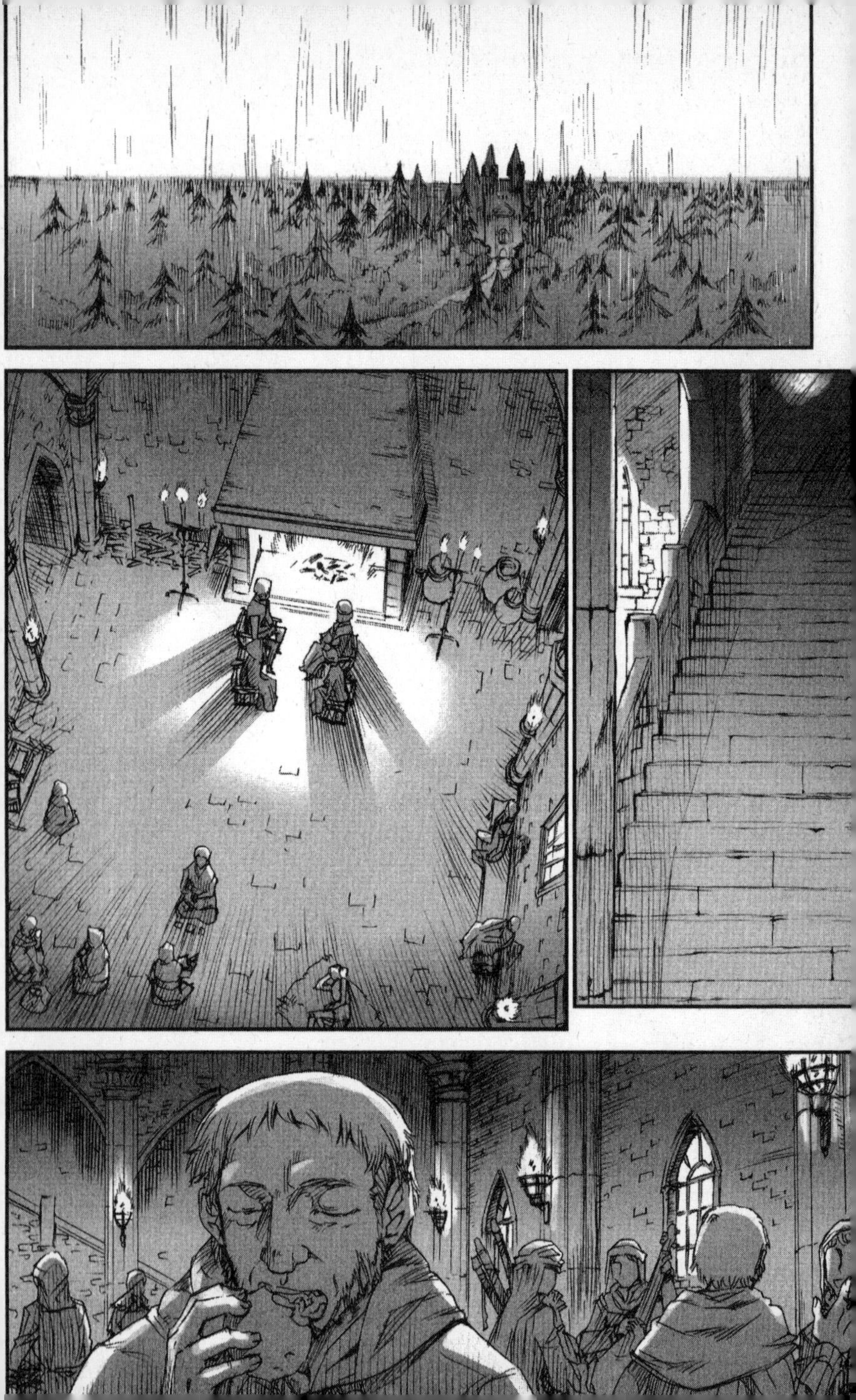

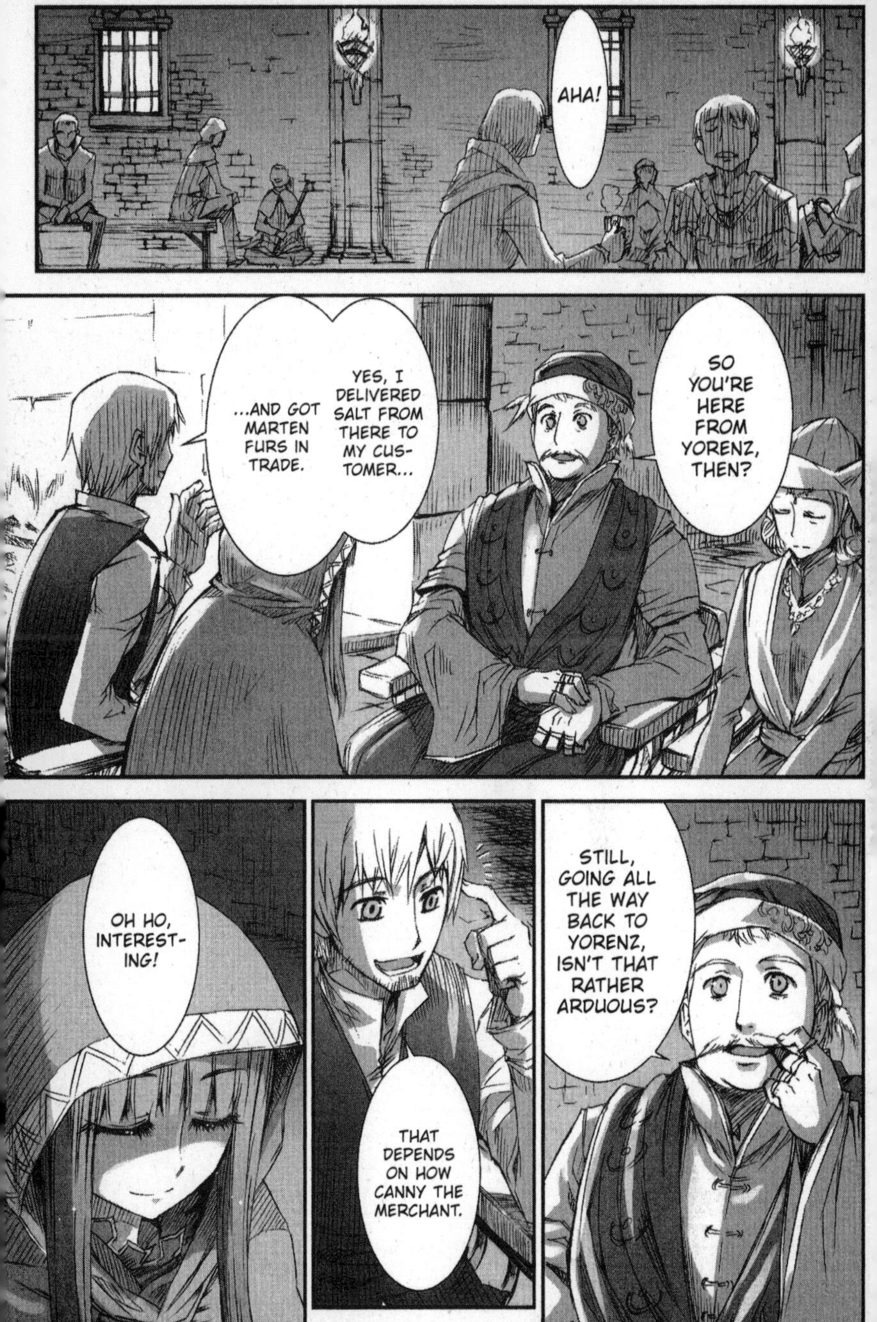
AHA!
SO YOU'RE HERE FROM YORENZ, THEN?
YES, I DELIVERED SALT FROM THERE TO MY CUSTOMER... ...AND GOT MARTEN FURS IN TRADE.
STILL, GOING ALL THE WAY BACK TO YORENZ, ISN'T THAT RATHER ARDUOUS?
THAT DEPENDS ON HOW CANNY THE MERCHANT.
OH HO, INTERESTING!

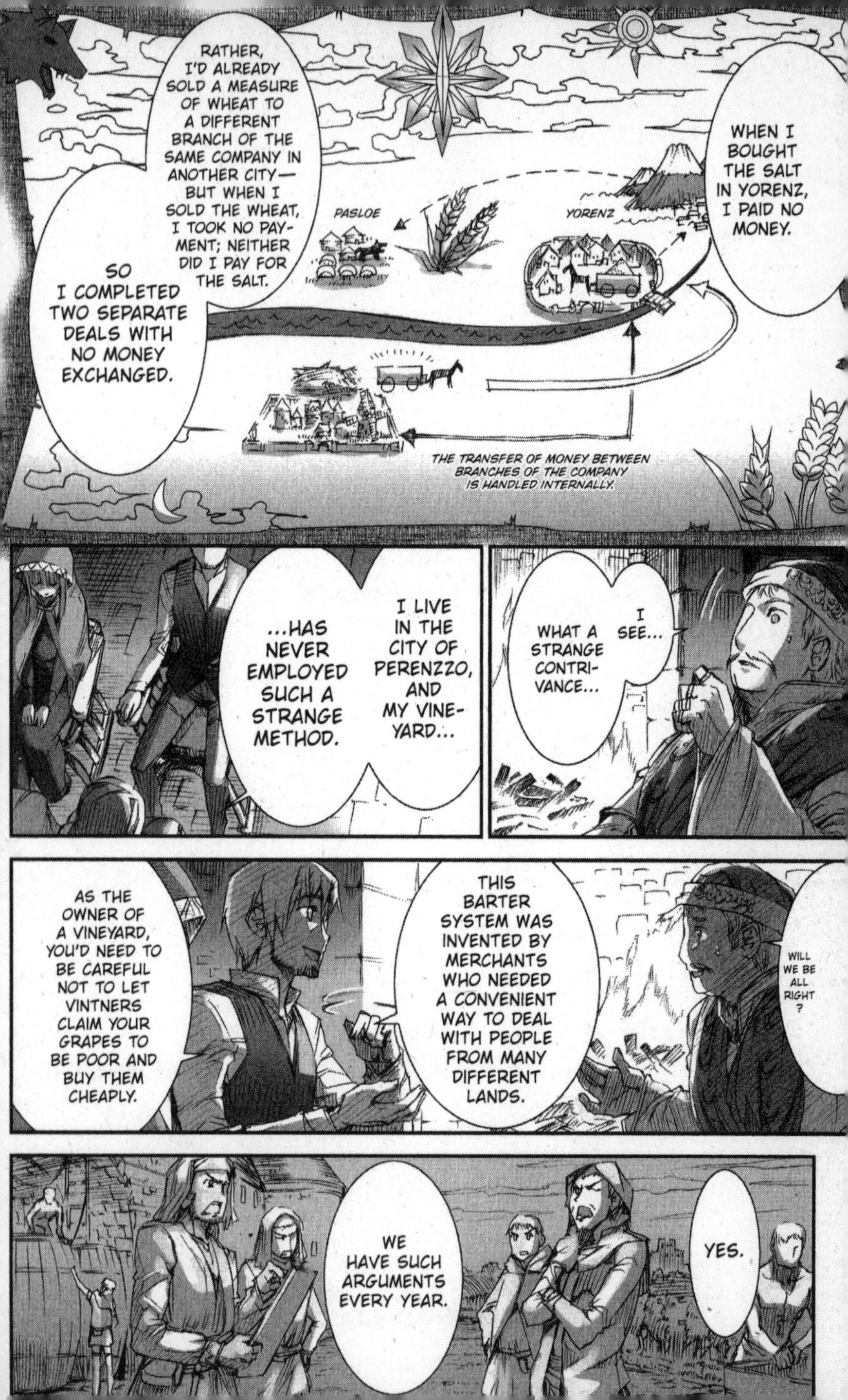
WHEN I BOUGHT THE SALT IN YORENZ, I PAID NO MONEY.
RATHER, I'D ALREADY SOLD A MEASURE OF WHEAT TO A DIFFERENT BRANCH OF THE SAME COMPANY IN ANOTHER CITY— BUT WHEN I SOLD THE WHEAT, I TOOK NO PAY-MENT; NEITHER DID I PAY FOR THE SALT.
SO I COMPLETED TWO SEPARATE DEALS WITH NO MONEY EXCHANGED.
YORENZ
PASLOE
THE TRANSFER OF MONEY BETWEEN BRANCHES OF THE COMPANY IS HANDLED INTERNALLY.
I SEE...
WHAT A STRANGE CONTRI-VANCE...
I LIVE IN THE CITY OF PERENZZO, AND MY VINE-YARD...
...HAS NEVER EMPLOYED SUCH A STRANGE METHOD.
WILL WE BE ALL RIGHT?
THIS BARTER SYSTEM WAS INVENTED BY MERCHANTS WHO NEEDED A CONVENIENT WAY TO DEAL WITH PEOPLE FROM MANY DIFFERENT LANDS.
AS THE OWNER OF A VINEYARD, YOU'D NEED TO BE CAREFUL NOT TO LET VINTNERS CLAIM YOUR GRAPES TO BE POOR AND BUY THEM CHEAPLY.
YES.
WE HAVE SUCH ARGUMENTS EVERY YEAR.

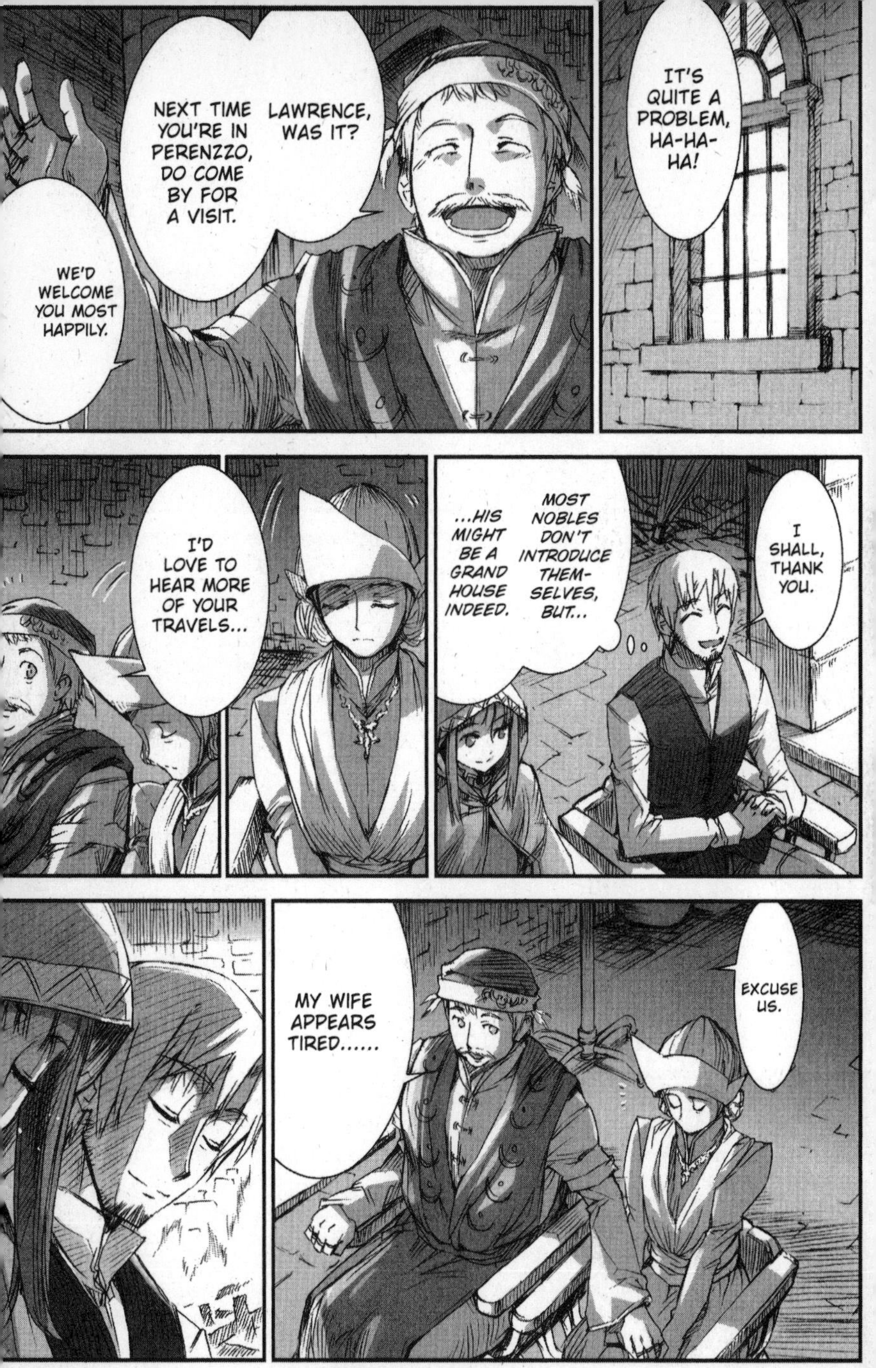
IT'S QUITE A PROBLEM, HA-HA-HA!
LAWRENCE, WAS IT?
NEXT TIME YOU'RE IN PERENZZO, DO COME BY FOR A VISIT.
WE'D WELCOME YOU MOST HAPPILY.
I SHALL, THANK YOU.
MOST NOBLES DON'T INTRODUCE THEM-SELVES, BUT...
...HIS MIGHT BE A GRAND HOUSE INDEED.
I'D LOVE TO HEAR MORE OF YOUR TRAVELS...
EXCUSE US.
MY WIFE APPEARS TIRED......

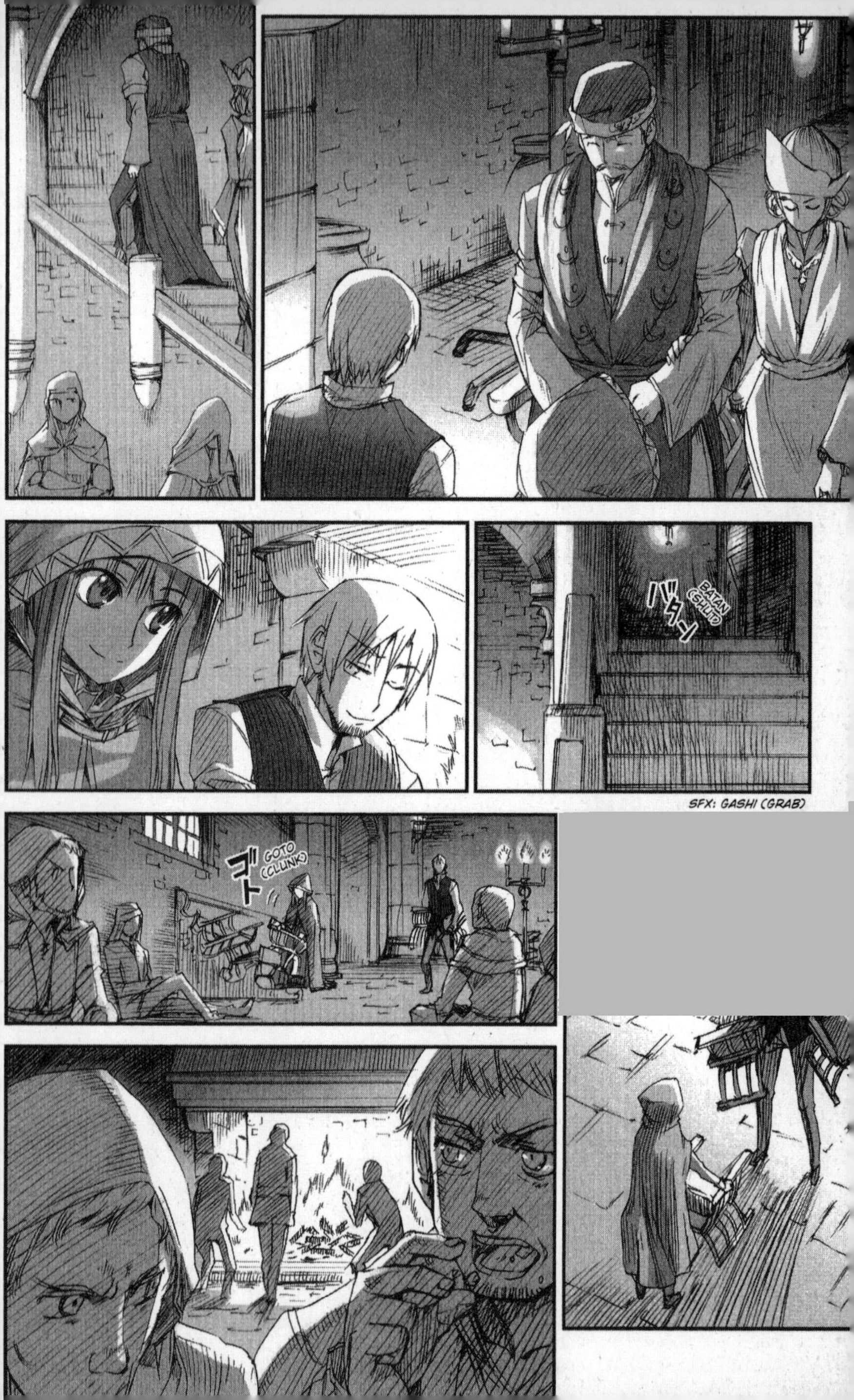
バターン
BATAN (SHUT)
SFX: GASHI (GRAB)
ゴトッ
GOTO (CLUNK)

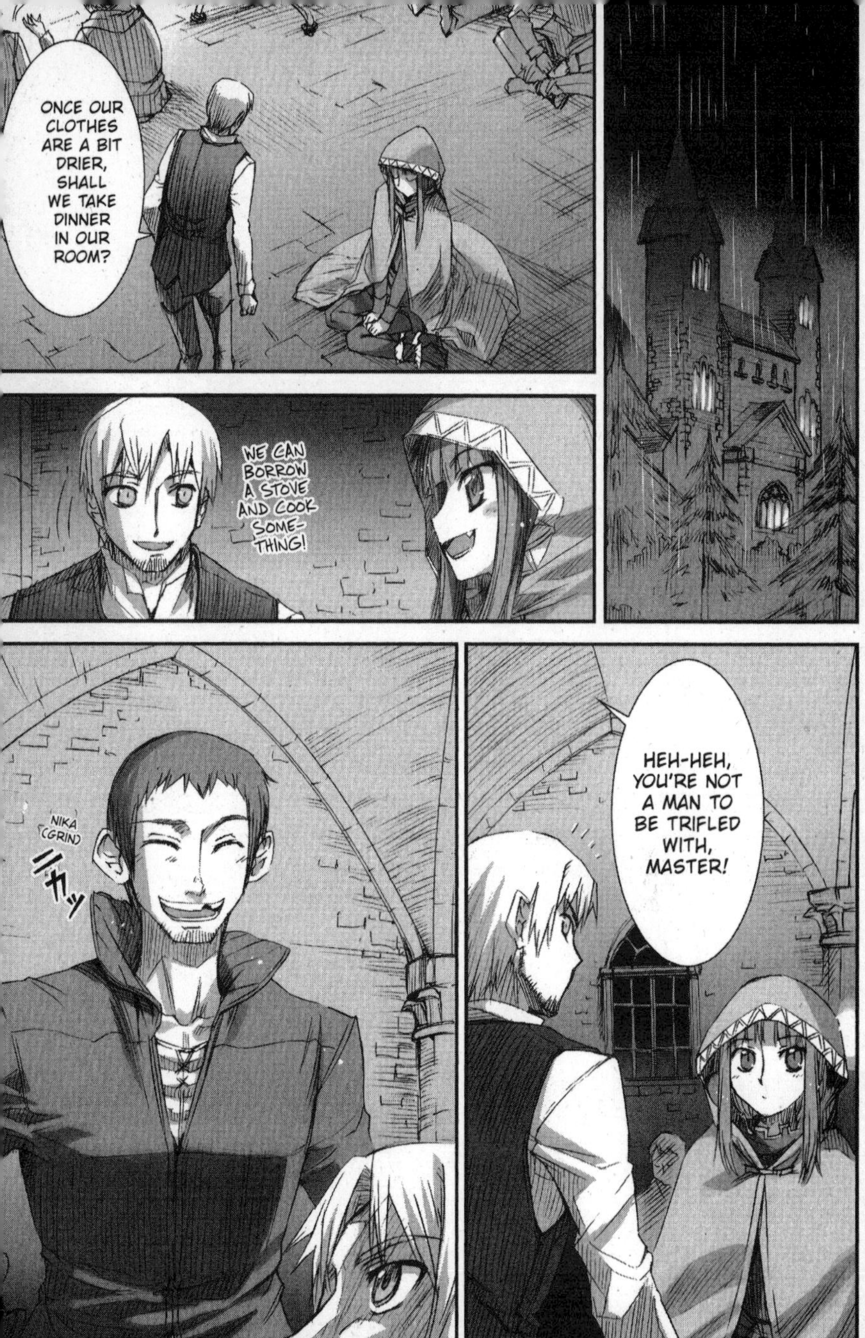
ONCE OUR CLOTHES ARE A BIT DRIER, SHALL WE TAKE DINNER IN OUR ROOM?
WE CAN BORROW A STOVE AND COOK SOME-THING!
HEH-HEH, YOU'RE NOT A MAN TO BE TRIFLED WITH, MASTER!
NIKA (GRIN)
ニカッ

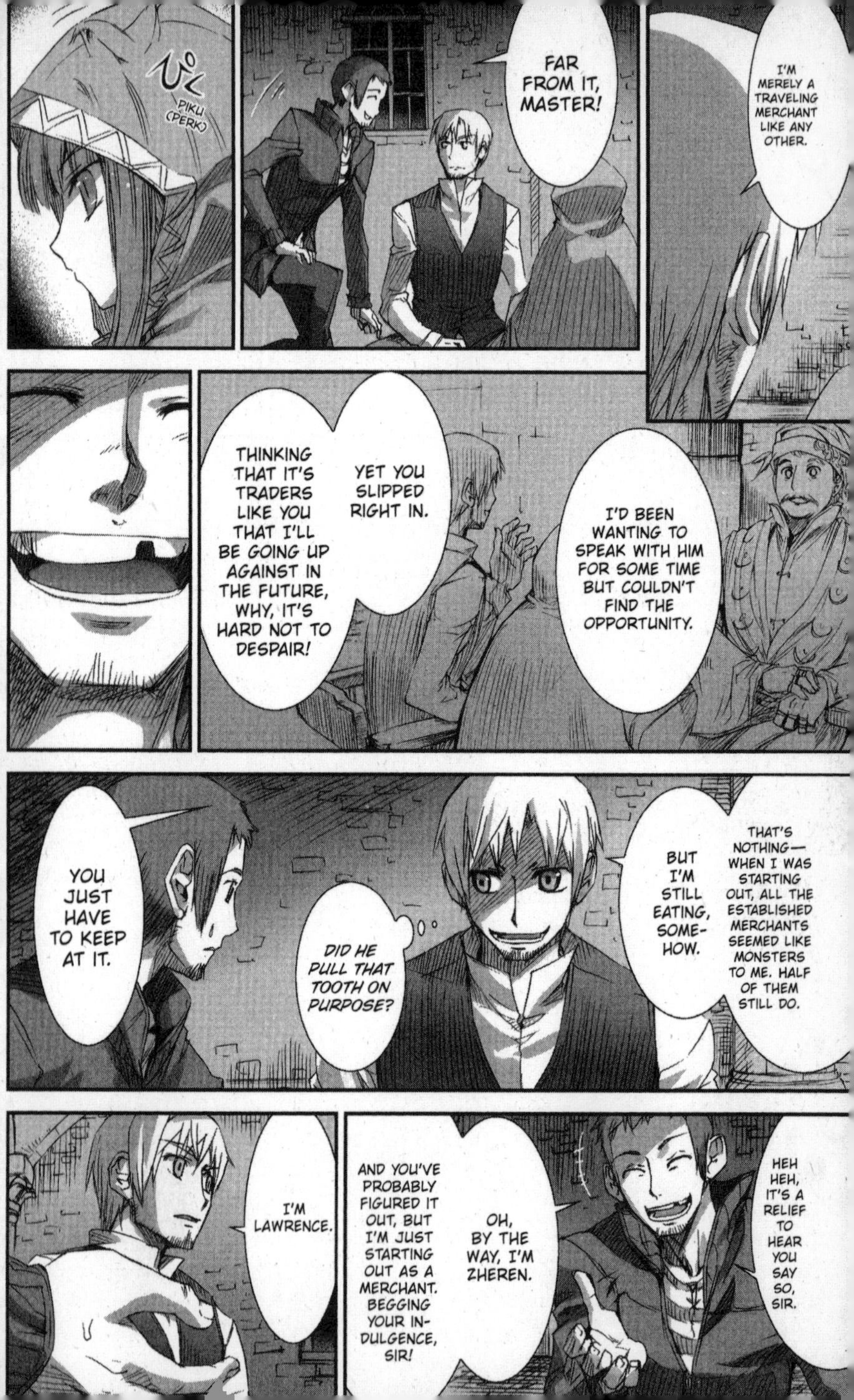
I'M MERELY A TRAVELING MERCHANT LIKE ANY OTHER.
FAR FROM IT, MASTER!
ぴく
PIKU (PERK)
I'D BEEN WANTING TO SPEAK WITH HIM FOR SOME TIME BUT COULDN'T FIND THE OPPORTUNITY.
YET YOU SLIPPED RIGHT IN.
THINKING THAT IT'S TRADERS LIKE YOU THAT I'LL BE GOING UP AGAINST IN THE FUTURE, WHY, IT'S HARD NOT TO DESPAIR!
THAT'S NOTHING—WHEN I WAS STARTING OUT, ALL THE ESTABLISHED MERCHANTS SEEMED LIKE MONSTERS TO ME. HALF OF THEM STILL DO.
BUT I'M STILL EATING, SOME-HOW.
DID HE PULL THAT TOOTH ON PURPOSE?
YOU JUST HAVE TO KEEP AT IT.
HEH HEH, IT'S A RELIEF TO HEAR YOU SAY SO, SIR.
OH, BY THE WAY, I'M ZHEREN.
AND YOU'VE PROBABLY FIGURED IT OUT, BUT I'M JUST STARTING OUT AS A MERCHANT. BEGGING YOUR IN-DULGENCE, SIR!
I'M LAWRENCE.

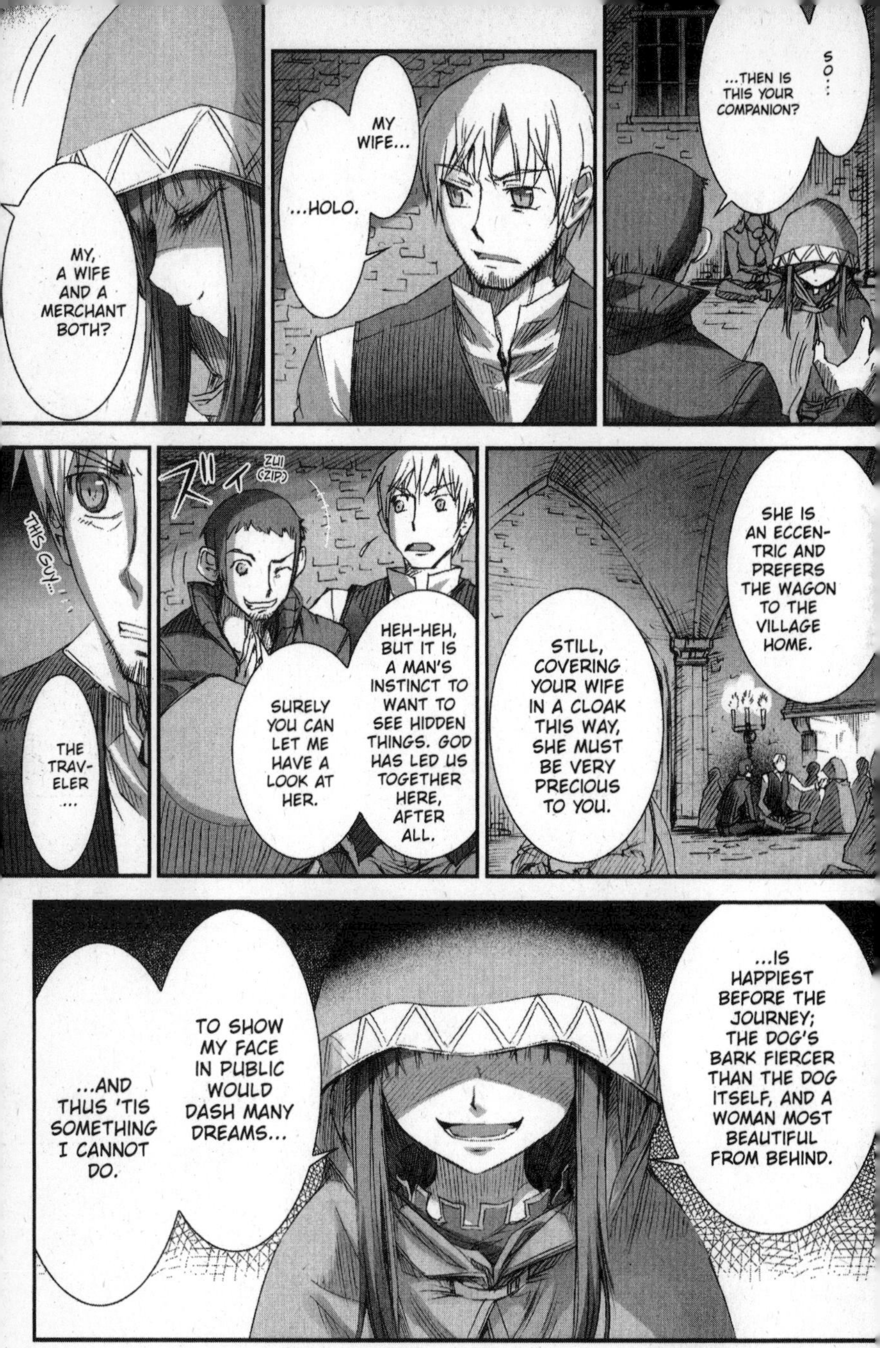
SO...
...THEN IS THIS YOUR COMPANION?
MY WIFE...
...HOLO.
MY, A WIFE AND A MERCHANT BOTH?
SHE IS AN ECCENTRIC AND PREFERS THE WAGON TO THE VILLAGE HOME.
STILL, COVERING YOUR WIFE IN A CLOAK THIS WAY, SHE MUST BE VERY PRECIOUS TO YOU.
ZUI (ZIP)
HEH-HEH, BUT IT IS A MAN'S INSTINCT TO WANT TO SEE HIDDEN THINGS. GOD HAS LED US TOGETHER HERE, AFTER ALL.
SURELY YOU CAN LET ME HAVE A LOOK AT HER.
THIS GUY...
THE TRAVELER....
...IS HAPPIEST BEFORE THE JOURNEY; THE DOG'S BARK FIERCER THAN THE DOG ITSELF, AND A WOMAN MOST BEAUTIFUL FROM BEHIND.
TO SHOW MY FACE IN PUBLIC WOULD DASH MANY DREAMS...
...AND THUS 'TIS SOMETHING I CANNOT DO.

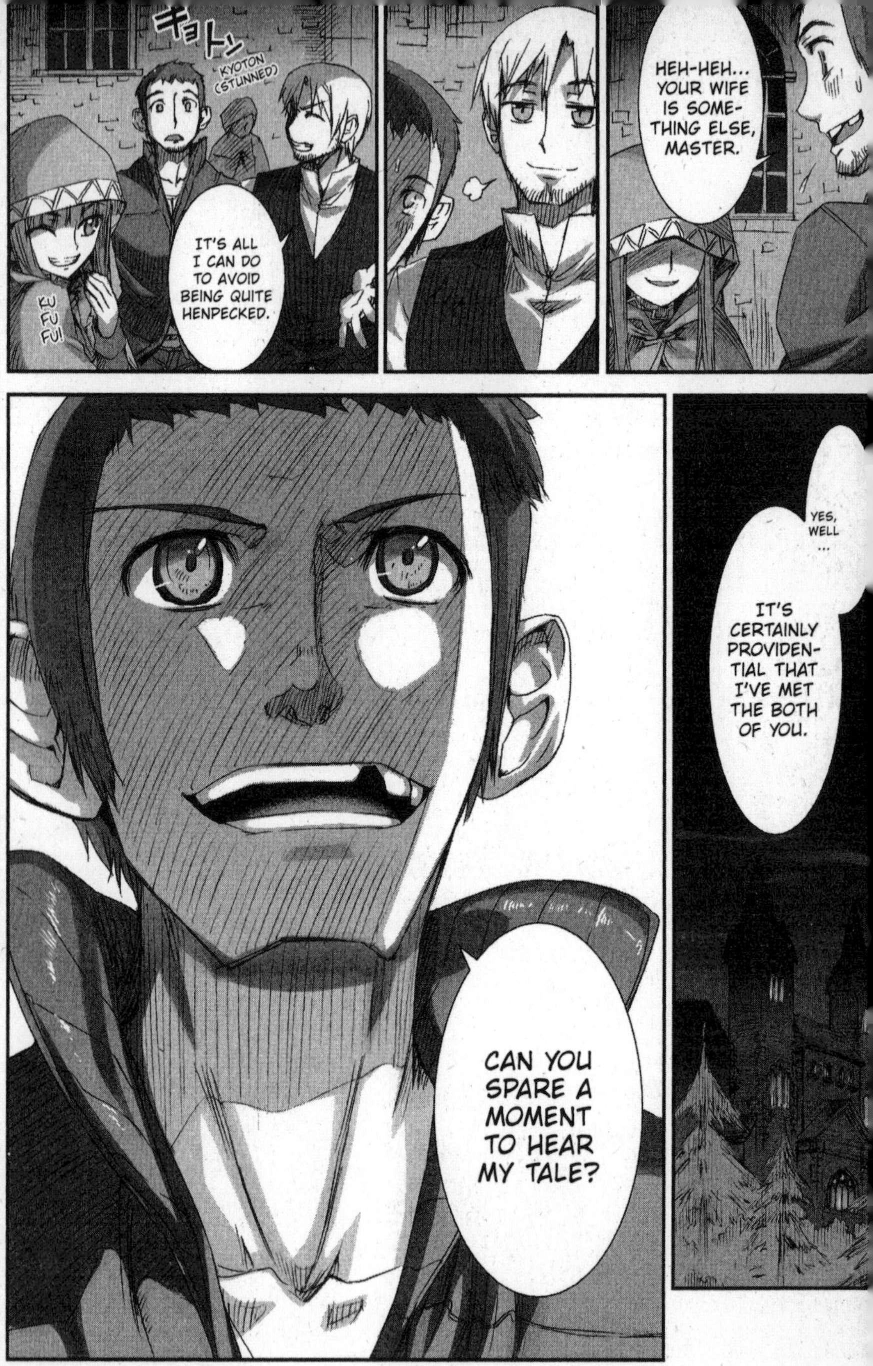
HEH-HEH... YOUR WIFE IS SOMETHING ELSE, MASTER.
キョトン
KYOTON (STUNNED)
IT'S ALL I CAN DO TO AVOID BEING QUITE HENPECKED.
KU FU FU!
YES, WELL ...
IT'S CERTAINLY PROVIDENTIAL THAT I'VE MET THE BOTH OF YOU.
CAN YOU SPARE A MOMENT TO HEAR MY TALE?

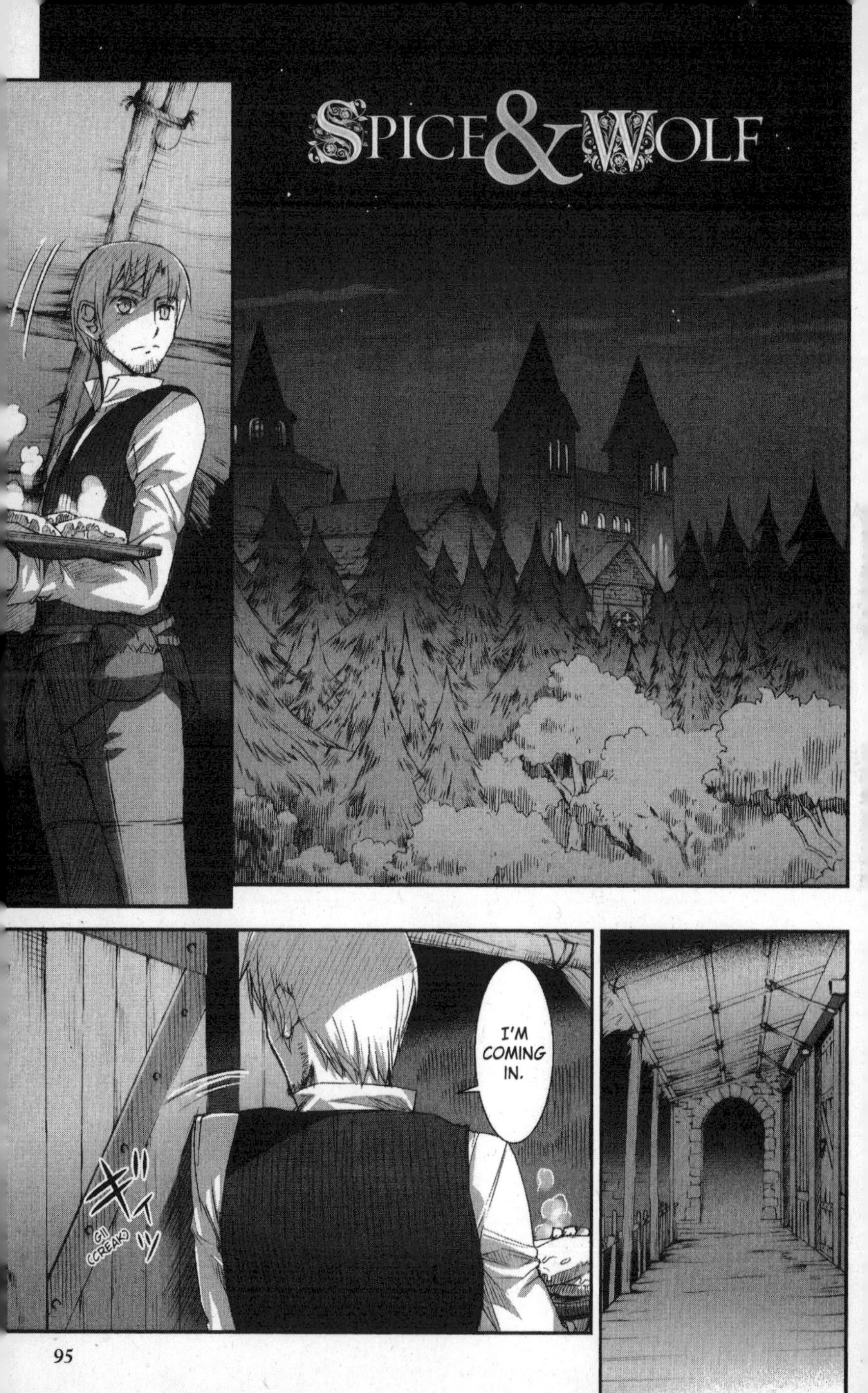
SPICE & WOLF
I'M COMING IN.
GII (CREAK)

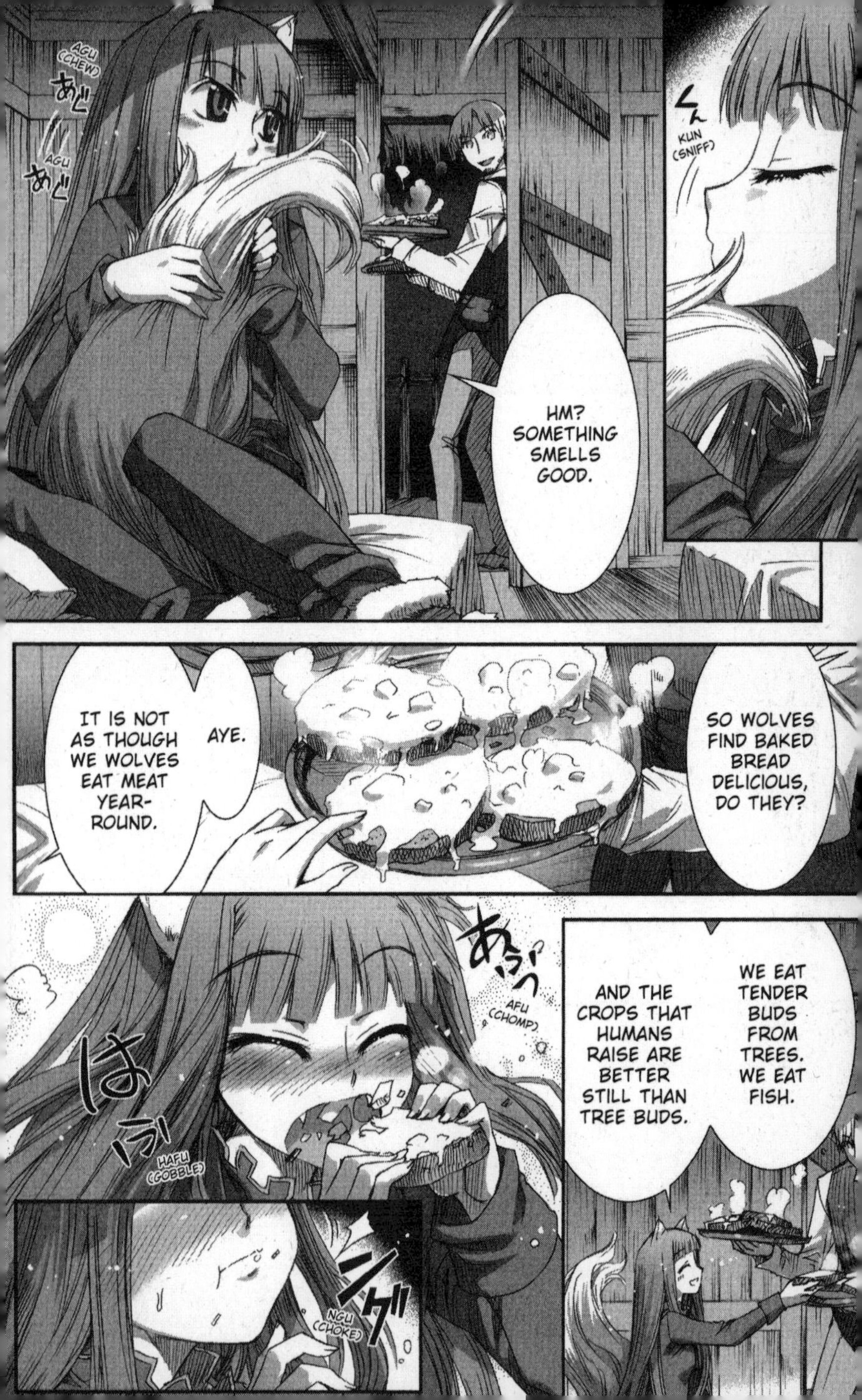
くん
KUN (SNIFF)
AGU (CHEW)
あぐ
AGU
あぐ
HM? SOMETHING SMELLS GOOD.
SO WOLVES FIND BAKED BREAD DELICIOUS, DO THEY?
AYE.
IT IS NOT AS THOUGH WE WOLVES EAT MEAT YEAR-ROUND.
WE EAT TENDER BUDS FROM TREES. WE EAT FISH.
AND THE CROPS THAT HUMANS RAISE ARE BETTER STILL THAN TREE BUDS.
あふっ
AFU (CHOMP)
はふ
HAFU (GOBBLE)
ング
NGU (CHOKE)

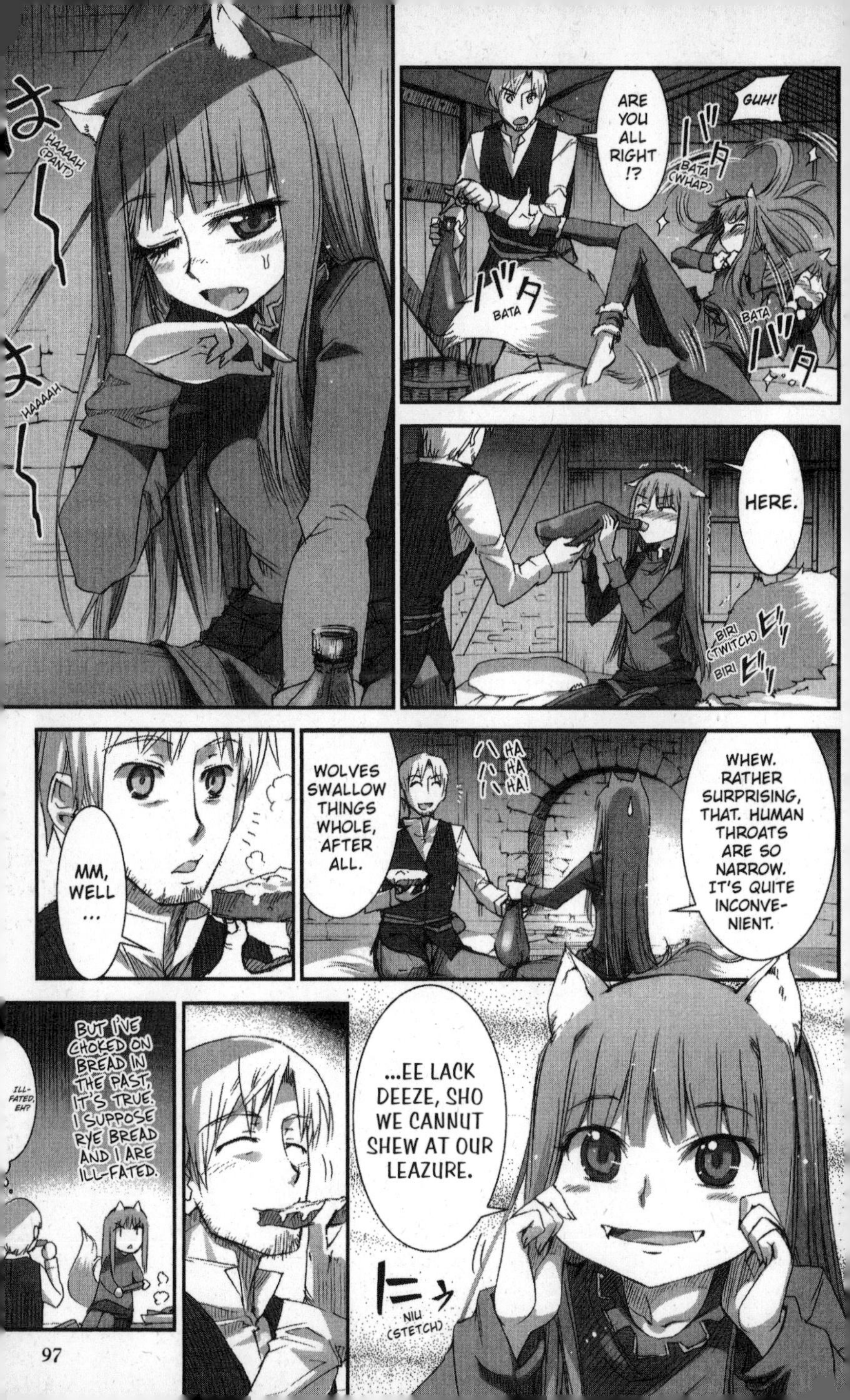

GUH!
バタ
BATA (WHAP)
ARE YOU ALL RIGHT!?
バタ
BATA
バタ
BATA
HERE.
ビリ
BIRI (TWITCH)
ビリ
BIRI
まぁ～
HAAAAH (PANT)
まぁ～
HAAAAH
WHEW. RATHER SURPRISING, THAT. HUMAN THROATS ARE SO NARROW. IT'S QUITE INCONVENIENT.
ハハハ
HA HA HA!
WOLVES SWALLOW THINGS WHOLE, AFTER ALL.
MM, WELL...
...EE LACK DEEZE, SHO WE CANNUT SHEW AT OUR LEAZURE.
にっ
NIU (STETCH)
BUT I'VE CHOKED ON BREAD IN THE PAST, IT'S TRUE. I SUPPOSE RYE BREAD AND I ARE ILL-FATED.
ILL-FATED, EH?

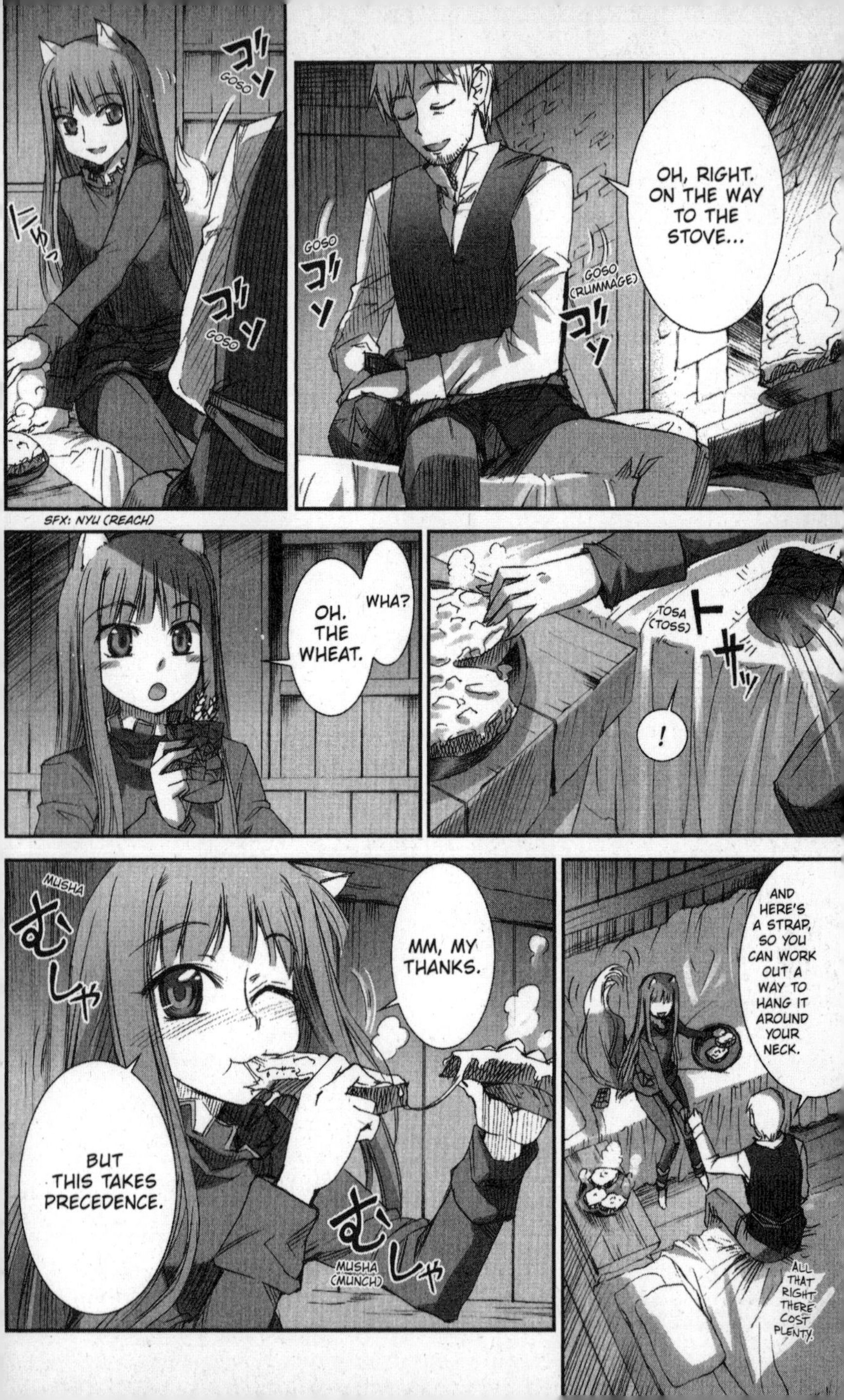
GOSO
OH, RIGHT. ON THE WAY TO THE STOVE...
GOSO (RUMMAGE)
GOSO
GOSO
SFX: NYU (REACH)
TOSA (TOSS)
!
WHA?
OH. THE WHEAT.
AND HERE'S A STRAP, SO YOU CAN WORK OUT A WAY TO HANG IT AROUND YOUR NECK.
ALL THAT RIGHT THERE COST PLENTY.
MUSHA
MM, MY THANKS.
BUT THIS TAKES PRECEDENCE.
MUSHA (MUNCH)

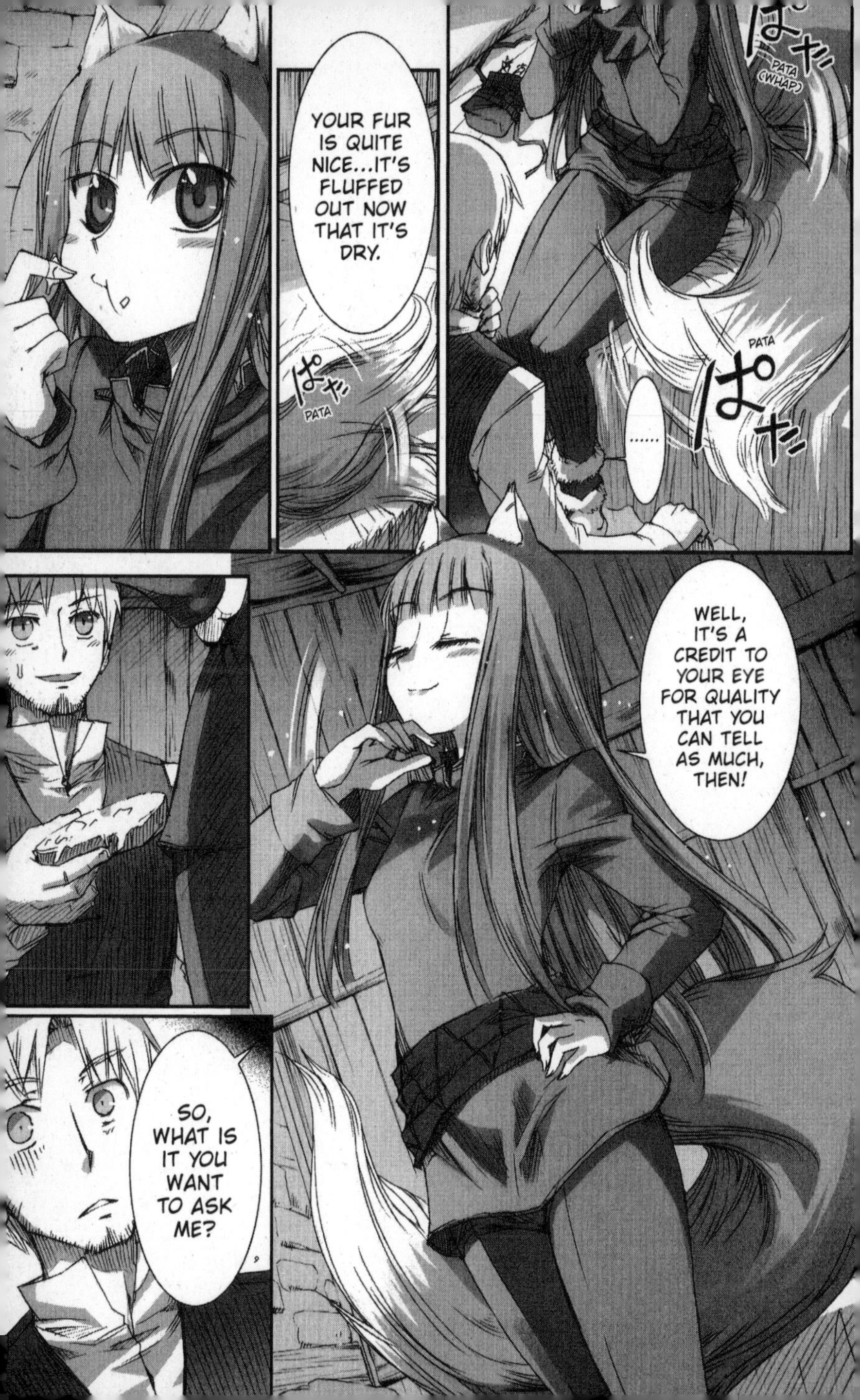

PATA
(WHAP)
PATA
......
YOUR FUR IS QUITE NICE...IT'S FLUFFED OUT NOW THAT IT'S DRY.
PATA
WELL, IT'S A CREDIT TO YOUR EYE FOR QUALITY THAT YOU CAN TELL AS MUCH, THEN!
SO, WHAT IS IT YOU WANT TO ASK ME?

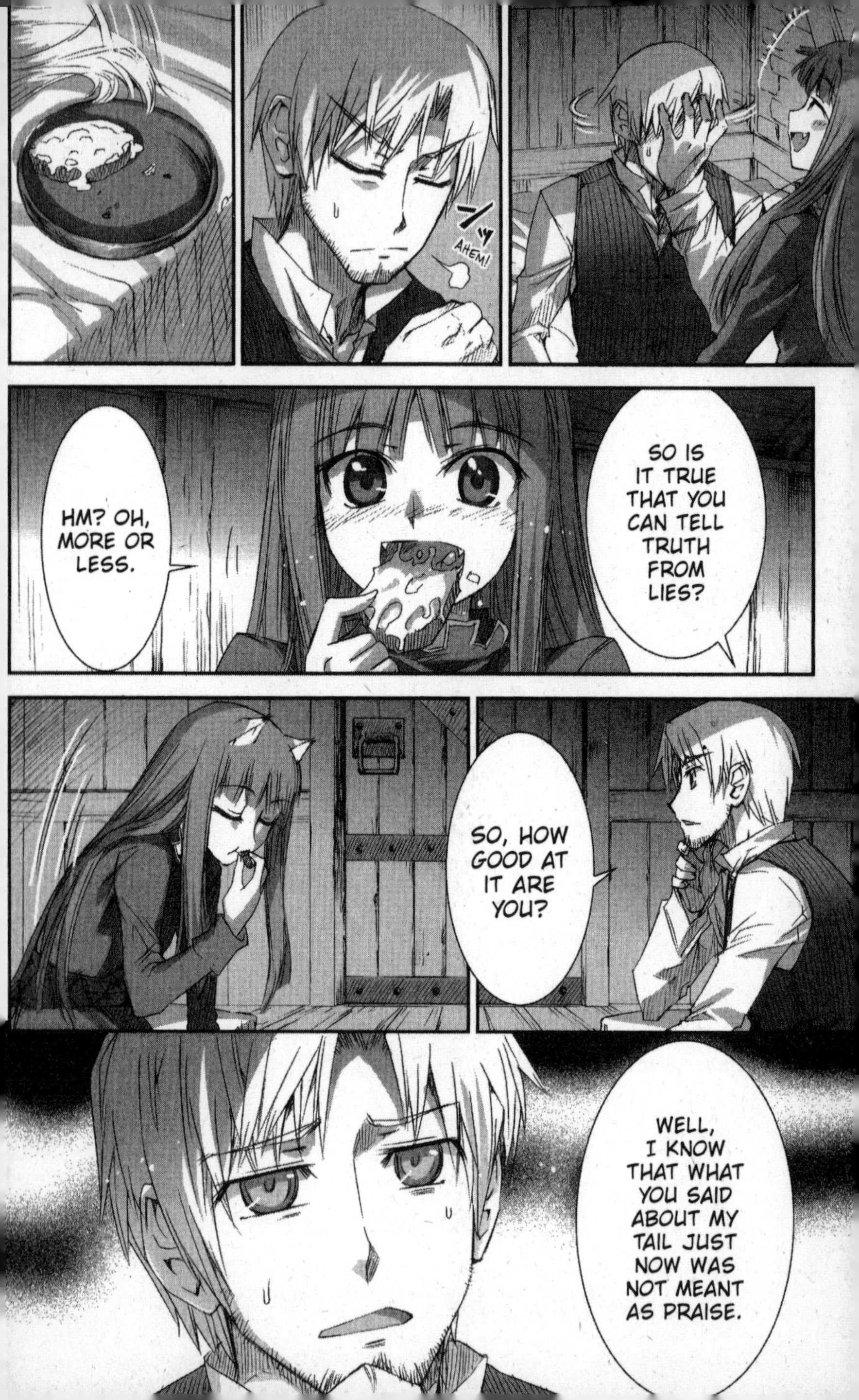
ンッ
AHEM!
SO IS IT TRUE THAT YOU CAN TELL TRUTH FROM LIES?
HM? OH, MORE OR LESS.
SO, HOW GOOD AT IT ARE YOU?
WELL, I KNOW THAT WHAT YOU SAID ABOUT MY TAIL JUST NOW WAS NOT MEANT AS PRAISE.

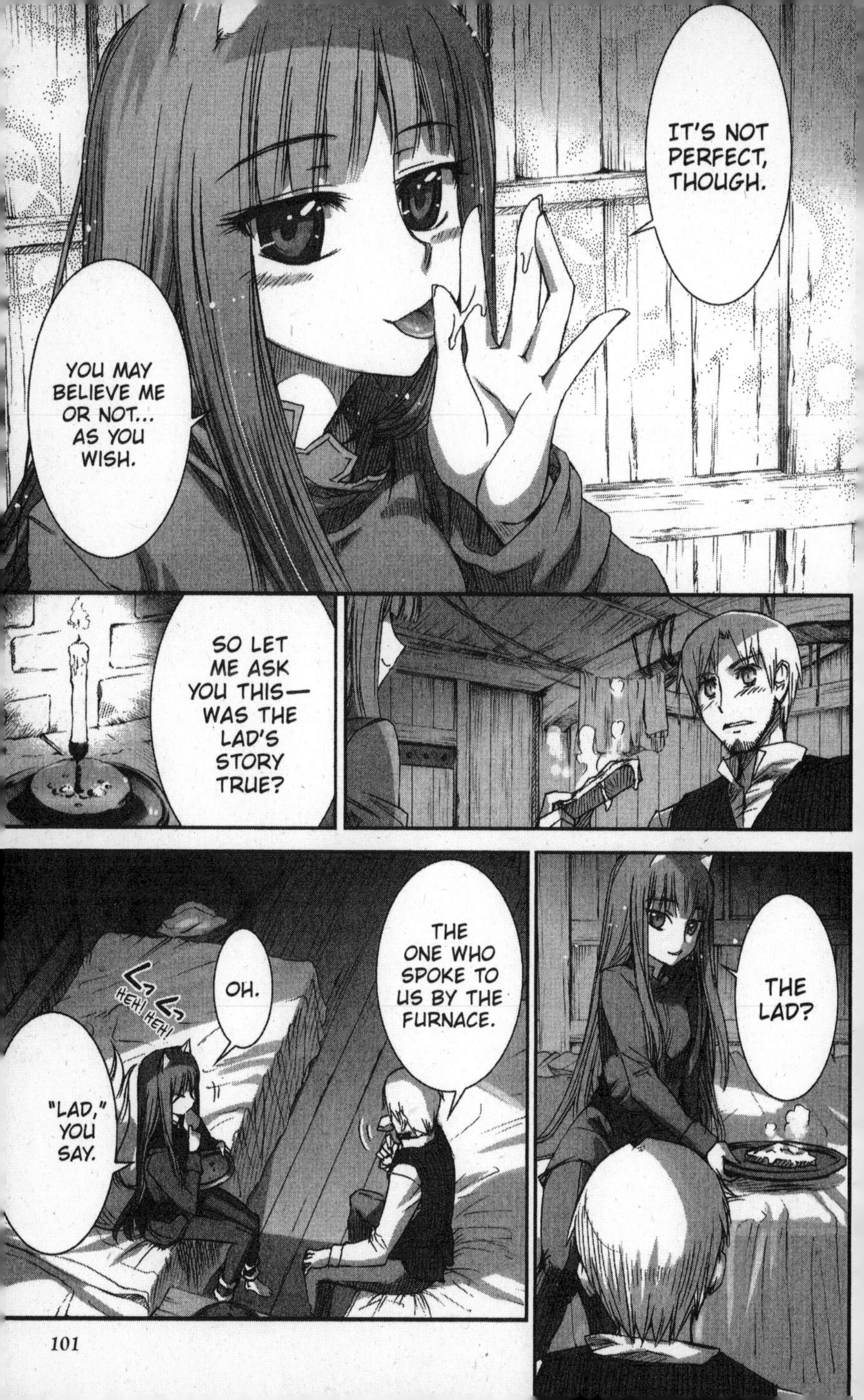
IT'S NOT PERFECT, THOUGH.
YOU MAY BELIEVE ME OR NOT... AS YOU WISH.
SO LET ME ASK YOU THIS—WAS THE LAD'S STORY TRUE?
THE LAD?
THE ONE WHO SPOKE TO US BY THE FURNACE.
OH.
HEH! HEH!
"LAD," YOU SAY.

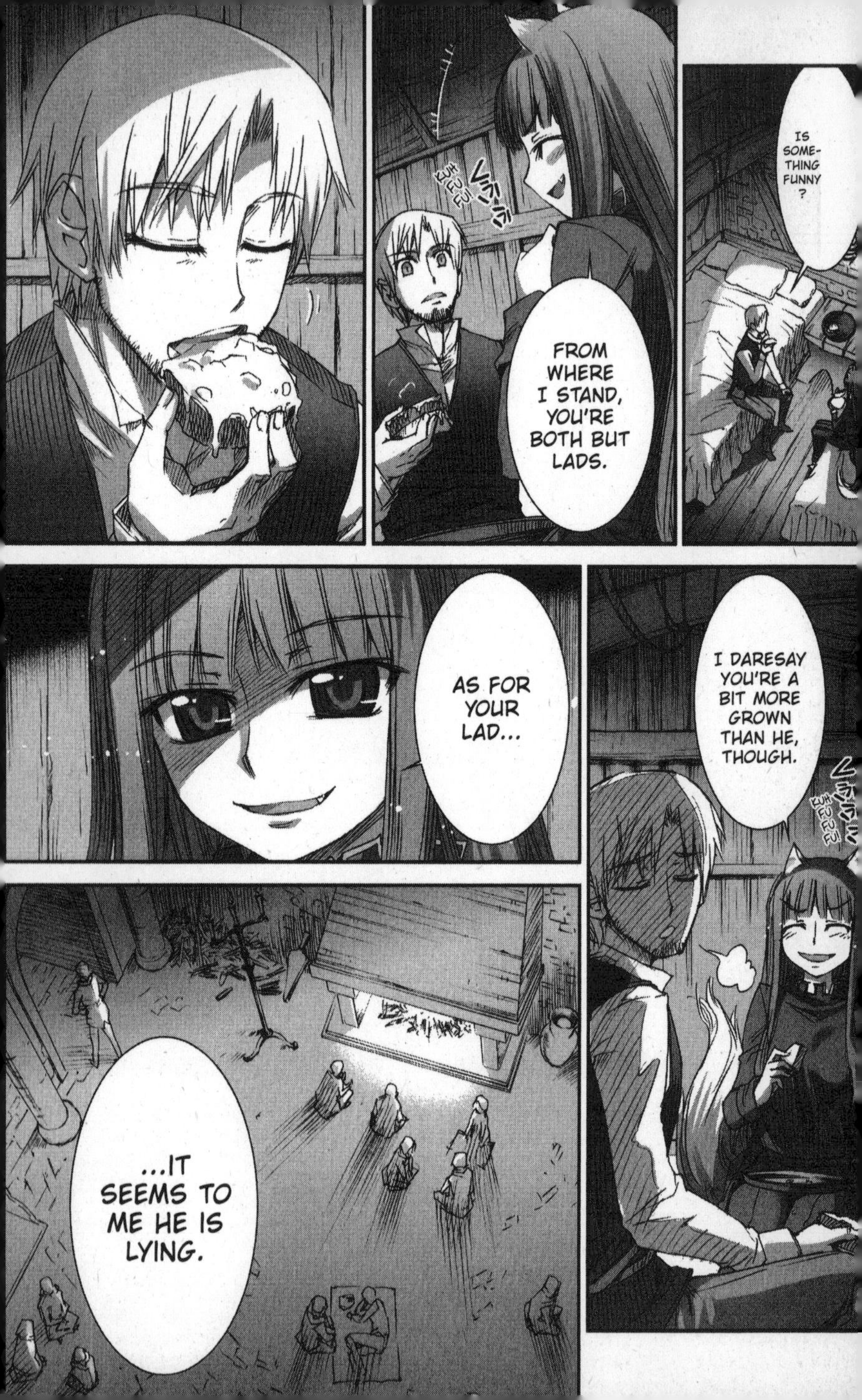
IS SOMETHING FUNNY?
KUH FU FU!
FROM WHERE I STAND, YOU'RE BOTH BUT LADS.
I DARESAY YOU'RE A BIT MORE GROWN THAN HE, THOUGH.
KUH FU FU FU!
AS FOR YOUR LAD...
...IT SEEMS TO ME HE IS LYING.

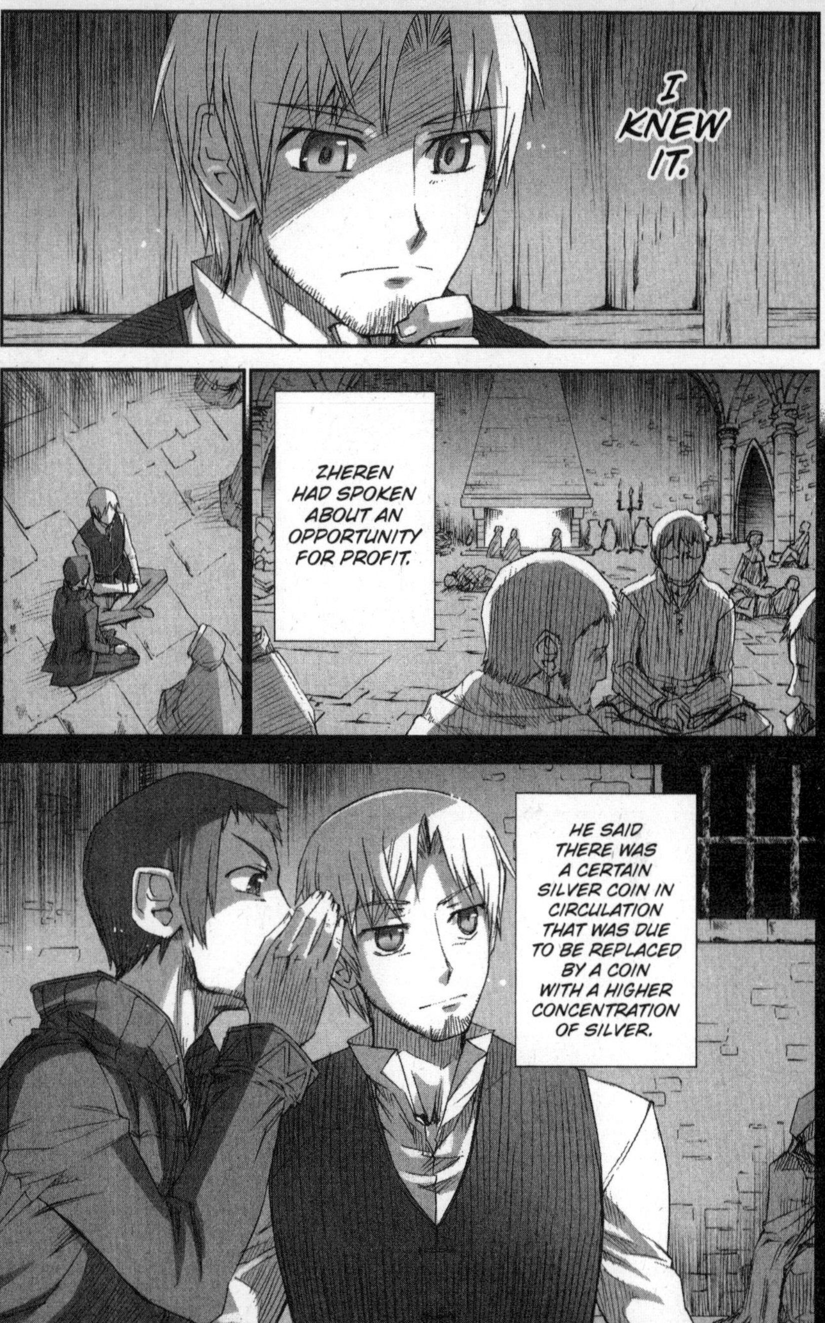
I KNEW IT.
ZHEREN HAD SPOKEN ABOUT AN OPPORTUNITY FOR PROFIT.
HE SAID THERE WAS A CERTAIN SILVER COIN IN CIRCULATION THAT WAS DUE TO BE REPLACED BY A COIN WITH A HIGHER CONCENTRATION OF SILVER.

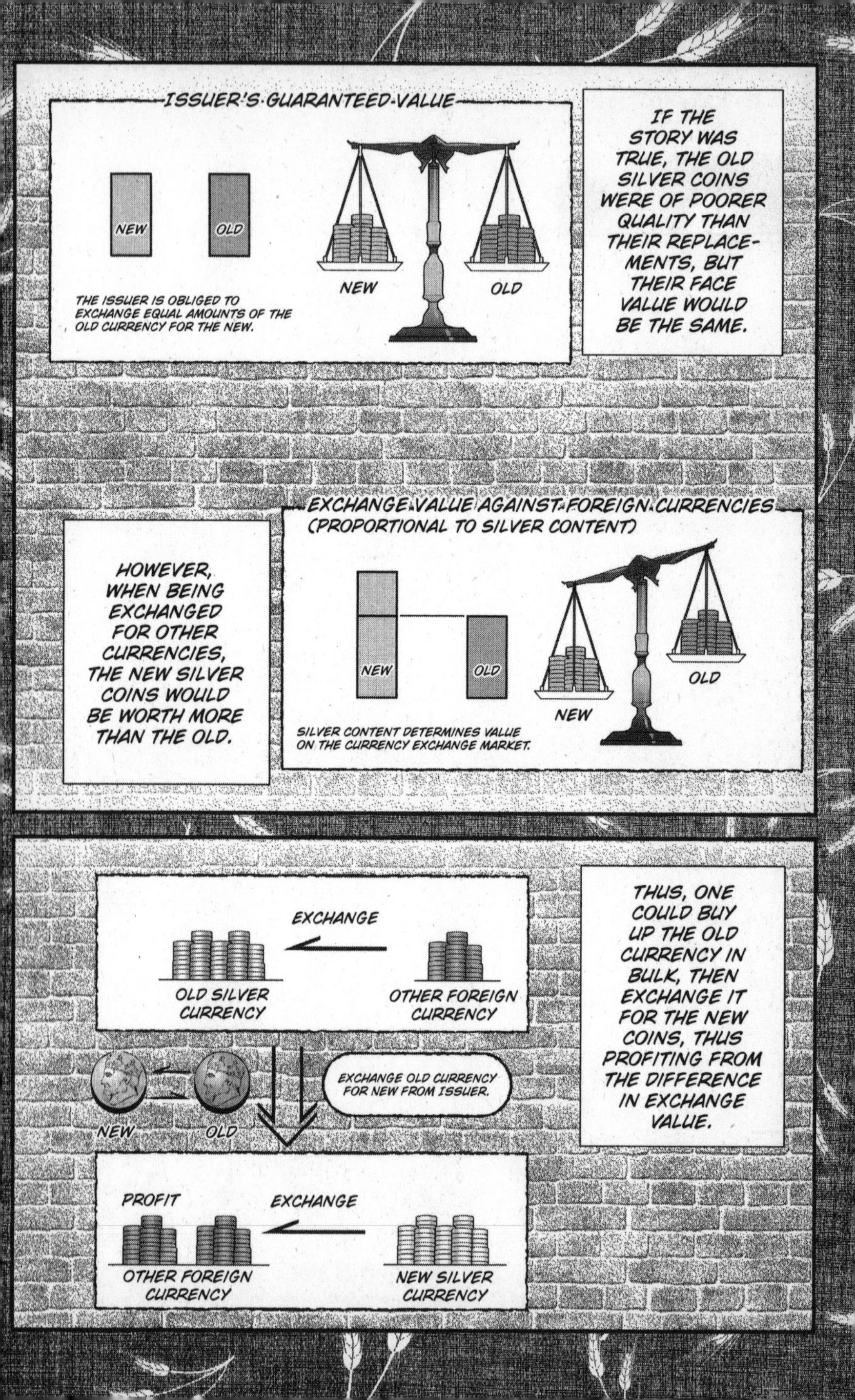
IF THE STORY WAS TRUE, THE OLD SILVER COINS WERE OF POORER QUALITY THAN THEIR REPLACEMENTS, BUT THEIR FACE VALUE WOULD BE THE SAME.
ISSUER'S GUARANTEED VALUE
NEW
OLD
NEW
OLD
THE ISSUER IS OBLIGED TO EXCHANGE EQUAL AMOUNTS OF THE OLD CURRENCY FOR THE NEW.
EXCHANGE VALUE AGAINST FOREIGN CURRENCIES (PROPORTIONAL TO SILVER CONTENT)
NEW
OLD
OLD
NEW
SILVER CONTENT DETERMINES VALUE ON THE CURRENCY EXCHANGE MARKET.
HOWEVER, WHEN BEING EXCHANGED FOR OTHER CURRENCIES, THE NEW SILVER COINS WOULD BE WORTH MORE THAN THE OLD.
THUS, ONE COULD BUY UP THE OLD CURRENCY IN BULK, THEN EXCHANGE IT FOR THE NEW COINS, THUS PROFITING FROM THE DIFFERENCE IN EXCHANGE VALUE.
EXCHANGE
OLD SILVER CURRENCY
OTHER FOREIGN CURRENCY
EXCHANGE OLD CURRENCY FOR NEW FROM ISSUER.
NEW
OLD
PROFIT
EXCHANGE
OTHER FOREIGN CURRENCY
NEW SILVER CURRENCY

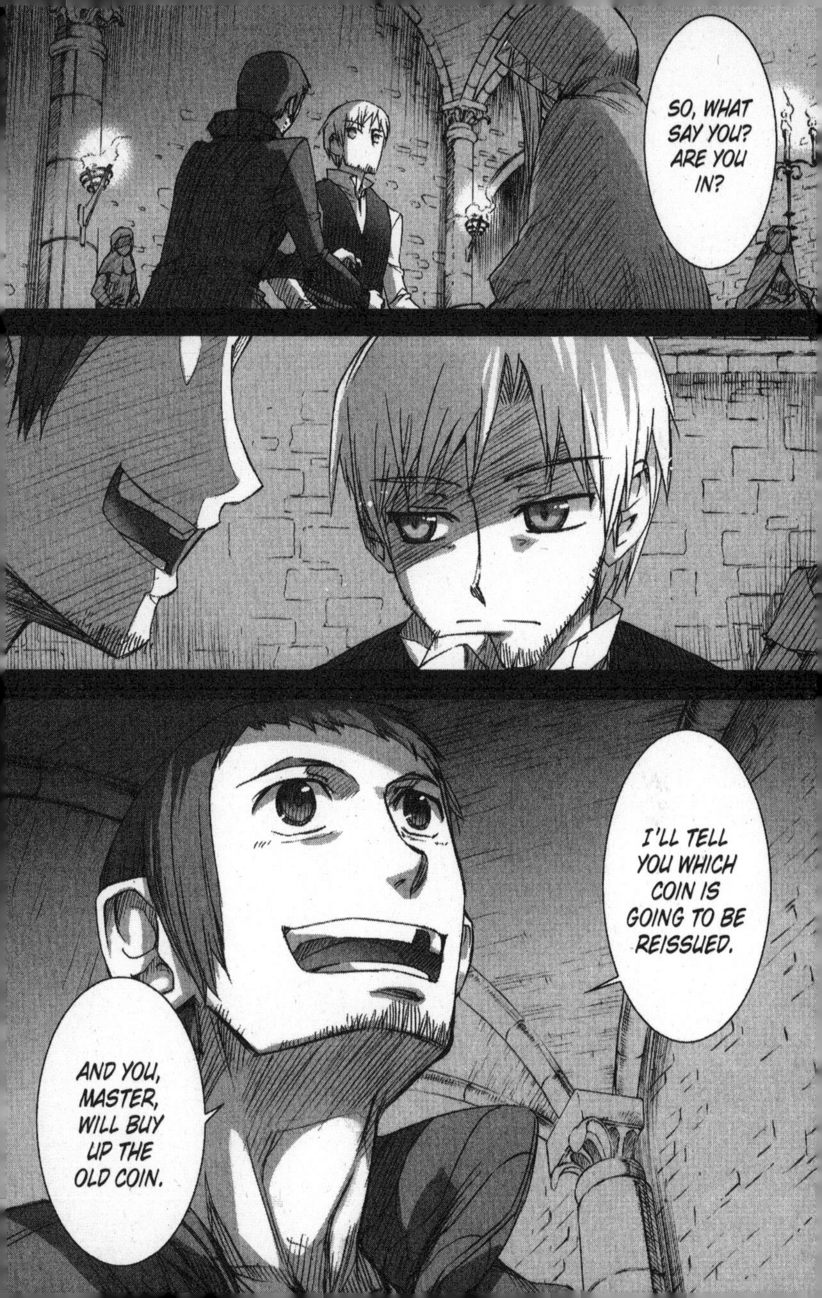
SO, WHAT SAY YOU? ARE YOU IN?
I'LL TELL YOU WHICH COIN IS GOING TO BE REISSUED.
AND YOU, MASTER, WILL BUY UP THE OLD COIN.

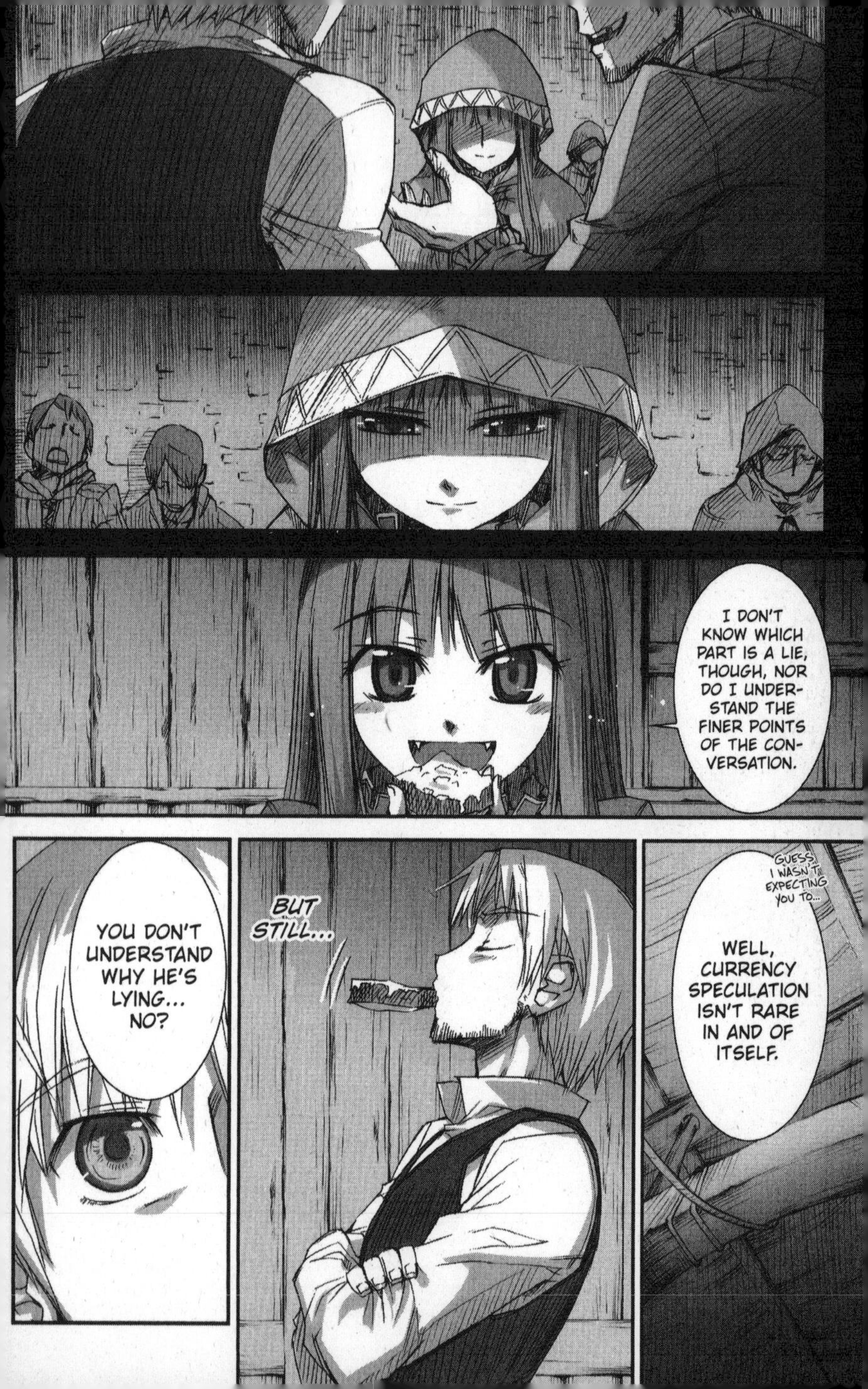
I DON'T KNOW WHICH PART IS A LIE, THOUGH, NOR DO I UNDERSTAND THE FINER POINTS OF THE CONVERSATION.
GUESS I WASN'T EXPECTING YOU TO...
WELL, CURRENCY SPECULATION ISN'T RARE IN AND OF ITSELF.
BUT STILL...
YOU DON'T UNDERSTAND WHY HE'S LYING... NO?

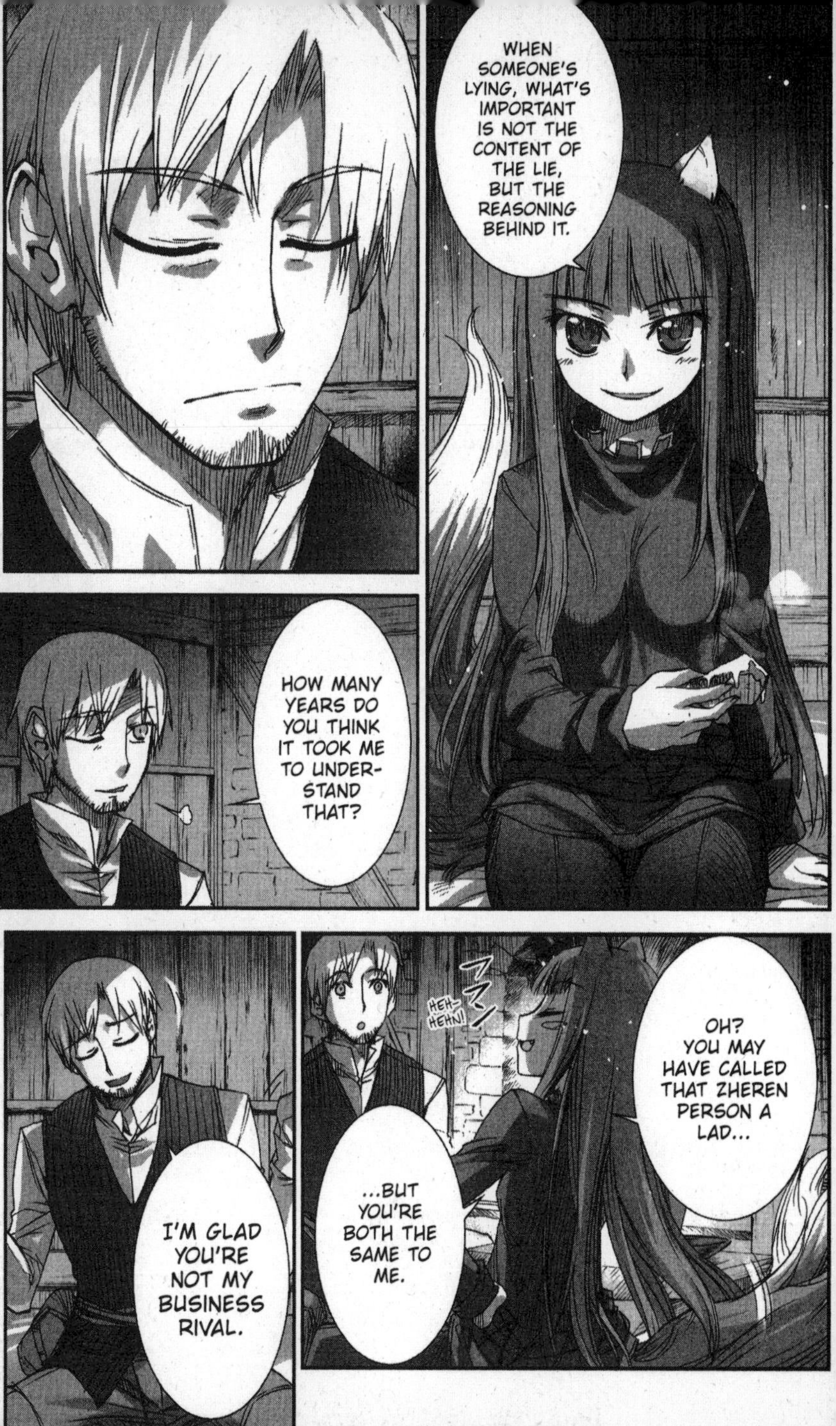
WHEN SOMEONE'S LYING, WHAT'S IMPORTANT IS NOT THE CONTENT OF THE LIE, BUT THE REASONING BEHIND IT.
HOW MANY YEARS DO YOU THINK IT TOOK ME TO UNDER-STAND THAT?
OH? YOU MAY HAVE CALLED THAT ZHEREN PERSON A LAD...
HEH-HEHN!
...BUT YOU'RE BOTH THE SAME TO ME.
I'M GLAD YOU'RE NOT MY BUSINESS RIVAL.

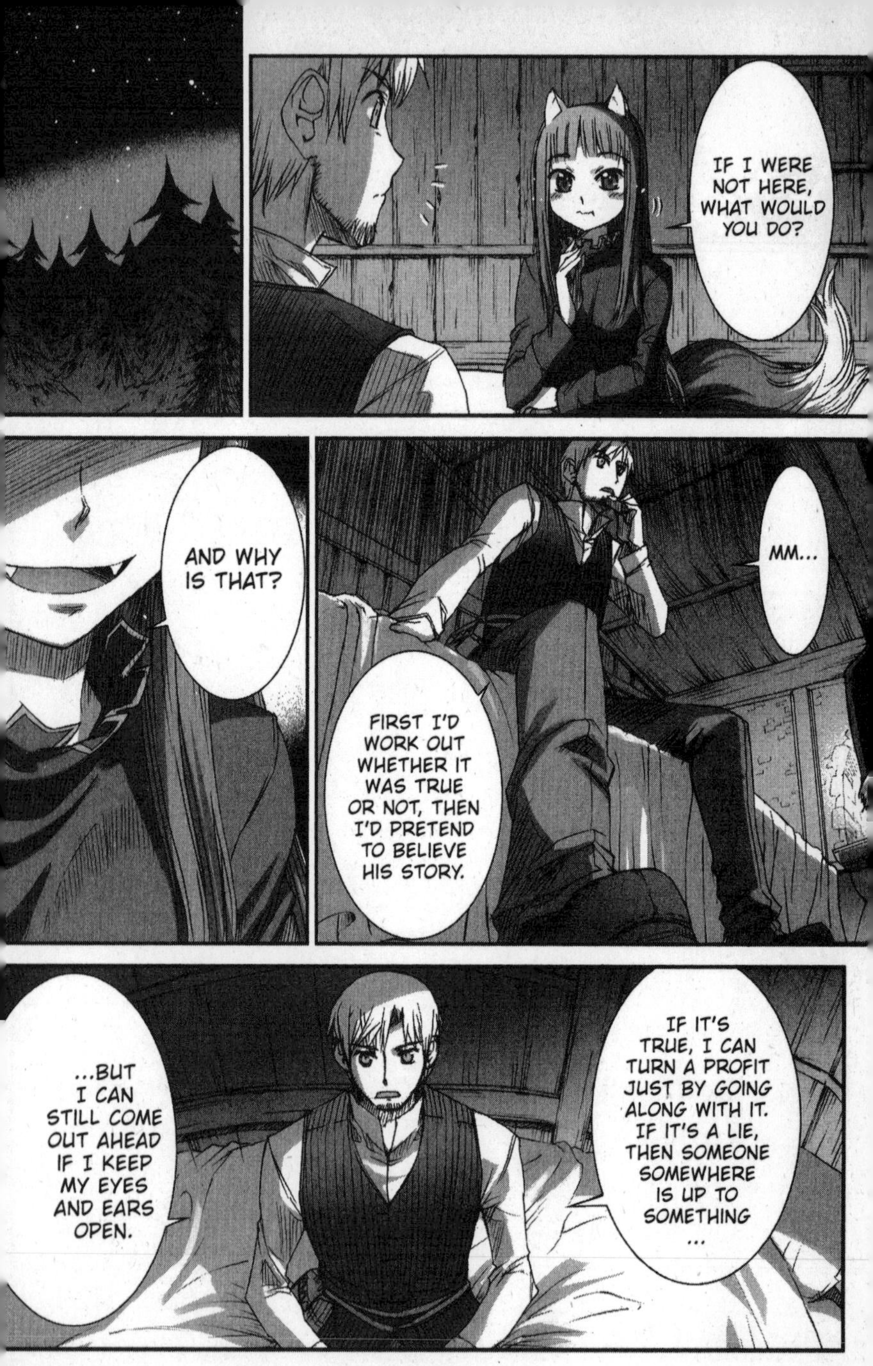
IF I WERE NOT HERE, WHAT WOULD YOU DO?
MM...
FIRST I'D WORK OUT WHETHER IT WAS TRUE OR NOT, THEN I'D PRETEND TO BELIEVE HIS STORY.
AND WHY IS THAT?
IF IT'S TRUE, I CAN TURN A PROFIT JUST BY GOING ALONG WITH IT. IF IT'S A LIE, THEN SOMEONE SOMEWHERE IS UP TO SOMETHING ...
...BUT I CAN STILL COME OUT AHEAD IF I KEEP MY EYES AND EARS OPEN.

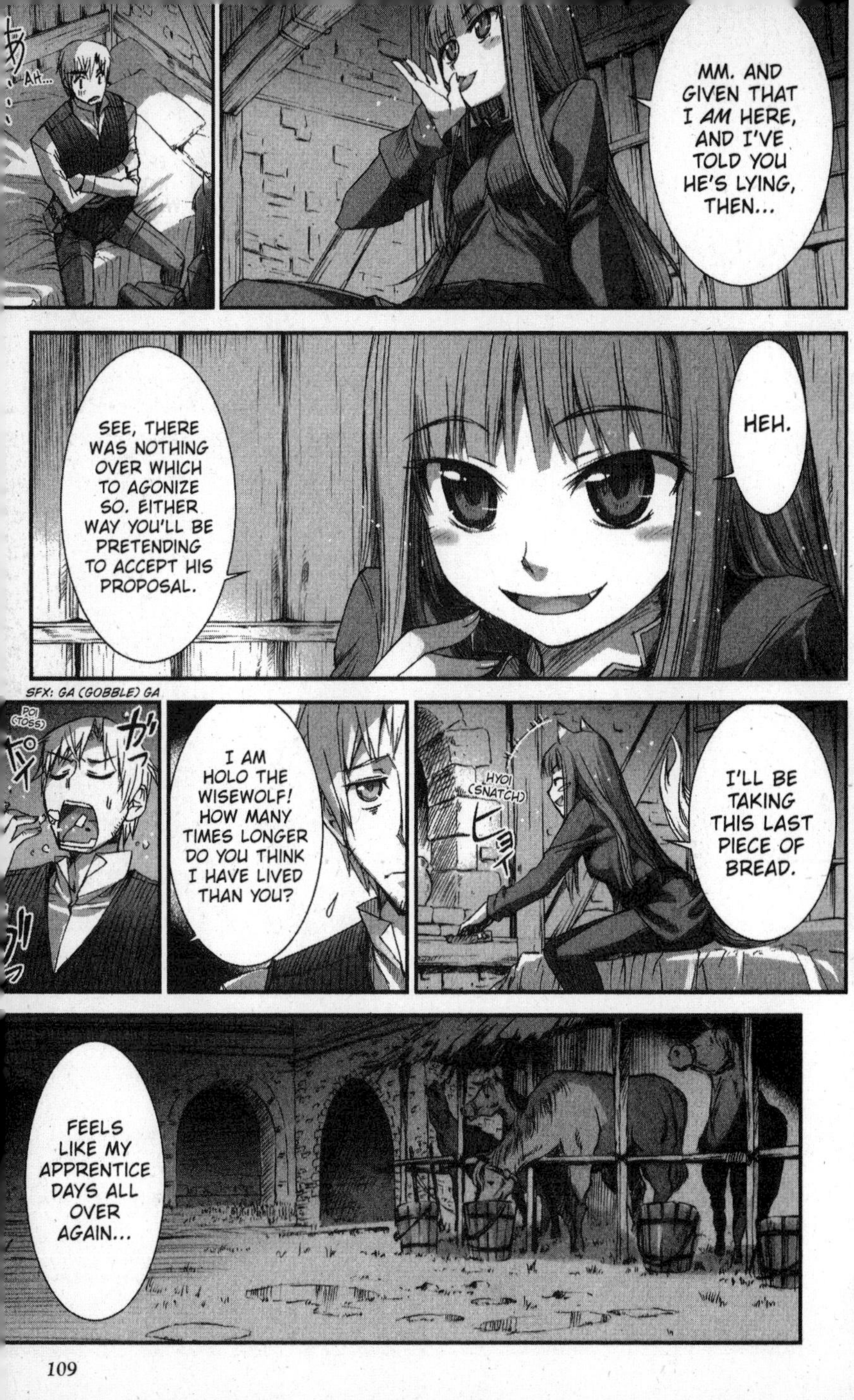

MM. AND GIVEN THAT I *AM* HERE, AND I'VE TOLD YOU HE'S LYING, THEN...
AH...
HEH.
SEE, THERE WAS NOTHING OVER WHICH TO AGONIZE SO. EITHER WAY YOU'LL BE PRETENDING TO ACCEPT HIS PROPOSAL.
SFX: GA (GOBBLE) GA
I'LL BE TAKING THIS LAST PIECE OF BREAD.
HYOI (SNATCH)
I AM HOLO THE WISEWOLF! HOW MANY TIMES LONGER DO YOU THINK I HAVE LIVED THAN YOU?
POI (TOSS)
FEELS LIKE MY APPRENTICE DAYS ALL OVER AGAIN...

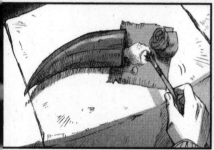

GASHI
(BRUSH)
ガシ

ガシ
GASHI

CHIRI
(SCRAPE)
チリ

チー
CHIRI

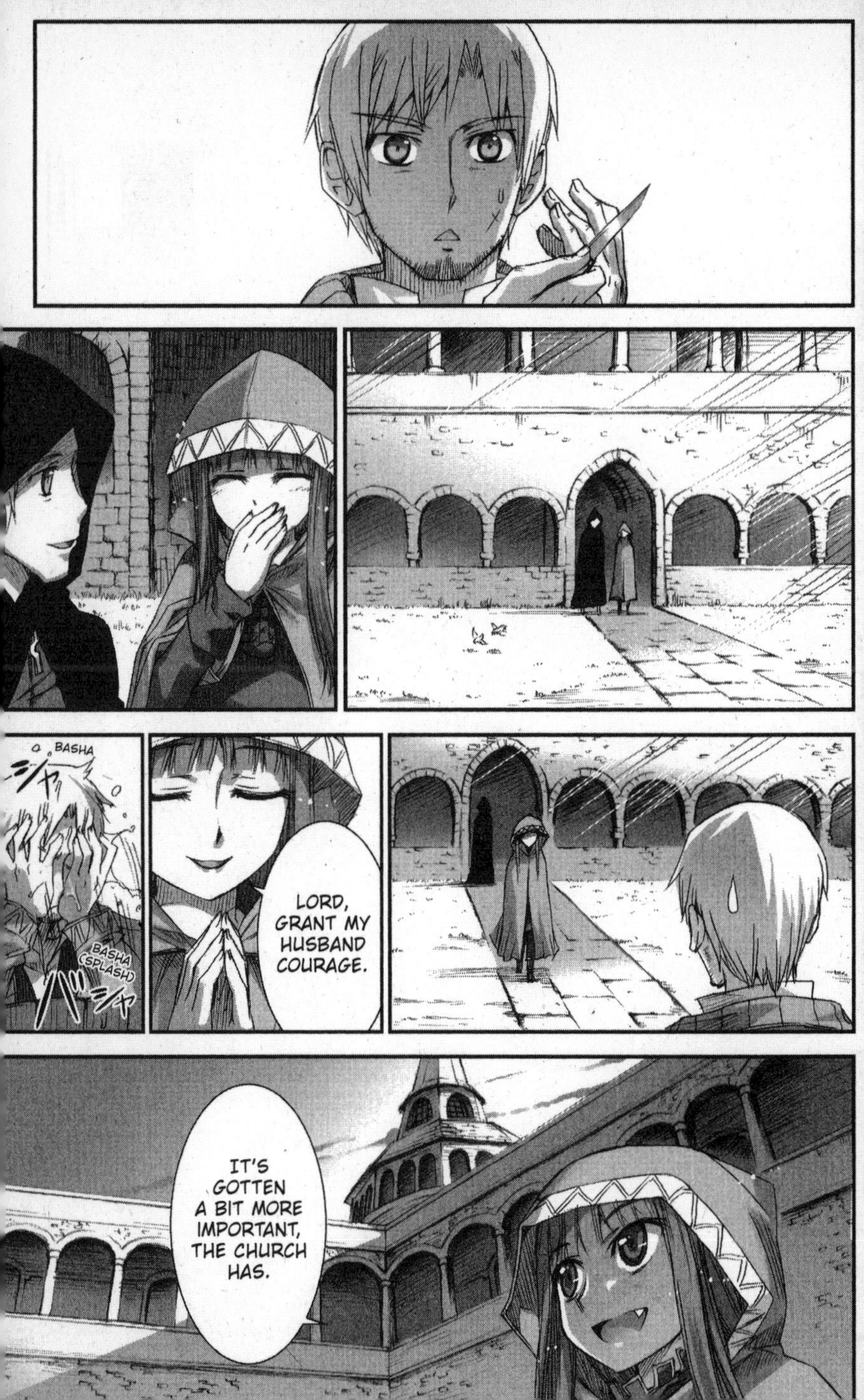
LORD, GRANT MY HUSBAND COURAGE.
BASHA
BASHA (SPLASH)
IT'S GOTTEN A BIT MORE IMPORTANT, THE CHURCH HAS.

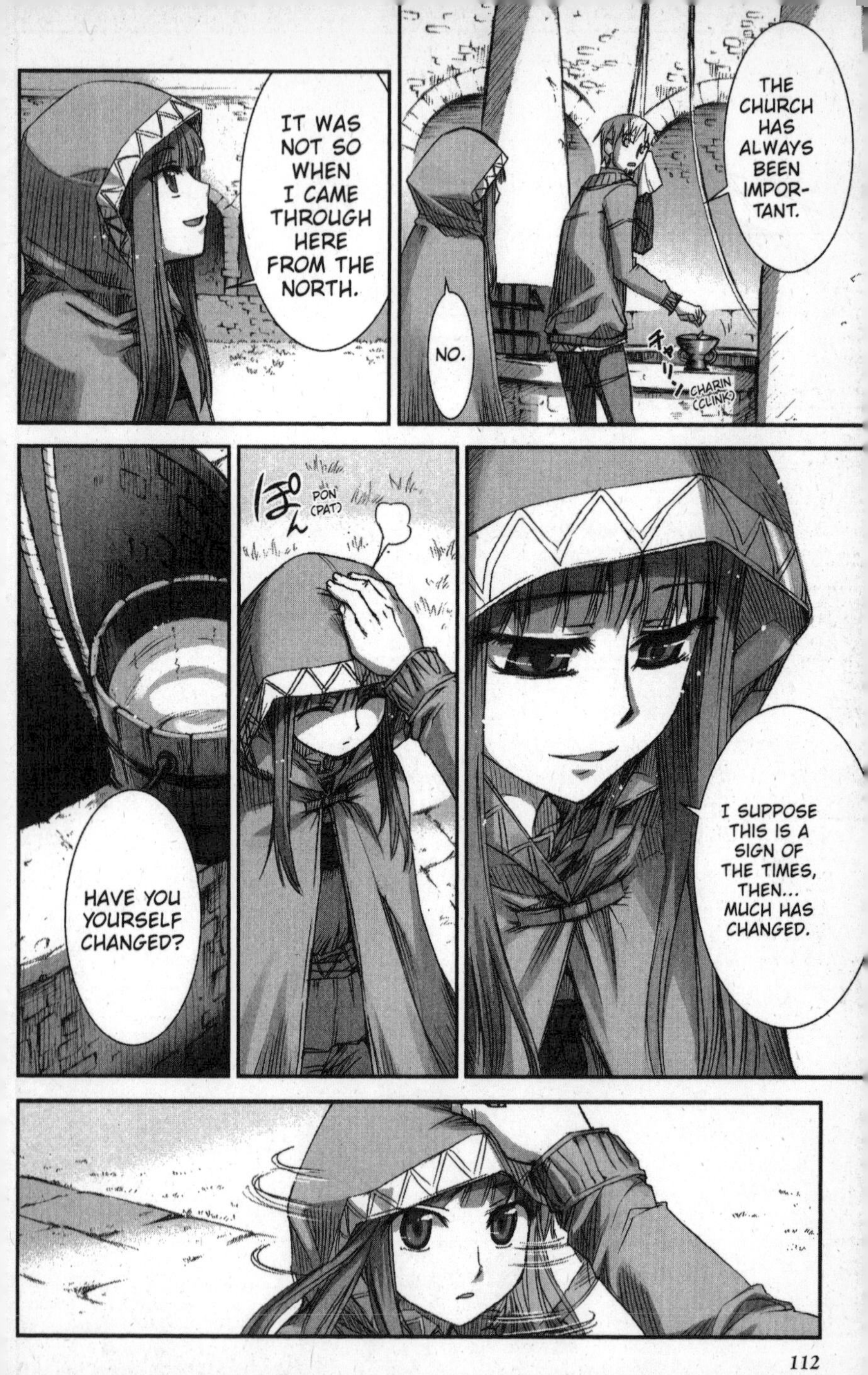
THE CHURCH HAS ALWAYS BEEN IMPORTANT.
NO.
チャリーン
CHARIN (CLINK)
IT WAS NOT SO WHEN I CAME THROUGH HERE FROM THE NORTH.
I SUPPOSE THIS IS A SIGN OF THE TIMES, THEN... MUCH HAS CHANGED.
ぽん
PON (PAT)
HAVE YOU YOURSELF CHANGED?

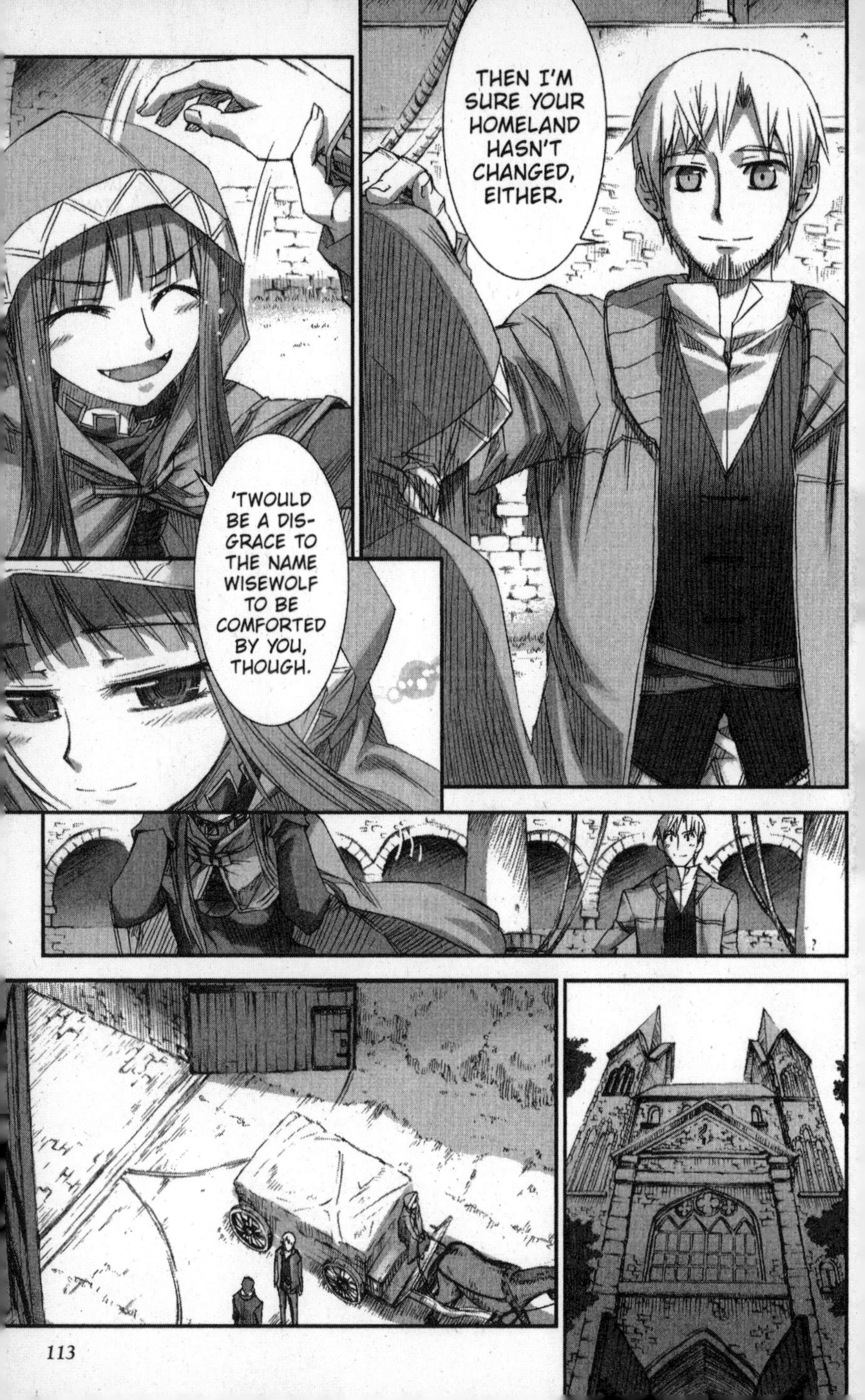
THEN I'M SURE YOUR HOMELAND HASN'T CHANGED, EITHER.
'TWOULD BE A DIS-GRACE TO THE NAME WISEWOLF TO BE COMFORTED BY YOU, THOUGH.

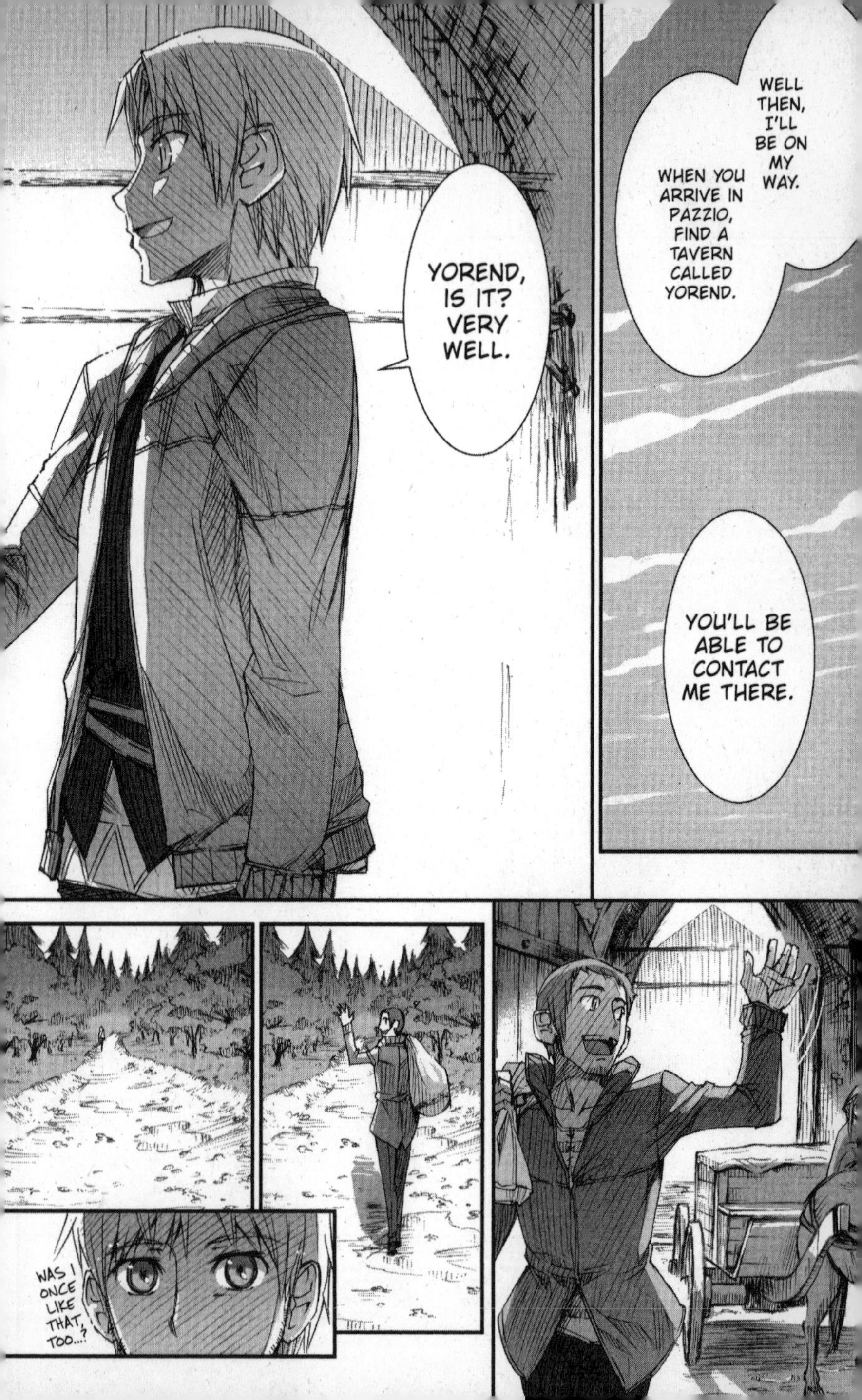
WELL THEN, I'LL BE ON MY WAY.
WHEN YOU ARRIVE IN PAZZIO, FIND A TAVERN CALLED YOREND.
YOU'LL BE ABLE TO CONTACT ME THERE.
YOREND, IS IT? VERY WELL.
WAS I ONCE LIKE THAT, TOO...?

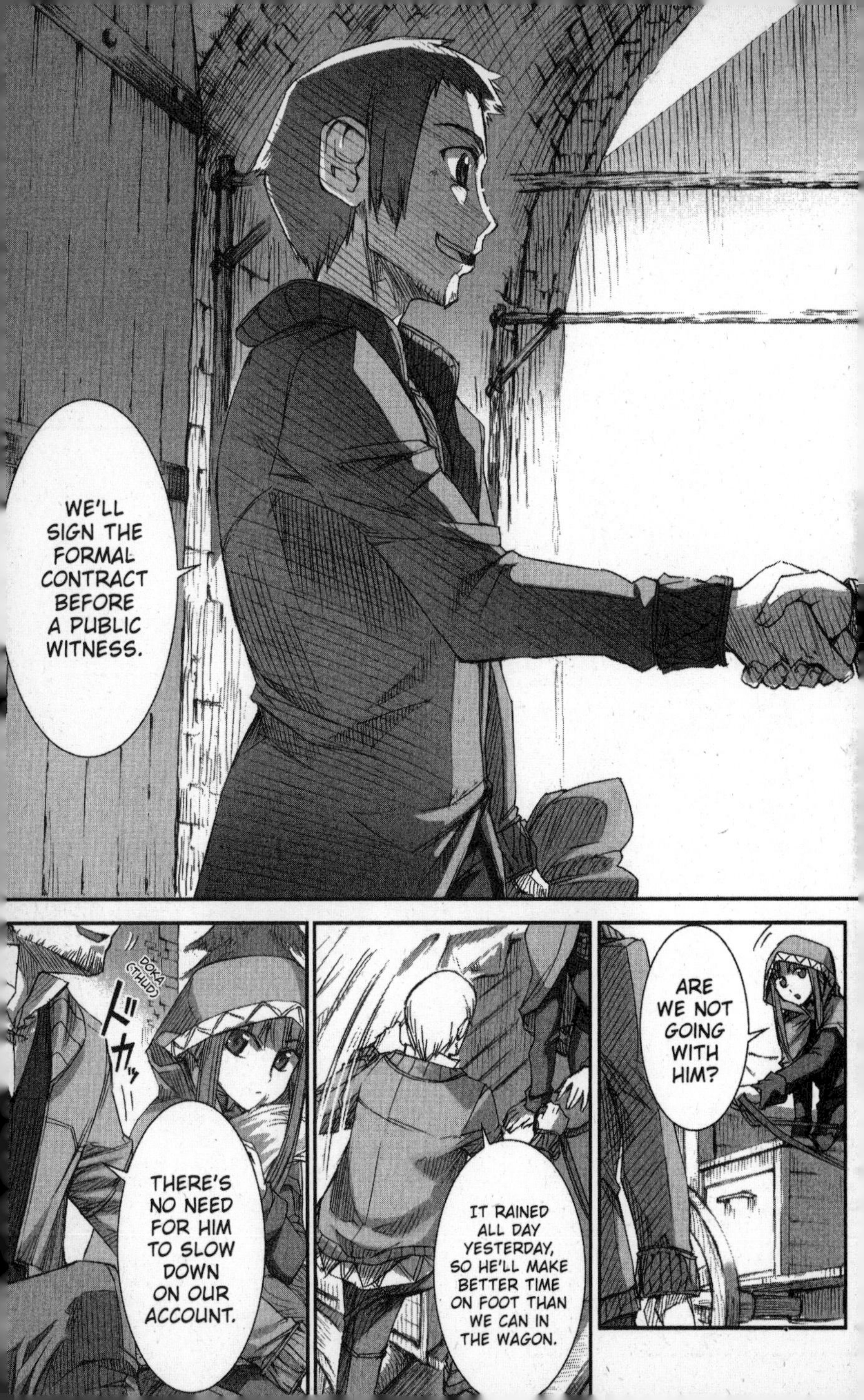
WE'LL SIGN THE FORMAL CONTRACT BEFORE A PUBLIC WITNESS.
ARE WE NOT GOING WITH HIM?
IT RAINED ALL DAY YESTERDAY, SO HE'LL MAKE BETTER TIME ON FOOT THAN WE CAN IN THE WAGON.
ドカッ
DOKA (THUD)
THERE'S NO NEED FOR HIM TO SLOW DOWN ON OUR ACCOUNT.

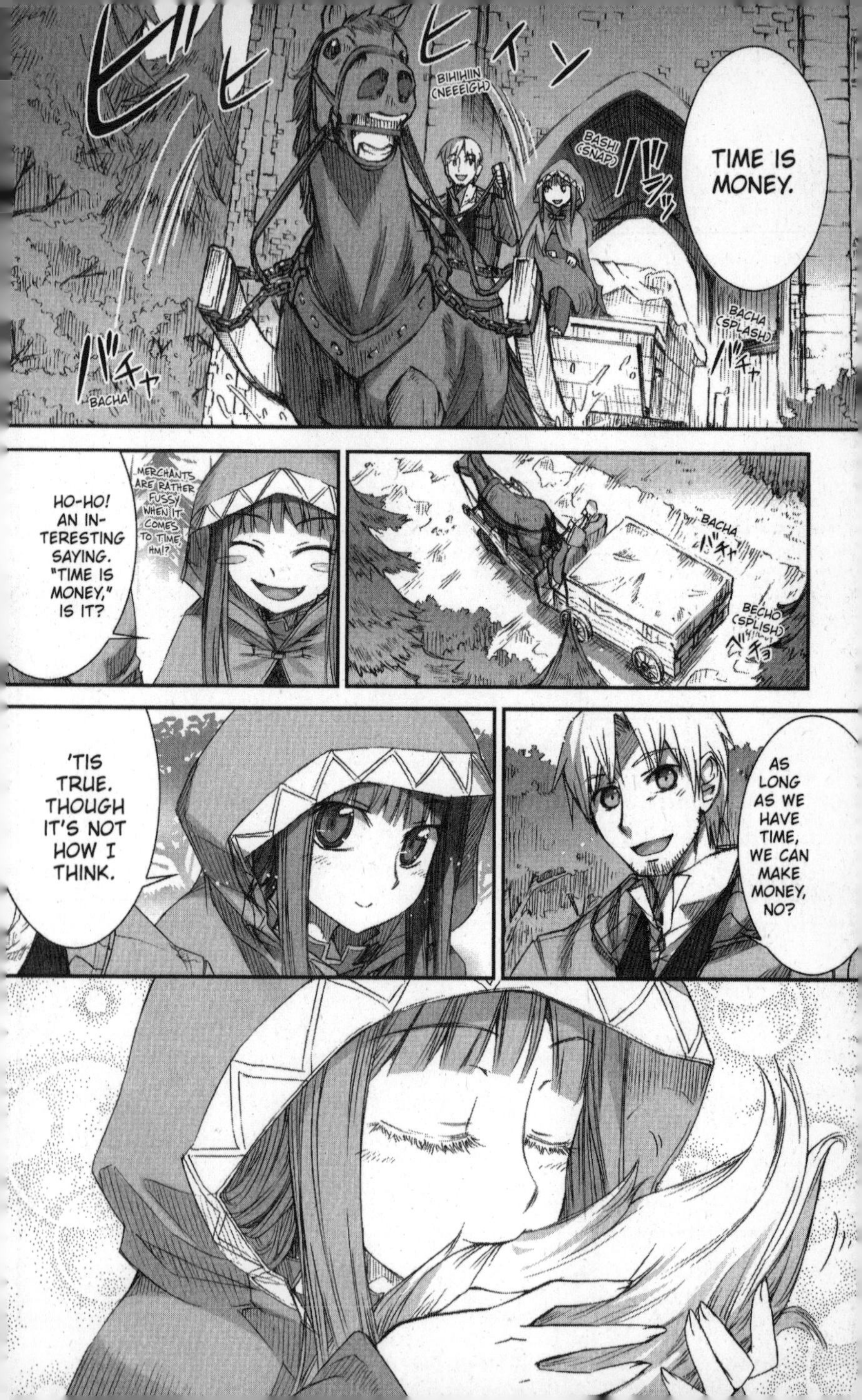
TIME IS MONEY.
BASHI (SNAP)
BIHIHIIN (NEEEIGH)
BACHA (SPLASH)
BACHA
BACHA
BECHO (SPLISH)
HO-HO! AN IN-TERESTING SAYING. "TIME IS MONEY," IS IT?
MERCHANTS ARE RATHER FUSSY WHEN IT COMES TO TIME. HM!?
AS LONG AS WE HAVE TIME, WE CAN MAKE MONEY, NO?
'TIS TRUE. THOUGH IT'S NOT HOW I THINK.

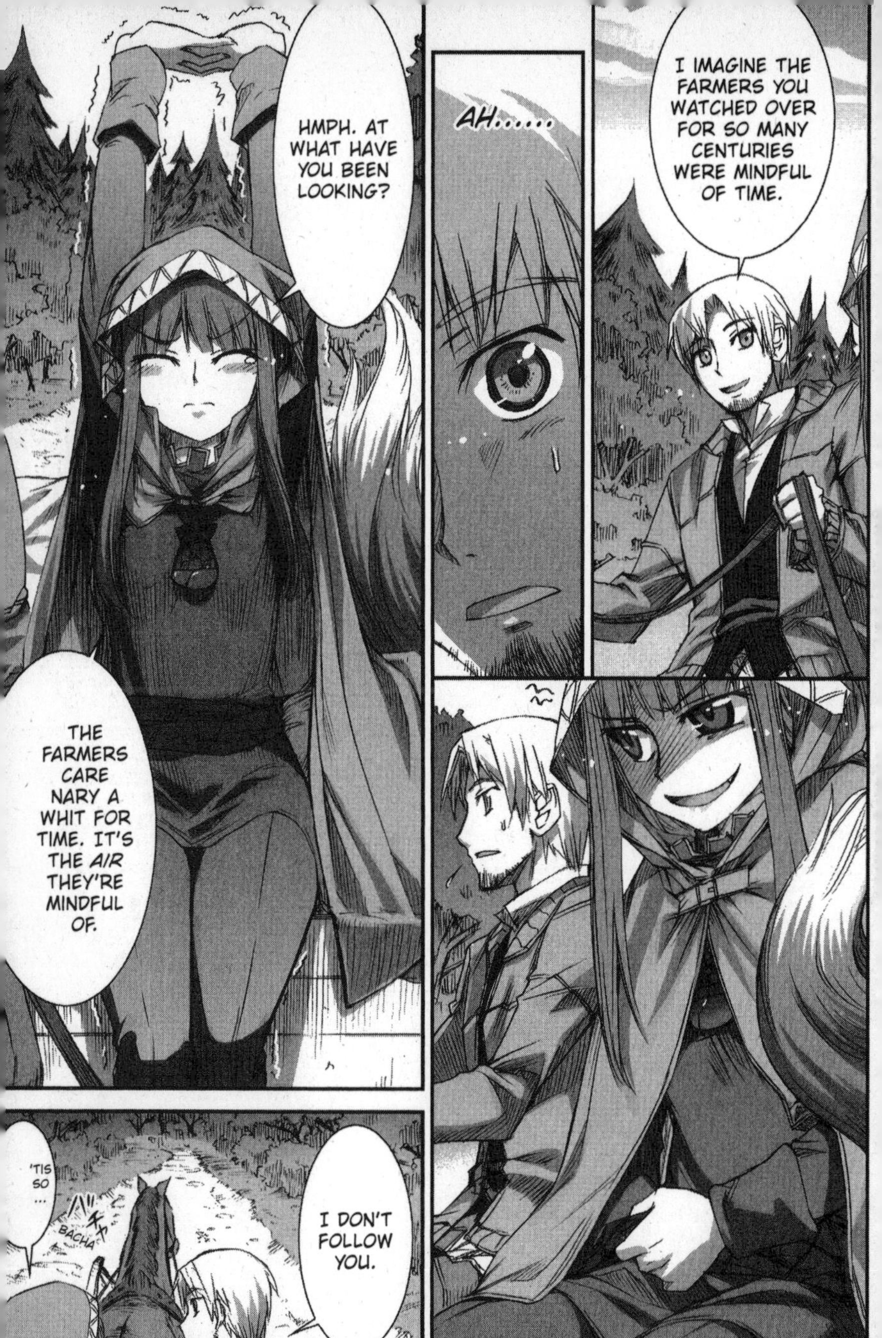
I IMAGINE THE FARMERS YOU WATCHED OVER FOR SO MANY CENTURIES WERE MINDFUL OF TIME.
AH......
HMPH. AT WHAT HAVE YOU BEEN LOOKING?
THE FARMERS CARE NARY A WHIT FOR TIME. IT'S THE *AIR* THEY'RE MINDFUL OF.
BACHA
I DON'T FOLLOW YOU.
BACHA
'TIS SO ...

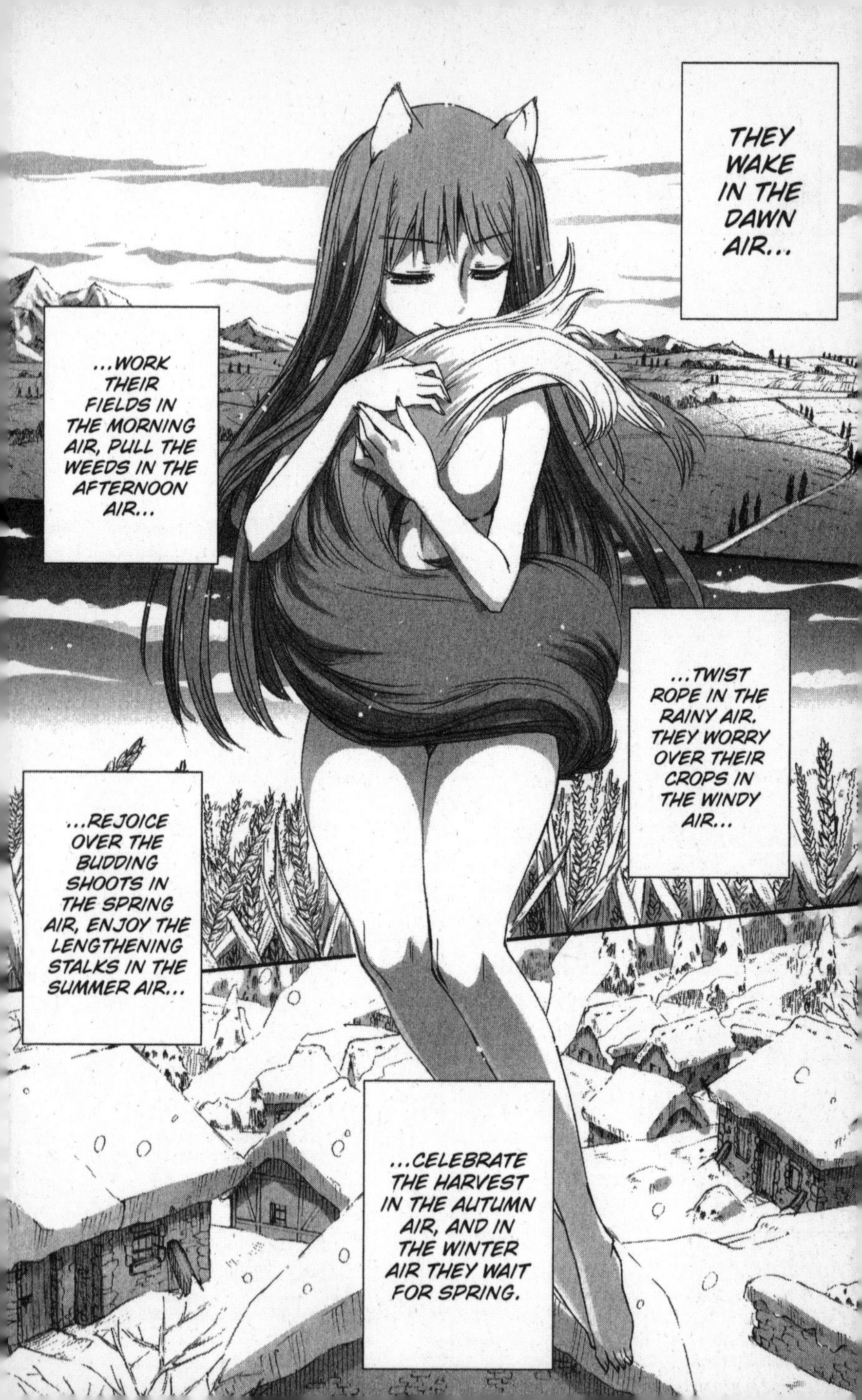
THEY WAKE IN THE DAWN AIR...
...WORK THEIR FIELDS IN THE MORNING AIR, PULL THE WEEDS IN THE AFTERNOON AIR...
...TWIST ROPE IN THE RAINY AIR. THEY WORRY OVER THEIR CROPS IN THE WINDY AIR...
...REJOICE OVER THE BUDDING SHOOTS IN THE SPRING AIR, ENJOY THE LENGTHENING STALKS IN THE SUMMER AIR...
...CELEBRATE THE HARVEST IN THE AUTUMN AIR, AND IN THE WINTER AIR THEY WAIT FOR SPRING.

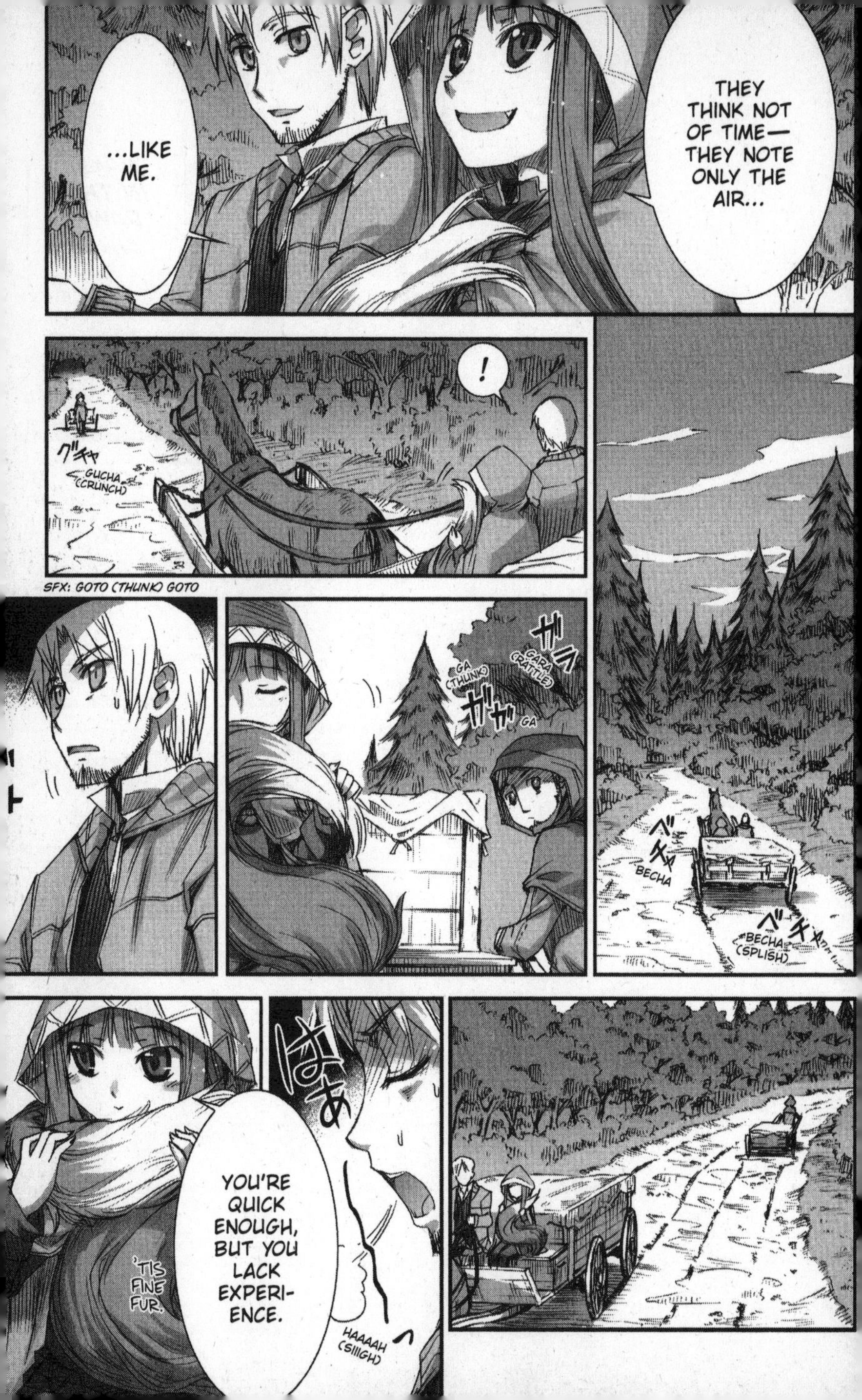
THEY THINK NOT OF TIME—THEY NOTE ONLY THE AIR...
...LIKE ME.
BECHA
BECHA (SPLISH)
!
GUCHA (CRUNCH)
SFX: GOTO (THUNK) GOTO
GARA (RATTLE)
GA (THUNK)
GA
YOU'RE QUICK ENOUGH, BUT YOU LACK EXPERI-ENCE.
HAAAAH (SIIIGH)
'TIS FINE FUR.

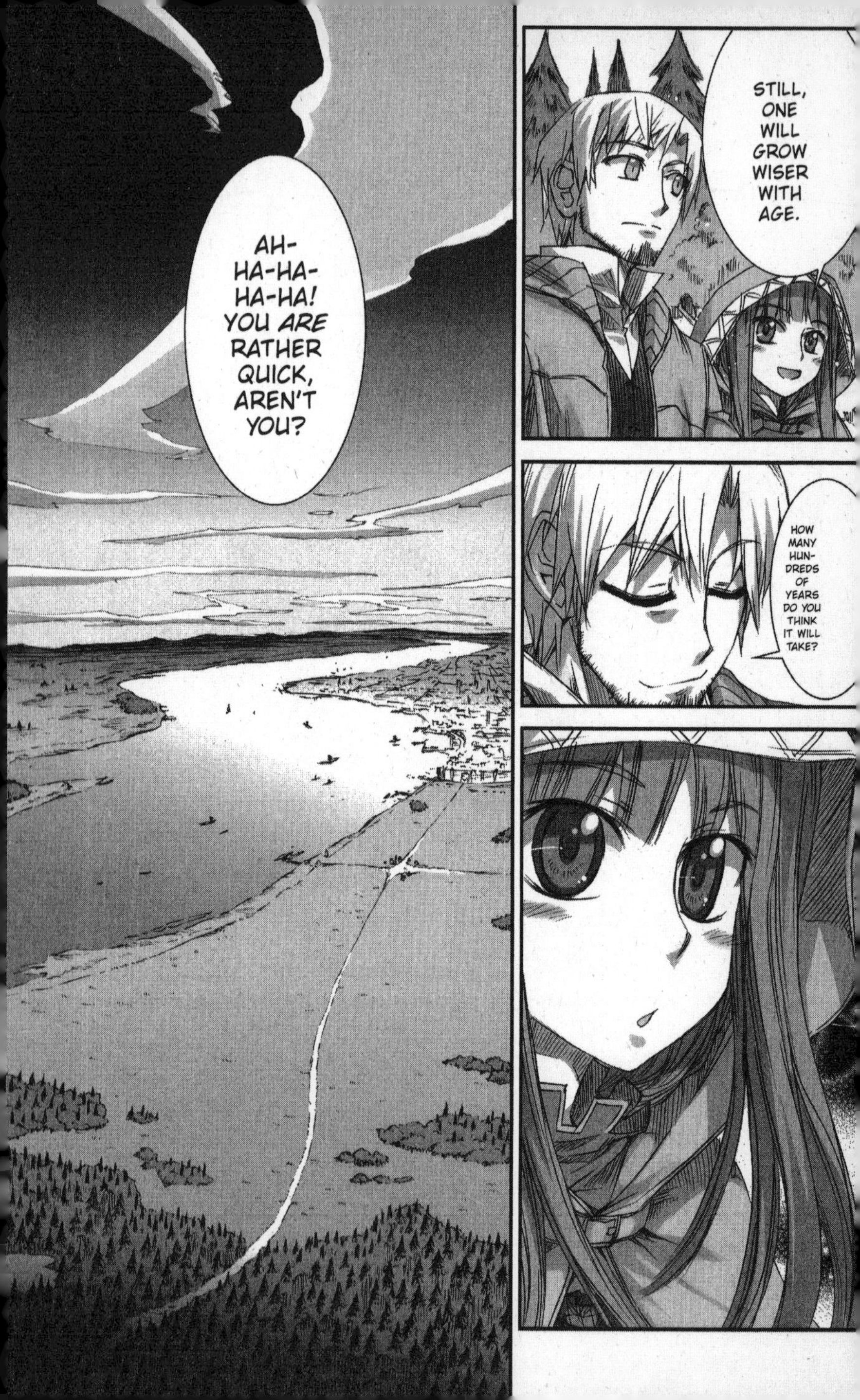
STILL, ONE WILL GROW WISER WITH AGE.
HOW MANY HUNDREDS OF YEARS DO YOU THINK IT WILL TAKE?
AH-HA-HA-HA-HA! YOU *ARE* RATHER QUICK, AREN'T YOU?

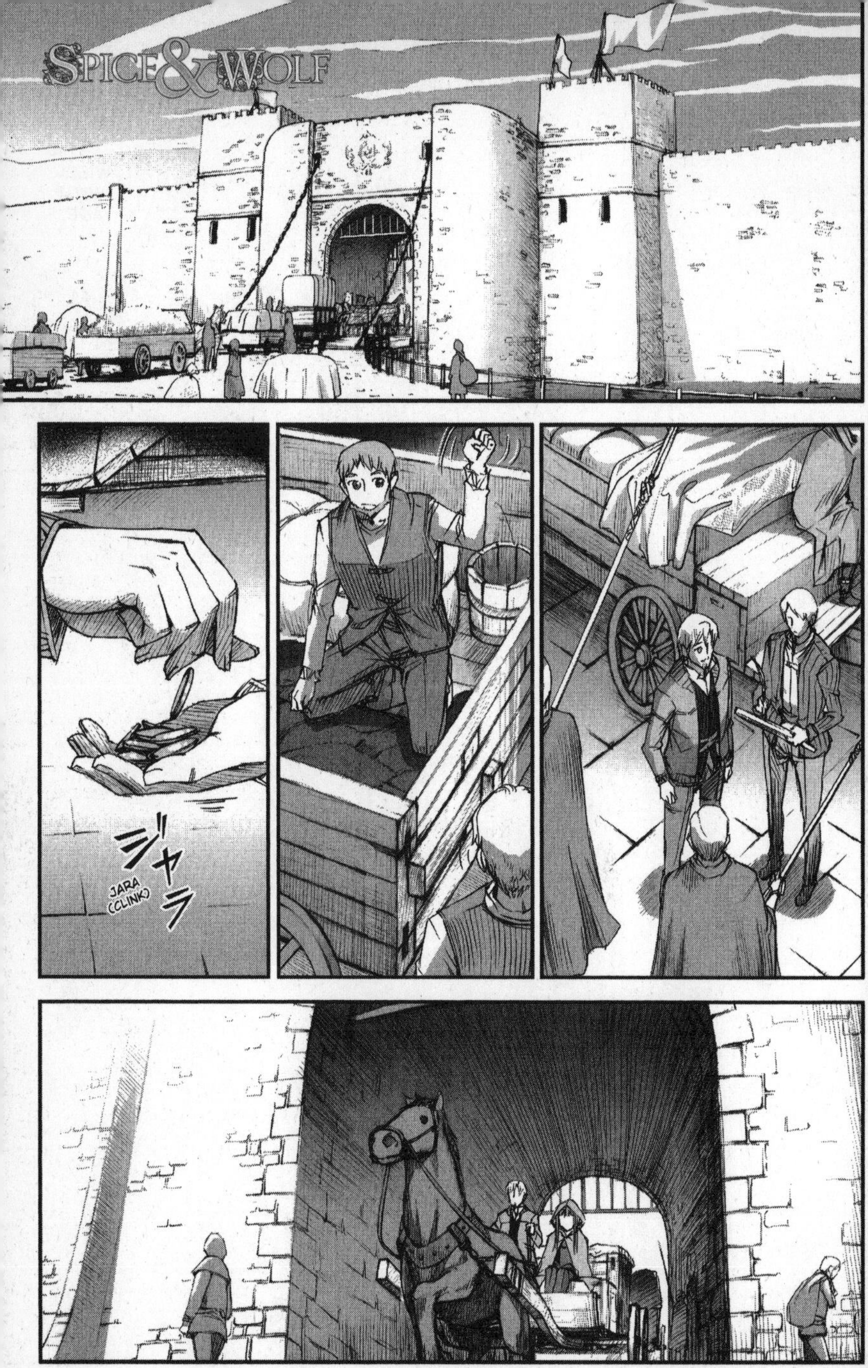
SPICE & WOLF
ジャラ
JARA (CLINK)

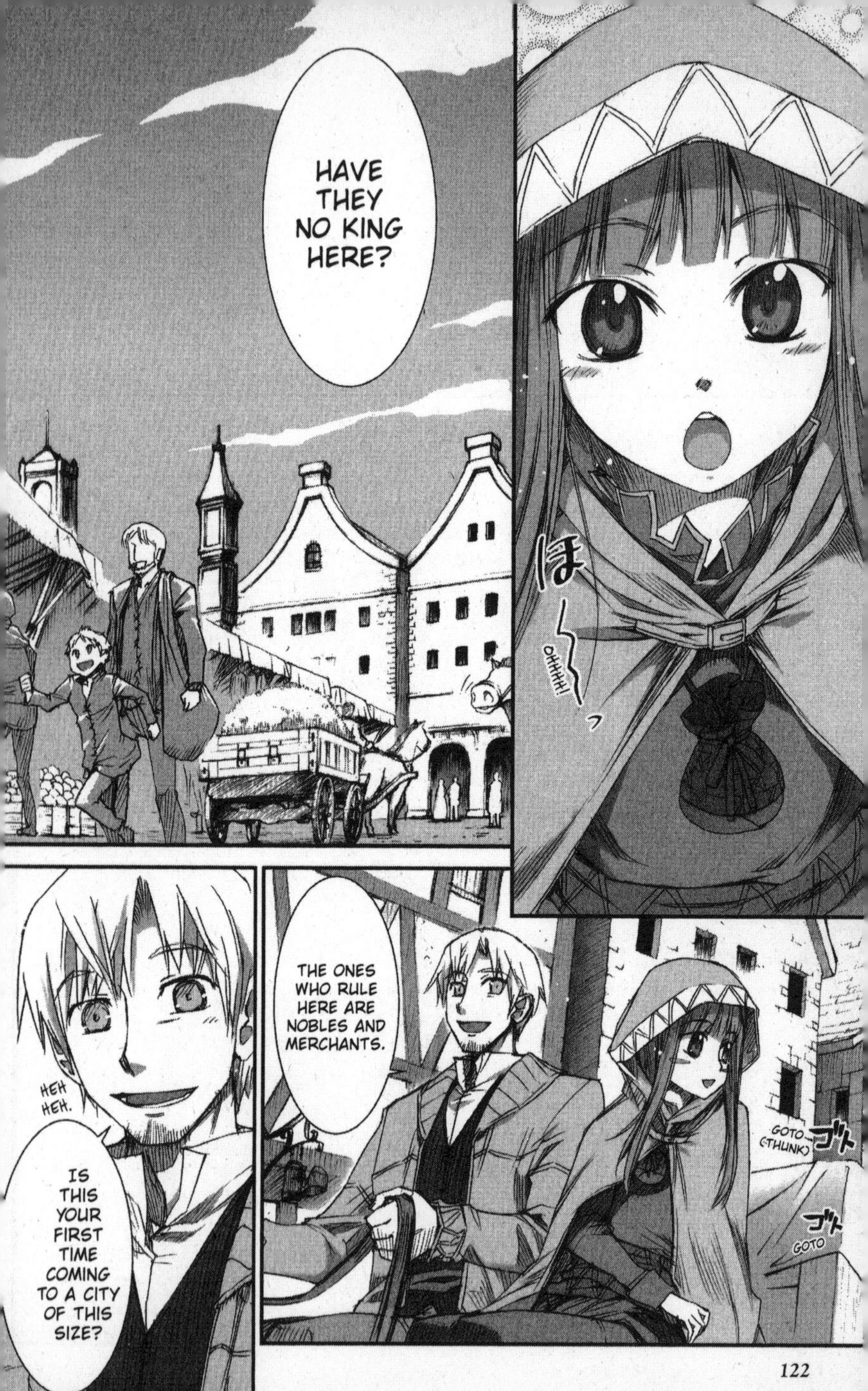
ほ～～っ
OHHHH!
HAVE THEY NO KING HERE?
THE ONES WHO RULE HERE ARE NOBLES AND MERCHANTS.
ゴト
GOTO (THUNK)
ゴト
GOTO
HEH HEH.
IS THIS YOUR FIRST TIME COMING TO A CITY OF THIS SIZE?

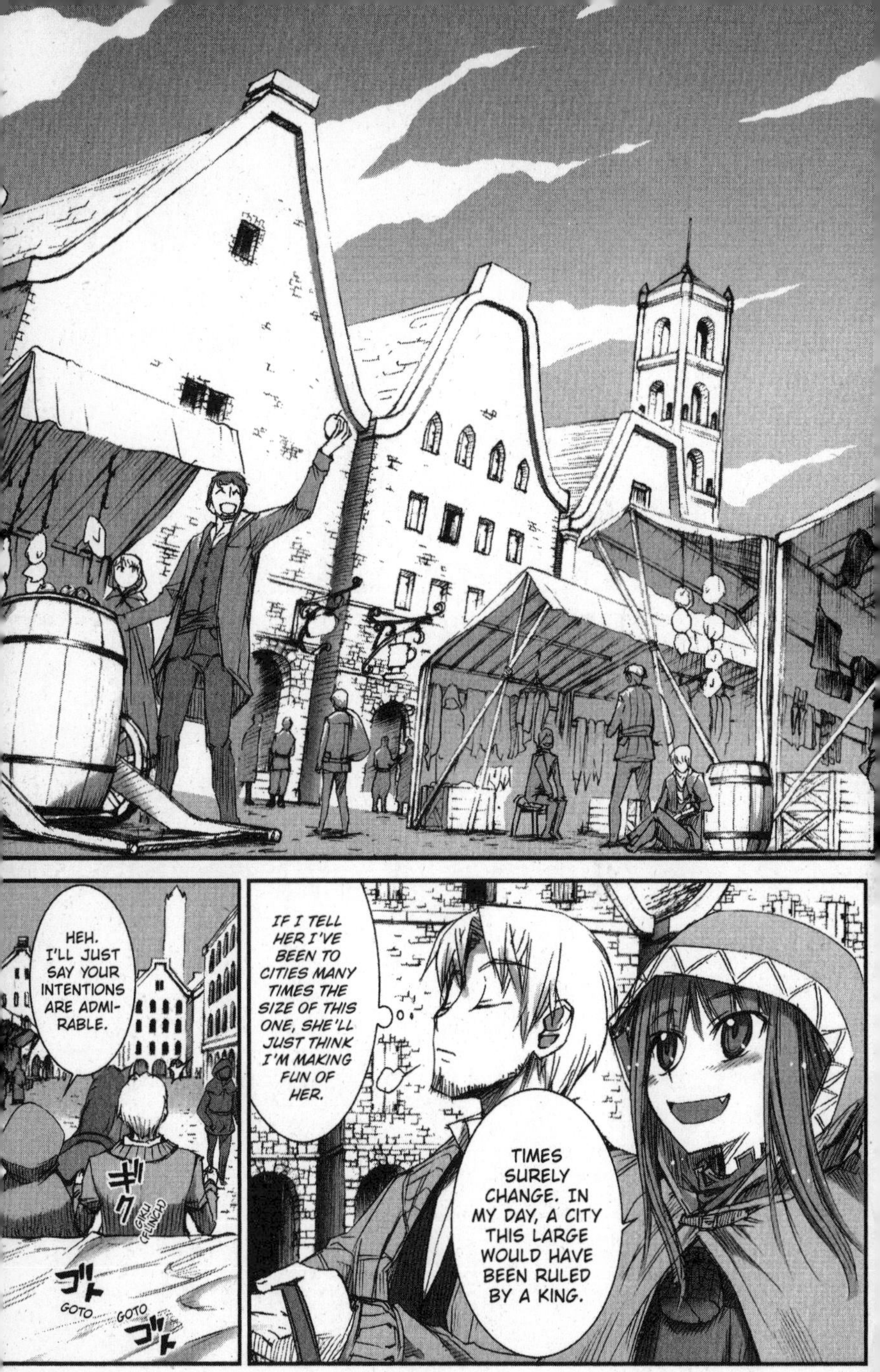
TIMES SURELY CHANGE. IN MY DAY, A CITY THIS LARGE WOULD HAVE BEEN RULED BY A KING.
IF I TELL HER I'VE BEEN TO CITIES MANY TIMES THE SIZE OF THIS ONE, SHE'LL JUST THINK I'M MAKING FUN OF HER.
HEH. I'LL JUST SAY YOUR INTENTIONS ARE ADMI-RABLE.
ギク
GIKU (FLINCH)
ゴト
GOTO
GOTO
ゴト

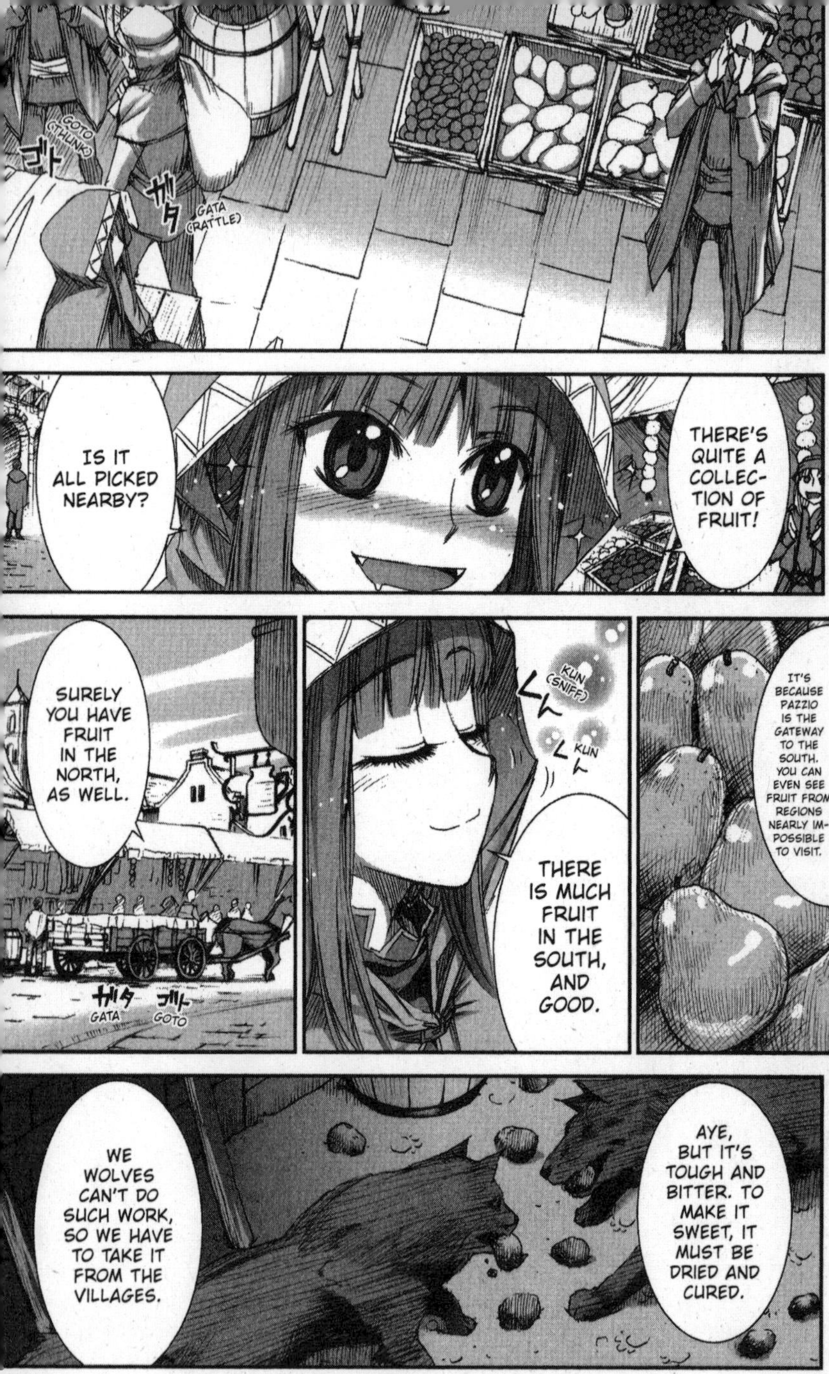
ガタ
GATA (RATTLE)
ゴト
GOTO (THUNK)
THERE'S QUITE A COLLEC-TION OF FRUIT!
IS IT ALL PICKED NEARBY?
IT'S BECAUSE PAZZIO IS THE GATEWAY TO THE SOUTH. YOU CAN EVEN SEE FRUIT FROM REGIONS NEARLY IM-POSSIBLE TO VISIT.
くん
KUN (SNIFF)
くん
KUN
THERE IS MUCH FRUIT IN THE SOUTH, AND GOOD.
SURELY YOU HAVE FRUIT IN THE NORTH, AS WELL.
ゴト
GOTO
ガタ
GATA
AYE, BUT IT'S TOUGH AND BITTER. TO MAKE IT SWEET, IT MUST BE DRIED AND CURED.
WE WOLVES CAN'T DO SUCH WORK, SO WE HAVE TO TAKE IT FROM THE VILLAGES.

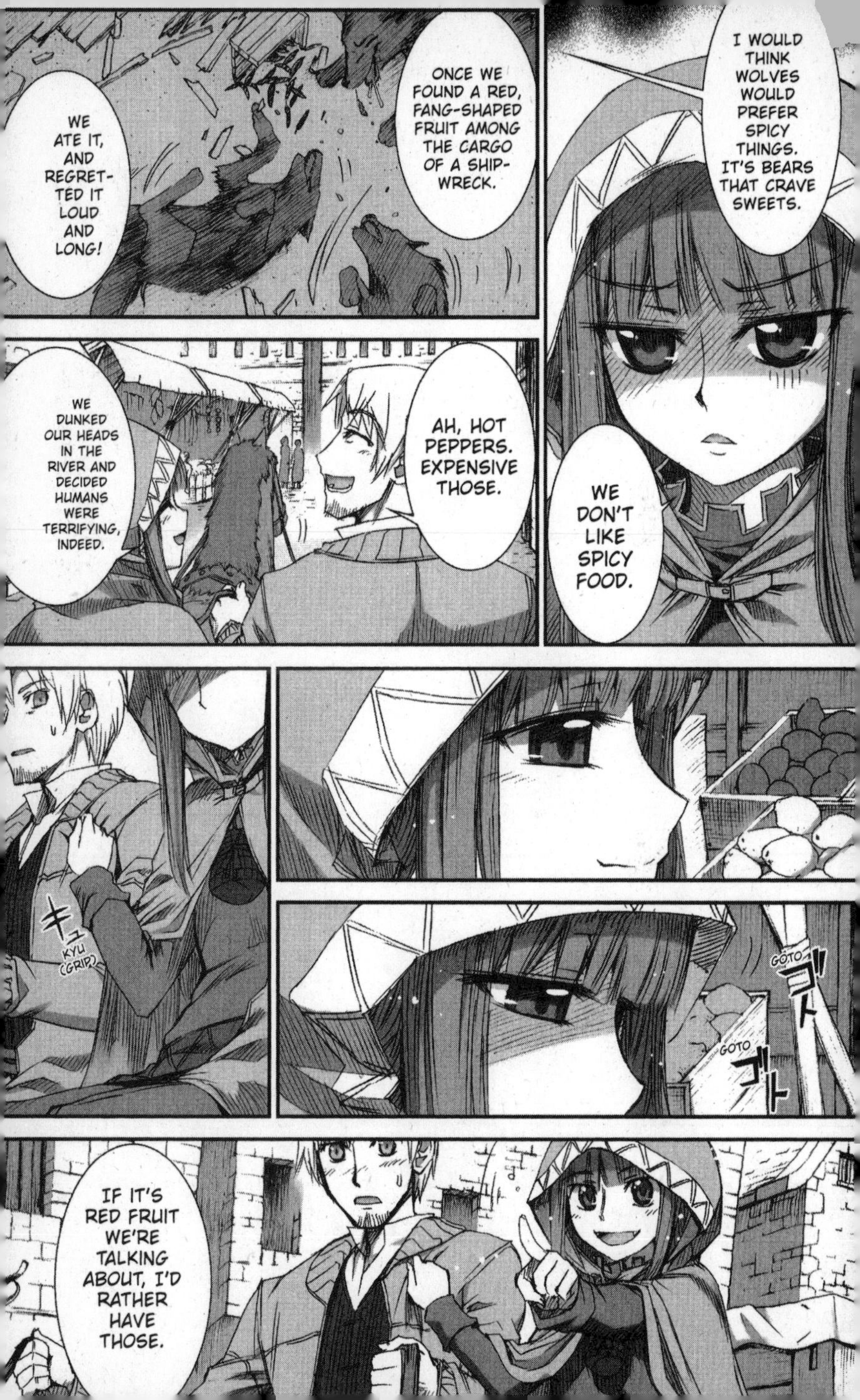
I WOULD THINK WOLVES WOULD PREFER SPICY THINGS. IT'S BEARS THAT CRAVE SWEETS.
WE DON'T LIKE SPICY FOOD.
ONCE WE FOUND A RED, FANG-SHAPED FRUIT AMONG THE CARGO OF A SHIP-WRECK.
WE ATE IT, AND REGRET-TED IT LOUD AND LONG!
AH, HOT PEPPERS. EXPENSIVE THOSE.
WE DUNKED OUR HEADS IN THE RIVER AND DECIDED HUMANS WERE TERRIFYING, INDEED.
ゴト GOTO
ゴト GOTO
キュ KYU (GRIP)
IF IT'S RED FRUIT WE'RE TALKING ABOUT, I'D RATHER HAVE THOSE.

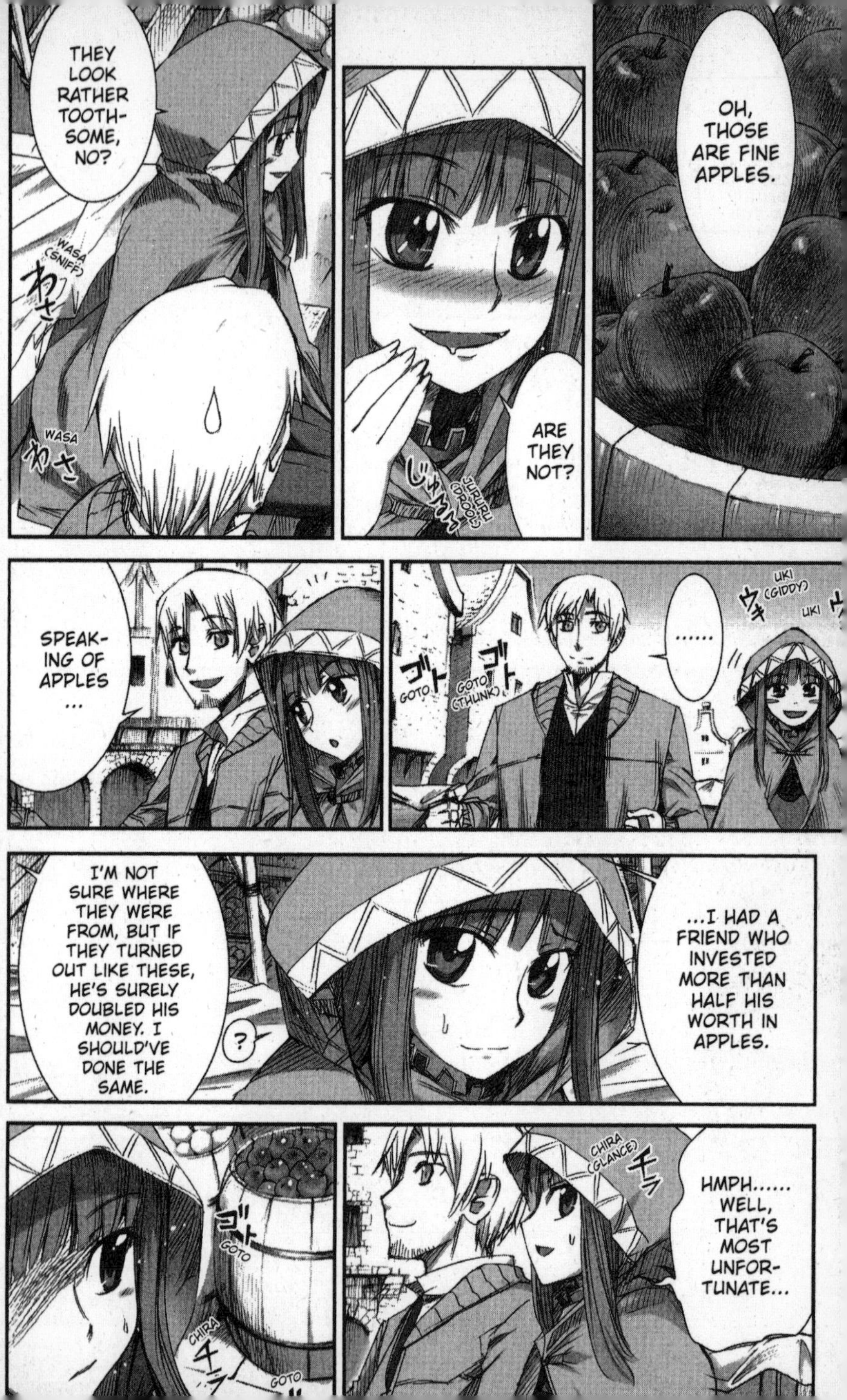
OH, THOSE ARE FINE APPLES.
ARE THEY NOT?
JURURU (DROOL)
じゅるる
THEY LOOK RATHER TOOTH-SOME, NO?
WASA (SNIFF)
わさ
WASA
わさ
......
UKI (GIDDY)
ウキ
UKI
GOTO (THUNK)
ゴト
GOTO
ゴト
SPEAK-ING OF APPLES ...
...I HAD A FRIEND WHO INVESTED MORE THAN HALF HIS WORTH IN APPLES.
?
I'M NOT SURE WHERE THEY WERE FROM, BUT IF THEY TURNED OUT LIKE THESE, HE'S SURELY DOUBLED HIS MONEY. I SHOULD'VE DONE THE SAME.
HMPH...... WELL, THAT'S MOST UNFOR-TUNATE...
CHIRA (GLANCE)
チラ
ゴト
GOTO
CHIRA
チラ
GOTO

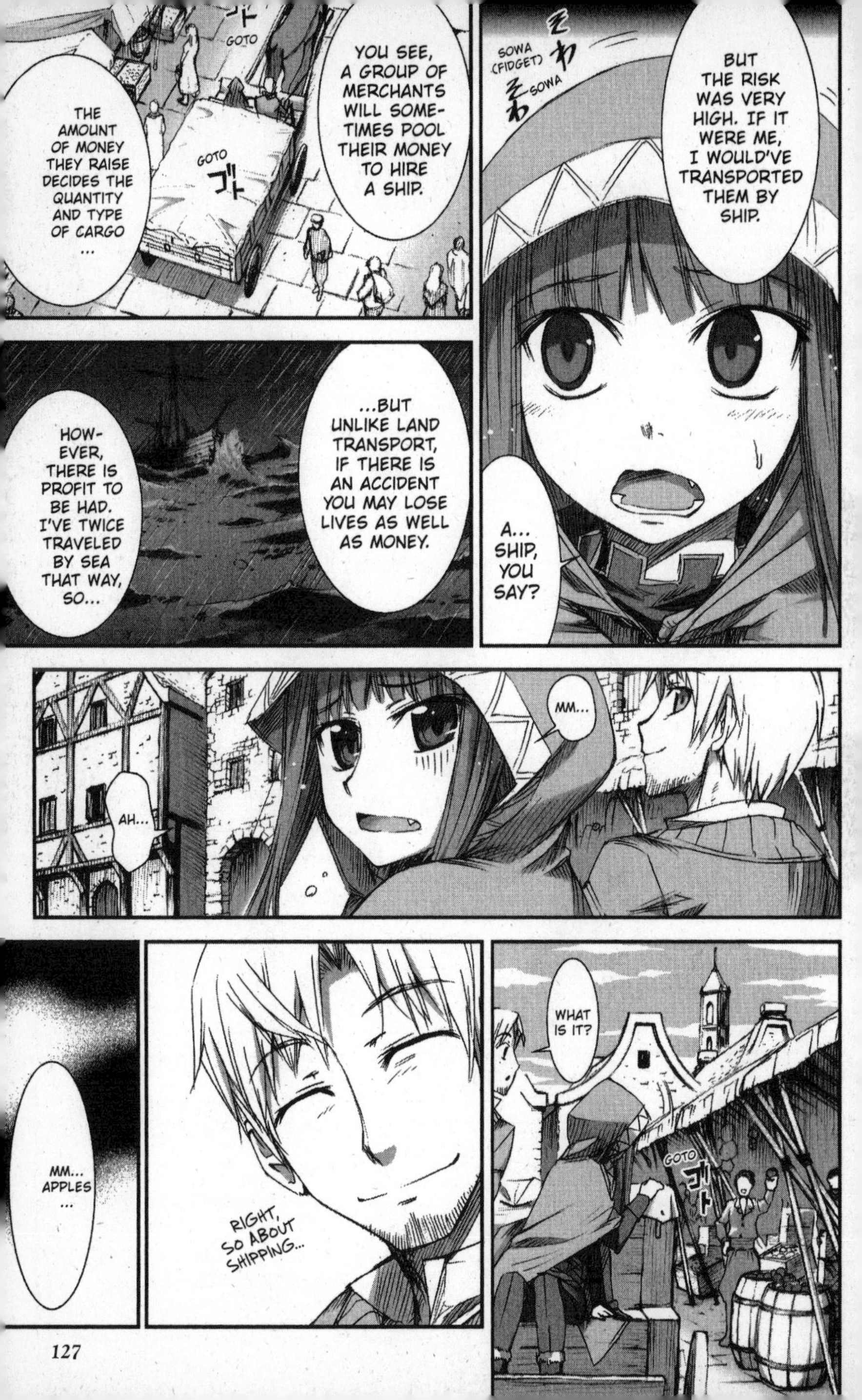
SOWA (FIDGET)
SOWA
BUT THE RISK WAS VERY HIGH. IF IT WERE ME, I WOULD'VE TRANSPORTED THEM BY SHIP.
A... SHIP, YOU SAY?
GOTO
YOU SEE, A GROUP OF MERCHANTS WILL SOME-TIMES POOL THEIR MONEY TO HIRE A SHIP.
GOTO
THE AMOUNT OF MONEY THEY RAISE DECIDES THE QUANTITY AND TYPE OF CARGO ...
...BUT UNLIKE LAND TRANSPORT, IF THERE IS AN ACCIDENT YOU MAY LOSE LIVES AS WELL AS MONEY.
HOW-EVER, THERE IS PROFIT TO BE HAD. I'VE TWICE TRAVELED BY SEA THAT WAY, SO...
MM...
AH...
WHAT IS IT?
GOTO
RIGHT, SO ABOUT SHIPPING...
MM... APPLES ...

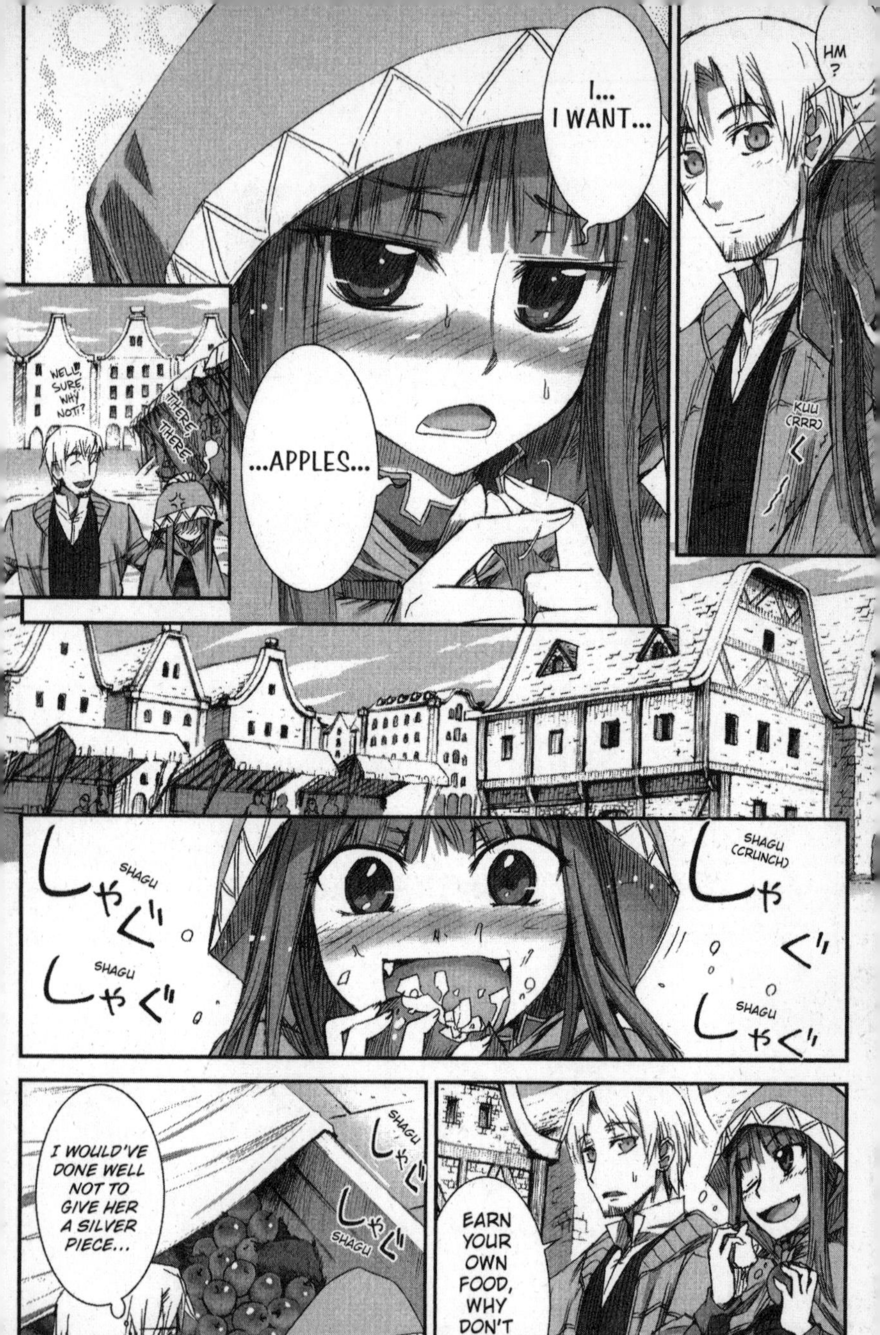
HM?
KUU (RRR)
I... I WANT...
...APPLES...
THERE, THERE.
WELL, SURE, WHY NOT!?
SHAGU (CRUNCH)
しゃぐ
SHAGU
しゃぐ
SHAGU
しゃぐ
SHAGU
しゃぐ
EARN YOUR OWN FOOD, WHY DON'T YOU.
SHAGU
しゃぐ
しゃぐ
SHAGU
I WOULD'VE DONE WELL NOT TO GIVE HER A SILVER PIECE...

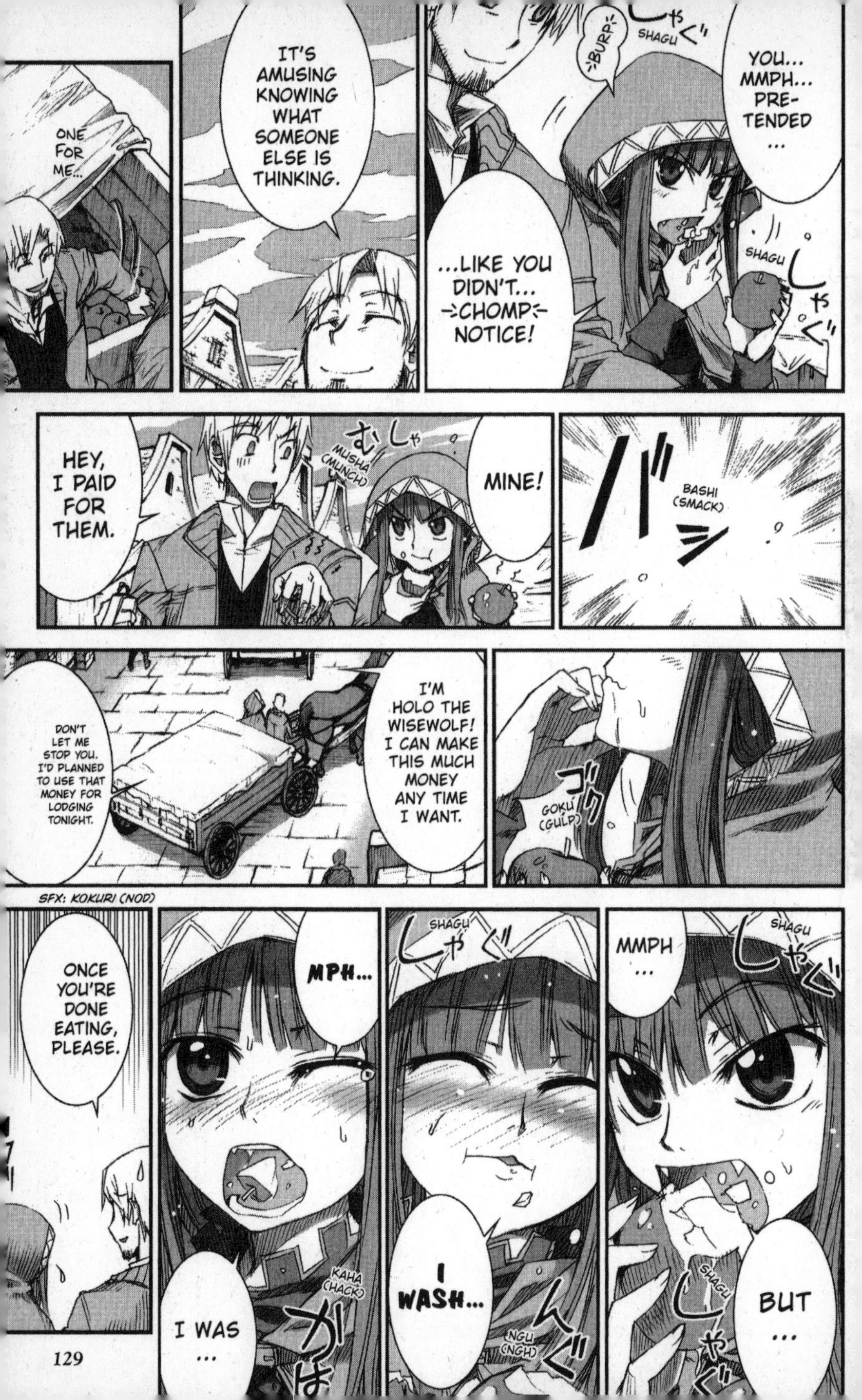
SHAGU
YOU... MMPH... PRE-TENDED...
BURP
...LIKE YOU DIDN'T... CHOMP NOTICE!
SHAGU
IT'S AMUSING KNOWING WHAT SOMEONE ELSE IS THINKING.
ONE FOR ME...
BASHI (SMACK)
MINE!
MUSHA (MUNCH)
HEY, I PAID FOR THEM.
GOKU (GULP)
I'M HOLO THE WISEWOLF! I CAN MAKE THIS MUCH MONEY ANY TIME I WANT.
DON'T LET ME STOP YOU. I'D PLANNED TO USE THAT MONEY FOR LODGING TONIGHT.
SFX: KOKURI (NOD)
SHAGU
MMPH...
SHAGU
BUT...
SHAGU
MPH...
NGU (NGH)
I WASH...
KAHA (HACK)
I WAS...
ONCE YOU'RE DONE EATING, PLEASE.

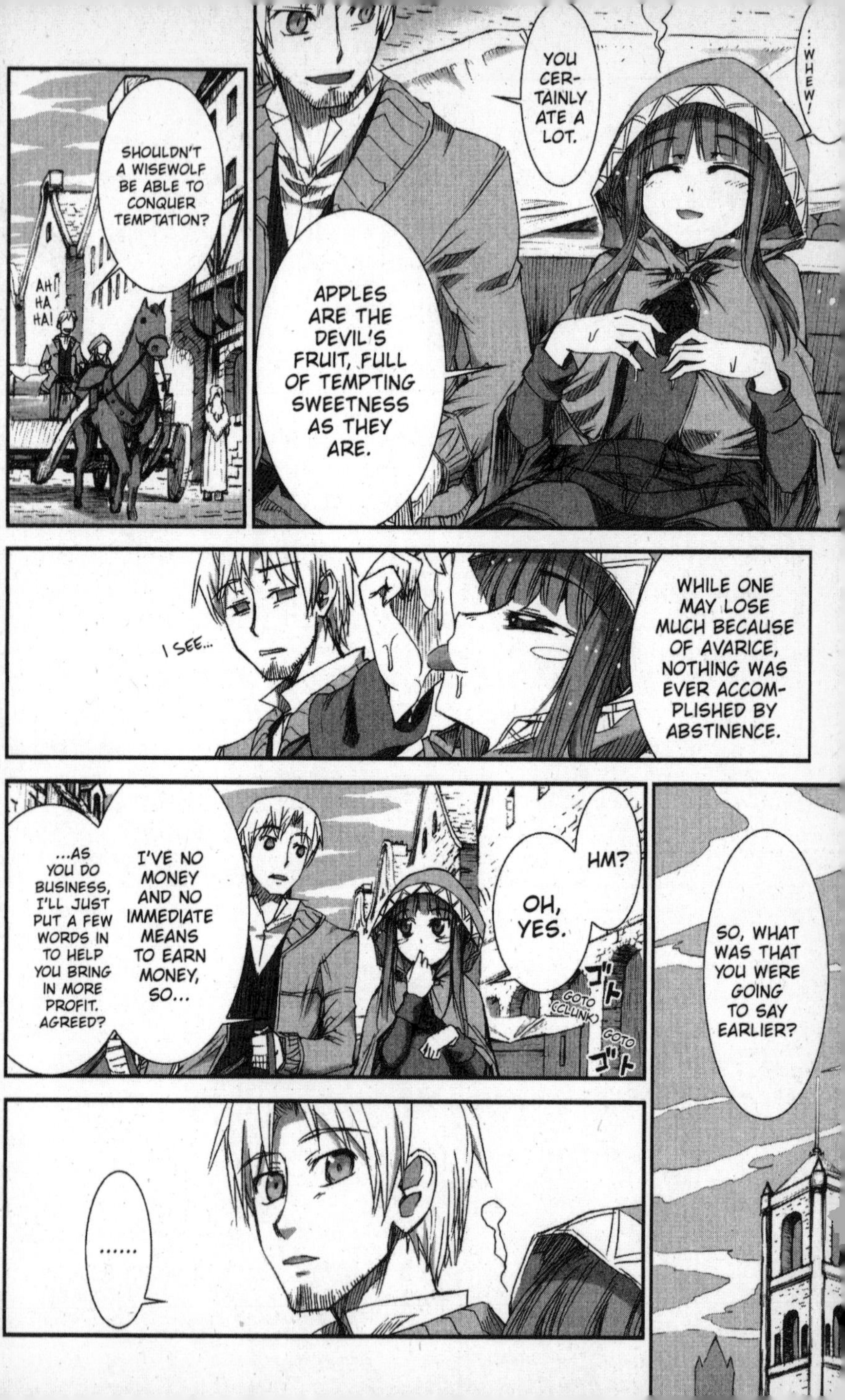
...WHEW!
YOU CER-TAINLY ATE A LOT.
APPLES ARE THE DEVIL'S FRUIT, FULL OF TEMPTING SWEETNESS AS THEY ARE.
SHOULDN'T A WISEWOLF BE ABLE TO CONQUER TEMPTATION?
AH HA HA!
WHILE ONE MAY LOSE MUCH BECAUSE OF AVARICE, NOTHING WAS EVER ACCOM-PLISHED BY ABSTINENCE.
I SEE...
SO, WHAT WAS THAT YOU WERE GOING TO SAY EARLIER?
HM?
OH, YES.
GOTO (CLUNK)
GOTO
I'VE NO MONEY AND NO IMMEDIATE MEANS TO EARN MONEY, SO...
...AS YOU DO BUSINESS, I'LL JUST PUT A FEW WORDS IN TO HELP YOU BRING IN MORE PROFIT. AGREED?
......

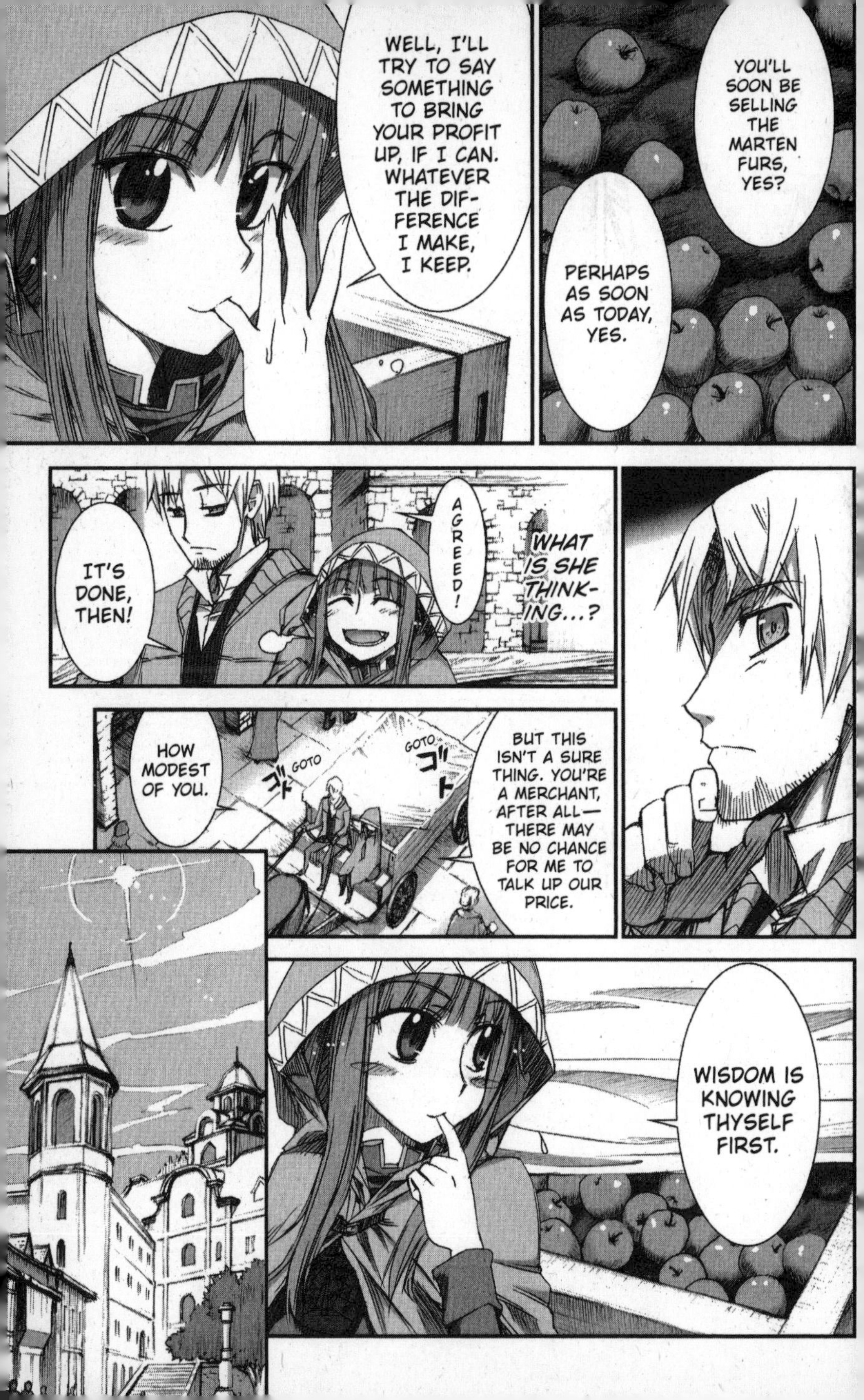
YOU'LL SOON BE SELLING THE MARTEN FURS, YES?
PERHAPS AS SOON AS TODAY, YES.
WELL, I'LL TRY TO SAY SOMETHING TO BRING YOUR PROFIT UP, IF I CAN. WHATEVER THE DIF-FERENCE I MAKE, I KEEP.
AGREED!
WHAT IS SHE THINK-ING...?
IT'S DONE, THEN!
BUT THIS ISN'T A SURE THING. YOU'RE A MERCHANT, AFTER ALL—THERE MAY BE NO CHANCE FOR ME TO TALK UP OUR PRICE.
GOTO
GOTO
HOW MODEST OF YOU.
WISDOM IS KNOWING THYSELF FIRST.

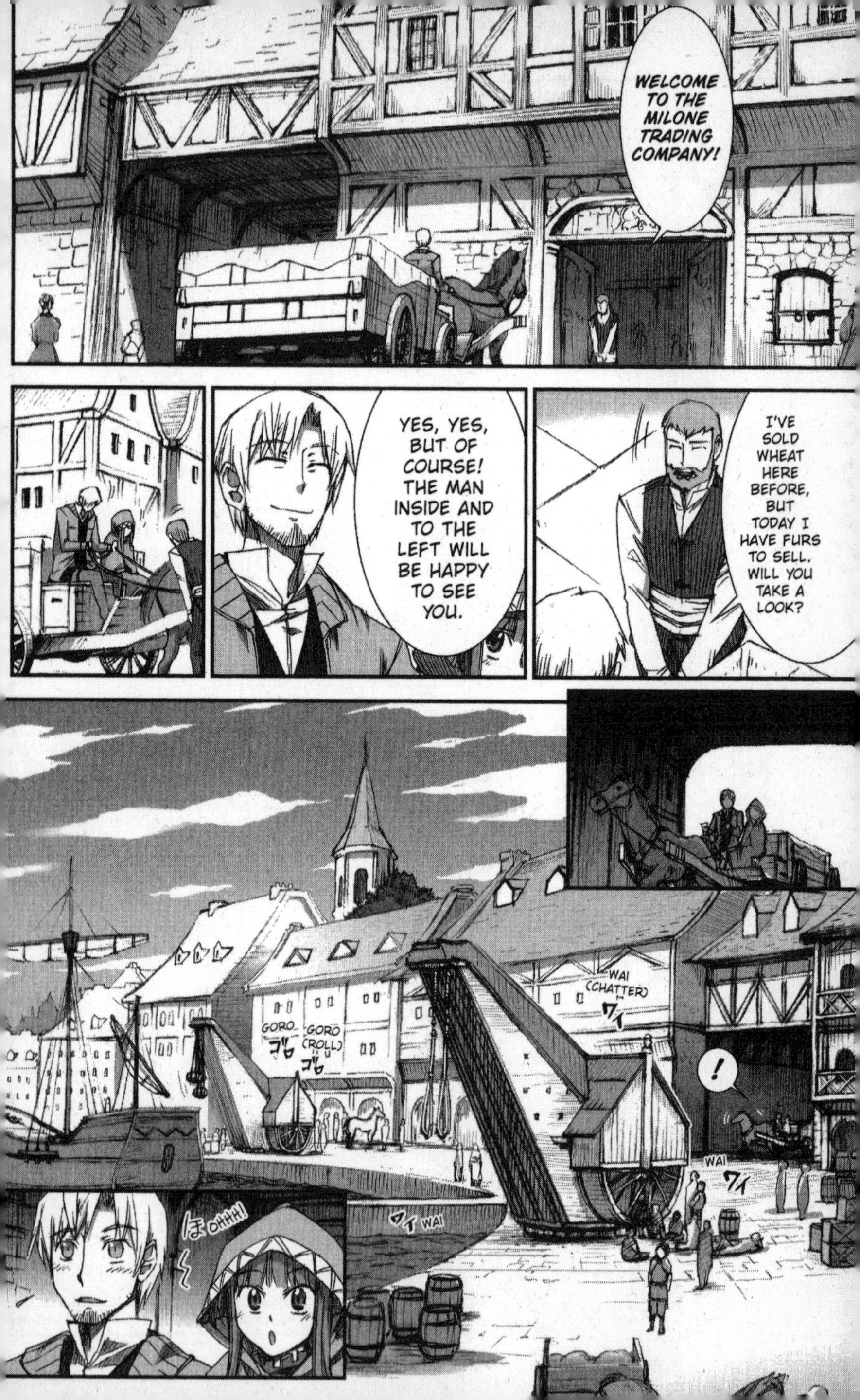
WELCOME TO THE MILONE TRADING COMPANY!
I'VE SOLD WHEAT HERE BEFORE, BUT TODAY I HAVE FURS TO SELL. WILL YOU TAKE A LOOK?
YES, YES, BUT OF COURSE! THE MAN INSIDE AND TO THE LEFT WILL BE HAPPY TO SEE YOU.
WAI (CHATTER) ワイ
!
WAI ワイ
GORO ゴロ
GORO (ROLL) ゴロ
ワイ WAI
ほOHHH!

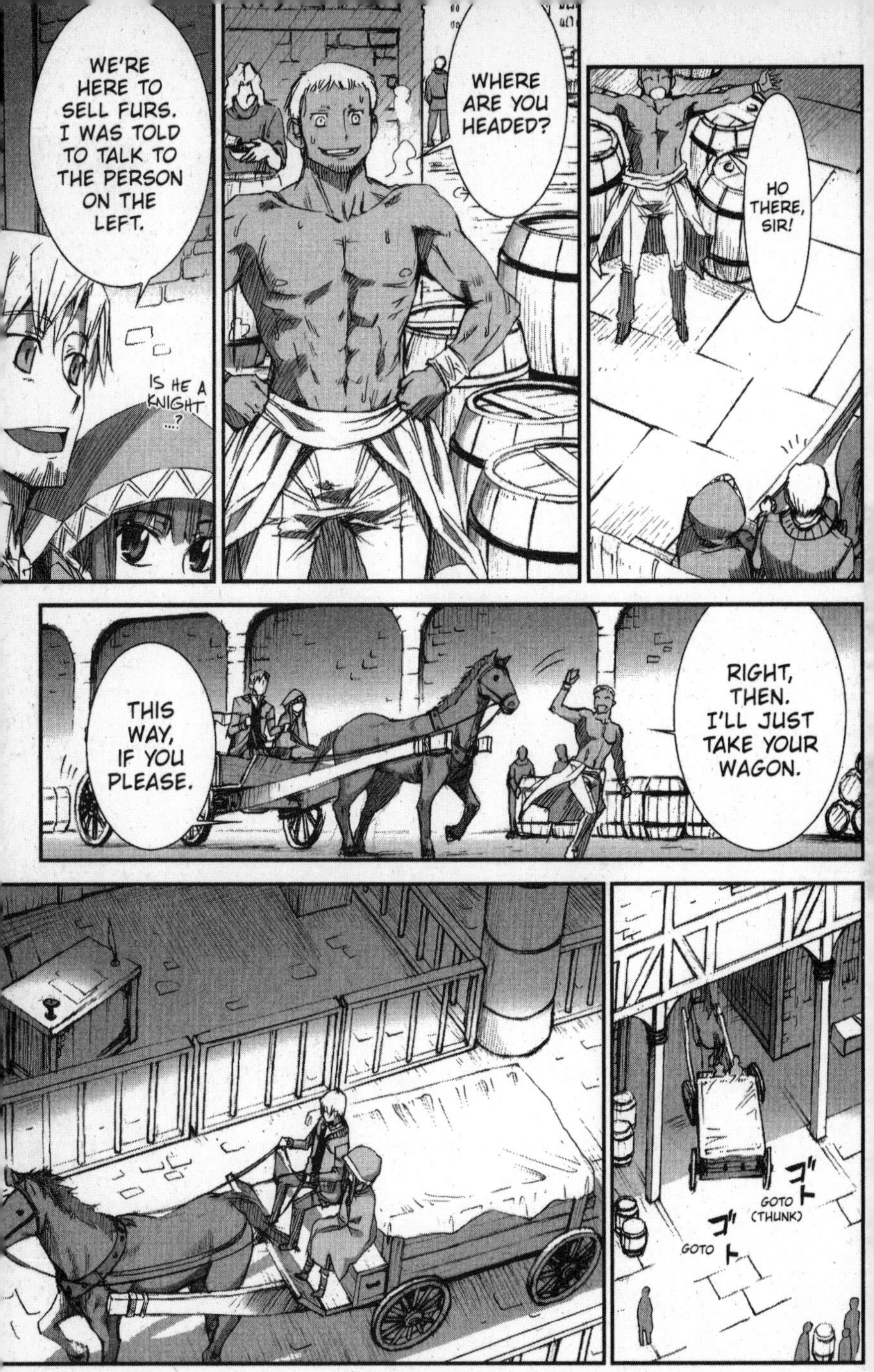
HO THERE, SIR!
WHERE ARE YOU HEADED?
WE'RE HERE TO SELL FURS. I WAS TOLD TO TALK TO THE PERSON ON THE LEFT.
IS HE A KNIGHT ...?
RIGHT, THEN. I'LL JUST TAKE YOUR WAGON.
THIS WAY, IF YOU PLEASE.
ゴト
GOTO (THUNK)
ゴト
GOTO

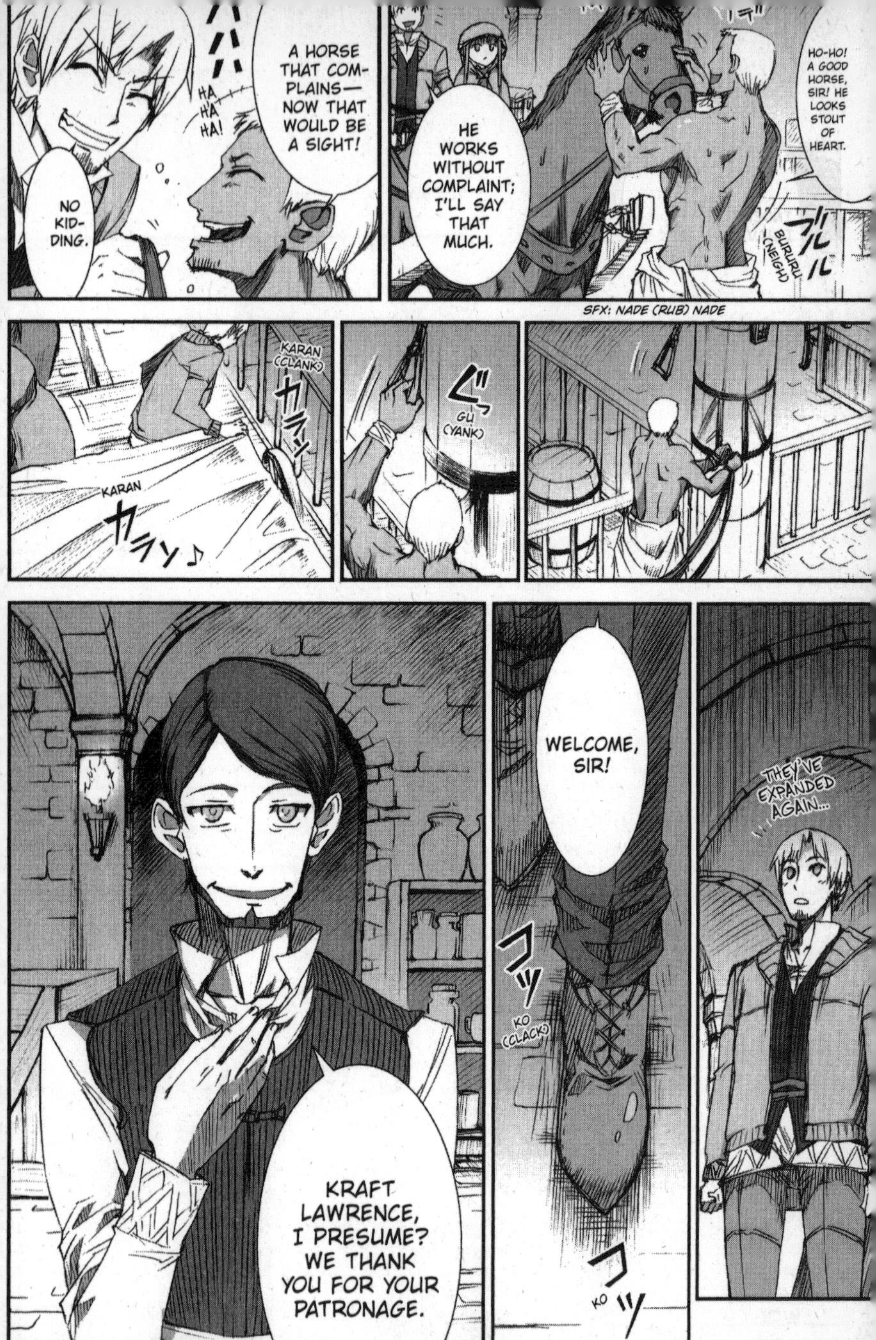
HO-HO! A GOOD HORSE, SIR! HE LOOKS STOUT OF HEART.
BURURU (NEIGH)
HE WORKS WITHOUT COMPLAINT; I'LL SAY THAT MUCH.
SFX: NADE (RUB) NADE
A HORSE THAT COMPLAINS— NOW THAT WOULD BE A SIGHT!
HA HA HA!
NO KIDDING.
GU (YANK)
KARAN (CLANK)
KARAN
THEY'VE EXPANDED AGAIN...
WELCOME, SIR!
KO (CLACK)
KO
KRAFT LAWRENCE, I PRESUME? WE THANK YOU FOR YOUR PATRONAGE.

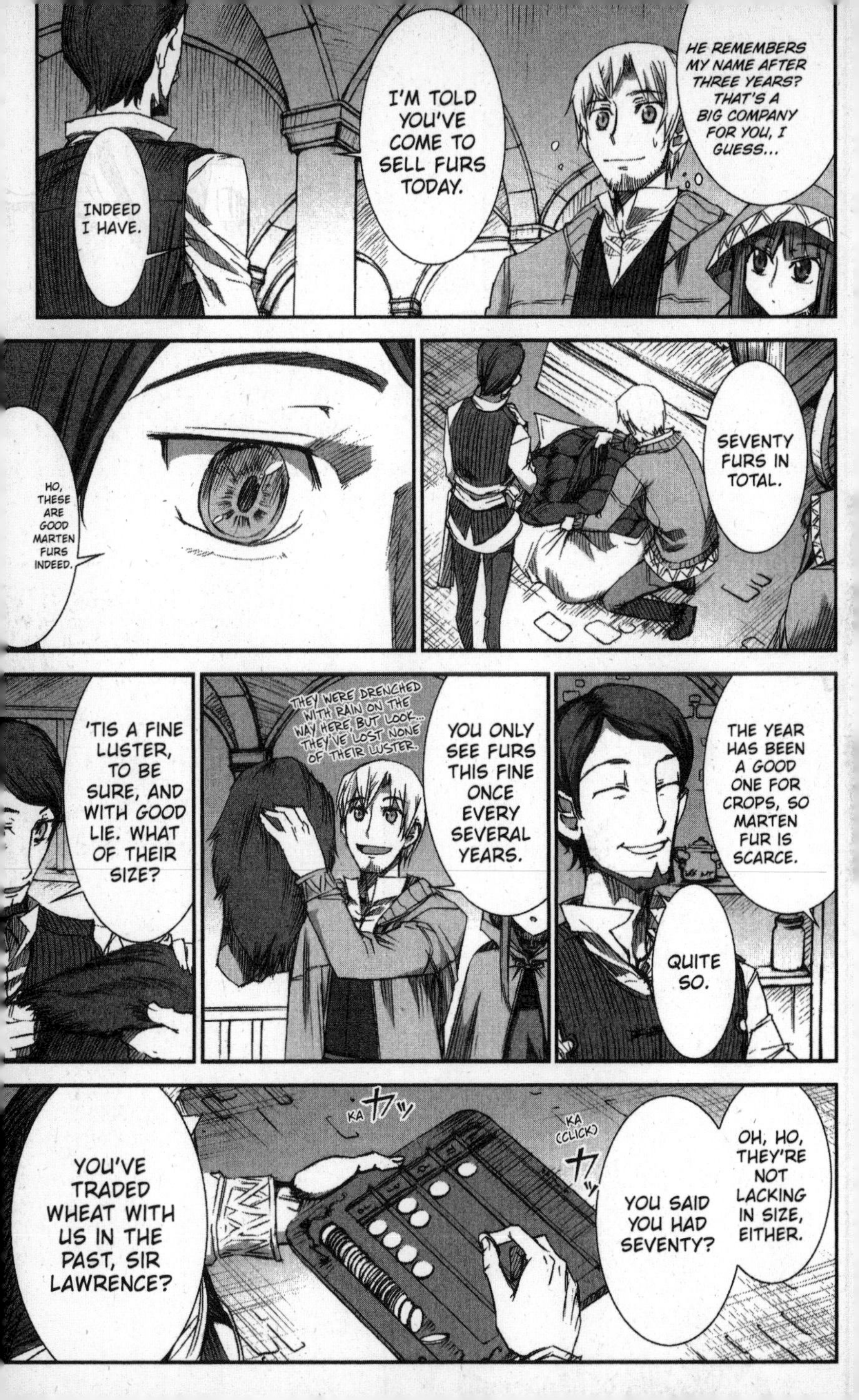
HE REMEMBERS MY NAME AFTER THREE YEARS? THAT'S A BIG COMPANY FOR YOU, I GUESS...
I'M TOLD YOU'VE COME TO SELL FURS TODAY.
INDEED I HAVE.
SEVENTY FURS IN TOTAL.
HO, THESE ARE GOOD MARTEN FURS INDEED.
THE YEAR HAS BEEN A GOOD ONE FOR CROPS, SO MARTEN FUR IS SCARCE.
QUITE SO.
YOU ONLY SEE FURS THIS FINE ONCE EVERY SEVERAL YEARS.
THEY WERE DRENCHED WITH RAIN ON THE WAY HERE, BUT LOOK... THEY'VE LOST NONE OF THEIR LUSTER.
'TIS A FINE LUSTER, TO BE SURE, AND WITH GOOD LIE. WHAT OF THEIR SIZE?
OH, HO, THEY'RE NOT LACKING IN SIZE, EITHER.
KA (CLICK)
YOU SAID YOU HAD SEVENTY?
KA
YOU'VE TRADED WHEAT WITH US IN THE PAST, SIR LAWRENCE?

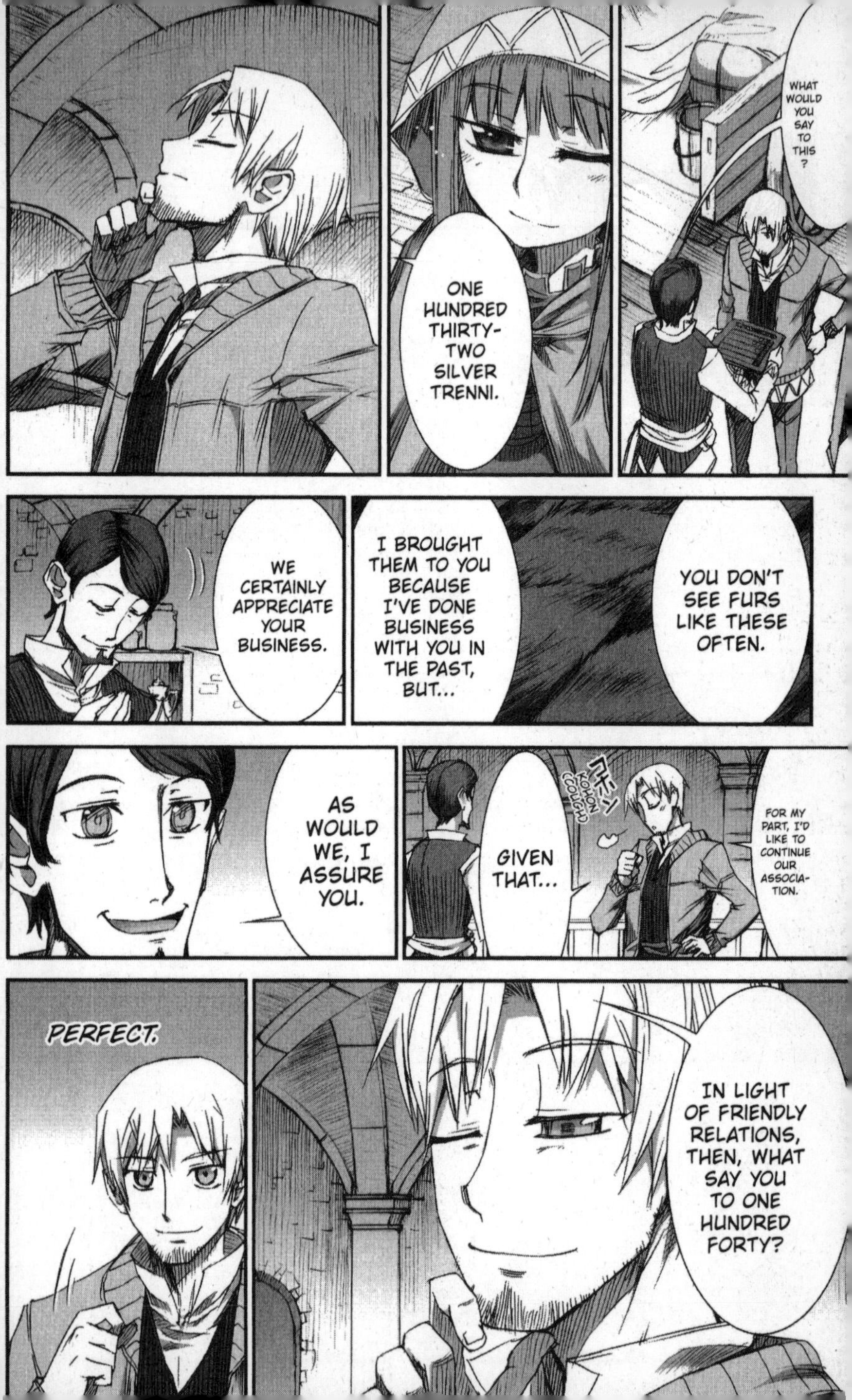
WHAT WOULD YOU SAY TO THIS?
ONE HUNDRED THIRTY-TWO SILVER TRENNI.
YOU DON'T SEE FURS LIKE THESE OFTEN.
I BROUGHT THEM TO YOU BECAUSE I'VE DONE BUSINESS WITH YOU IN THE PAST, BUT...
WE CERTAINLY APPRECIATE YOUR BUSINESS.
FOR MY PART, I'D LIKE TO CONTINUE OUR ASSOCIATION.
KOHON (COUGH)
GIVEN THAT...
AS WOULD WE, I ASSURE YOU.
IN LIGHT OF FRIENDLY RELATIONS, THEN, WHAT SAY YOU TO ONE HUNDRED FORTY?
PERFECT.

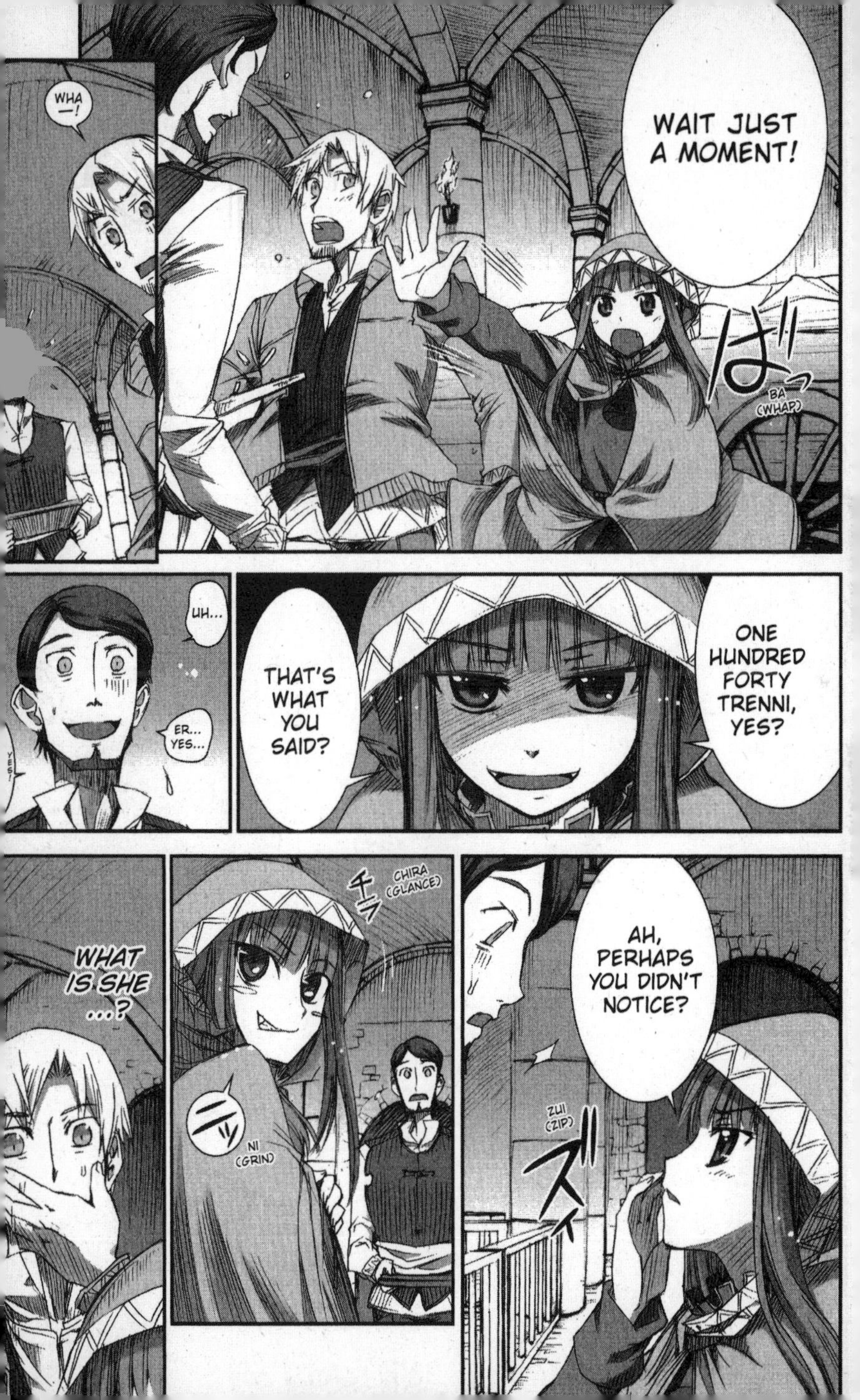

WAIT JUST A MOMENT!
BA (WHAP)
WHA—!
ONE HUNDRED FORTY TRENNI, YES?
THAT'S WHAT YOU SAID?
UH...
ER... YES...
YES!
AH, PERHAPS YOU DIDN'T NOTICE?
ZUI (ZIP)
CHIRA (GLANCE)
NI (GRIN)
WHAT IS SHE ...?

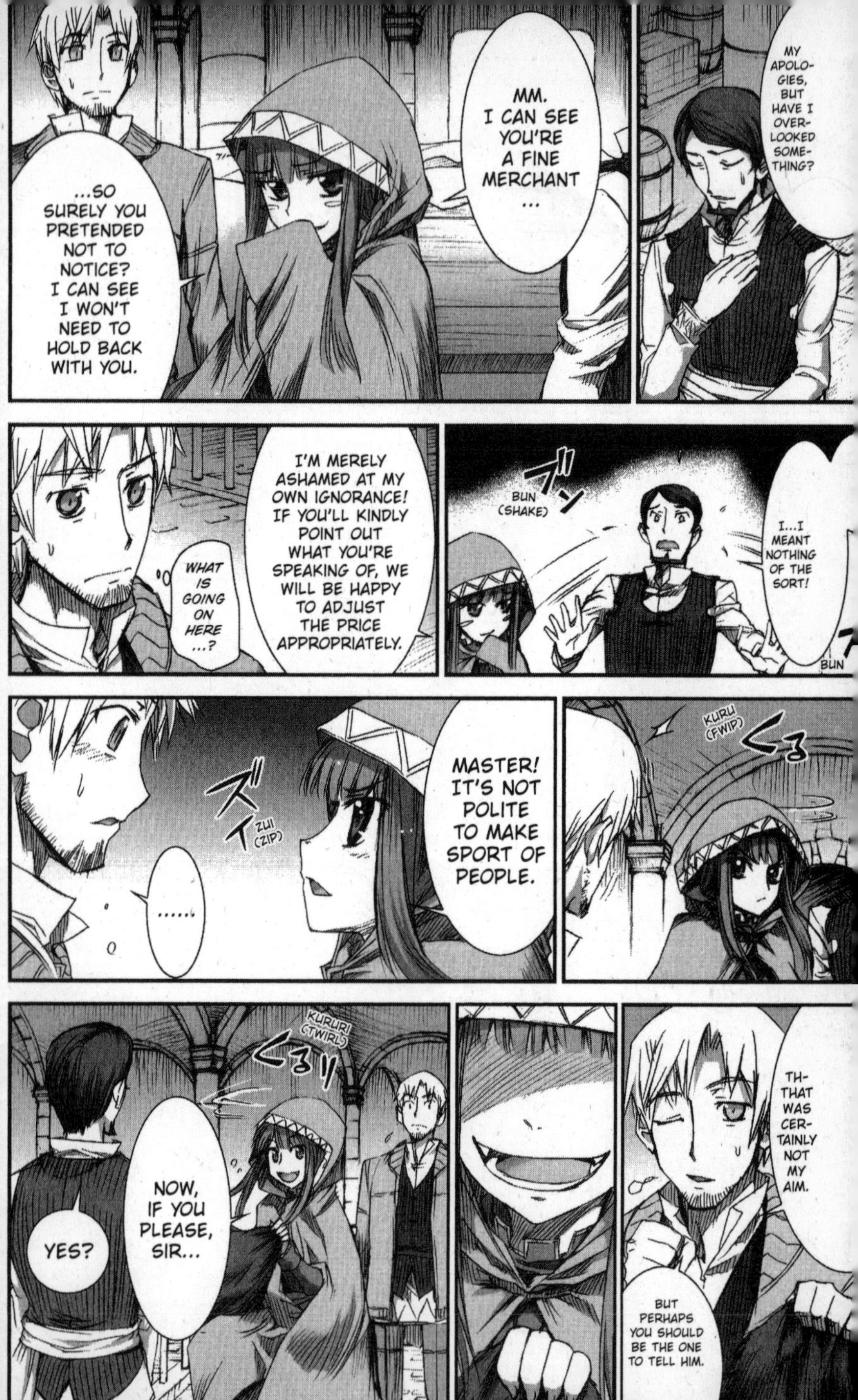
MY APOLOGIES, BUT HAVE I OVERLOOKED SOMETHING?
MM. I CAN SEE YOU'RE A FINE MERCHANT ...
...SO SURELY YOU PRETENDED NOT TO NOTICE? I CAN SEE I WON'T NEED TO HOLD BACK WITH YOU.
BUN (SHAKE)
I...I MEANT NOTHING OF THE SORT!
BUN
I'M MERELY ASHAMED AT MY OWN IGNORANCE! IF YOU'LL KINDLY POINT OUT WHAT YOU'RE SPEAKING OF, WE WILL BE HAPPY TO ADJUST THE PRICE APPROPRIATELY.
WHAT IS GOING ON HERE ...?
KURU (FWIP)
MASTER! IT'S NOT POLITE TO MAKE SPORT OF PEOPLE.
ZUI (ZIP)
......
TH-THAT WAS CERTAINLY NOT MY AIM.
BUT PERHAPS YOU SHOULD BE THE ONE TO TELL HIM.
KURURI (TWIRL)
NOW, IF YOU PLEASE, SIR...
YES?

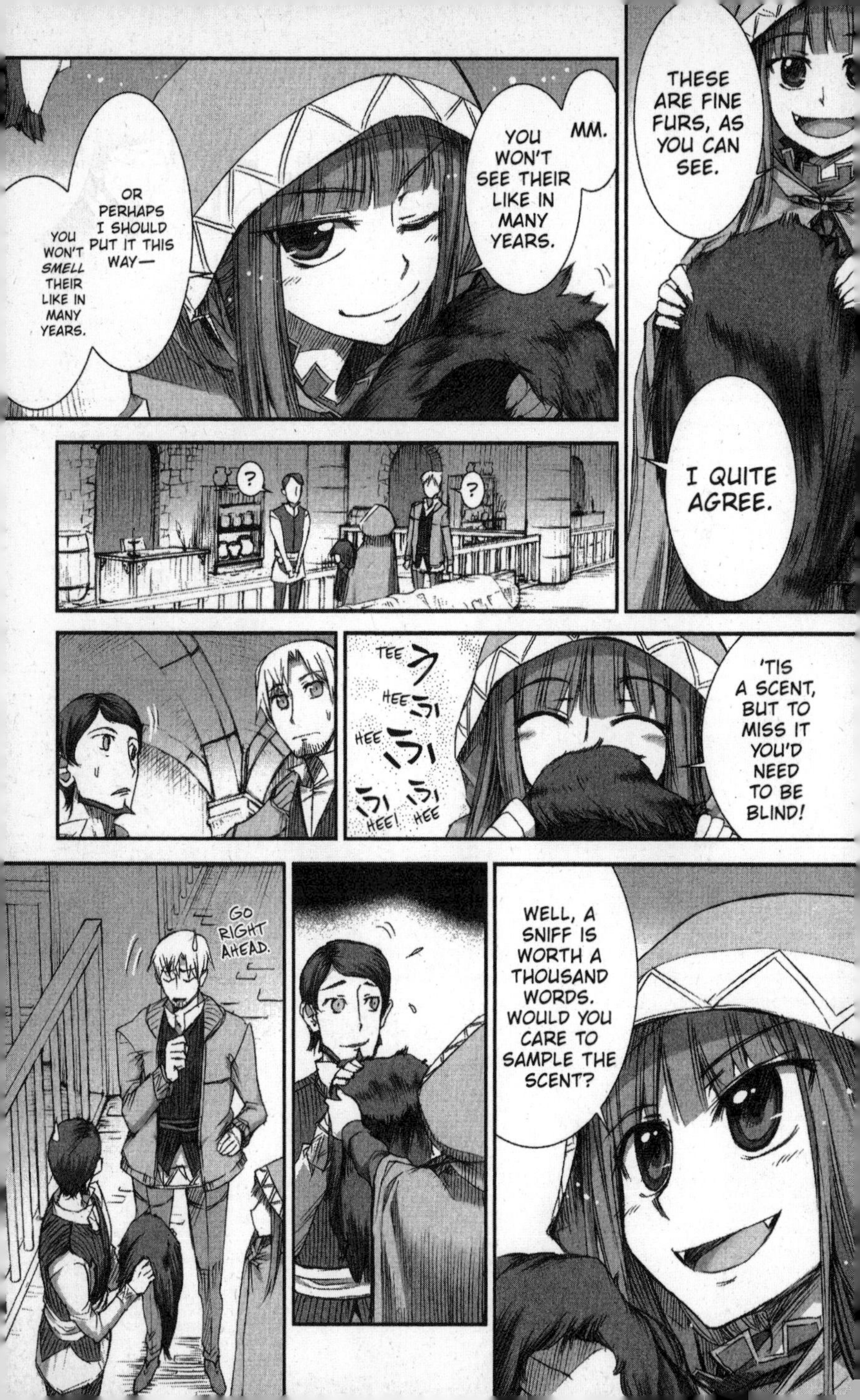
THESE ARE FINE FURS, AS YOU CAN SEE.
I QUITE AGREE.
MM.
YOU WON'T SEE THEIR LIKE IN MANY YEARS.
OR PERHAPS I SHOULD PUT IT THIS WAY—
YOU WON'T *SMELL* THEIR LIKE IN MANY YEARS.
?
?
'TIS A SCENT, BUT TO MISS IT YOU'D NEED TO BE BLIND!
TEE
HEE
HEE
HEE!
HEE
WELL, A SNIFF IS WORTH A THOUSAND WORDS. WOULD YOU CARE TO SAMPLE THE SCENT?
GO RIGHT AHEAD.

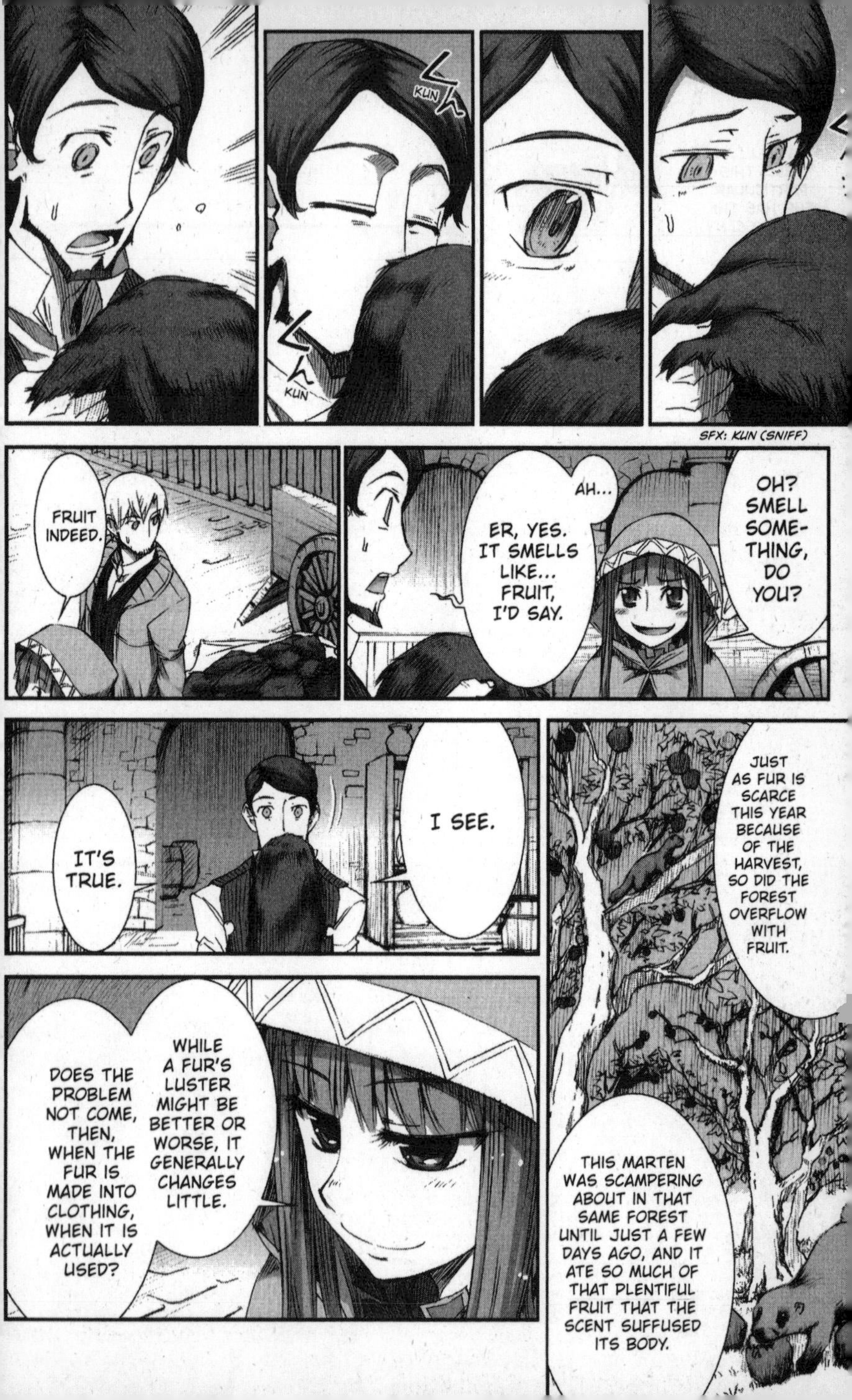
KUN
KUN
SFX: KUN (SNIFF)
OH? SMELL SOMETHING, DO YOU?
AH...
ER, YES. IT SMELLS LIKE... FRUIT, I'D SAY.
FRUIT INDEED.
JUST AS FUR IS SCARCE THIS YEAR BECAUSE OF THE HARVEST, SO DID THE FOREST OVERFLOW WITH FRUIT.
THIS MARTEN WAS SCAMPERING ABOUT IN THAT SAME FOREST UNTIL JUST A FEW DAYS AGO, AND IT ATE SO MUCH OF THAT PLENTIFUL FRUIT THAT THE SCENT SUFFUSED ITS BODY.
I SEE.
IT'S TRUE.
WHILE A FUR'S LUSTER MIGHT BE BETTER OR WORSE, IT GENERALLY CHANGES LITTLE.
DOES THE PROBLEM NOT COME, THEN, WHEN THE FUR IS MADE INTO CLOTHING, WHEN IT IS ACTUALLY USED?

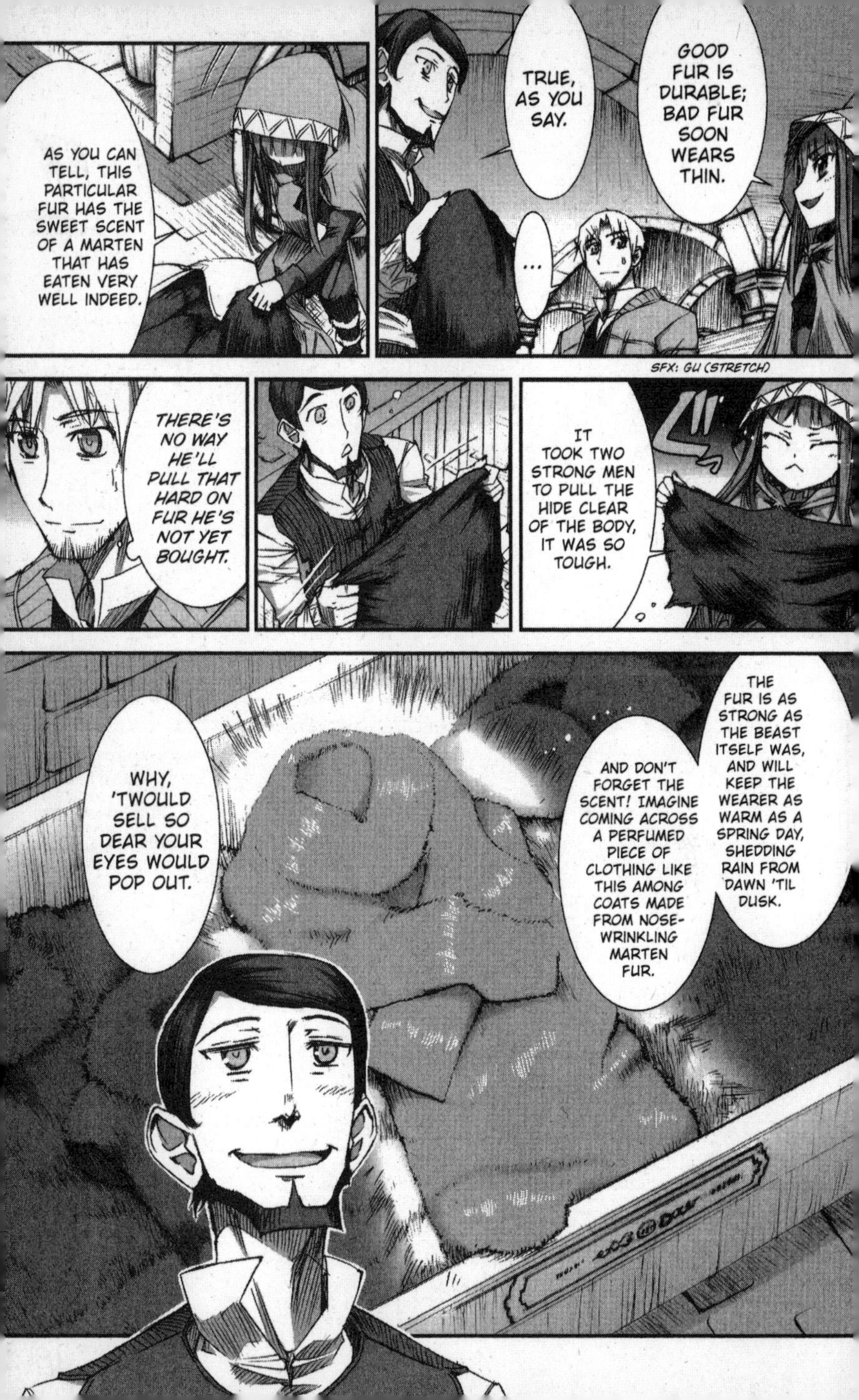
GOOD FUR IS DURABLE; BAD FUR SOON WEARS THIN.
TRUE, AS YOU SAY.
...
AS YOU CAN TELL, THIS PARTICULAR FUR HAS THE SWEET SCENT OF A MARTEN THAT HAS EATEN VERY WELL INDEED.
SFX: GU (STRETCH)
IT TOOK TWO STRONG MEN TO PULL THE HIDE CLEAR OF THE BODY, IT WAS SO TOUGH.
THERE'S NO WAY HE'LL PULL THAT HARD ON FUR HE'S NOT YET BOUGHT.
THE FUR IS AS STRONG AS THE BEAST ITSELF WAS, AND WILL KEEP THE WEARER AS WARM AS A SPRING DAY, SHEDDING RAIN FROM DAWN 'TIL DUSK.
AND DON'T FORGET THE SCENT! IMAGINE COMING ACROSS A PERFUMED PIECE OF CLOTHING LIKE THIS AMONG COATS MADE FROM NOSE-WRINKLING MARTEN FUR.
WHY, 'TWOULD SELL SO DEAR YOUR EYES WOULD POP OUT.

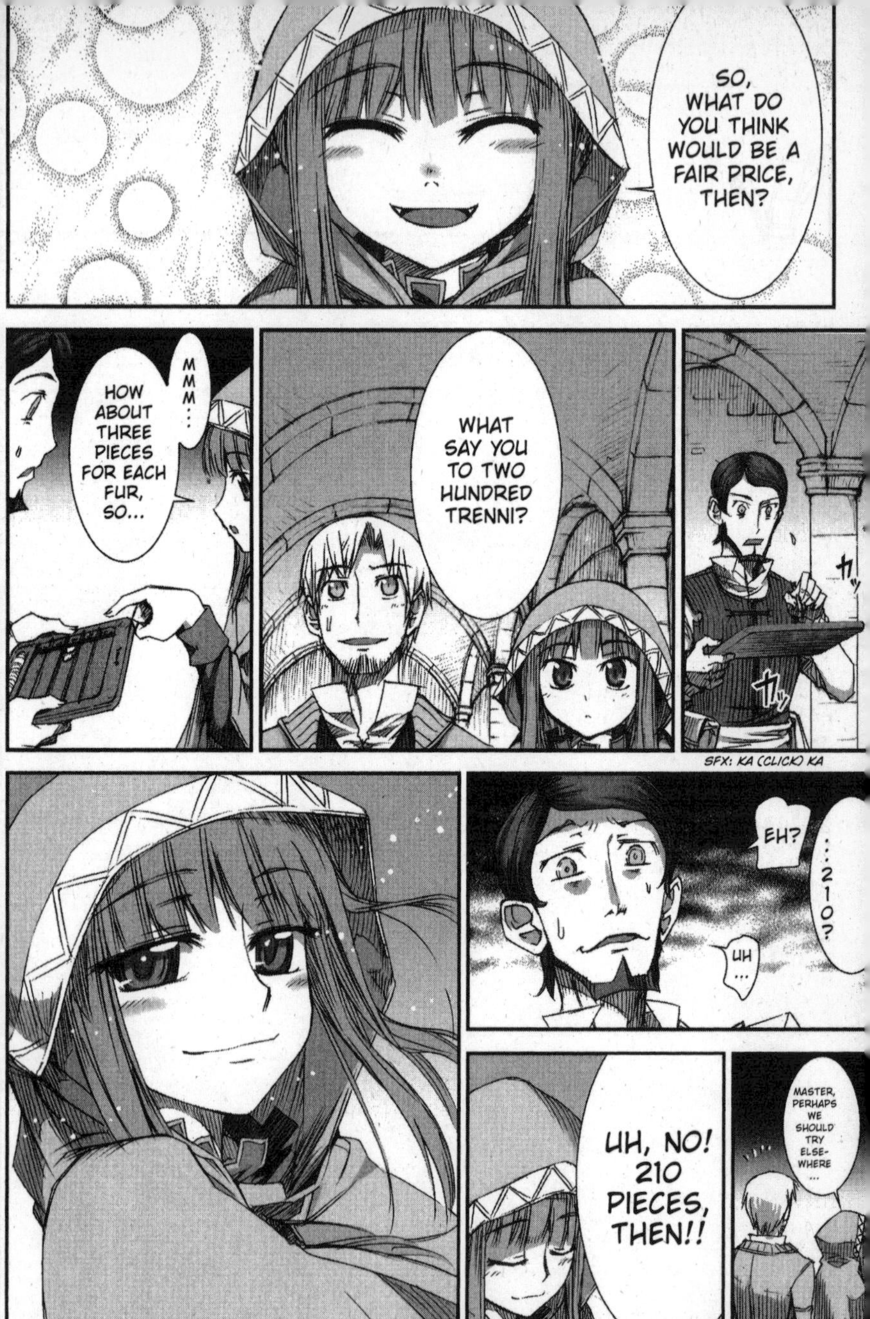
SO, WHAT DO YOU THINK WOULD BE A FAIR PRICE, THEN?
WHAT SAY YOU TO TWO HUNDRED TRENNI?
MMM...
HOW ABOUT THREE PIECES FOR EACH FUR, SO...
SFX: KA (CLICK) KA
...210?
EH?
UH...
MASTER, PERHAPS WE SHOULD TRY ELSE-WHERE...
UH, NO! 210 PIECES, THEN!!

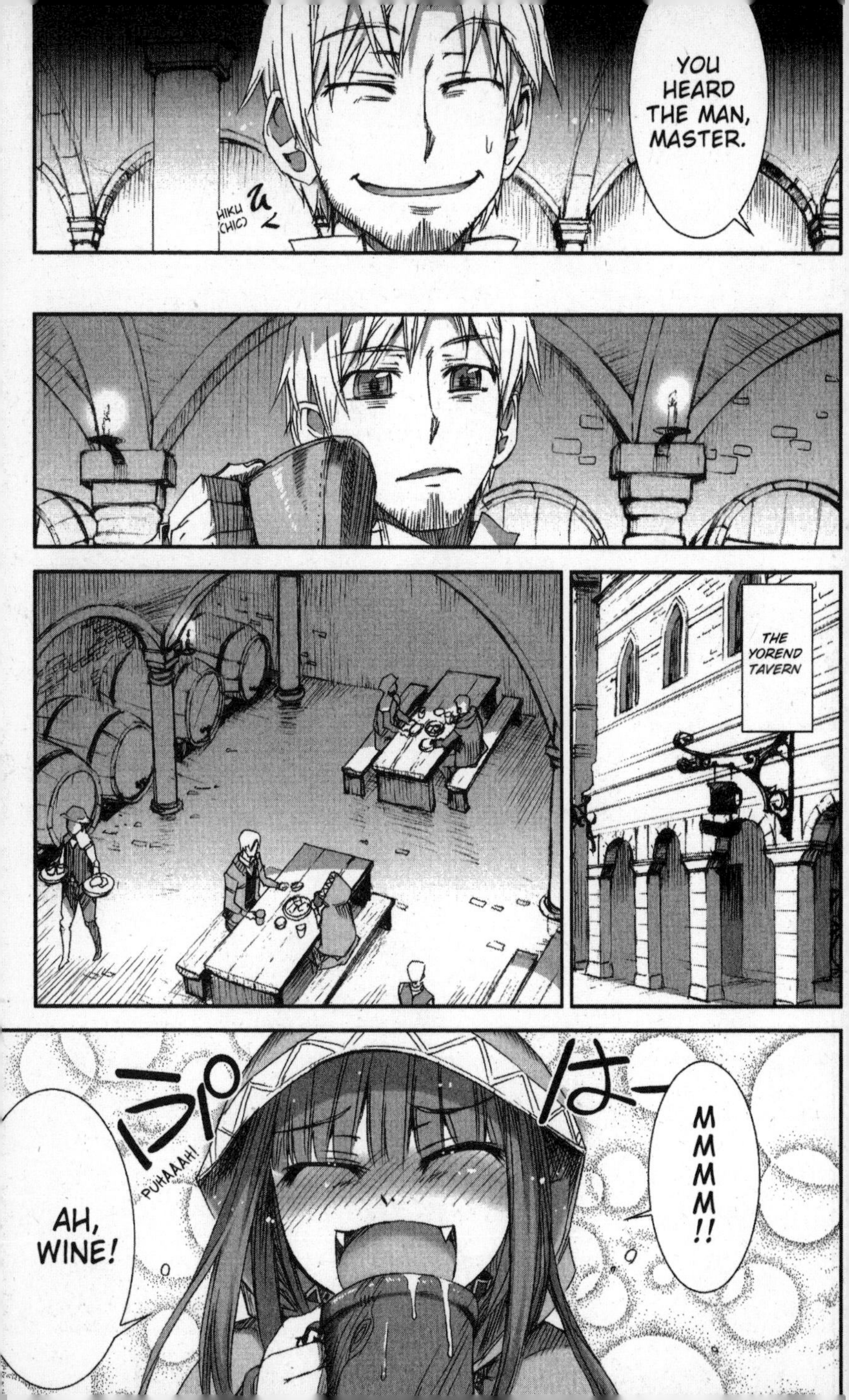
YOU HEARD THE MAN, MASTER.
ひく
HIKU (HIC)
THE YOREND TAVERN
MMMM!!
はー
ぷ
PUHAAAH!
AH, WINE!

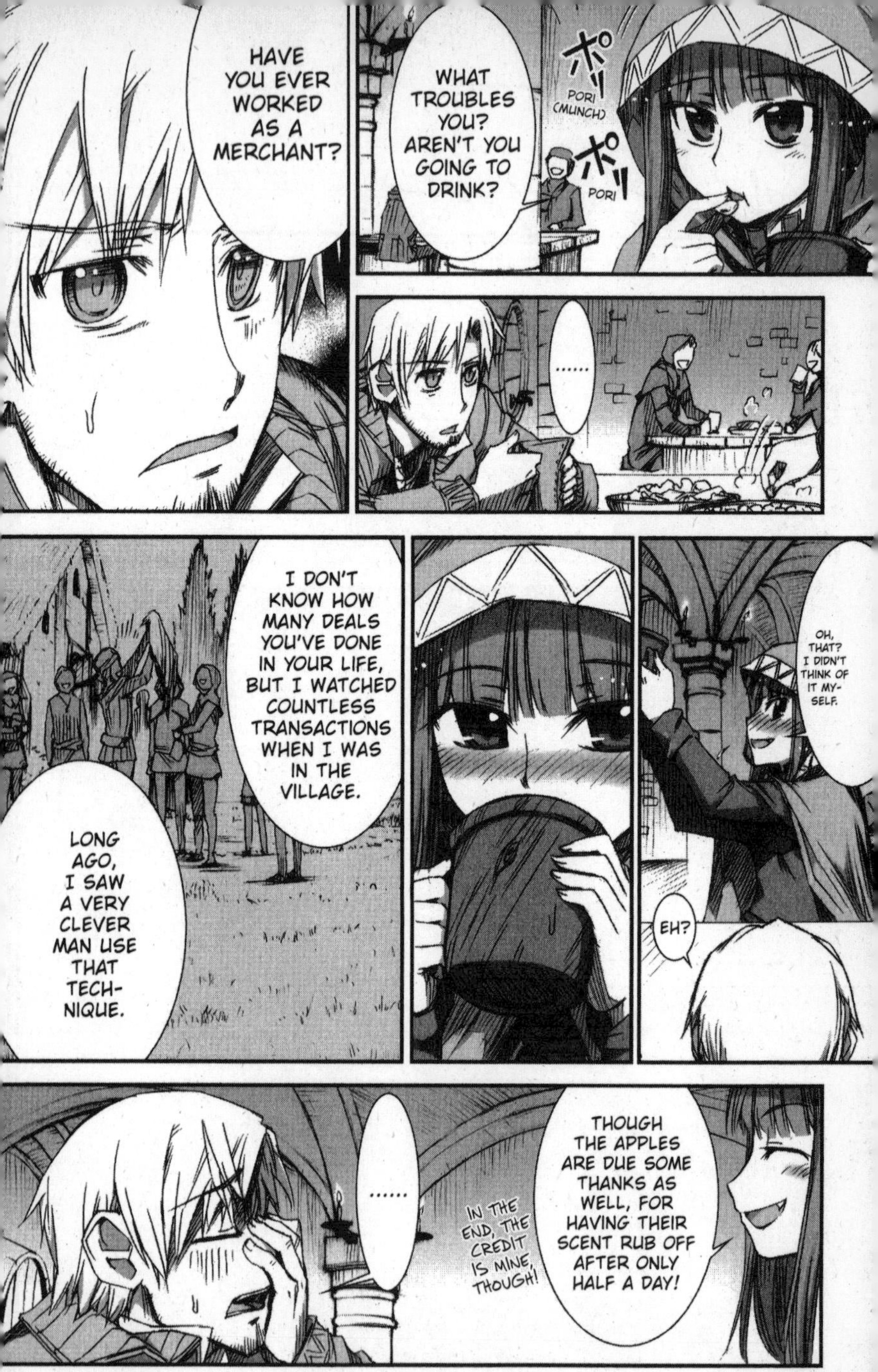
ポリ
PORI (MUNCH)
ポリ
PORI
WHAT TROUBLES YOU? AREN'T YOU GOING TO DRINK?
......
HAVE YOU EVER WORKED AS A MERCHANT?
OH, THAT? I DIDN'T THINK OF IT MY-SELF.
EH?
I DON'T KNOW HOW MANY DEALS YOU'VE DONE IN YOUR LIFE, BUT I WATCHED COUNTLESS TRANSACTIONS WHEN I WAS IN THE VILLAGE.
LONG AGO, I SAW A VERY CLEVER MAN USE THAT TECH-NIQUE.
THOUGH THE APPLES ARE DUE SOME THANKS AS WELL, FOR HAVING THEIR SCENT RUB OFF AFTER ONLY HALF A DAY!
IN THE END, THE CREDIT IS MINE, THOUGH!
......

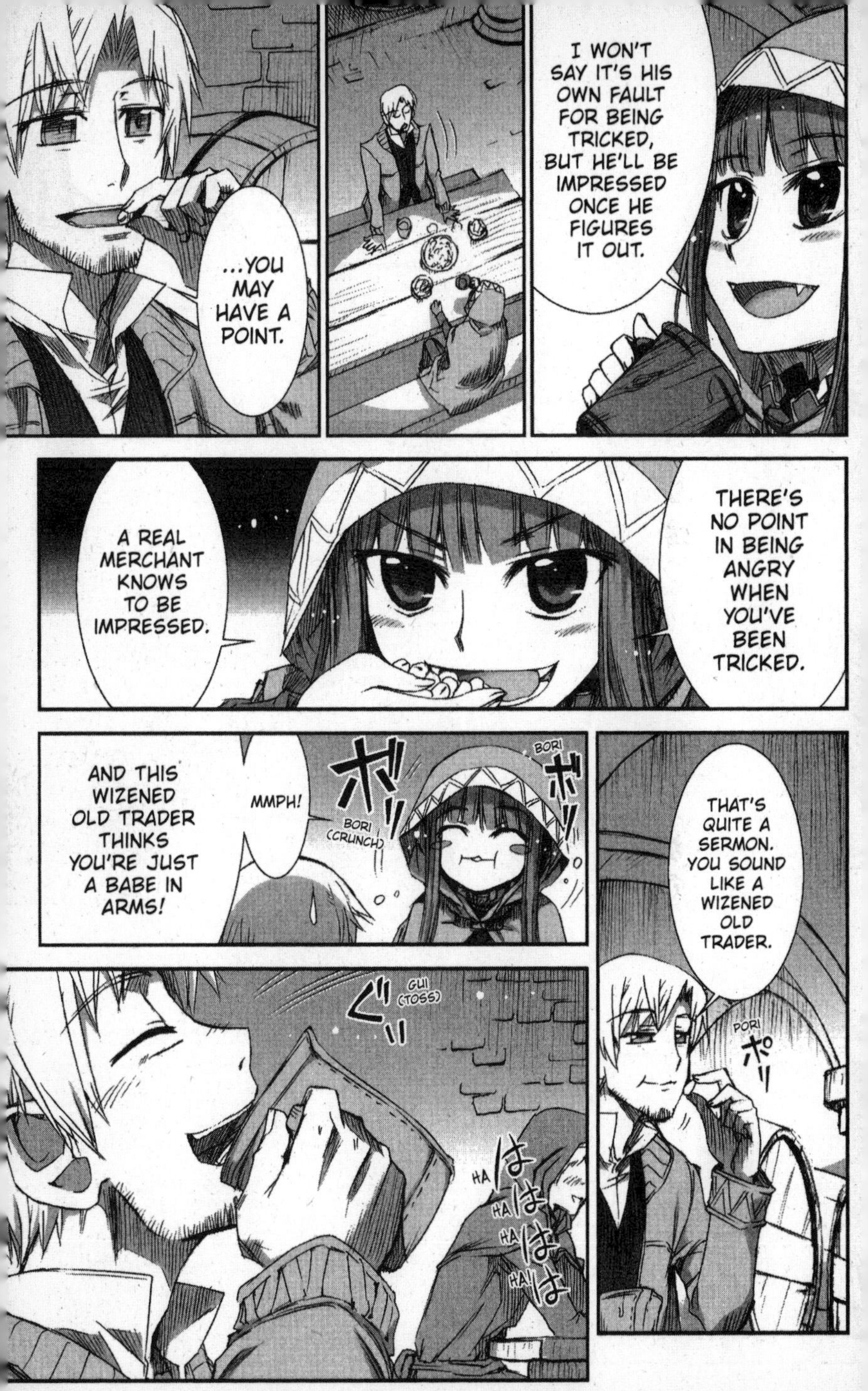
I WON'T SAY IT'S HIS OWN FAULT FOR BEING TRICKED, BUT HE'LL BE IMPRESSED ONCE HE FIGURES IT OUT.
...YOU MAY HAVE A POINT.
THERE'S NO POINT IN BEING ANGRY WHEN YOU'VE BEEN TRICKED.
A REAL MERCHANT KNOWS TO BE IMPRESSED.
THAT'S QUITE A SERMON. YOU SOUND LIKE A WIZENED OLD TRADER.
PORI
BORI
BORI (CRUNCH)
MMPH!
AND THIS WIZENED OLD TRADER THINKS YOU'RE JUST A BABE IN ARMS!
GUI (TOSS)
HA HA HA HA

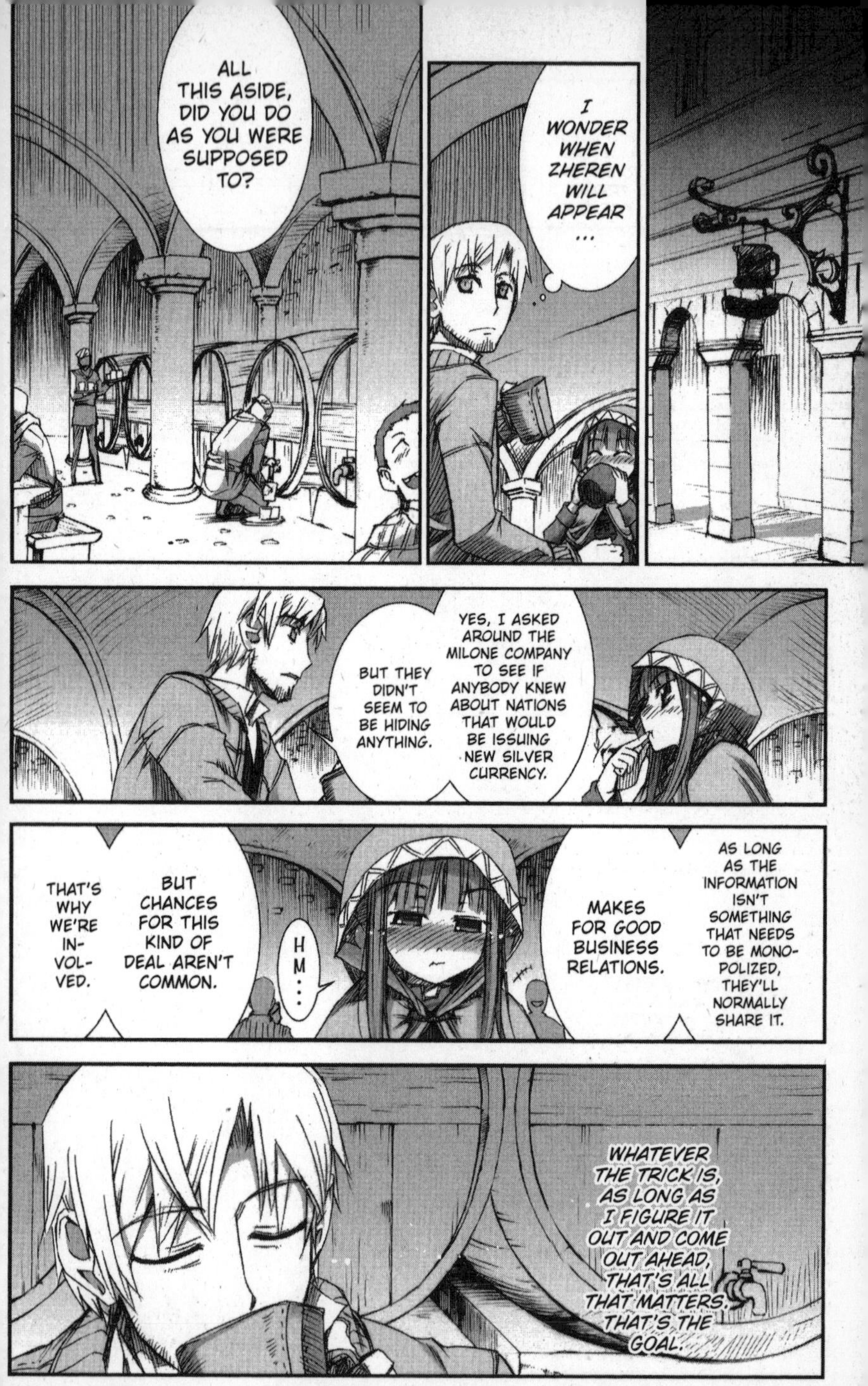
I WONDER WHEN ZHEREN WILL APPEAR...
ALL THIS ASIDE, DID YOU DO AS YOU WERE SUPPOSED TO?
YES, I ASKED AROUND THE MILONE COMPANY TO SEE IF ANYBODY KNEW ABOUT NATIONS THAT WOULD BE ISSUING NEW SILVER CURRENCY.
BUT THEY DIDN'T SEEM TO BE HIDING ANYTHING.
AS LONG AS THE INFORMATION ISN'T SOMETHING THAT NEEDS TO BE MONOPOLIZED, THEY'LL NORMALLY SHARE IT.
MAKES FOR GOOD BUSINESS RELATIONS.
HM...
BUT CHANCES FOR THIS KIND OF DEAL AREN'T COMMON.
THAT'S WHY WE'RE INVOLVED.
WHATEVER THE TRICK IS, AS LONG AS I FIGURE IT OUT AND COME OUT AHEAD, THAT'S ALL THAT MATTERS. THAT'S THE GOAL.

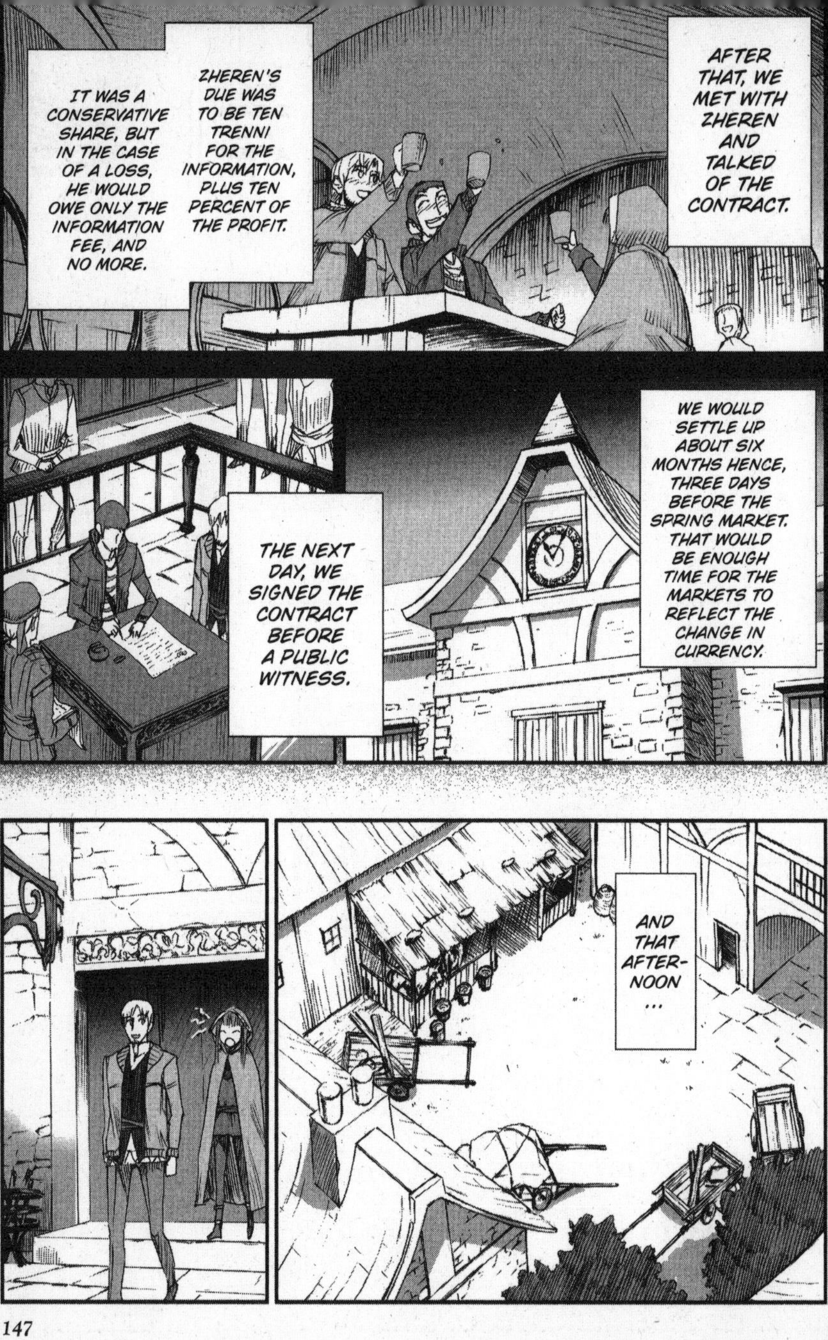
AFTER THAT, WE MET WITH ZHEREN AND TALKED OF THE CONTRACT.
ZHEREN'S DUE WAS TO BE TEN TRENNI FOR THE INFORMATION, PLUS TEN PERCENT OF THE PROFIT.
IT WAS A CONSERVATIVE SHARE, BUT IN THE CASE OF A LOSS, HE WOULD OWE ONLY THE INFORMATION FEE, AND NO MORE.
WE WOULD SETTLE UP ABOUT SIX MONTHS HENCE, THREE DAYS BEFORE THE SPRING MARKET. THAT WOULD BE ENOUGH TIME FOR THE MARKETS TO REFLECT THE CHANGE IN CURRENCY.
THE NEXT DAY, WE SIGNED THE CONTRACT BEFORE A PUBLIC WITNESS.
AND THAT AFTER-NOON ...

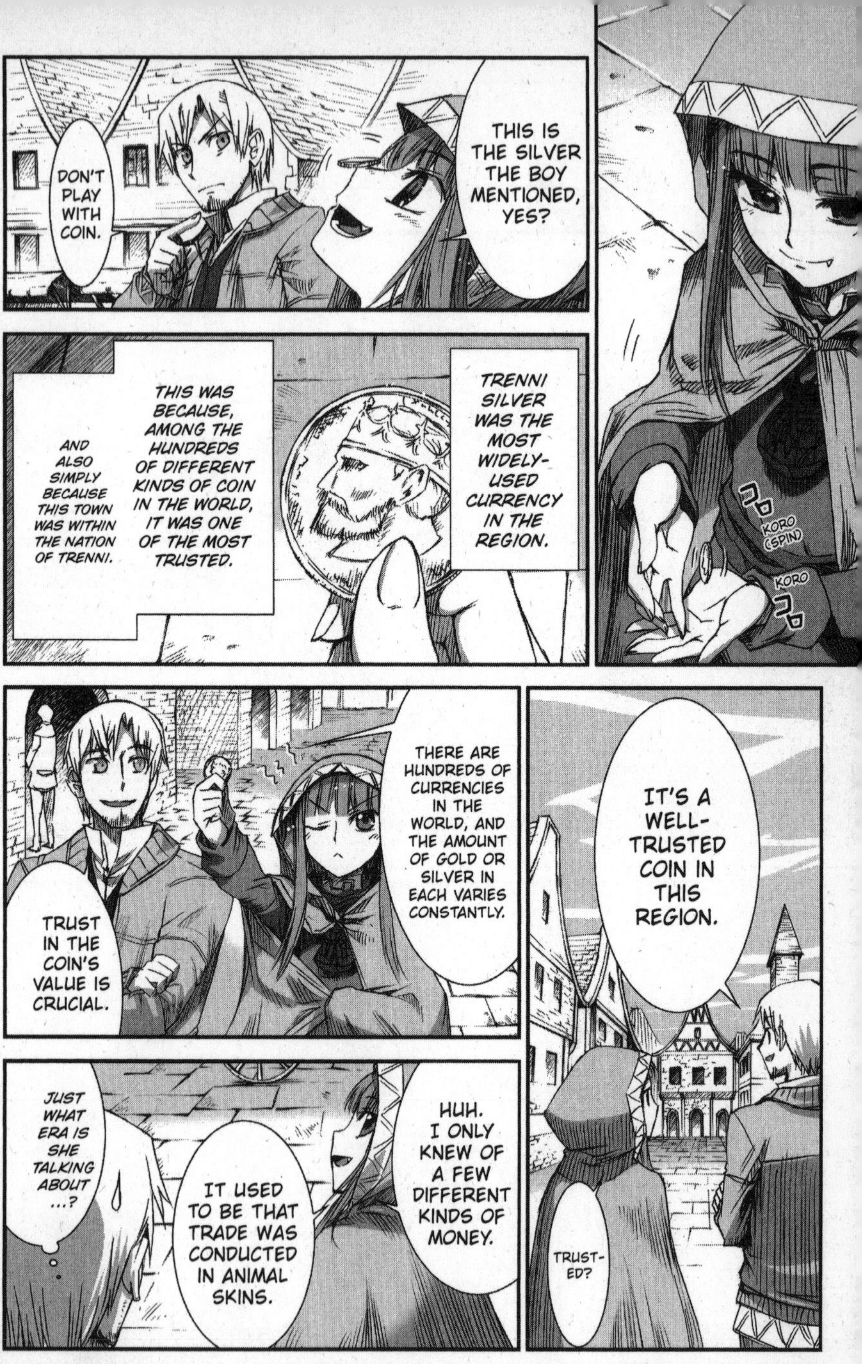

コロ
KORO (SPIN)
KORO
コロ
THIS IS THE SILVER THE BOY MENTIONED, YES?
DON'T PLAY WITH COIN.
TRENNI SILVER WAS THE MOST WIDELY-USED CURRENCY IN THE REGION.
THIS WAS BECAUSE, AMONG THE HUNDREDS OF DIFFERENT KINDS OF COIN IN THE WORLD, IT WAS ONE OF THE MOST TRUSTED.
AND ALSO SIMPLY BECAUSE THIS TOWN WAS WITHIN THE NATION OF TRENNI.
IT'S A WELL-TRUSTED COIN IN THIS REGION.
TRUST-ED?
THERE ARE HUNDREDS OF CURRENCIES IN THE WORLD, AND THE AMOUNT OF GOLD OR SILVER IN EACH VARIES CONSTANTLY.
TRUST IN THE COIN'S VALUE IS CRUCIAL.
HUH. I ONLY KNEW OF A FEW DIFFERENT KINDS OF MONEY.
IT USED TO BE THAT TRADE WAS CONDUCTED IN ANIMAL SKINS.
JUST WHAT ERA IS SHE TALKING ABOUT ...?

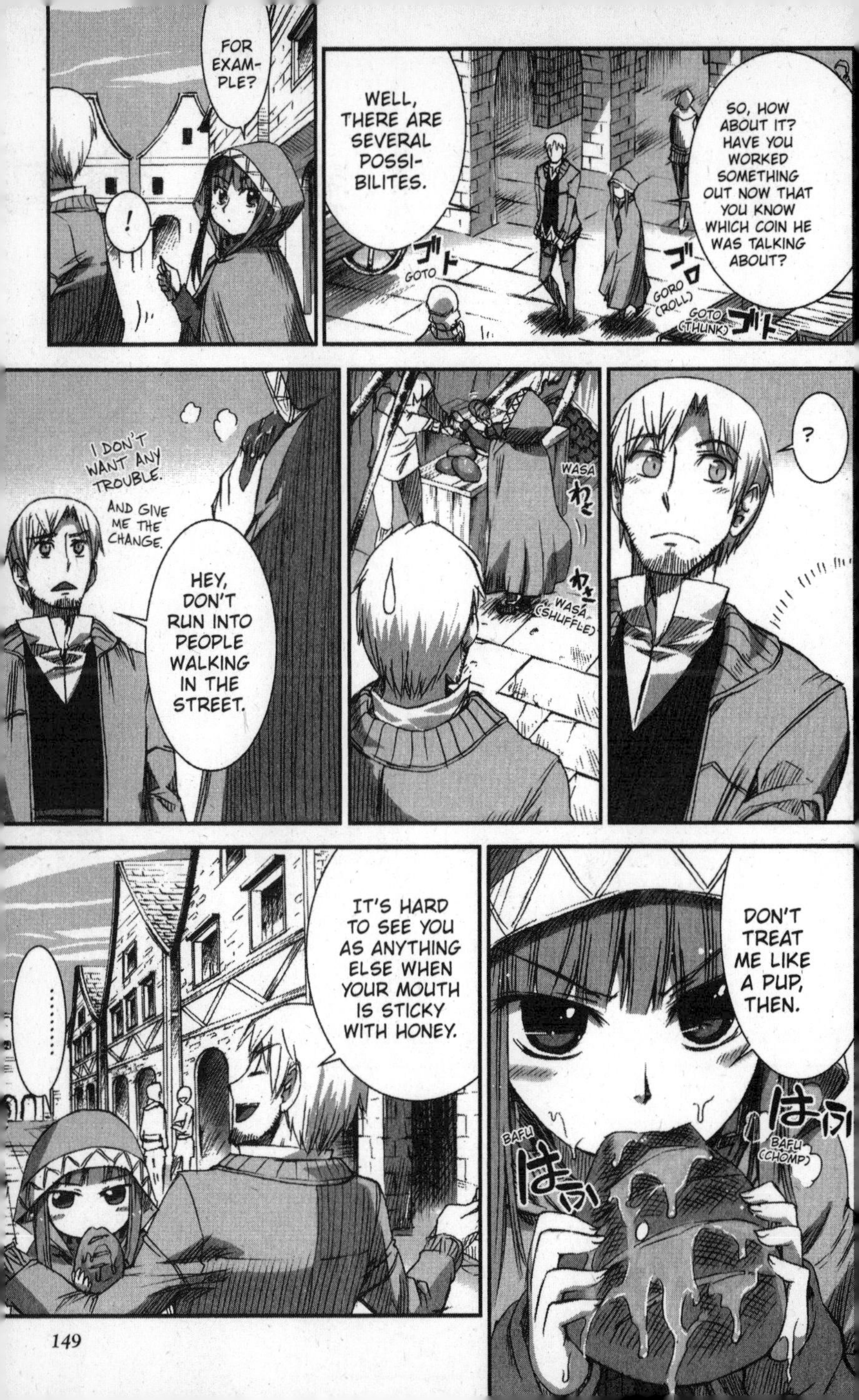
SO, HOW ABOUT IT? HAVE YOU WORKED SOMETHING OUT NOW THAT YOU KNOW WHICH COIN HE WAS TALKING ABOUT?
GOTO (THUNK)
GORO (ROLL)
GOTO
WELL, THERE ARE SEVERAL POSSI-BILITES.
FOR EXAM-PLE?
!
?
WASA
WASA (SHUFFLE)
HEY, DON'T RUN INTO PEOPLE WALKING IN THE STREET.
I DON'T WANT ANY TROUBLE.
AND GIVE ME THE CHANGE.
DON'T TREAT ME LIKE A PUP, THEN.
BAFU (CHOMP)
BAFU
IT'S HARD TO SEE YOU AS ANYTHING ELSE WHEN YOUR MOUTH IS STICKY WITH HONEY.
......

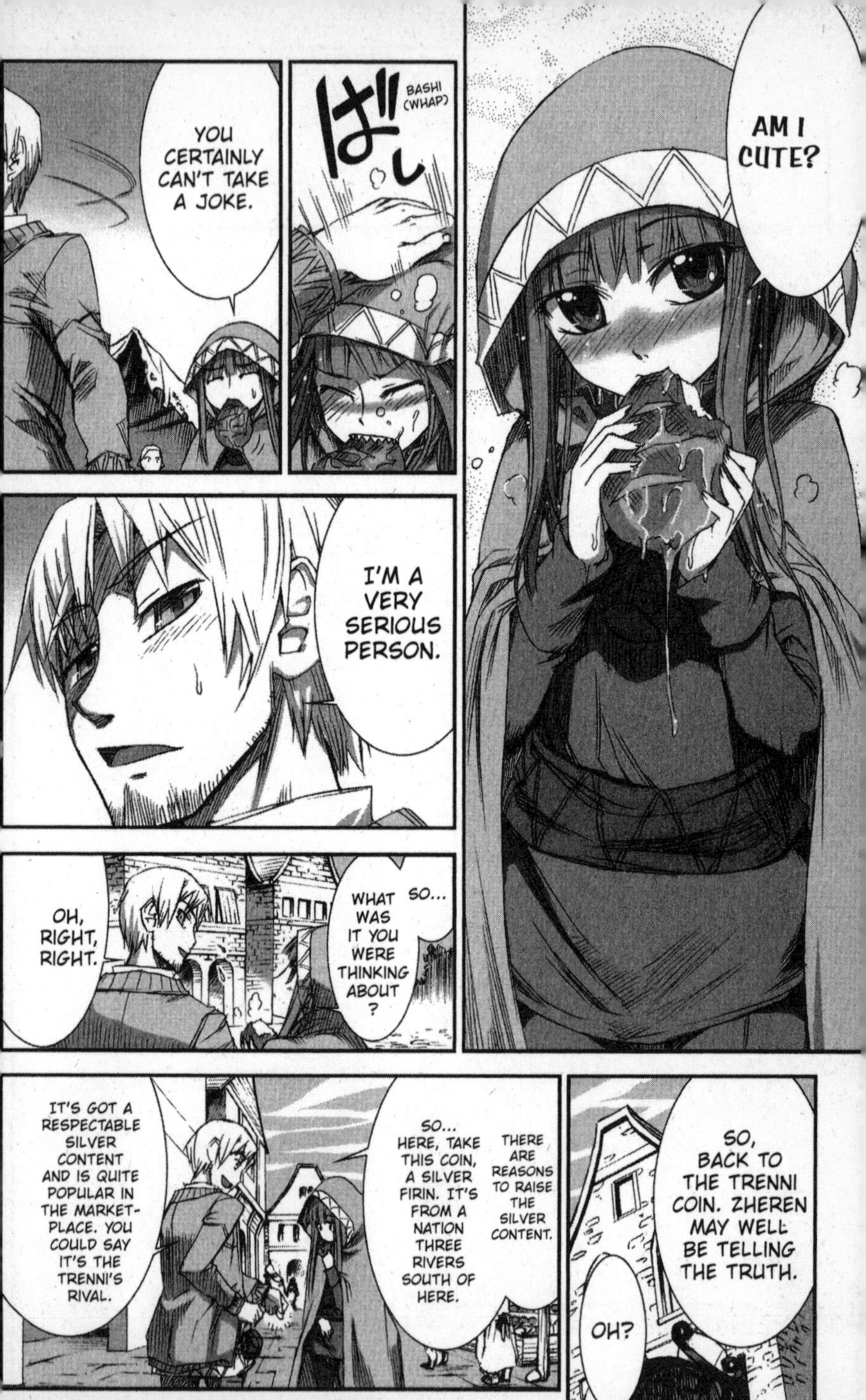
AM I CUTE?
ばし
BASHI (WHAP)
YOU CERTAINLY CAN'T TAKE A JOKE.
I'M A VERY SERIOUS PERSON.
SO...
WHAT WAS IT YOU WERE THINKING ABOUT ?
OH, RIGHT, RIGHT.
SO, BACK TO THE TRENNI COIN. ZHEREN MAY WELL BE TELLING THE TRUTH.
OH?
THERE ARE REASONS TO RAISE THE SILVER CONTENT.
SO... HERE, TAKE THIS COIN, A SILVER FIRIN. IT'S FROM A NATION THREE RIVERS SOUTH OF HERE.
IT'S GOT A RESPECTABLE SILVER CONTENT AND IS QUITE POPULAR IN THE MARKET-PLACE. YOU COULD SAY IT'S THE TRENNI'S RIVAL.

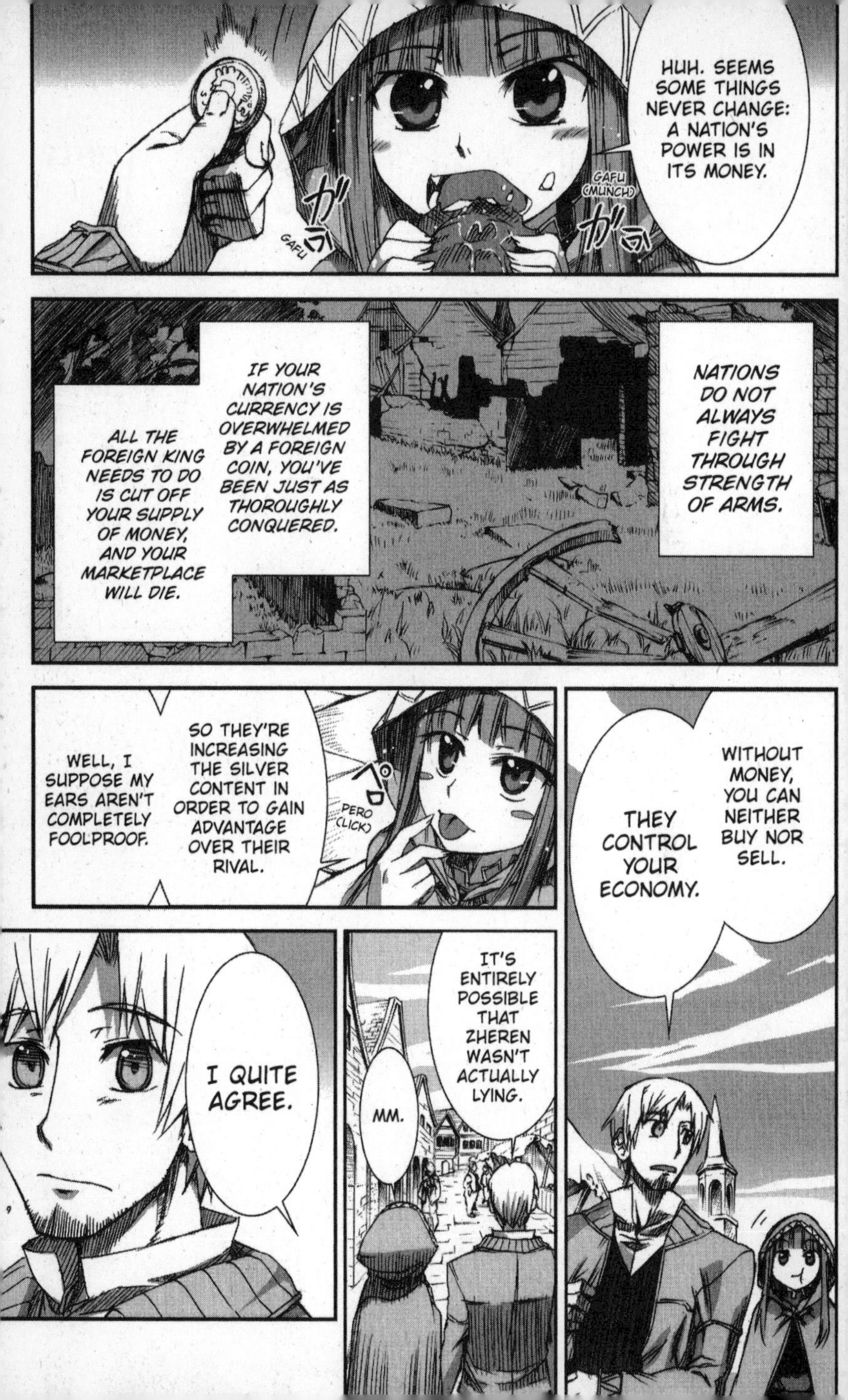
HUH. SEEMS SOME THINGS NEVER CHANGE: A NATION'S POWER IS IN ITS MONEY.
GAFU (MUNCH)
GAFU
NATIONS DO NOT ALWAYS FIGHT THROUGH STRENGTH OF ARMS.
IF YOUR NATION'S CURRENCY IS OVERWHELMED BY A FOREIGN COIN, YOU'VE BEEN JUST AS THOROUGHLY CONQUERED.
ALL THE FOREIGN KING NEEDS TO DO IS CUT OFF YOUR SUPPLY OF MONEY, AND YOUR MARKETPLACE WILL DIE.
WITHOUT MONEY, YOU CAN NEITHER BUY NOR SELL.
THEY CONTROL YOUR ECONOMY.
PERO (LICK)
SO THEY'RE INCREASING THE SILVER CONTENT IN ORDER TO GAIN ADVANTAGE OVER THEIR RIVAL.
WELL, I SUPPOSE MY EARS AREN'T COMPLETELY FOOLPROOF.
IT'S ENTIRELY POSSIBLE THAT ZHEREN WASN'T ACTUALLY LYING.
MM.
I QUITE AGREE.

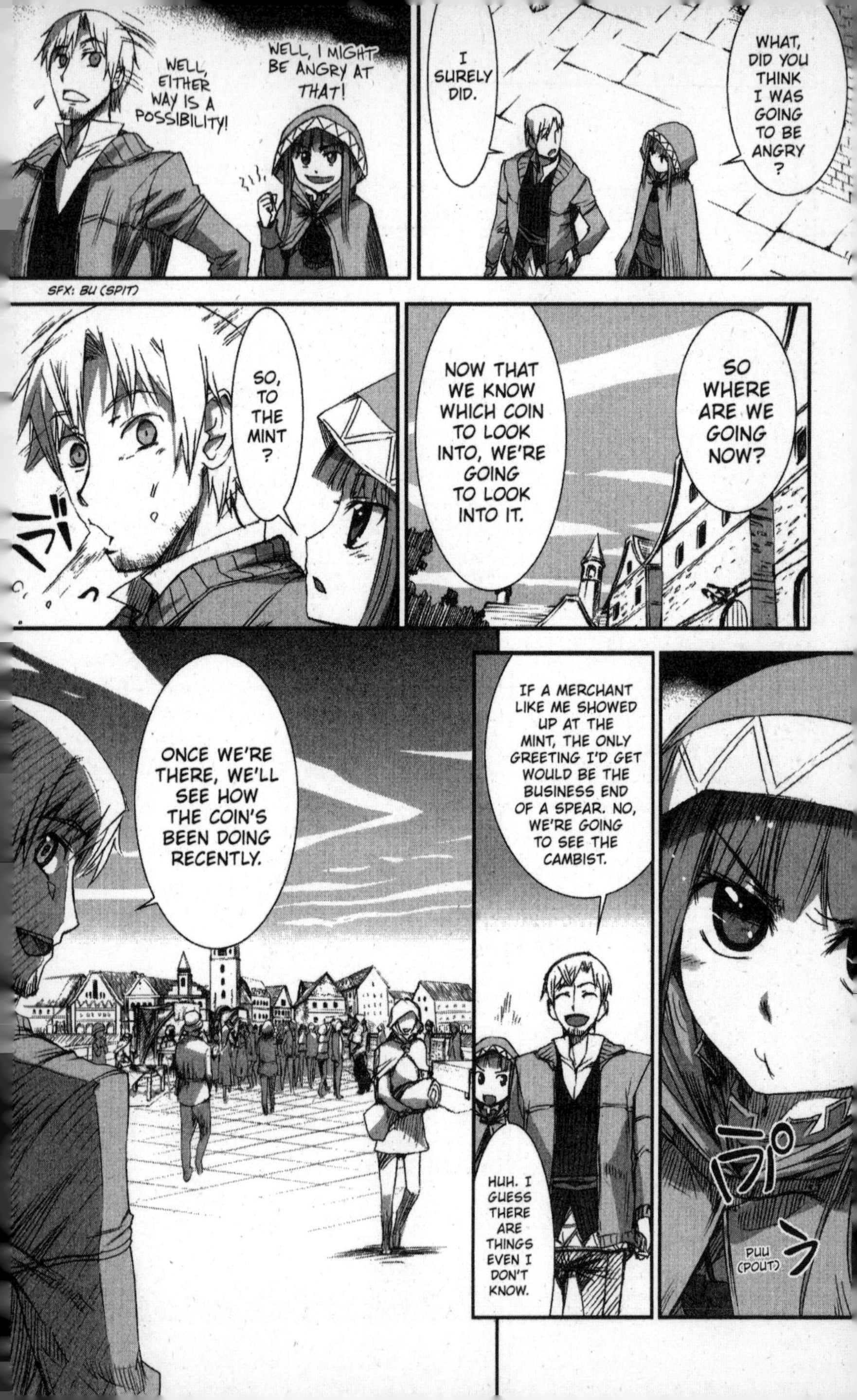
WHAT, DID YOU THINK I WAS GOING TO BE ANGRY?
I SURELY DID.
WELL, I MIGHT BE ANGRY AT THAT!
WELL, EITHER WAY IS A POSSIBILITY!
SFX: BU (SPIT)
SO WHERE ARE WE GOING NOW?
NOW THAT WE KNOW WHICH COIN TO LOOK INTO, WE'RE GOING TO LOOK INTO IT.
SO, TO THE MINT?
PUU (POUT)
IF A MERCHANT LIKE ME SHOWED UP AT THE MINT, THE ONLY GREETING I'D GET WOULD BE THE BUSINESS END OF A SPEAR. NO, WE'RE GOING TO SEE THE CAMBIST.
HUH. I GUESS THERE ARE THINGS EVEN I DON'T KNOW.
ONCE WE'RE THERE, WE'LL SEE HOW THE COIN'S BEEN DOING RECENTLY.

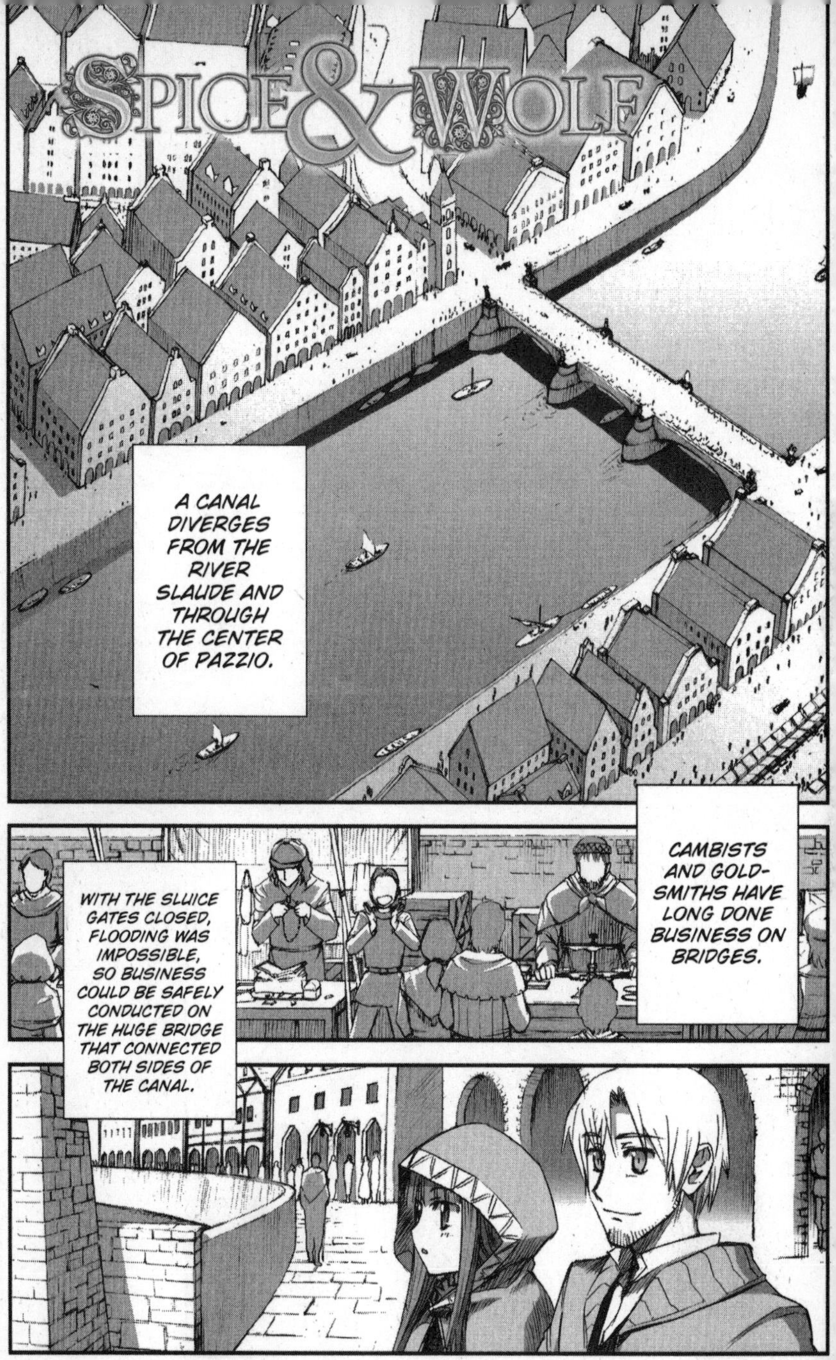
SPICE & WOLF
A CANAL DIVERGES FROM THE RIVER SLAUDE AND THROUGH THE CENTER OF PAZZIO.
CAMBISTS AND GOLD-SMITHS HAVE LONG DONE BUSINESS ON BRIDGES.
WITH THE SLUICE GATES CLOSED, FLOODING WAS IMPOSSIBLE, SO BUSINESS COULD BE SAFELY CONDUCTED ON THE HUGE BRIDGE THAT CONNECTED BOTH SIDES OF THE CANAL.

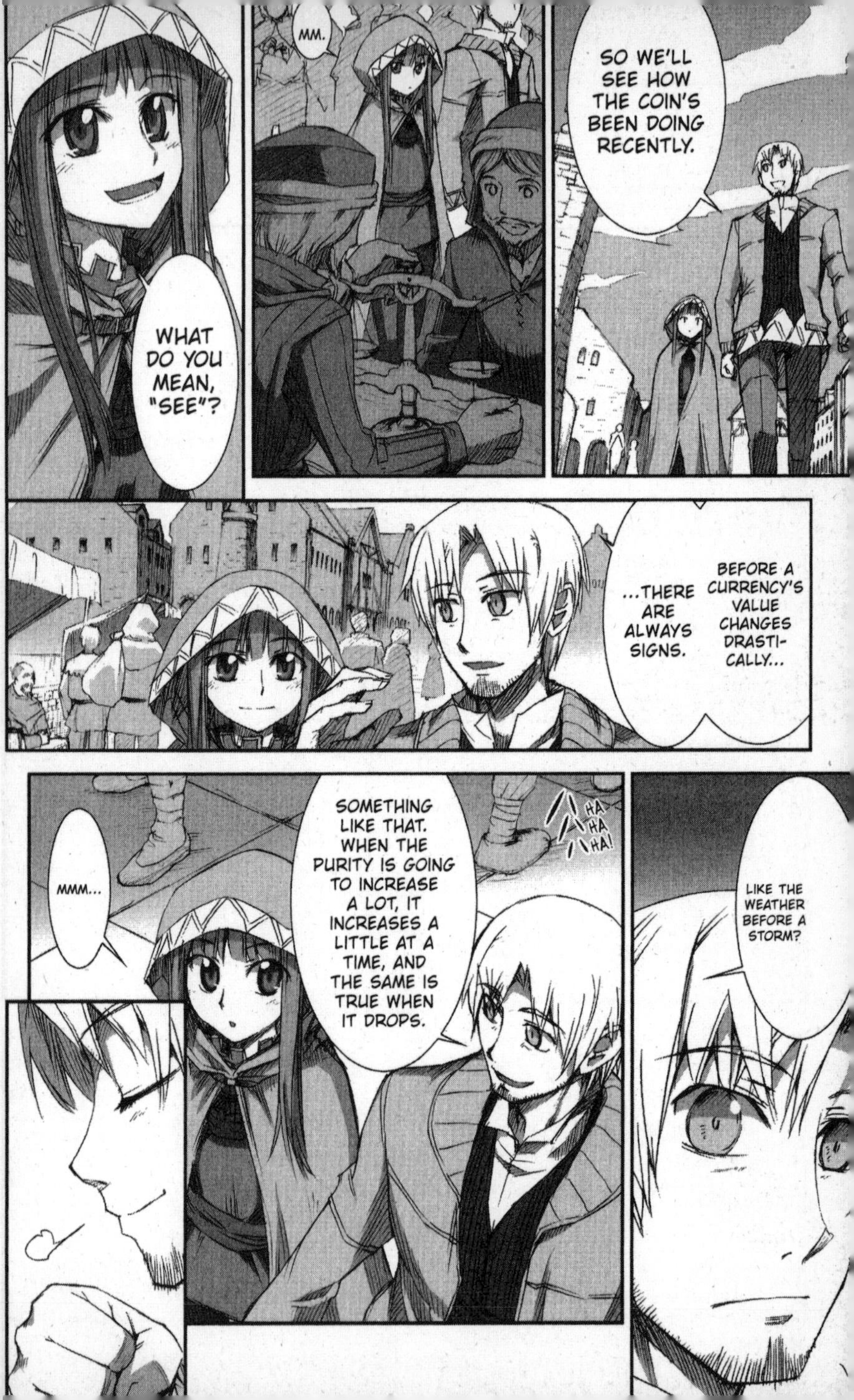
SO WE'LL SEE HOW THE COIN'S BEEN DOING RECENTLY.
MM.
WHAT DO YOU MEAN, "SEE"?
BEFORE A CURRENCY'S VALUE CHANGES DRASTICALLY...
...THERE ARE ALWAYS SIGNS.
LIKE THE WEATHER BEFORE A STORM?
HA HA HA!
SOMETHING LIKE THAT. WHEN THE PURITY IS GOING TO INCREASE A LOT, IT INCREASES A LITTLE AT A TIME, AND THE SAME IS TRUE WHEN IT DROPS.
MMM...

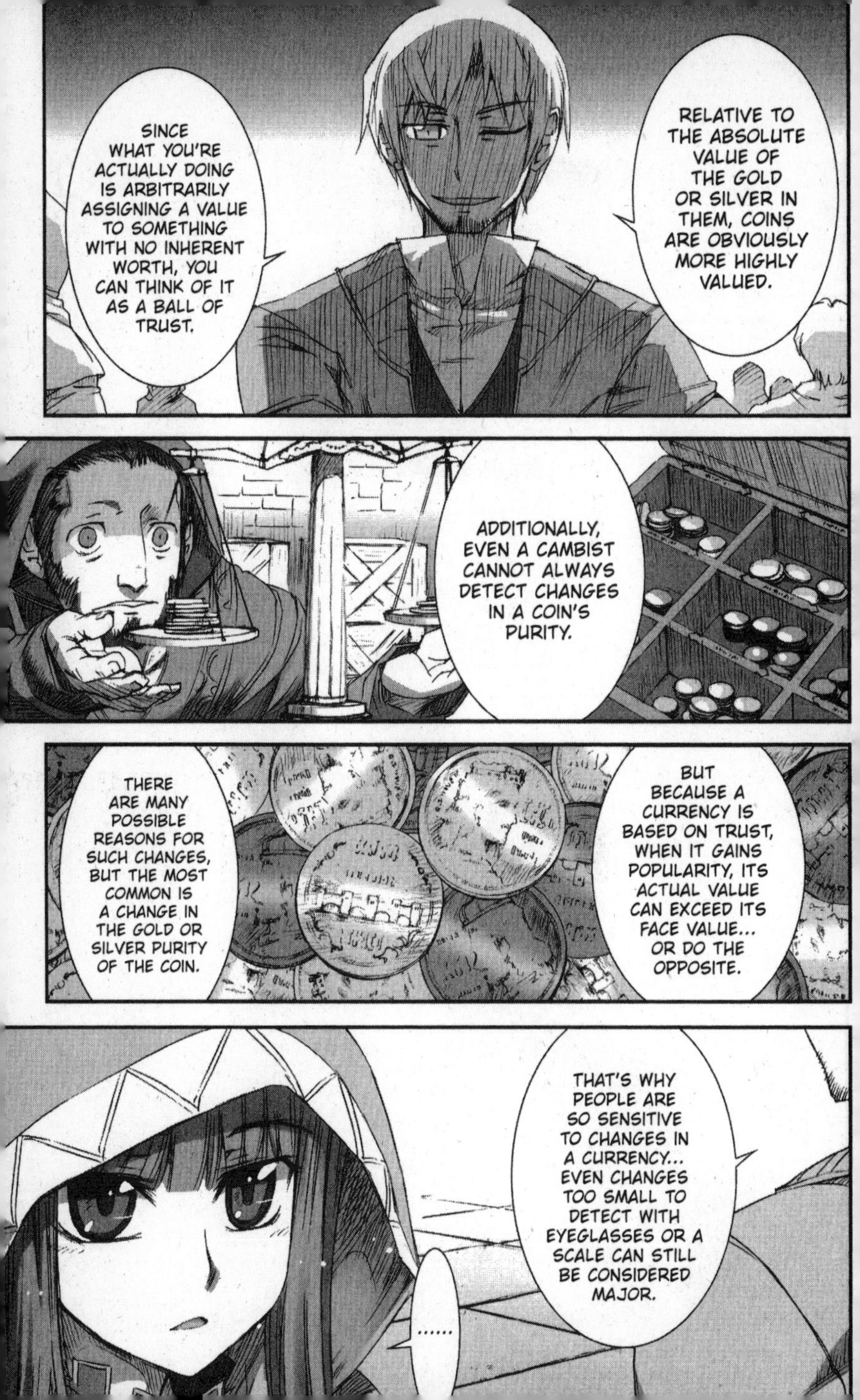
RELATIVE TO THE ABSOLUTE VALUE OF THE GOLD OR SILVER IN THEM, COINS ARE OBVIOUSLY MORE HIGHLY VALUED.
SINCE WHAT YOU'RE ACTUALLY DOING IS ARBITRARILY ASSIGNING A VALUE TO SOMETHING WITH NO INHERENT WORTH, YOU CAN THINK OF IT AS A BALL OF TRUST.
ADDITIONALLY, EVEN A CAMBIST CANNOT ALWAYS DETECT CHANGES IN A COIN'S PURITY.
BUT BECAUSE A CURRENCY IS BASED ON TRUST, WHEN IT GAINS POPULARITY, ITS ACTUAL VALUE CAN EXCEED ITS FACE VALUE... OR DO THE OPPOSITE.
THERE ARE MANY POSSIBLE REASONS FOR SUCH CHANGES, BUT THE MOST COMMON IS A CHANGE IN THE GOLD OR SILVER PURITY OF THE COIN.
THAT'S WHY PEOPLE ARE SO SENSITIVE TO CHANGES IN A CURRENCY... EVEN CHANGES TOO SMALL TO DETECT WITH EYEGLASSES OR A SCALE CAN STILL BE CONSIDERED MAJOR.
......

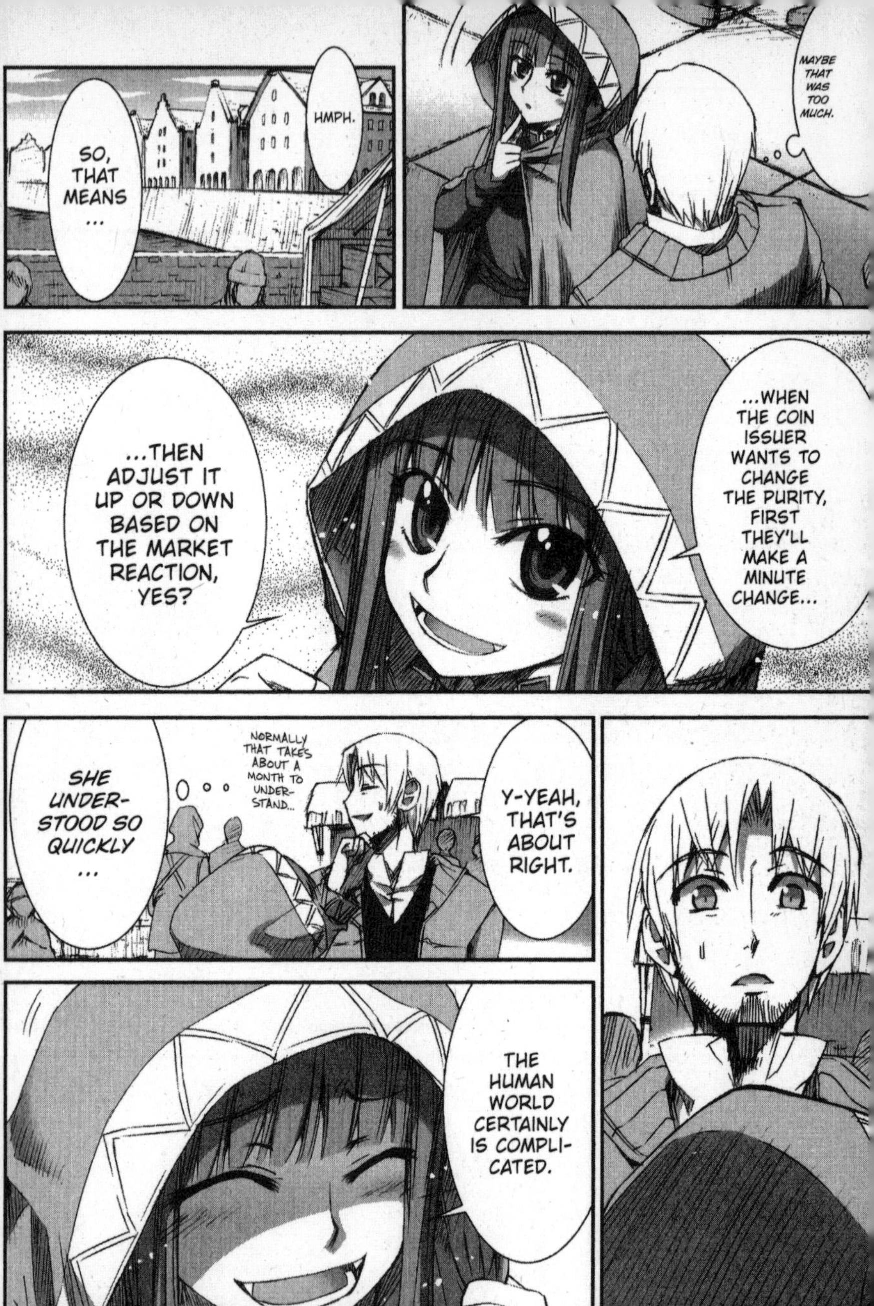
MAYBE THAT WAS TOO MUCH.
HMPH.
SO, THAT MEANS...
...WHEN THE COIN ISSUER WANTS TO CHANGE THE PURITY, FIRST THEY'LL MAKE A MINUTE CHANGE...
...THEN ADJUST IT UP OR DOWN BASED ON THE MARKET REACTION, YES?
Y-YEAH, THAT'S ABOUT RIGHT.
NORMALLY THAT TAKES ABOUT A MONTH TO UNDER-STAND...
SHE UNDER-STOOD SO QUICKLY...
THE HUMAN WORLD CERTAINLY IS COMPLI-CATED.

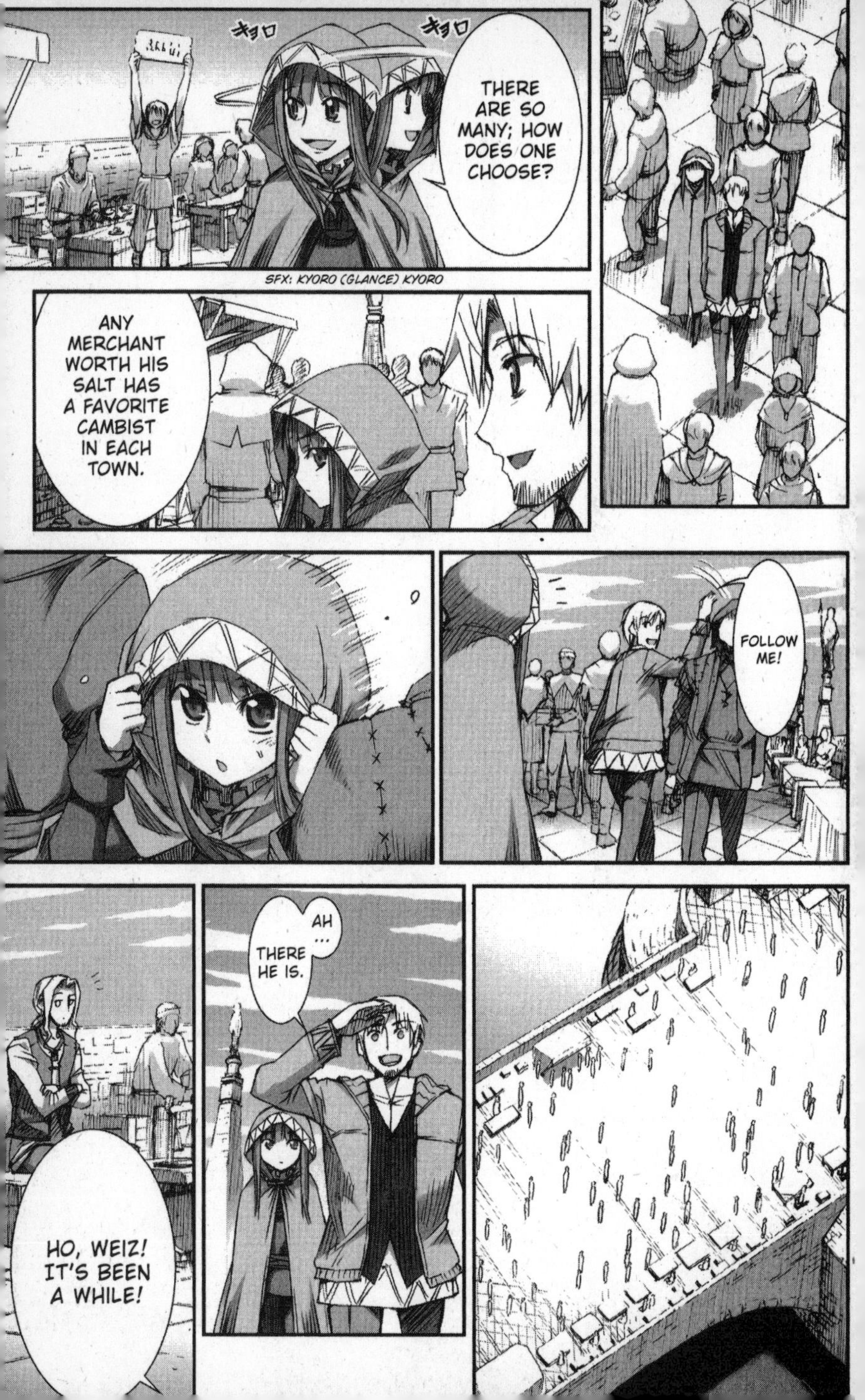
キョロ
キョロ
THERE ARE SO MANY; HOW DOES ONE CHOOSE?
SFX: KYORO (GLANCE) KYORO
ANY MERCHANT WORTH HIS SALT HAS A FAVORITE CAMBIST IN EACH TOWN.
FOLLOW ME!
AH ... THERE HE IS.
HO, WEIZ! IT'S BEEN A WHILE!

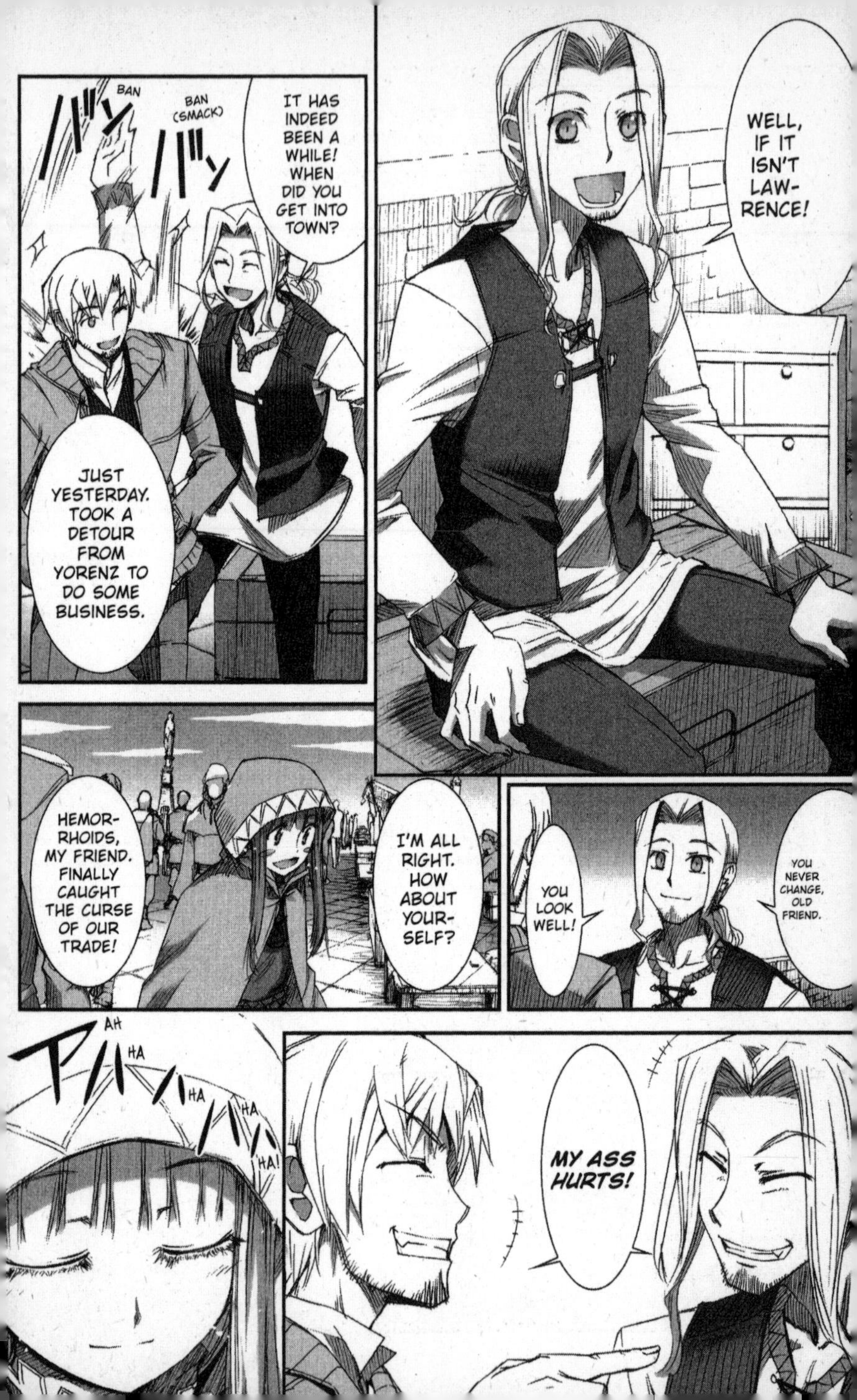
WELL, IF IT ISN'T LAWRENCE!
BAN
BAN (SMACK)
IT HAS INDEED BEEN A WHILE! WHEN DID YOU GET INTO TOWN?
JUST YESTERDAY. TOOK A DETOUR FROM YORENZ TO DO SOME BUSINESS.
YOU NEVER CHANGE, OLD FRIEND.
YOU LOOK WELL!
I'M ALL RIGHT. HOW ABOUT YOURSELF?
HEMORRHOIDS, MY FRIEND. FINALLY CAUGHT THE CURSE OF OUR TRADE!
MY ASS HURTS!
AH HA HA HA HA!

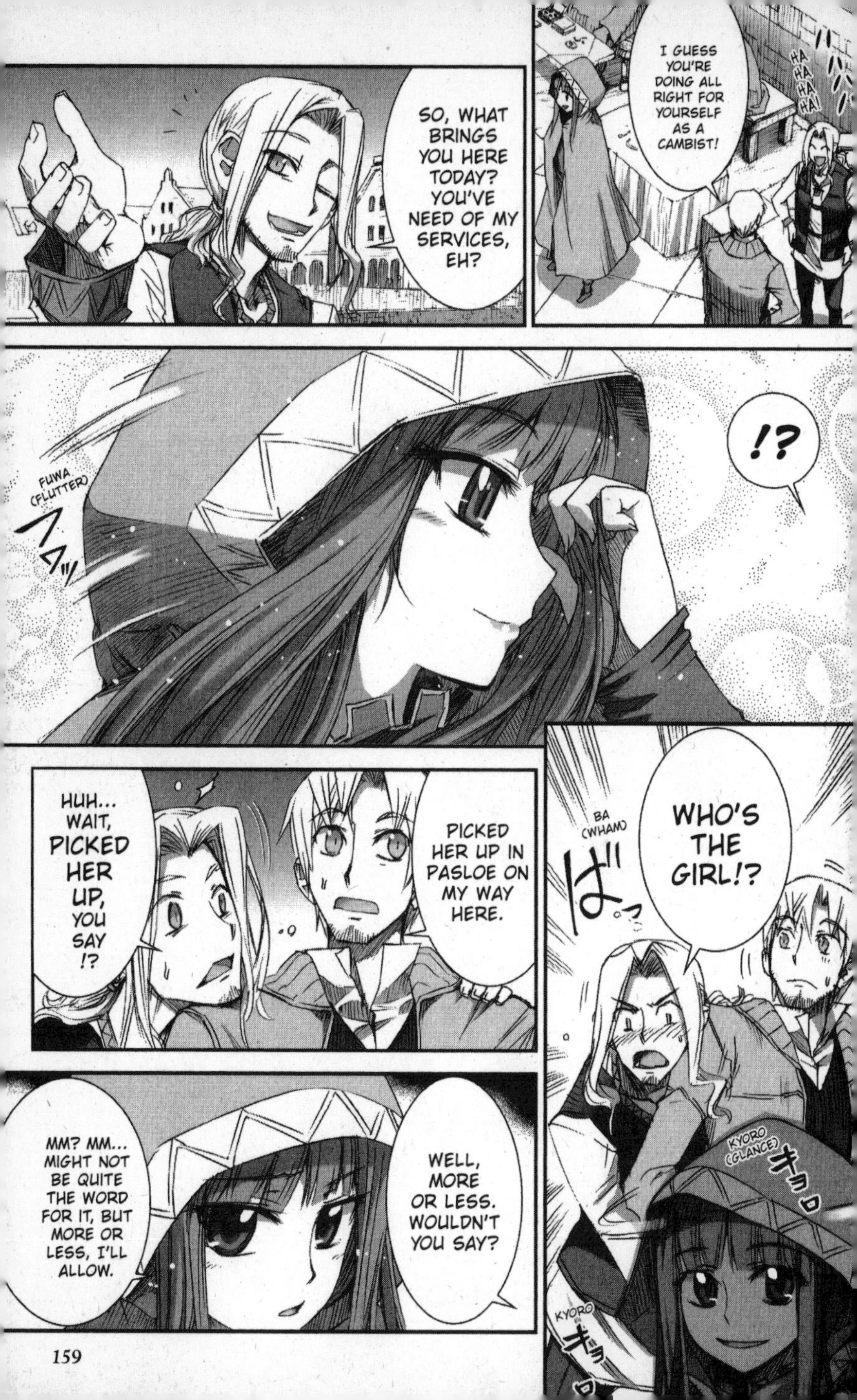
HA HA HA HA!
I GUESS YOU'RE DOING ALL RIGHT FOR YOURSELF AS A CAMBIST!
SO, WHAT BRINGS YOU HERE TODAY? YOU'VE NEED OF MY SERVICES, EH?
!?
FUWA (FLUTTER)
BA (WHAM)
WHO'S THE GIRL!?
KYORO (GLANCE)
KYORO
PICKED HER UP IN PASLOE ON MY WAY HERE.
HUH... WAIT, PICKED HER UP, YOU SAY!?
WELL, MORE OR LESS. WOULDN'T YOU SAY?
MM? MM... MIGHT NOT BE QUITE THE WORD FOR IT, BUT MORE OR LESS, I'LL ALLOW.

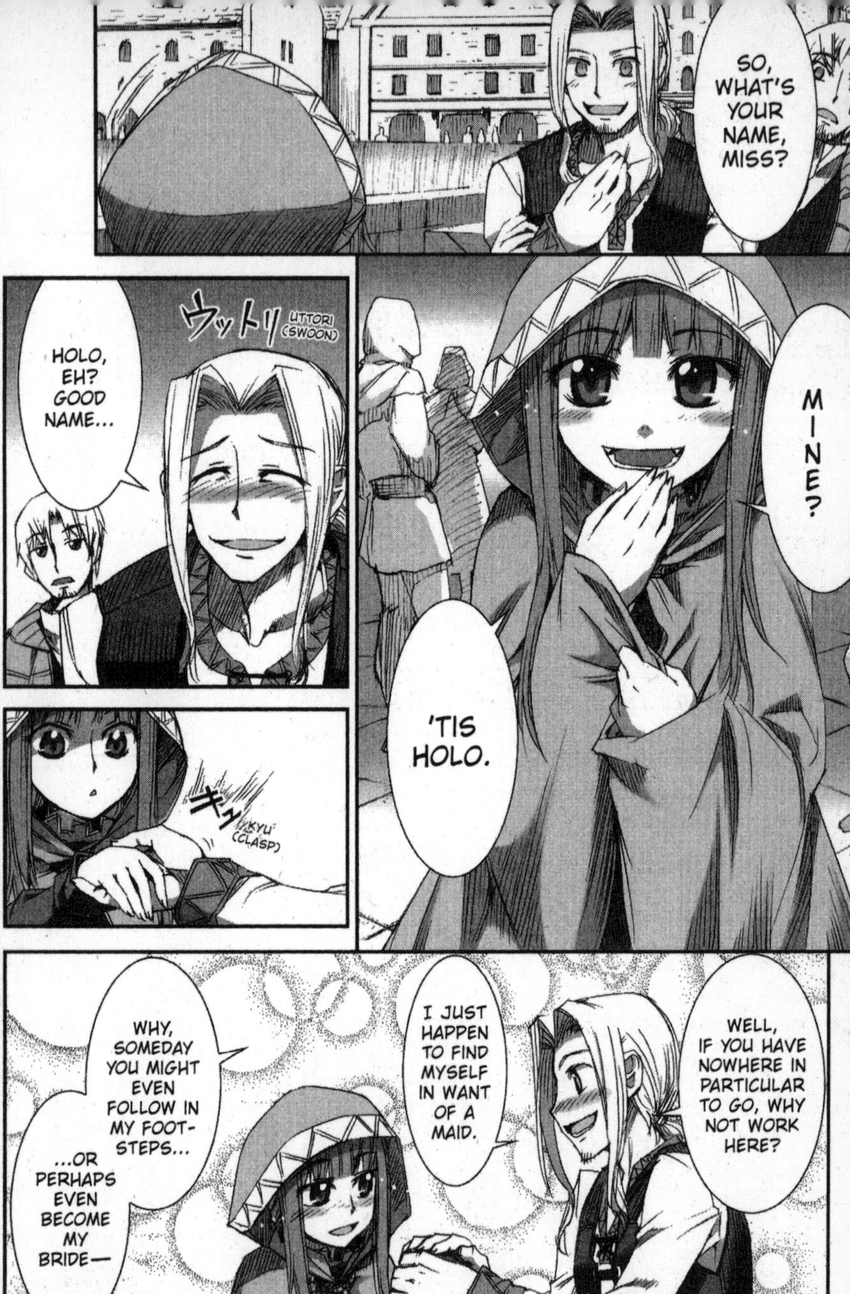
SO, WHAT'S YOUR NAME, MISS?
MINE?
'TIS HOLO.
ウットリ UTTORI (SWOON)
HOLO, EH? GOOD NAME...
キュッ KYU (CLASP)
WELL, IF YOU HAVE NOWHERE IN PARTICULAR TO GO, WHY NOT WORK HERE?
I JUST HAPPEN TO FIND MYSELF IN WANT OF A MAID.
WHY, SOMEDAY YOU MIGHT EVEN FOLLOW IN MY FOOT-STEPS...
...OR PERHAPS EVEN BECOME MY BRIDE—

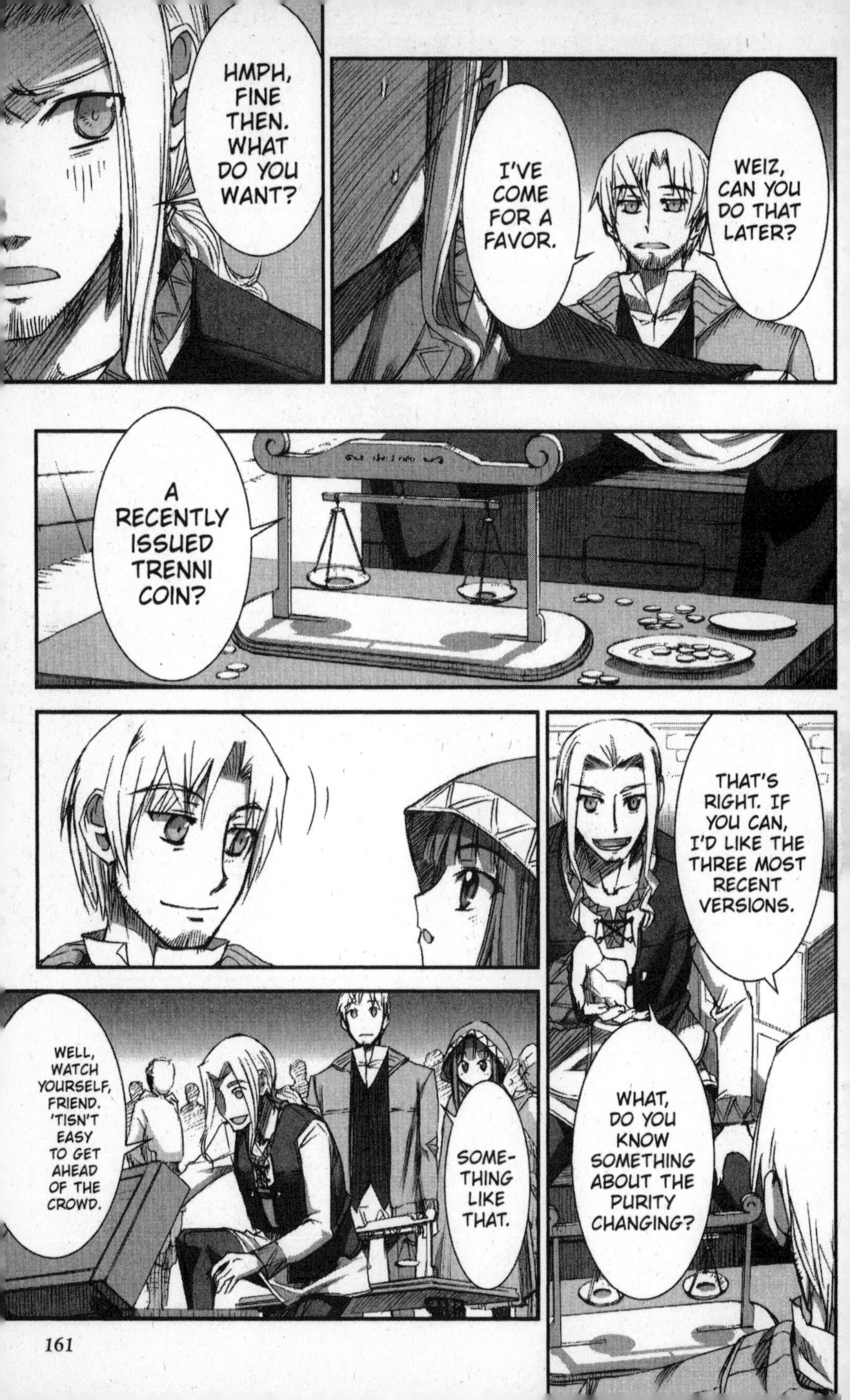
WEIZ, CAN YOU DO THAT LATER?
I'VE COME FOR A FAVOR.
HMPH, FINE THEN. WHAT DO YOU WANT?
A RECENTLY ISSUED TRENNI COIN?
THAT'S RIGHT. IF YOU CAN, I'D LIKE THE THREE MOST RECENT VERSIONS.
WHAT, DO YOU KNOW SOMETHING ABOUT THE PURITY CHANGING?
SOME-THING LIKE THAT.
WELL, WATCH YOURSELF, FRIEND. 'TISN'T EASY TO GET AHEAD OF THE CROWD.

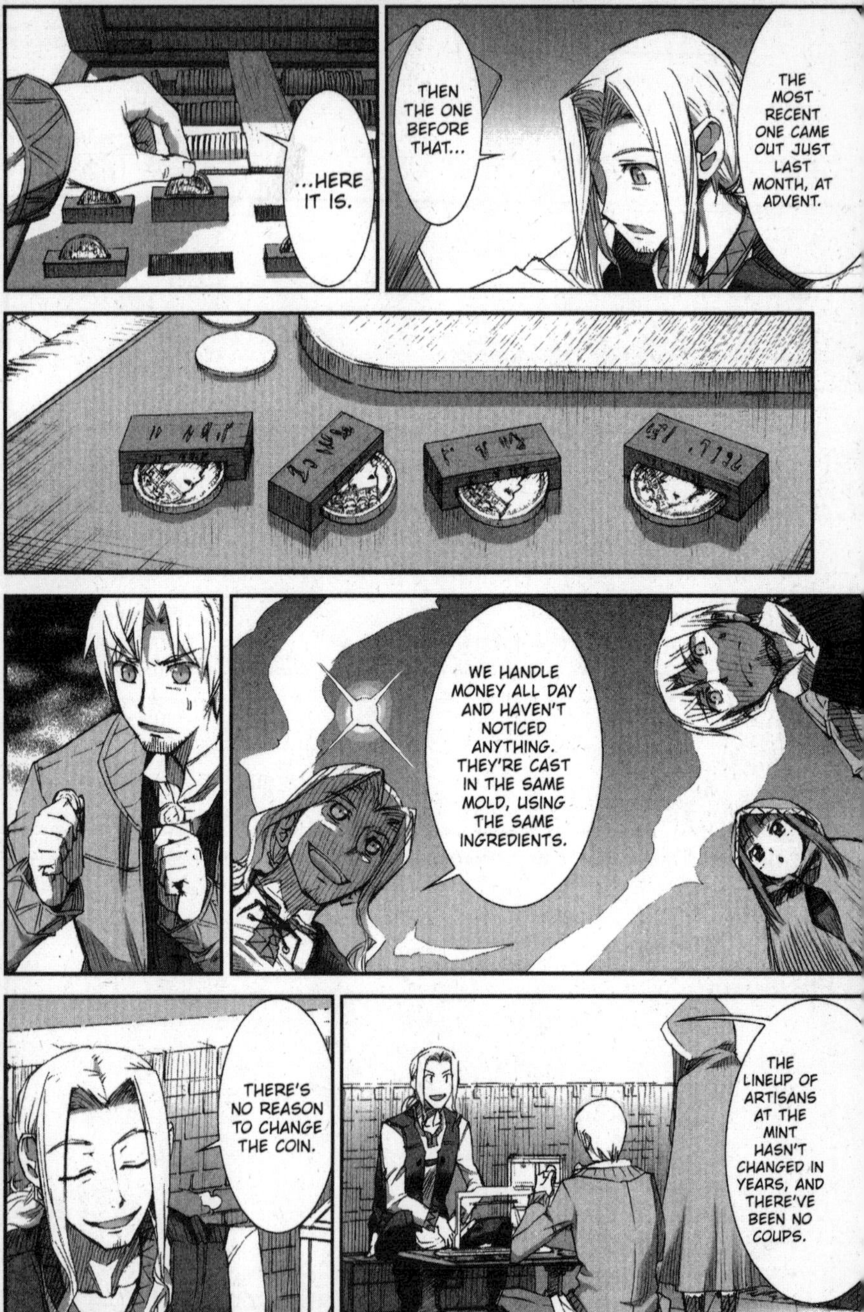
THE MOST RECENT ONE CAME OUT JUST LAST MONTH, AT ADVENT.
THEN THE ONE BEFORE THAT...
...HERE IT IS.
WE HANDLE MONEY ALL DAY AND HAVEN'T NOTICED ANYTHING. THEY'RE CAST IN THE SAME MOLD, USING THE SAME INGREDIENTS.
THE LINEUP OF ARTISANS AT THE MINT HASN'T CHANGED IN YEARS, AND THERE'VE BEEN NO COUPS.
THERE'S NO REASON TO CHANGE THE COIN.

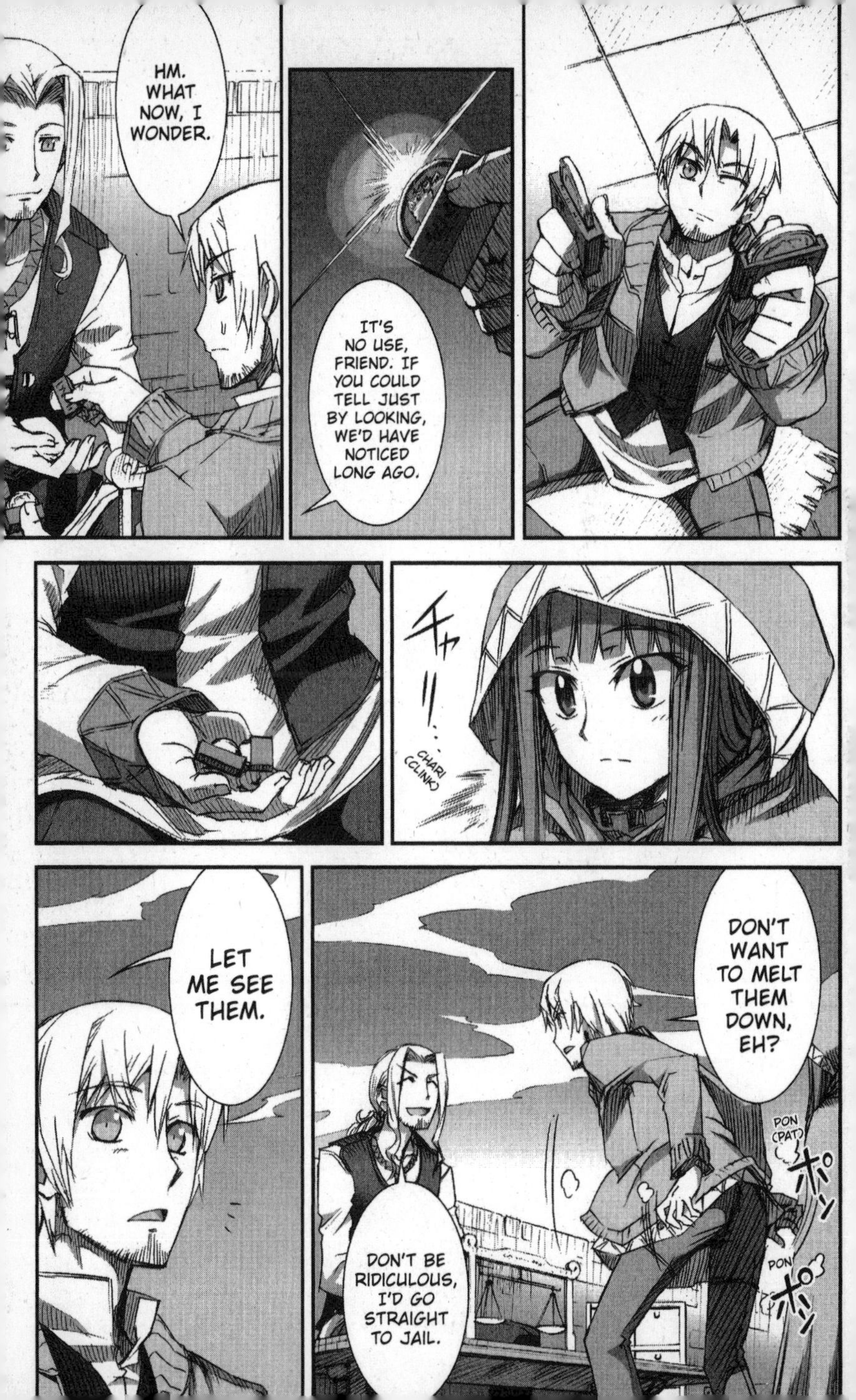
IT'S NO USE, FRIEND. IF YOU COULD TELL JUST BY LOOKING, WE'D HAVE NOTICED LONG AGO.
HM. WHAT NOW, I WONDER.
CHARI (CLINK)
DON'T WANT TO MELT THEM DOWN, EH?
PON (PAT)
PON
DON'T BE RIDICULOUS, I'D GO STRAIGHT TO JAIL.
LET ME SEE THEM.

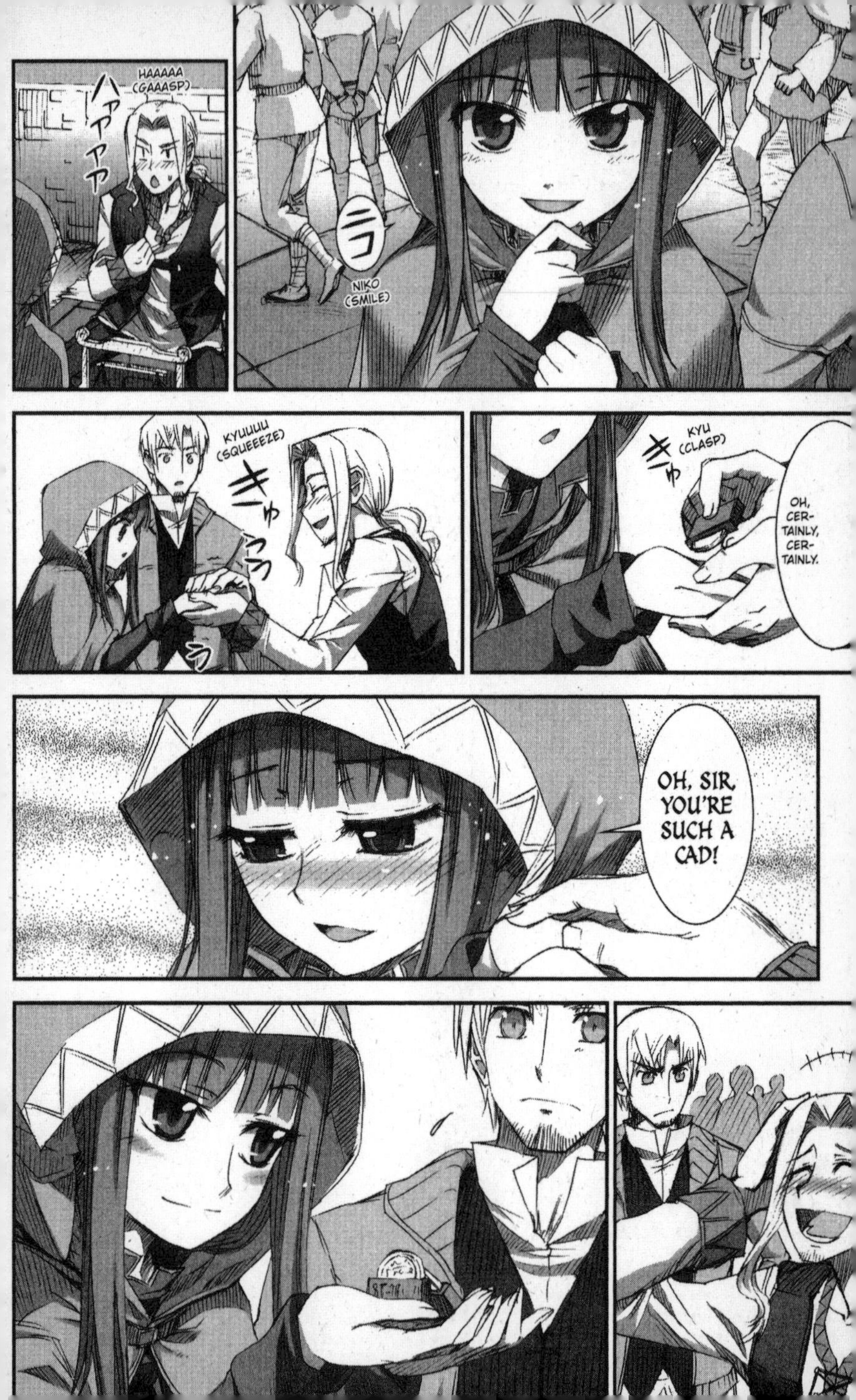
ニコ
NIKO (SMILE)
ハァァァ
HAAAAA (GAAASP)
OH, CER-TAINLY, CER-TAINLY.
KYU (CLASP)
KYUUUU (SQUEEEZE)
OH, SIR, YOU'RE SUCH A CAD!

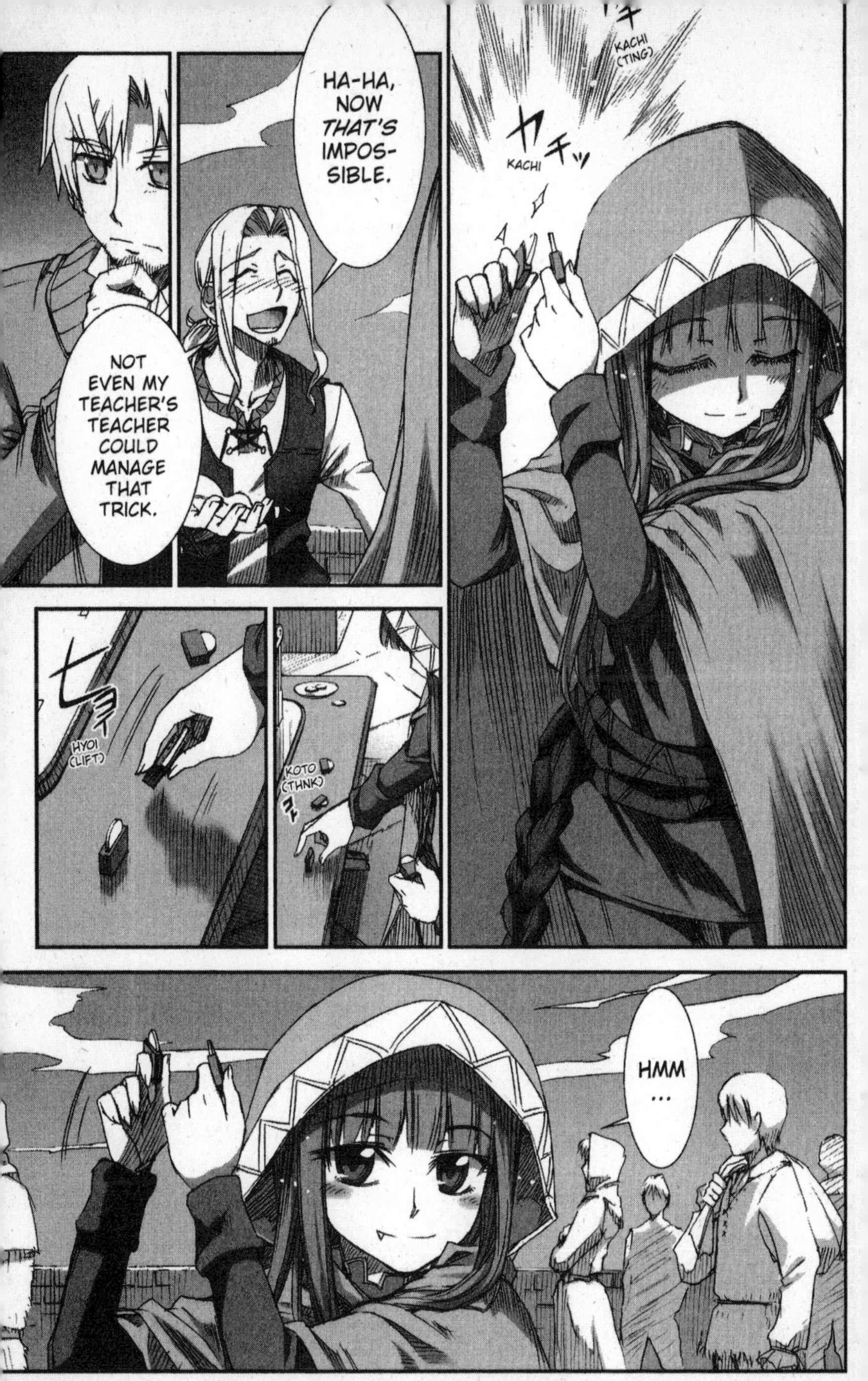
KACHI (TING)
KACHI
HA-HA, NOW THAT'S IMPOSSIBLE.
NOT EVEN MY TEACHER'S TEACHER COULD MANAGE THAT TRICK.
KOTO (THNK)
HYOI (LIFT)
HMM...

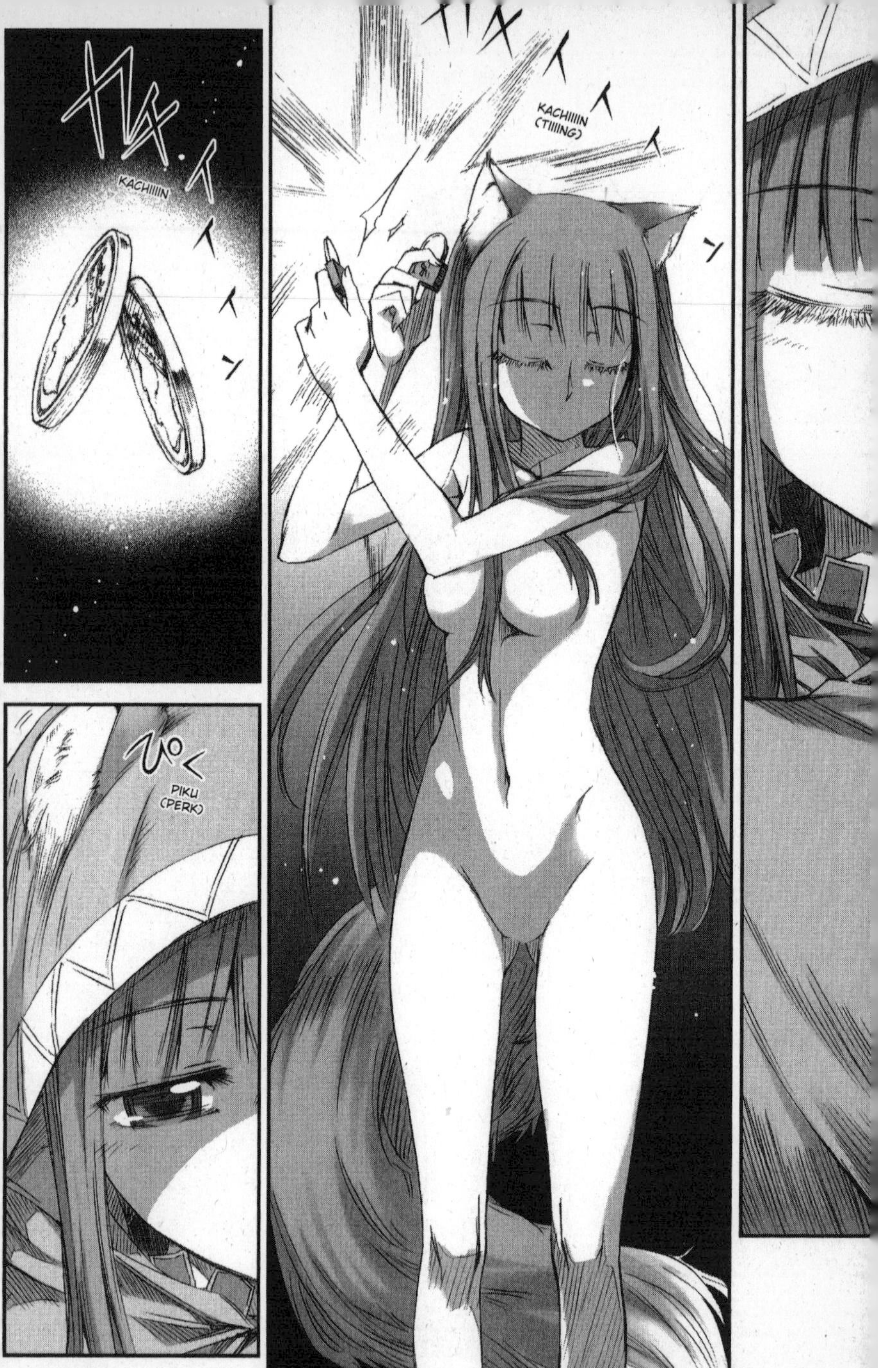
KACHIIIIN
(TIIIING)
KACHIIIIN
ぴく
PIKU
(PERK)

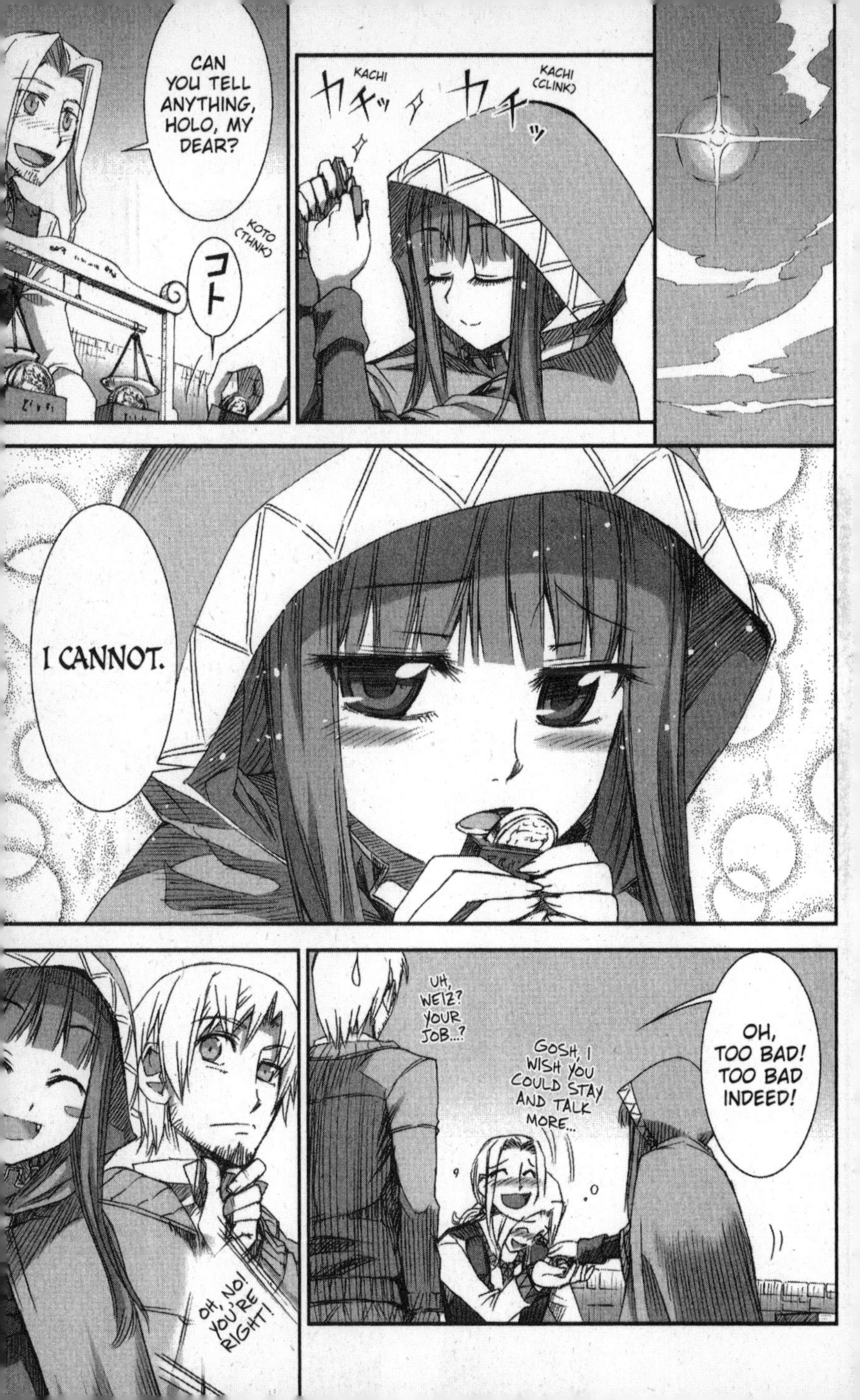
KACHI (CLINK)
KACHI
CAN YOU TELL ANYTHING, HOLO, MY DEAR?
KOTO (THNK)
コト
I CANNOT.
OH, TOO BAD! TOO BAD INDEED!
GOSH, I WISH YOU COULD STAY AND TALK MORE...
UH, WEIZ? YOUR JOB...?
OH, NO! YOU'RE RIGHT!

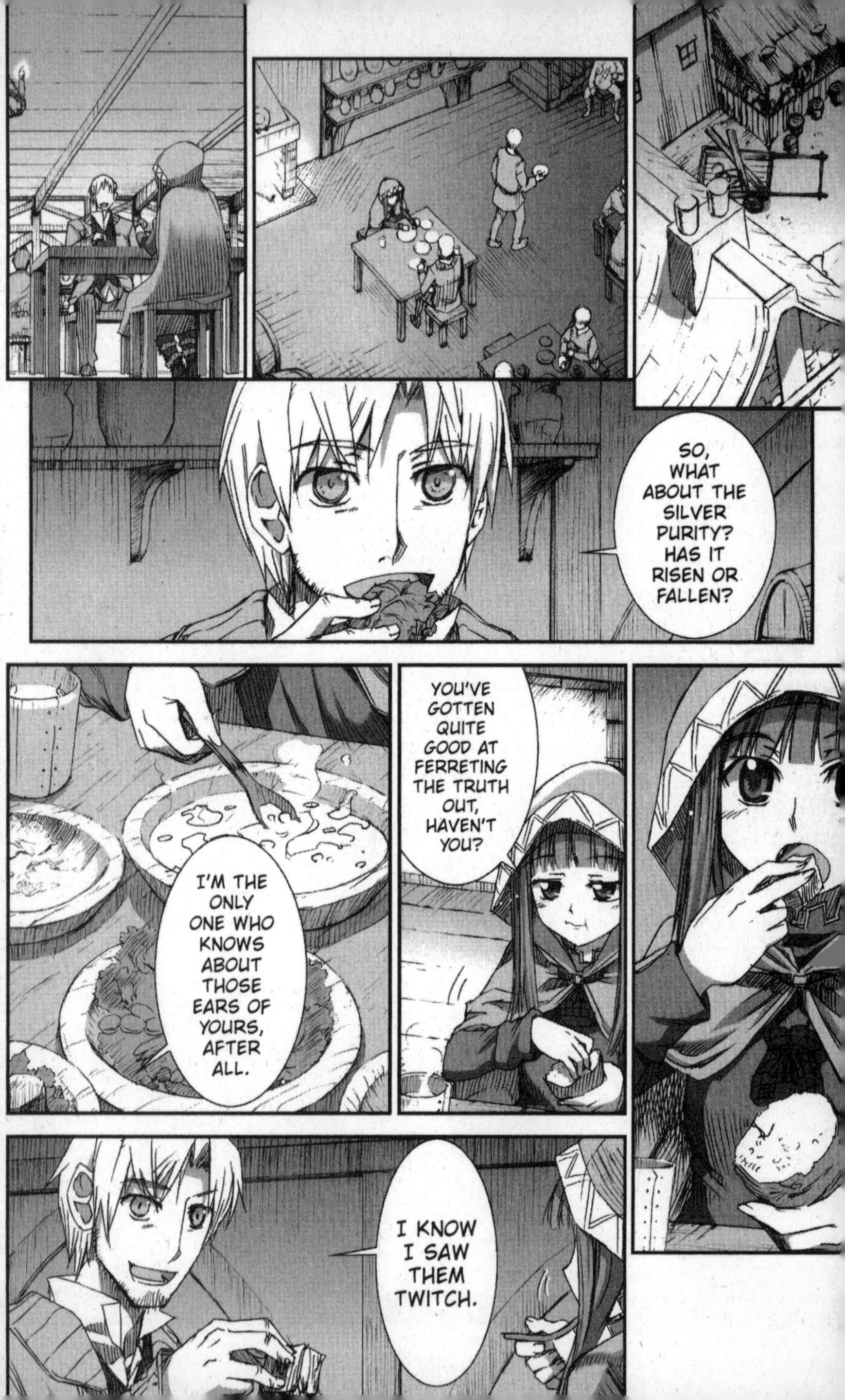
SO, WHAT ABOUT THE SILVER PURITY? HAS IT RISEN OR FALLEN?
YOU'VE GOTTEN QUITE GOOD AT FERRETING THE TRUTH OUT, HAVEN'T YOU?
I'M THE ONLY ONE WHO KNOWS ABOUT THOSE EARS OF YOURS, AFTER ALL.
I KNOW I SAW THEM TWITCH.

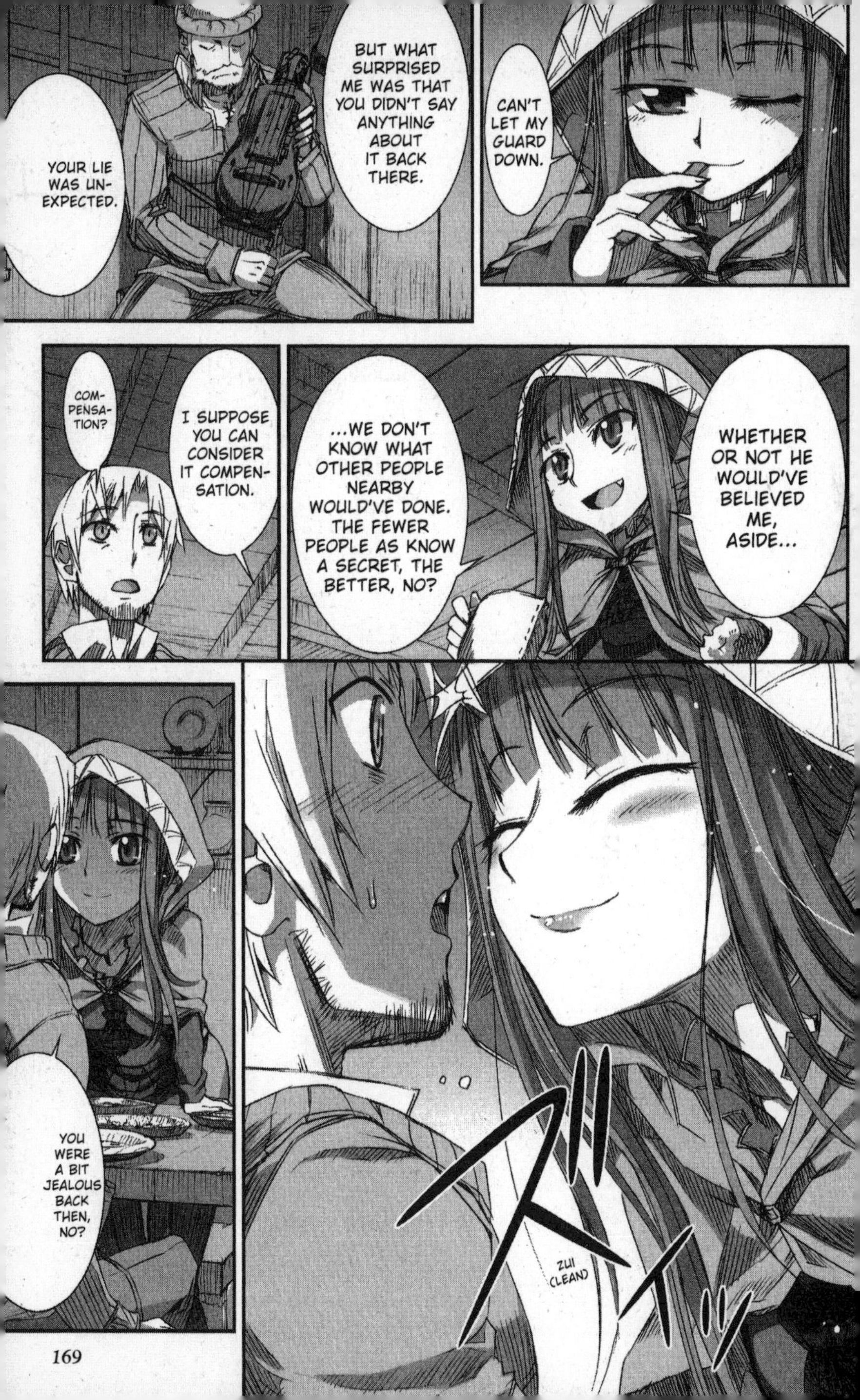
CAN'T LET MY GUARD DOWN.
BUT WHAT SURPRISED ME WAS THAT YOU DIDN'T SAY ANYTHING ABOUT IT BACK THERE.
YOUR LIE WAS UN-EXPECTED.
WHETHER OR NOT HE WOULD'VE BELIEVED ME, ASIDE...
...WE DON'T KNOW WHAT OTHER PEOPLE NEARBY WOULD'VE DONE. THE FEWER PEOPLE AS KNOW A SECRET, THE BETTER, NO?
I SUPPOSE YOU CAN CONSIDER IT COMPEN-SATION.
COM-PENSA-TION?
ZUI (LEAN)
YOU WERE A BIT JEALOUS BACK THEN, NO?

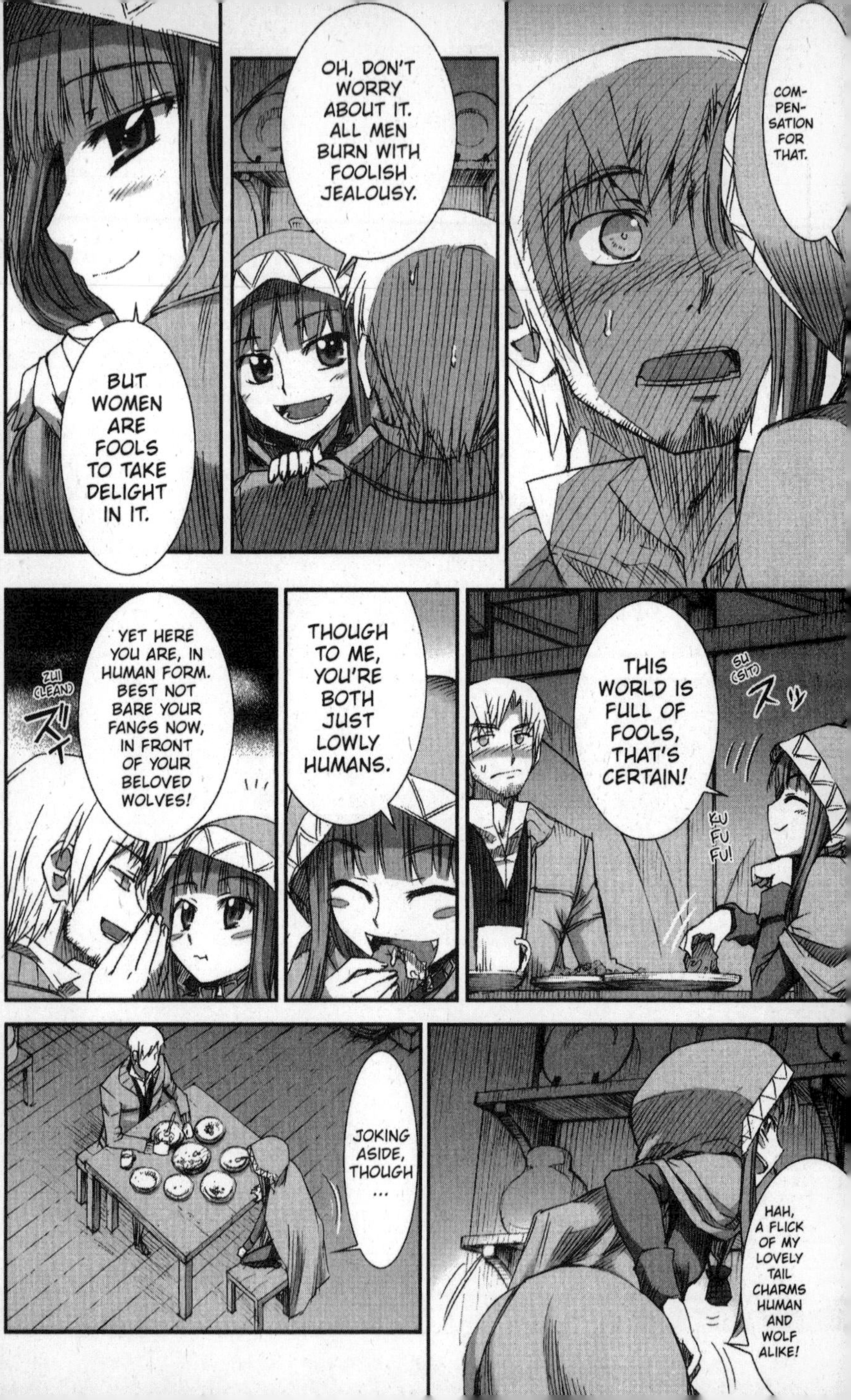
COMPENSATION FOR THAT.
OH, DON'T WORRY ABOUT IT. ALL MEN BURN WITH FOOLISH JEALOUSY.
BUT WOMEN ARE FOOLS TO TAKE DELIGHT IN IT.
SU (SIT)
スッ
THIS WORLD IS FULL OF FOOLS, THAT'S CERTAIN!
KU FU FU!
THOUGH TO ME, YOU'RE BOTH JUST LOWLY HUMANS.
ZUI (LEAN)
ズイ
YET HERE YOU ARE, IN HUMAN FORM. BEST NOT BARE YOUR FANGS NOW, IN FRONT OF YOUR BELOVED WOLVES!
HAH, A FLICK OF MY LOVELY TAIL CHARMS HUMAN AND WOLF ALIKE!
JOKING ASIDE, THOUGH ...

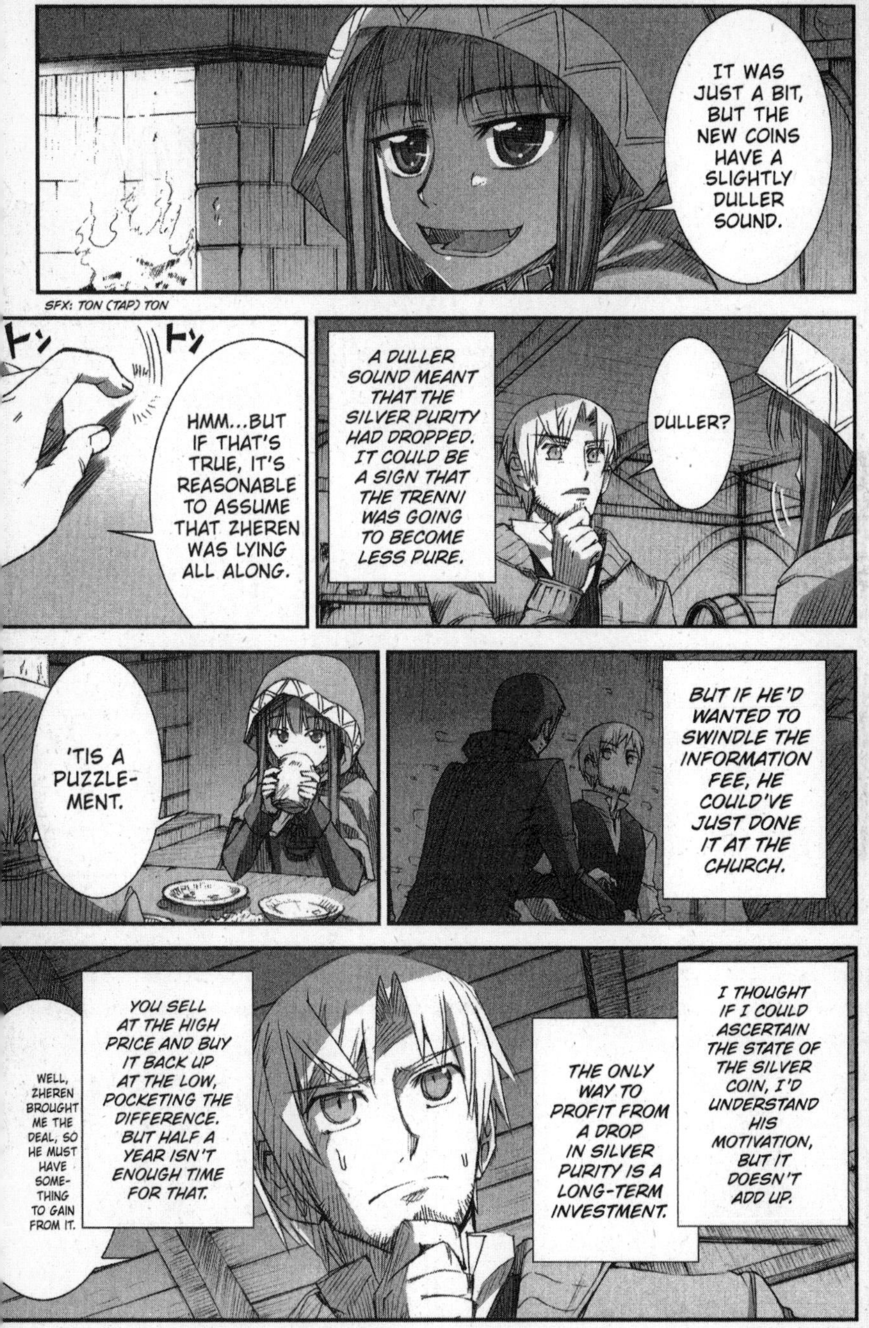
IT WAS JUST A BIT, BUT THE NEW COINS HAVE A SLIGHTLY DULLER SOUND.
SFX: TON (TAP) TON
DULLER?
A DULLER SOUND MEANT THAT THE SILVER PURITY HAD DROPPED. IT COULD BE A SIGN THAT THE TRENNI WAS GOING TO BECOME LESS PURE.
トン トン
HMM...BUT IF THAT'S TRUE, IT'S REASONABLE TO ASSUME THAT ZHEREN WAS LYING ALL ALONG.
BUT IF HE'D WANTED TO SWINDLE THE INFORMATION FEE, HE COULD'VE JUST DONE IT AT THE CHURCH.
'TIS A PUZZLEMENT.
I THOUGHT IF I COULD ASCERTAIN THE STATE OF THE SILVER COIN, I'D UNDERSTAND HIS MOTIVATION, BUT IT DOESN'T ADD UP.
THE ONLY WAY TO PROFIT FROM A DROP IN SILVER PURITY IS A LONG-TERM INVESTMENT.
YOU SELL AT THE HIGH PRICE AND BUY IT BACK UP AT THE LOW, POCKETING THE DIFFERENCE. BUT HALF A YEAR ISN'T ENOUGH TIME FOR THAT.
WELL, ZHEREN BROUGHT ME THE DEAL, SO HE MUST HAVE SOME-THING TO GAIN FROM IT.

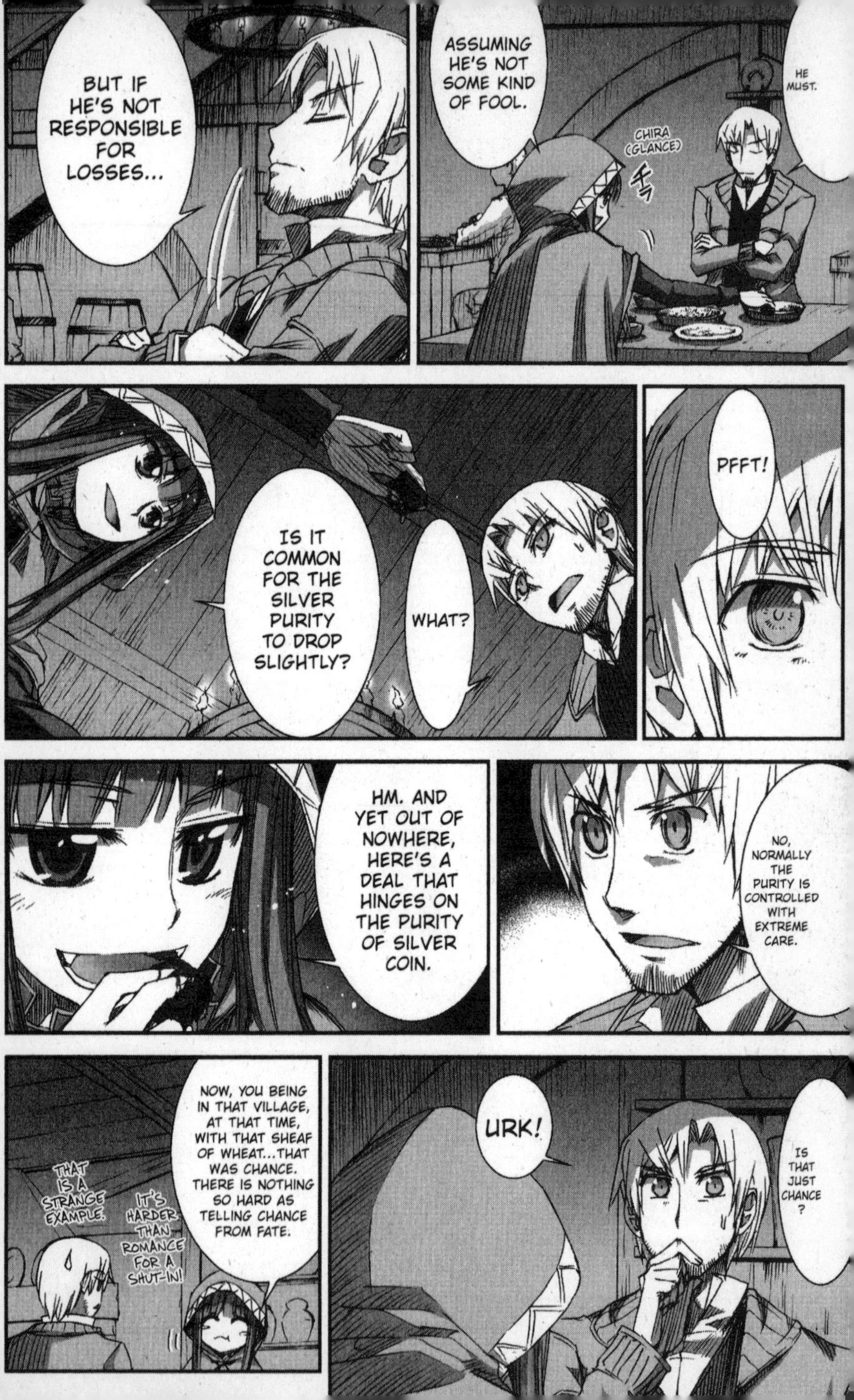
HE MUST.
ASSUMING HE'S NOT SOME KIND OF FOOL.
CHIRA (GLANCE)
BUT IF HE'S NOT RESPONSIBLE FOR LOSSES...
PFFT!
WHAT?
IS IT COMMON FOR THE SILVER PURITY TO DROP SLIGHTLY?
NO, NORMALLY THE PURITY IS CONTROLLED WITH EXTREME CARE.
HM. AND YET OUT OF NOWHERE, HERE'S A DEAL THAT HINGES ON THE PURITY OF SILVER COIN.
IS THAT JUST CHANCE?
URK!
NOW, YOU BEING IN THAT VILLAGE, AT THAT TIME, WITH THAT SHEAF OF WHEAT...THAT WAS CHANCE. THERE IS NOTHING SO HARD AS TELLING CHANCE FROM FATE.
IT'S HARDER THAN ROMANCE FOR A SHUT-IN!
THAT IS A STRANGE EXAMPLE.

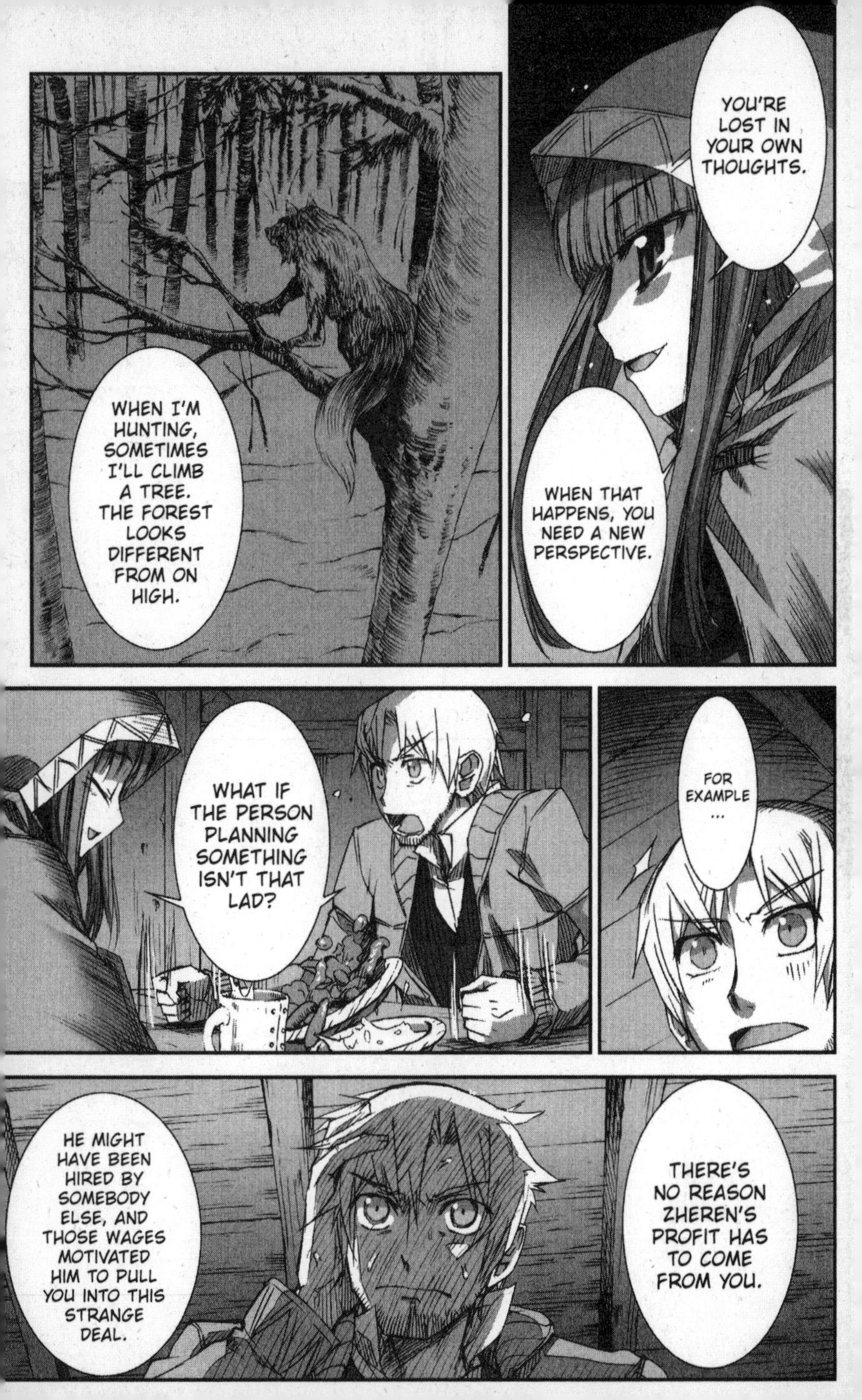

YOU'RE LOST IN YOUR OWN THOUGHTS.
WHEN THAT HAPPENS, YOU NEED A NEW PERSPECTIVE.
WHEN I'M HUNTING, SOMETIMES I'LL CLIMB A TREE. THE FOREST LOOKS DIFFERENT FROM ON HIGH.
FOR EXAMPLE ...
WHAT IF THE PERSON PLANNING SOMETHING ISN'T THAT LAD?
THERE'S NO REASON ZHEREN'S PROFIT HAS TO COME FROM YOU.
HE MIGHT HAVE BEEN HIRED BY SOMEBODY ELSE, AND THOSE WAGES MOTIVATED HIM TO PULL YOU INTO THIS STRANGE DEAL.

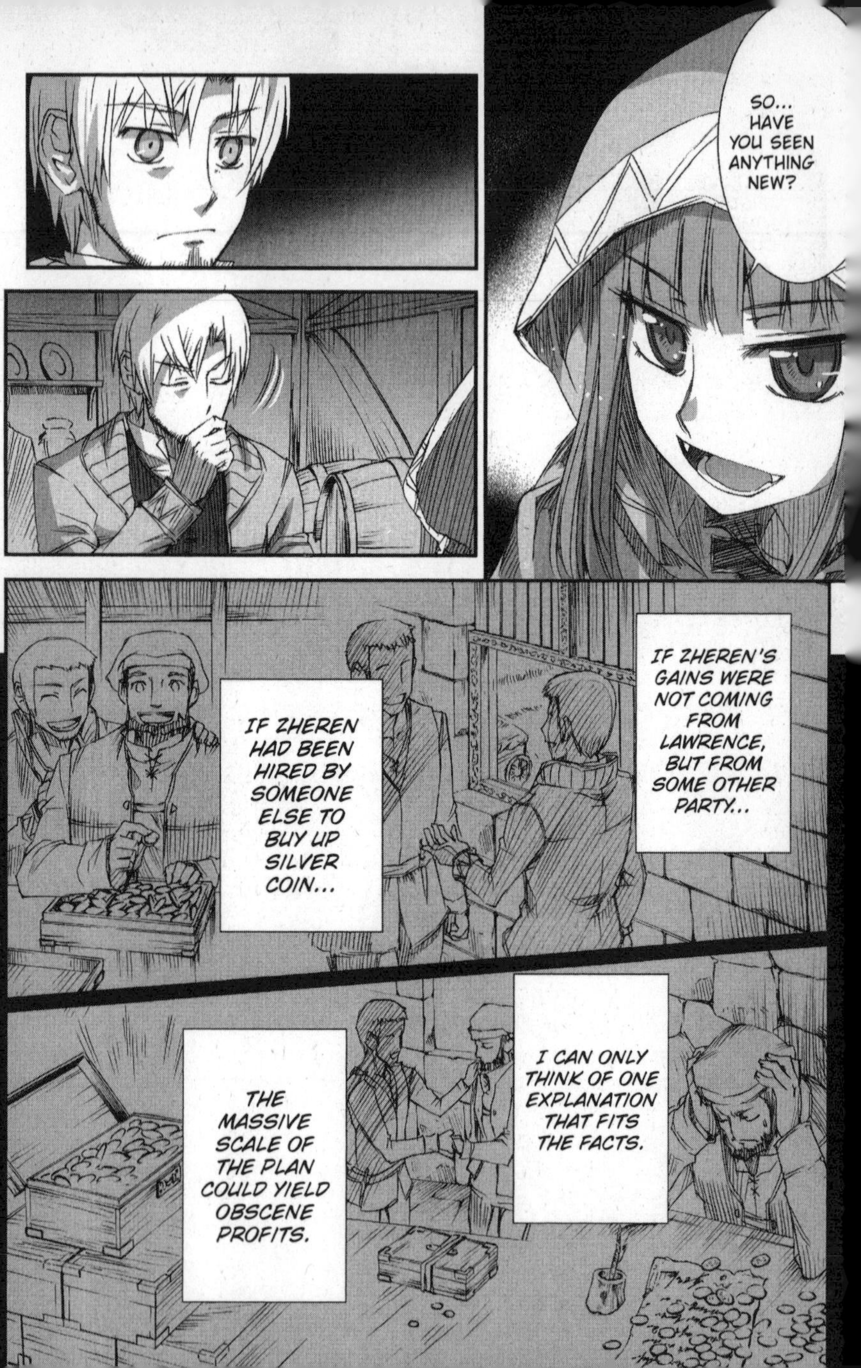
SO... HAVE YOU SEEN ANYTHING NEW?
IF ZHEREN'S GAINS WERE NOT COMING FROM LAWRENCE, BUT FROM SOME OTHER PARTY...
IF ZHEREN HAD BEEN HIRED BY SOMEONE ELSE TO BUY UP SILVER COIN...
I CAN ONLY THINK OF ONE EXPLANATION THAT FITS THE FACTS.
THE MASSIVE SCALE OF THE PLAN COULD YIELD OBSCENE PROFITS.

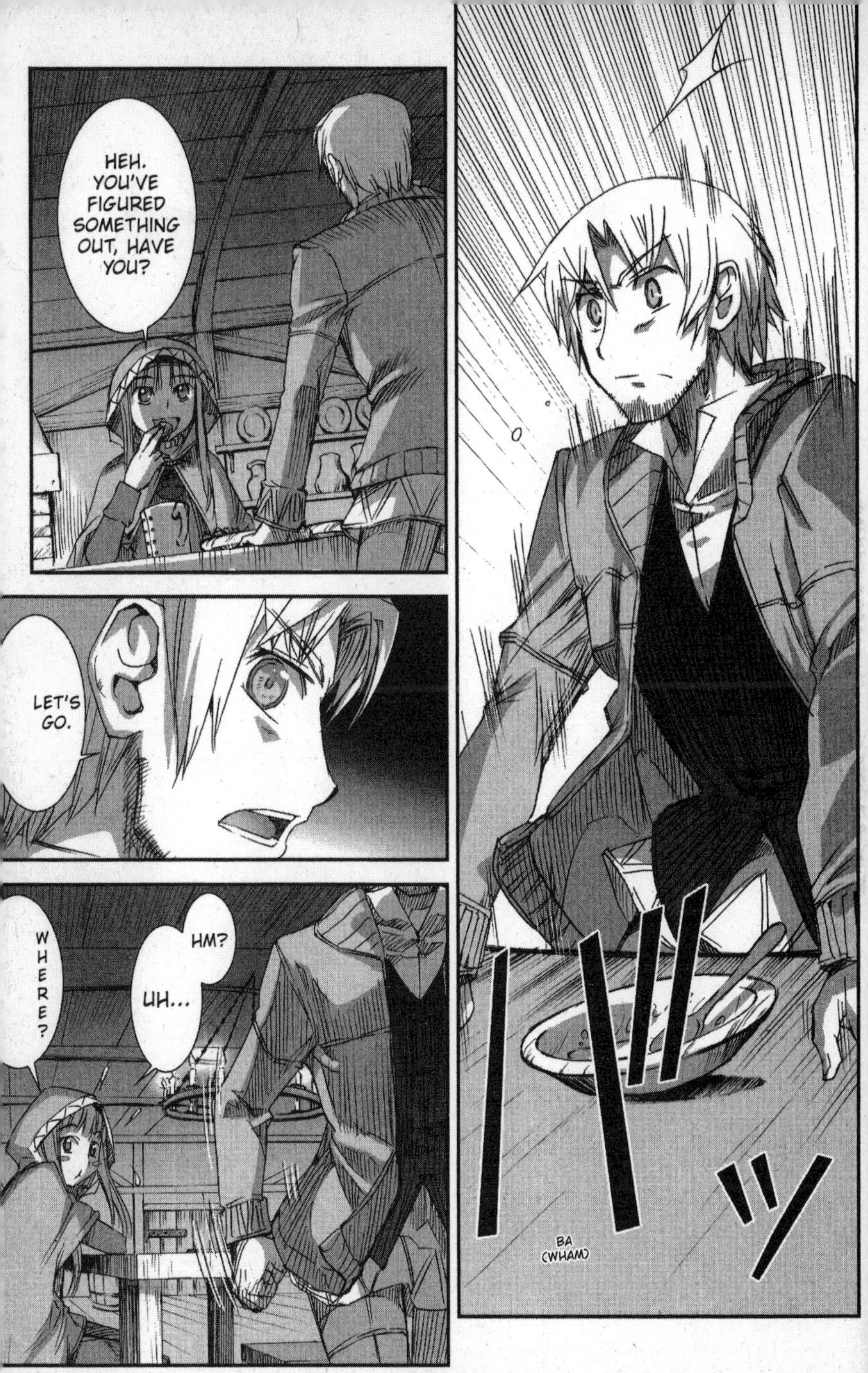
BA
(WHAM)
HEH. YOU'VE FIGURED SOMETHING OUT, HAVE YOU?
LET'S GO.
HM?
UH...
WHERE?

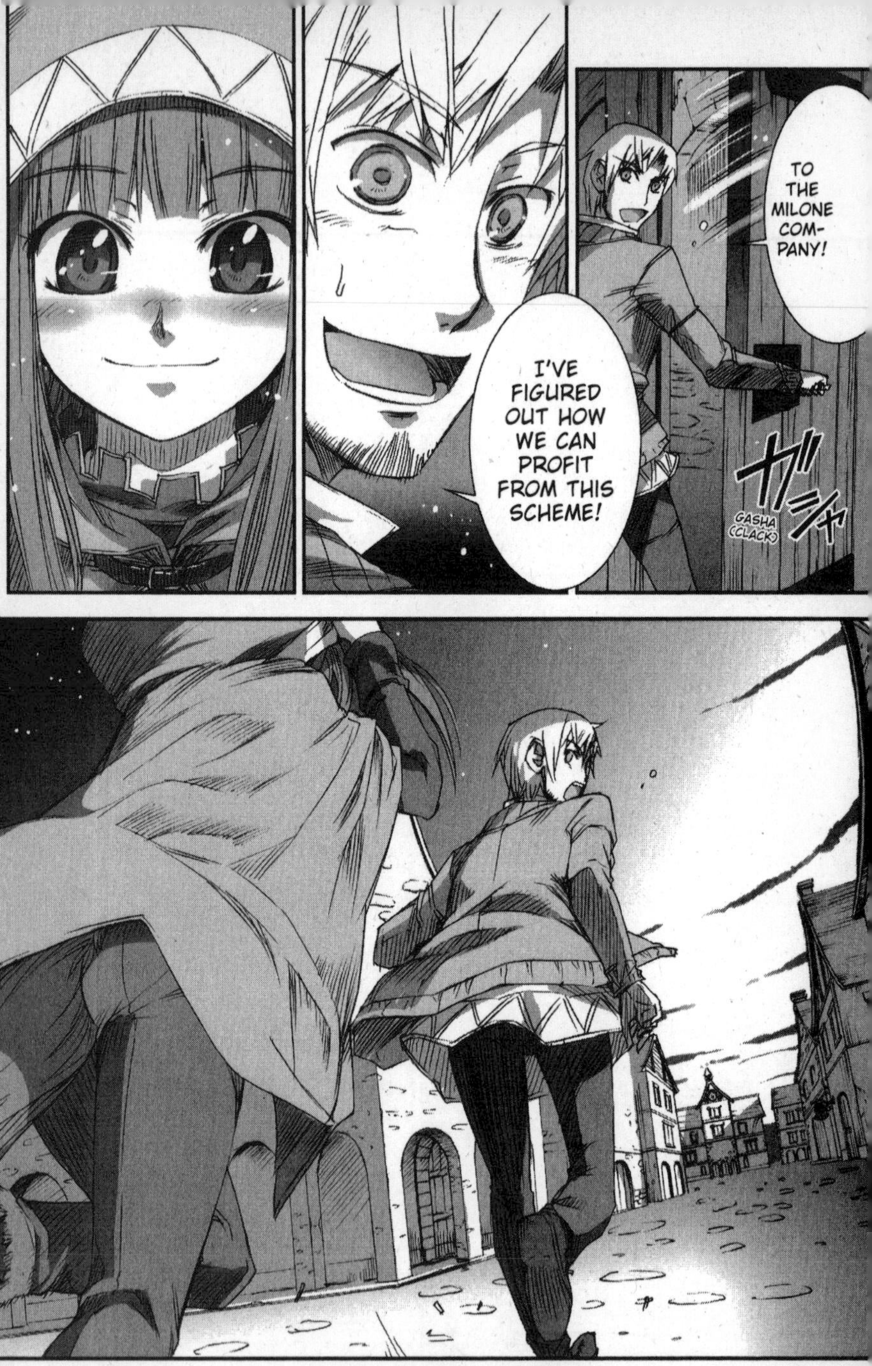
TO THE MILONE COMPANY!
ガシャ
GASHA (CLACK)
I'VE FIGURED OUT HOW WE CAN PROFIT FROM THIS SCHEME!

To be continued in Volume 2...

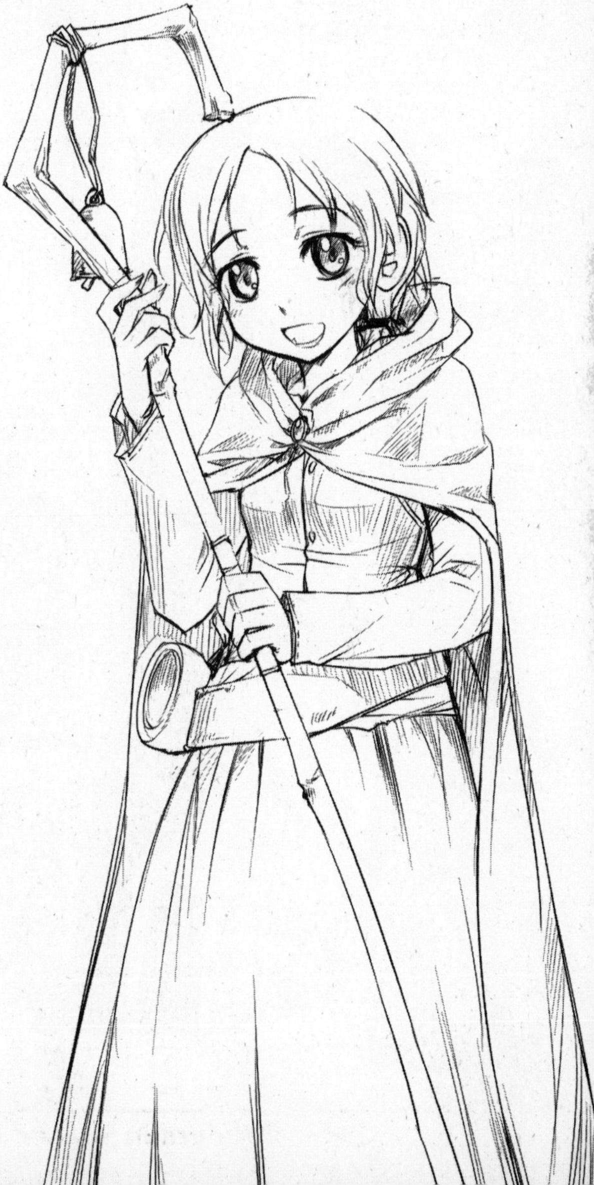

STAFF

KOUMEKEITO

TOITENTSU

S.T

YAKKUN

THANKS

VOLUME 1 OF THE SPICE AND WOLF MANGA IS FINALLY, FINALLY ON SALE. IN THE YEAR OR SO THAT IT'S BEEN IN PROGRESS, I'VE HAD THE SUPPORT OF MANY, MANY PEOPLE. THANK YOU SO MUCH. TO THE AUTHOR, ISUNA HASEKURA, THE ILLUSTRATOR JYUU AYAKURA, AND MY VARIOUS EDITORS AND ILLUSTRATION STAFF, AND ESPECIALLY TO ALL THE FANS OF SPICE AND WOLF, I WANT TO EXTEND MY DEEPEST AND MOST HEARTFELT THANKS. I'LL DO MY BEST AS WE HEAD INTO THE SECOND VOLUME!

小梅けいと
KEITO KOUME
2008.3

■ WHEN RESEARCHING MEDIEVAL HISTORY, I LEARNED ALL SORTS OF INTERESTING THINGS. FOR EXAMPLE, THE VARIOUS KINDS OF IMPLEMENTS THAT WERE CARVED FROM ANIMAL HORN. HORN WAS THE PLASTIC OF THE MIDDLE AGES, AND IT WAS USED FOR EVERYTHING FROM SPOONS TO WINDOW GLASS!

IN THE MEDIEVAL DAYS, EVERYONE HAD THEIR OWN PERSONAL SPOON, APPARENTLY. (ALTHOUGH GENERALLY THEY JUST ATE WITH THEIR HANDS, I GUESS.)

DO YOU SUPPOSE HOLO GOT LAWRENCE TO BUY HER HER OWN SPOON?

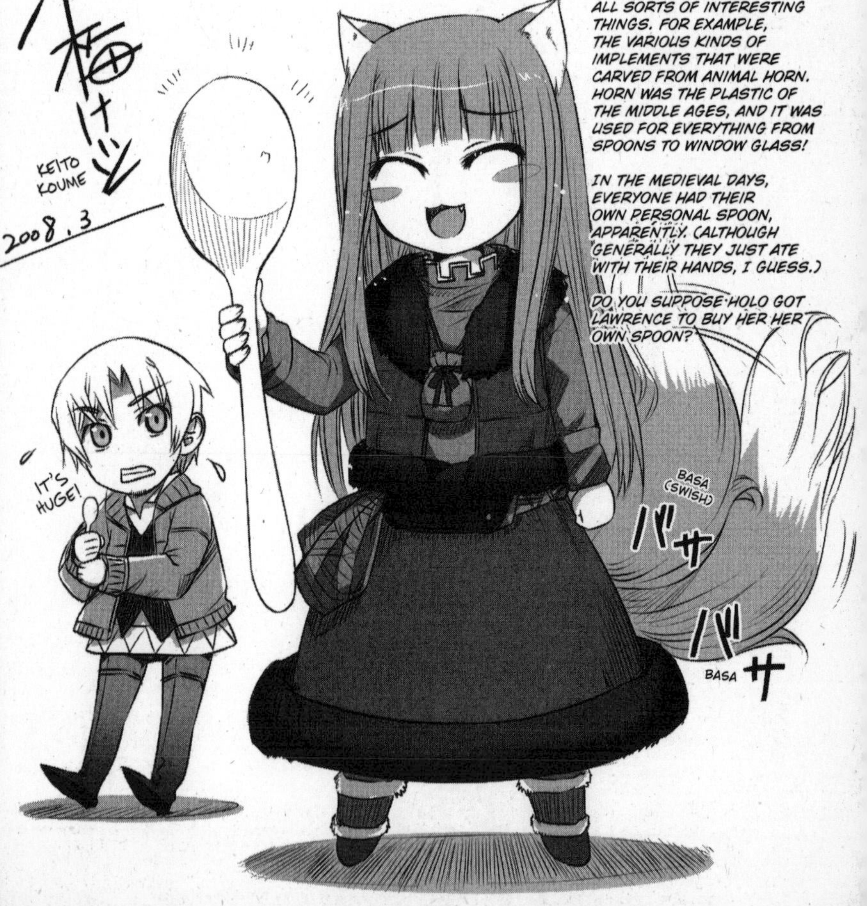
バサ
BASA (SWISH)
バサ
BASA
IT'S HUGE!

SPICE & WOLF

◎ HOORAY! THE FIRST VOLUME OF MANGA! I CAN'T HIDE MY SURPRISE AT HOW QUICKLY IT'S COME TO PUBLICATION, BUT MOST IMPRESSIVE OF ALL IS THE INCREDIBLE QUALITY OF MR. KOUME'S ARTWORK!

ISUNA HASEKURA

■ CONGRATULATIONS ON THE FIRST MANGA VOLUME! MR. KOUME'S VERSION OF HOLO IS JUST ADORABLE, AND ALWAYS GETTING THE BETTER OF EVERYBODY! I LOOK FORWARD TO SEEING MORE.

JYUU AYAKURA

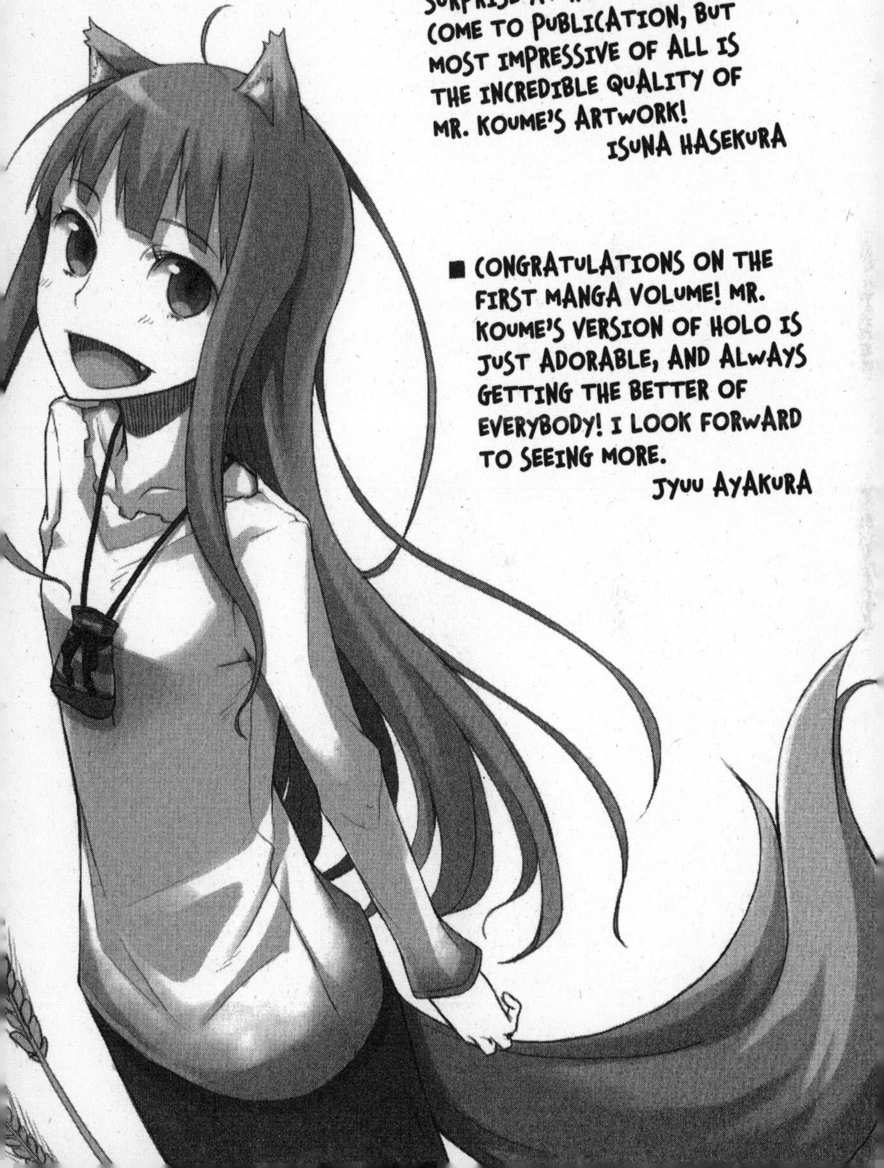

SPICE & WOLF ❶

Isuna Hasekura
Keito Koume

Translation: Paul Starr

Lettering: Alexis Eckerman

OOKAMI TO KOUSHINRYO Vol. 1 © Isuna Hasekura / ASCII
MEDIA WORKS 2008 © Keito Koume 2008. All rights reserved. First
published in Japan in 2008 by ASCII MEDIA WORKS INC., Tokyo.
English translation rights in USA, Canada, and UK arranged with
ASCII MEDIA WORKS INC. through Tuttle-Mori Agency, Inc., Tokyo.

Translation © 2010 by Hachette Book Group

Yen Press
Hachette Book Group
237 Park Avenue, New York, NY 10017

www.HachetteBookGroup.com
www.YenPress.com

Yen Press is an imprint of Hachette Book Group, Inc. The Yen Press
name and logo are trademarks of Hachette Book Group, Inc.

First Yen Press Edition: April 2010

ISBN-13: 978-0-316-07339-4

10 9 8 7 6 5 4 3 2 1

BVG

Printed in the United States of America

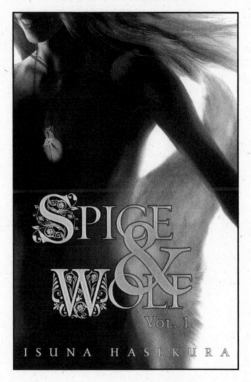

"Mind you, don't cut too far!"

"Holo flees from the greedy hand!"

"Who, who, who will catch the wolf?"

"It's Yarei! Yarei, Yarei, Yarei!"

Lawrence got off his wagon and peered at the crowd just as Yarei caught the last bundle of wheat. His face was black with sweat and soil as he grinned and hefted the wheat high, threw his head back, and howled.

"Awooooooo!"

"It's Holo! Holo, Holo, Holo!"

"Awooooooo!"

"Holo the wolf is here! Holo the wolf is here!"

"Catch it, now! Catch it quick!"

"Don't let it escape!"

The shouting men suddenly gave chase after Yarei.

The god of the bountiful harvest, once cornered, would possess a human and try to escape. Capture it and it would remain for another year.

None knew if this god truly existed. But this was an old tradition in the area.

Lawrence had traveled far and wide, so he put no stock in the teachings of the Church, but his faith in superstition was greater even than that of the farmers here. Too many times had he crossed mountains only to arrive in towns and find the price of his goods dropping precipitously. It was enough to make anyone superstitious.

Thus he didn't bat an eye at traditions that true believers or Church officials would've found outrageous.

But it was inconvenient that Yarei was this year's Holo. Now Yarei would be locked in a granary stocked with treats until the festival was over — close to a week — and would be impossible to talk to.

"Ho there, good work!" Lawrence called out to a farmer driving a cart heaped high with wheat in the corner of one of the fields. It was well-ripened wheat. Those who had invested in wheat futures could breath a sigh of relief.

"What's that?"

"Might you tell me where to find Yarei?" Lawrence asked.

"Oh, Yarei'll be over yonder — see where the crowd is gathering? That field. It's all youngsters at his place this year. Whoever's slowest will wind up being the Holo!" said the farmer good-naturedly, his tan face smiling. It was the kind of guileless smile a merchant could never manage.

Lawrence thanked the farmer with his best trader's smile, and turned his horse toward Yarei's place.

Just as the farmer had said, there was a crowd gathering within its confines, and they were shouting something. They seemed to be making sport of the few who were still working the field, but it wasn't ridicule at their lateness. The jeering was part of the festival.

As Lawrence lazily approached the crowd, he was able to make out their shouting.

"There's a wolf! A wolf!"

"A wolf lies there!"

"Who will be the last and catch the wolf? Who, who, who?" the villagers shouted, their faces so cheerful one wondered if they were drunk. None of them noticed Lawrence pulling his cart up behind the crowd.

What they so enthusiastically called a wolf was in fact not a wolf at all. Had it been real, no one would have been laughing.

The wolf was the harvest god, and according to village legend, it resided within the last stalk of wheat to be reaped. Whoever cut that stalk down would be possessed by the wolf, it was said.

"It's the last bundle!"

unable to keep control over the area, which undoubtedly made it all the more nervous about goings-on.

Indeed, the Church had been eager to hold inquisitions and convert heathens, and clashes between natural philosophers and theologians in the city were far from rare. The time when the Church could command the populace's unconditional submission was vanishing.

The dignity of the institution was beginning to crumble — even if the inhabitants of the cities said nothing, all were gradually beginning to realize it. In fact, the pope had recently had to petition the monarchs of several nations for funds when tithes had come in below expectations. Such a tale would have been preposterous even ten years before.

Thus the Church was desperate to regain its authority.

"Business everywhere will suffer," said Lawrence with a rueful smile, popping another honey drop into his mouth.

The western skies were a more beautiful golden hue than the wheat in the fields by the time Lawrence arrived in the plains. Distant birds became tiny shadows as they hurried home, and here and there the frogs sang themselves to sleep.

It appeared that the wheat fields had been mostly harvested, so the festival would undoubtedly begin soon — perhaps even as soon as the day after tomorrow.

Before Lawrence lay the expanses of the village of Pasloe's fertile wheat fields. The more abundant the harvest, the more prosperous the villagers. Furthermore, the noble who managed the land, one Count Ehrendott, was a famous area eccentric who enjoyed working in the fields himself. Naturally the festival also enjoyed his support, and every year it was a riot of wine and song.

Lawrence had not once participated in it, though. Unfortunately, outsiders were not permitted.

"The monks have caught wind of a big pagan festival that's approaching. Thus the increased guard. Do you know anything of this festival?"

If his face had betrayed any hint of his disappointment at the explanation, calling it a third-rate performance would have been generous. So Lawrence only affected a pained expression and answered, "Sadly, I know nothing." This was of course a huge lie, but the knight was just as mistaken, so there was nothing for it.

"Perhaps it truly is being held in secret, then. Pagans are a cowardly lot, after all." The knight was so mistaken it was amusing, but Lawrence merely agreed and took his leave.

The knight nodded and thanked him again for the honey drops.

Undoubtedly they had been delicious. Most of a knight's money went to equipment and lodging; even an apprentice cobbler lived a better life. It had surely been a long time since the knight had eaten anything sweet.

Not that Lawrence had any intention of giving him another piece.

"Still, a pagan festival, they say?" Lawrence repeated the knight's words to himself once the monastery was well behind him.

Lawrence had an inkling of what the knight was talking about. Actually, anyone from this area would know about it.

But it was no "pagan festival." For one thing, true pagans were farther north, or farther east.

The festival that happened here was hardly something one needed knights to guard against.

It was a simple harvest festival, of the sort to be found nearly anywhere.

True, this area's festival was somewhat grander than the typical celebration, which is probably why the monastery was keeping an eye on it and reporting to the city. The Church had long been

"Mmm," said the knight, hesitating momentarily before his desire for the sweet candy won out.

Still, perhaps because of his position as a knight, a considerable amount of time passed between his initial nod and when he actually reached out and took a honey drop.

"A half-day's travel east of here there's a small village in the mountains. I was trading salt there."

"Ah. I see you've a load in your cart. Salt as well?"

"No, but furs. Look," said Lawrence, turning around and removing the tarp that covered his load, revealing a bundle of magnificent marten pelts. A year's salary of the knight before him was paltry compared with its worth.

"Mm. And this?"

"Ah, this is wheat I received from the village."

The sheaf of wheat in the corner of the mountain of furs had been harvested in the village where Lawrence had traded his salt. It was hardy in cold weather and resisted insects. He planned to sell it in the northwest, where crops had sustained heavy frost damage.

"Hm. Very well. You may pass."

It was a strange way of speaking for someone who'd summoned him over so high-handedly earlier, but if Lawrence were to meekly say, "Yes, sir," now, a fine merchant he'd be.

"So, what occasions your post here, sir knight?"

The knight's brow knitted in consternation at the question and furrowed still deeper as he glanced at the bag of honey drops.

He was well and truly caught now. Lawrence undid the bag's string closure and plucked out another sweet, giving it to the knight.

"Mmm. Delicious. I should thank you."

The knight was being reasonable. Lawrence inclined his head gratefully, using his best trader's smile.

As he approached the monastery and the figure became clearer, Lawrence muttered in spite of himself:

". . . a knight?"

He at first dismissed the idea as ridiculous, but as he drew nearer he saw that it was unmistakably a knight. The gray clothing was in fact silver armor.

"You, there! What's your business here?"

The distance between them was still too far for conversation, which is why the knight yelled. He apparently felt no need to introduce himself, as if his position were obvious.

"I am Lawrence, a traveling merchant. Do you require my service?"

The monastery was now directly in front of him. He was close enough to count the number of servants working in the fields to the south.

He also noted that the knight in front of him was not alone. There was another one past the monastery, perhaps standing guard.

"A merchant? There's no town in the direction you came from, merchant," said the knight haughtily, sticking out his chest as if to display the golden cross that was engraved there.

But the mantle draped over his shoulders was gray, indicating a knight of low rank. His blond hair looked freshly cut, and his body did not look as if it had been though many battles; so his pride most likely came from being a new knight. It was important to deal with such men carefully. They tended to be excitable.

So instead of replying, Lawrence took a leather pouch out of his breast pocket and slowly undid the twine that held it closed. Inside were candies made of crystallized honey. He plucked one out and popped it in his mouth, then offered the open bag to the knight.

"Care for one?"

He didn't know what young noble was cloistered in this remote location. The masonry of the building was magnificent, and unbelievably it even had an iron gate. Lawrence seemed to remember that roughly twenty monks lived there, attended to by a similar number of manservants.

When the monastery had first been built, Lawrence had anticipated fresh clientele; the monks were somehow able to secure supplies without employing independent merchants, though, so his dreams were fleeting.

Admittedly the monks lived simply, tilling their fields, so trade with them would not be especially profitable. There was another problem in that they would probably solicit donations and leave their bills unpaid.

As far as simple trade went, they were worse partners than out-and-out thieves. Still, there were times when trade with them was convenient.

Thus Lawrence looked in the direction of the monastery with some small regret, but then his eyes narrowed.

From the direction of the monastery, someone was waving at him.

"What's this?"

The figure did not look like a manservant. They wore dark brown work clothes. The waving figure was covered in gray clothing. His deliberate approach likely meant some hassle, but ignoring him could make matters worse later. Lawrence reluctantly turned his horse toward the figure.

Perhaps having realized that Lawrence was now headed his way, the figure stopped waving but made no move to approach. He appeared to be waiting for the cart's arrival. It would hardly be the first time that a Church-associated person demonstrated arrogance. Lawrence was in no mood to take every such insult personally.

"So that's the last, then?"

"Hm, looks like . . . seventy pelts, on the nose. Always a pleasure."

"Hey, anytime. You're the only one who'll come this far into the mountains, Lawrence. I should be thanking *you*."

"Ah, but for my trouble I get truly fine pelts. I'll come again."

The usual pleasantries concluded, Lawrence managed to leave the village just around five o'clock. The sun was just beginning its climb when he left, and it was midday by the time he descended from the mountains and entered the plains.

The weather was good; there was no wind. It was a perfect day for dozing in the wagon as he crossed the plains. It seemed absurd that only recently he had felt the chill of the approaching winter.

This was Lawrence's seventh year as a traveling merchant, and his twenty-fifth since birth. He gave a huge yawn in the driver's box.

There were few grasses or trees of any notable height, so he had an expansive view. At the very edge of his field of vision, he could see a monastery that had been built some years earlier.

CHAPTER ONE

Maybe that is why there is no need for them to honor the ancient agreement, *she thought.*

In any case, she knew she no longer had a place here.

The mountains that rose in the east caused the clouds over the village to drift mostly north.

She thought of her homeland beyond those drifting clouds and sighed.

Returning her gaze from the sky to the fields, her eyes fell upon her magnificent tail, which twitched just past her nose.

With nothing better to do, she set to grooming it.

The autumn sky was high and clear.

Harvest time had come again.

Many wolves were running through the wheat fields.

In this village, when the ripened ears of wheat sway in the breeze, it is said that a wolf runs through them.

This is because one can make out the form of a running wolf in the shifting stalks of the wheat fields.

When the wind is too strong and the stalks are blown over, it is said that the wolf has trampled them. When the harvest is poor, it is said that the wolf has eaten it.

It was a nice turn of phrase, but it had a troublesome aspect that flawed it, she felt.

Still, lately it was a popular sort of expression, and there were few remaining who wielded it with the sort of familiarity or awe it had held in the past.

Although the autumn sky that was visible between the swaying stalks of wheat had not changed in hundreds of years, conditions below that sky had indeed changed.

The villagers who tended the wheat as the years passed lived for seventy years at the most.

Perhaps it would be worse for them to go centuries without changing.

BEGIN READING HERE
FOR AN EXCERPT FROM

SPICE&WOLF

VOLUME 1

AVAILABLE NOW!

PROLOGUE